GUY GAUNT

Anthony Delano was a third-generation Australian newspaperman when he went to London to join the *Daily Mirror*, which at that time sold nearly five million copies daily. His career included the most glamorous jobs in journalism: Chief European Correspondent, Chief American Correspondent and Managing Editor. Later he taught journalism and researched it academically, gaining first a Master's degree at Queensland University of Technology then a PhD from the University of Westminster (his 2001 doctoral thesis, 'The Formation of the British Journalist 1900–2000', is widely cited). He became senior lecturer, senior research fellow and finally visiting professor at the London College of Communication. He lives in the South of France.

www.anthonydelano.info

Also by the Author—

GUY GAUNT

THE BOY FROM BALLARAT
WHO TALKED AMERICA
INTO THE GREAT WAR

ANTHONY DELANO

ARCADIA

First published 2016 by ARCADIA
the general books' imprint of
Australian Scholarly Publishing Pty Ltd
7 Lt Lothian St Nth, North Melbourne, Victoria 3051

tel 03 9329 6963 / *fax* 03 9329 5452
aspic@ozemail.com / www.scholarly.info

ISBN: 978-1-925333-20-6

Cover design Wayne Saunders

[ASP]

Contents

Conspirators converge

1914. The man trying to decide if it would be safe to sit down in the seemingly empty apartment on New York's Upper West Side was called Victor Voska. He had spent more than half his life in the United States, first chiselling inscriptions on tombstones for a living then buying into marble quarries in Kansas, Vermont and New York state, working up a stonemasonry business that he managed from Manhattan. He was thirty-nine and rich, a strongly built, bullet-headed man in his late thirties with distinctive light-grey eyes. Much of the money he made went towards trying to free Bohemia, the land of the Czechs where he had been born, from the Hapsburg monarchy in Vienna that ruled over it. In the early days of the Great War many Americans barely noticed that Britain and her allies France and Russia were fighting not only Germany but the Austro-Hungarian Empire, a far greater spread of real estate that ran from south of Serbia, where the fuse had been lit, to Galicia, the posterior of Poland: a common market of 42 million people so diverse that its banknotes were printed in ten languages.

Voska was nervous and rightly so. A lot of people in Manhattan would be happy to kill him if they discovered what he was up to. It took courage to follow the instructions he had been given by a woman he was not certain he could trust. Mabel Slávko Gruich was married to someone in the embassy of Serbia, a nervously independent kingdom overshadowed by Austro-Hungary. She also belonged, Voska soon found out, to a political clan, some of which had taken part in the 1903 assassination of their king and queen with a savagery that shocked even the turbulent Balkans. He had been introduced to her at a diplomatic soirée. She asked him to tea and without any reference to his patriotic activities mentioned that 'a man' she knew would like to meet him. Voska should go alone the very next afternoon to 103 West 76 Street at exactly four o'clock. Take the elevator to the third floor, she said, as though instructing a delivery boy. The door of the first apartment on the right would be unlocked. He should enter and wait. It says much for Voska's nerve and his readiness to go to the help of his country's enemies that he did as he was told, not knowing what would happen next.

In the apartment Voska moved cautiously down the hallway to an underfurnished living room. He was deciding whether to sit on a straight-backed chair, ready to spring up in self-defence, when a stranger came bouncing in, turning to lock the door behind him. 'I am Captain Guy Gaunt,' he said, holding out a hand to Voska. 'Naval attaché of the British Embassy in Washington.'

'He was young, slim, tanned, smartly but quietly dressed, Voska remembered, 'and even his voice seemed to radiate energy'. That reassuring impression was to last through three mischievous and momentous years for which they conspired to get the world's most powerful nation to see things their way.

Guy and Voska talked for nearly two hours, one in the sonorous register of *mittleuropa*, the other in the clipped tones of the quarterdeck. When they parted, Guy, a seagoing officer with no experience of espionage and not much of politics or diplomacy, had been handed control of a ready-made spy ring and propaganda network that was just what Britain needed at that moment to counter the strident efforts being made by Germany and German-Americans to keep the United States from supporting the Allies. It was a sharp career detour but there was no one else to grasp the opportunity. As things turned out, the metaphorical cloak and dagger suited Guy perfectly, as did the role of salesman for Britain's war. With the help of Voska and a third—even less probable—conspirator he became, for the long wait before America could be induced to join the war, the most powerful British intelligence agent in the world. 'I have no brains', he liked to say, in cheerful deprecation of his achievements. 'But I possess a certain amount of low cunning.' Voska did not buy that. Guy, as he was to see many times, had 'one of the sharpest minds I ever encountered'.

A few weeks after the Allied victory, David Lloyd George, prime minister for the crucial latter half of the conflict, shook Guy's hand and hailed him as 'the man who brought America into the war'. Or so Guy claimed in the autobiography he produced twenty years later. Was it true that Lloyd George ever said such a thing? Or, if he did, that he believed it? George was a notorious massager of egos, always ready with a nifty soundbite for people he wanted to flatter, and naturally enough Guy's version of events was tightly trimmed in his own favour. His account has to be balanced against other evidence—when it can be found. In the bashful way of gentlemanly memoirs, Guy preferred not to use the names of many people he wrote about in order—usually just when things were getting interesting—to 'save his blushes' or 'avoid embarrassment'. Crucial events simply went unmentioned: two marriages and a couple of steamy divorces, for instance.

An only slightly less momentous assertion about Guy is that he was responsible for the creation of the Central Intelligence Agency. It was not a claim he made himself; he was dead by the time the CIA came into being. But his exploits in America were greatly admired—and abetted—by Franklin Delano Roosevelt, who at the time of Guy's greatest influence was Assistant Secretary of the Navy. Roosevelt carried a revolver whenever they met in case the stalkers on Guy's tail went for him as well. Guy certainly tried to get across to FDR the idea that the security of the United States needed better protection than it could hope for from the Secret Service, whose main task was to protect the president and preserve the currency. And Roosevelt did hugely expand the Office of Naval Intelligence that in World War Two—by which time he had become the president—developed into the Office of Strategic Services that in turn morphed into the CIA. Roosevelt had fond memories of Guy, reminiscing about their time together with Winston Churchill, who by then was Britain's wartime prime minister.

Guy's version of his extraordinary life and achievements was 'put into shape' after a gap of thirty years by a shadowy spinner of early espionage fiction, Sidney Theodore Felstead, who had to sift through shaky recollections going back half a century earlier. There were no diaries, little correspondence and not much documentation. Plenty of senior officers in the Royal Navy admired Guy but the Admiralty was wary of mavericks and its archives remain frustratingly laconic. The Foreign Office, most secretive of ministries, had plenty to hide about the dirty tricks it was to play on Guy when he strayed on to its turf but the files in the National Archives have been thoroughly weeded. More might eventually be unearthed among the million or so documents that in 2014 the Foreign Office and the Ministry of Defence had to admit they had never—as the law required—got around to making publicly available.

The king pin of naval intelligence, Reginald 'Blinker' Hall, Guy's sheet-anchor in London, never completed his own account of the mischief they got up to together and a scholar who set out to do it for him, Ralph Strauss, gave up in frustration. Strauss found two boxes of letters and cables from Hall to Gaunt but where, he wanted to know, were another two boxes referred to that contained the far more relevant communications of Gaunt to Hall? Hall could not or would not say. Neither the boxes nor their contents made it to Hall's archive at Churchill College, Cambridge, or any other likely place. Whether the other side of that prolific correspondence was destroyed, lost or simply dumped, the way was left clear for Hall to make his own claim to be The Man Who Brought America In... which, it must be said, has quite a lot to support it. He had orchestrated the acquisition and disclosure of the Zimmermann Telegram, the crafty dealings that finally convinced Congress that the time had come for war.

The gap in the record is unfortunate since it means that much remains obscure about furtive British capers in the war-shy America of 1914–1917. But it proved a great help to some old school ties in the Foreign Office and the half-baked new intelligence services who swooped like gannets on garbage to snatch up credit for achievements that demonstrably belong to Guy. And when, in World War Two, Guy had the temerity to suggest from the sidelines that the smug mandarins of the diplomatic service might not be up to their task they made a comprehensively good job of wrecking his life. 'A handful of Foreign Office clerks have set out to ruin me,' he complained. 'And they have succeeded.'

In the main, Guy does not seem to have told many lies; just mixed up a few names and dates and left out plenty of details that might have been enlightening. An official CIA historian, Thomas Troy, made a beady-eyed analysis of the versions of key events provided by him and his antagonists and came down two to one in favour of Guy's accounts. In the case of the Lloyd George pronouncement Guy named two other people present who would have heard what was said. One was the rascally Australian newspaper proprietor Hugh D. McIntosh, known back home as 'Huge Deal', but the other was hewn from the bedrock of the British Establishment: the second Baron Burnham, editor of the *Daily Telegraph* and chairman of the Empire Press Union. So, on balance, Lloyd George probably did say what Guy said he had. Whether he meant it is something else again. But—on balance—Guy's claim to have changed the course of world events looks at least as good as Blinker Hall's and far better than that of the opportunist old school ties.

Enthralling as Guy's story is, it becomes even more remarkable when he is seen to be one of a tribe of young Gaunts that surged out of the turbulent goldfields of Australia at the end of the 19th Century. While the Australian colonies, yet to be assembled into a nation, were luring emigrants from Britain by the shipload the Gaunts, adventurous spirits every one, set out in the opposite direction. With no advantage beyond ambition and determination, they seized every opportunity the British Empire offered to its citizens who were young, adventurous—and, of course, white. They were unlike each other in more ways than they were similar but all of them had a steely determination to achieve the objective they singled out and a larger than usual supply of luck, less in the form of an assurance of good fortune than protection from the consequences of folly. By courage, low cunning and what patronage he could pick up along the way, Guy was able follow his older brother Ernest in becoming an admiral of the Royal Navy. By sheer swagger and horsemanship the eldest of the boys, Cecil, charged up through the ranks of a prestigious British cavalry regiment. The two youngest made careers out of law rather than disorder. Clive became Crown Prosecutor of Burma, a nabob of the Raj. Lancelot interspersed his Singapore legal career with bizarre escapades of the kind the Gaunts seemed unable to avoid.

That was just the brothers. The oldest sister, Mary—Minnie—was every bit as ambitious and wily. For her breakthrough as a writer she impersonated both Ernest and Guy to publish accounts of their adventures. Established under her own name, she made intrepid solo journeys across West Africa and China that enthralled readers by the thousand and made her a world-class literary star. Her sister Lucy, another alpha female, presided over Australia's first university college for women. No other family ever produced a generation like these Gaunts.

Of all the siblings, Guy and Minnie were the closest. The only welcome news from Britain in the early days of the war was that she was safely back from China having made her way across the sprawl of Russia from East to West alone except for a small dog. 'Alone' was Minnie's recent Unique Selling Point. *Alone in West Africa*, an account of an earlier journey, sold far more than any of her novels and she could expect to clean up again with *Alone in China*. One day Guy would hear the story, the real story rather than the one she would fashion for her devoted readers. 'Alone, my foot', he teased when she came back from Africa. 'Alone but for twenty-five native bearers and a pile of letters of introduction that got you a comfortable bed every night.'

He had gone to Euston station to see her off on that trip. She was fifty-one years old and built, as he would later hear said in New York, like a fire-plug. It had taken all his skill at cargo stowage to get a mountain of stuff into the luggage van, twenty items in all from her dinky portable typewriter to a folding bed, bath, chairs and table, their wooden casing stencilled 'Captain C. R. Gaunt'. Brother Cecil, on his way from Africa to India, had left her those indispensable comforts, even his medicine chest, a marvellous affair of polished mahogany whose drawers and compartments held every remedy the intrepid explorer might need.

Minnie knew Guy had the measure of her. She certainly had the affectionate measure of him—of all the boys. Until the first *Alone* her books had not sold in numbers like those of Conan Doyle, Hilaire Belloc, Jack London or Rider Haggard, but periodicals in which those names appeared accepted articles from her as well. Her pieces were strongly feminist, usually urging women to take control of their lives, an attitude she also struck in her novels, the earliest of which were fashioned from memories of a childhood in the Australian goldfields and the fanciful reworking of tales their father told.

PART ONE

Weeks to go

Guy Gaunt's superiors at the Admiralty decided to park him out of sight until a major setback to his career faded from memory. He arrived at the embassy in Washington in June 1914, just weeks before the great confrontation began. The swirling currents of the Entente Cordiale that Britain had established with France, Russian meddling in the Austro-Hungarian lands and Germany's aggressive colonial ambitions had forced the empires of Europe on to a collision course, a term Guy that would have made Guy wince. In London, the prospect of war with Germany had been the overwhelming topic, the volume of sabre-rattling pumped up over years by invasion fantasies: Erskine Childers's *The Riddle of the Sands* and William Le Queux's ludicrously exaggerated books. Popular newspapers did their worst to help. The *London Weekly News* appointed a Spy Editor and offered readers £10 to report a snooping German. Only the faintest echoes of this febrile clamour had reached Washington, however. The British ambassador had tootled off home on leave, as usual; the staff was thinning out, many already headed for cooler shores and woodlands.

Guy's first weeks there were dismal. Even as he was settling in, the huge British fleet from which he had been plucked—'the greatest assemblage of naval power ever witnessed' as Churchill, then First Lord of the Admiralty, boasted—began drawing together in the strategic anchorage of Scapa Flow ready to face the German High Seas Fleet in a mighty clash of guns and armour that, it was widely expected, would settle the conflict in a matter of hours. *Der Tag*, it would be for the Germans. The Day. Rear Admiral Ernest Gaunt's pennant flew over a squadron of dreadnought battleships and only a stroke of bad luck, something that until recently had been as unfamiliar to Guy as a guilty conscience, had cost him command of one of those mighty vessels. It was agonising to be so far from the prospect of action. Going to war would be the fulfilment of the lust for adventure that drove that entire generation of Gaunts like the wind in the sails of a great clipper ship.

Still, it was not in Guy's nature to brood. An attaché appointment normally ran for two years but he would keep himself prepared for a recall long before that. It was not a hardship post and he was not in disgrace; no one in Washington seemed aware that he had suffered the worst disaster a captain could sustain, short of losing his ship altogether. It helped that he was a youthful forty-five, toughly good-looking and temporarily unencumbered. His wife Margaret had been reluctant to leave the splendid house she had just inherited for a stay that might be cut short if her husband were ordered back to sea.

A personable naval officer was welcome at every port of call on the diplomatic circuit. The first years of the century had seen a frenzy of naval *folie de grandeur*. Children everywhere were dressed in sailor suits and straw boater hats and encouraged to collect the cards from candy packets that catalogued All the World's Warships. The balance of power between nations largely depended on the size of their fleets; developments in naval technology and spending were discussed by shapers of opinion as keenly as finance, fashion or blood sports. No diplomatic hostess could hope to keep the subject out of any conversation for long. As a dinner guest Guy deployed his salty charm assiduously.

'Do tell me, captain, what is a battle*cruiser*?'

'It is the latest kind of dreadnought, madame. It has the firepower of a battleship but it is much faster.'

'How exciting!'

'But that greater speed means a battlecruiser can carry very little armour to protect itself. It must hit and run. If it should be hit by a battleship it might not be able to run very far.'

'And does your navy have many of these ships?'

'I am not allowed to tell you that, madame. But you could count them on your fingers.'

'And how fast can they go?'

'You would have to count your toes as well. And your knees and elbows and a couple more points of interest.'

'Captain!'

He had plenty of good stories, particularly one about being the only British officer to command American troops in action since the War of Independence. That was in Samoa some years earlier when British and American ships joined in teaching the natives—and the German colonists there—a lesson. He kept quiet about outmanoeuvring the American admiral who wanted him to burn down Robert Louis Stevenson's old home, and a few other episodes in his career that would have sent the diplomatic matrons' fans into overdrive. Rather, he trotted out tales about the bear he had adopted in Siberia and raised as a ship's pet or his delight in discovering that in nearby Virginia he could ride to hounds, even in the summer.

Occasionally, though, hints emerged that his earlier life had been intriguingly different from that of officers like Ernest, whose career had been conventional: Royal Navy College cadet at thirteen, seagoing midshipman at sixteen, steady progress up the ranks. Guy had shaped a far less predictable course through the vast job-creation scheme of British imperialism at its zenith, the network of law, language and service that spanned the globe. Hauling himself up the reverse side of the ladder had made him streetwise as well as seawise. He had no doubt that the luck of the Gaunts would turn again. If he could only stick out the job he had been given he might soon get back to sea, perhaps in time for *Der Tag*. Meanwhile, the idea of taking control of a gang of Central European political desperados until someone better qualified came along appealed to his buccaneering streak. But once the extent of what Voska had to offer became apparent his prospects of returning to the fleet were scuppered. From then on it was intrigue unlimited: Guy Gaunt, spymaster, spychaser and plenty more.

New World

Guy had never been to New York, apart from the taxi ride from the pier to Penn Station for the train to Washington when he first arrived , never been bombarded by its brash demands for attention. Manhattan was shrill, clanging and impatient, automobiles wobbling noisily up and down the avenues, the Elevated Railroad rumbling over Third Avenue like endless big-gun broadsides. The old New York of the Four Hundred, families that ranked their generations like royalty II, III and IV were somewhere in the brownstone background but since the turn of the century money had been spread more widely and spent more wildly: hustling and rustling, buying and selling, making deals, playing the market, anything to make a buck or multiply it. Men were cocky but congenial, Guy's kinda guys; the women made to match, straight-talking and confident in their crimson lipstick: riding alone in cabs, smoking cigarettes in restaurants, downing cocktails, foxtrotting. The new fashions showed flashes of ankle and shapes from a new, more daring come-on: the brassiere. The city's heartland, Times Square and Broadway, full of action and opportunity, raucous, chaotic and out for a swell time, grabbed Guy by the lapels and let him know he was welcome.

Washington, by contrast, was staid and horse-drawn, steamy as a boiler room, soggy with overcooked politics. American public life was as turbulent and personalised in 1914 as ever thereafter. President Woodrow Wilson, a Democrat, was an academic historian, his only previous experience in office as governor of New Jersey. Before that, he had been president of Princeton University. He was a relentless idealist, convinced he could enforce ethical behaviour not only in government but in the way private businessmen conducted their affairs. America was coming of age and under his leadership would make its moral weight felt in the world. His zeal extended to the disorderly politics of neighbouring countries in the Caribbean and Latin America. 'I intend to make them elect good men', he declared.

In his first months in office he set out to apply this ethical vision in Mexico, where the previous Republican administration had conspired to place in power General Victoriano Huerta, a dictator with a stare as cold and flat as the blade of an Aztec sacrificial knife. In an effort to undo the mischief that caused, Wilson invited Huerta to give up the presidency into which he had been parachuted and allow a successor to be democratically elected. It would be inappropriate, Wilson added loftily, for Huerta himself to stand as a candidate. Unsurprisingly, Huerta rejected this suggestion, his response implying that it seemed hardly the kind of thing one sovereign head of state should ask of another.

Wilson shifted his attention to Europe to try to divert the adversaries from the dangerous course they seemed to have settled on. He sent an emissary to London and Berlin, slow-speaking but quick-thinking Colonel Edward House, the most effective backroom power ever seen in Washington—or more often *not* seen, since he preferred to lie low in New York—until Henry Kissinger sidled on to the scene half a century later. Like Kissinger, House was never elected to office (nor was he a colonel) but his views, deftly and discreetly submitted, were the greatest single influence on the president. And in the early months of the war, when House himself needed to be put on the right heading, the views that had the most influence on him were those of Guy Gaunt.

At the outset Guy was merely a bystander. Naval and military attachés were expected to do some discreet sniffing about but not pry too closely into a host nation's affairs. Doing so would be not only a breach of the protective bubble of diplomatic immunity but ungentlemanly, especially in well-disposed America. 'Secret service' was something governments left to freelance spies and shadowy peddlers of information that all of them used but none of them trusted. Nevertheless, he was not entirely ignorant of intelligence fieldcraft, such as it was at the time. In preparation for his shoreside posting he had spent a few weeks in the office of the Director of Naval Intelligence to whom he would report. Blinker Hall's new management was in the offing and amid the turmoil no one had time to show him much beyond some schoolboyish tricks with invisible messages written on seemingly blank paper or between the lines of an innocuous document. An early technical breakthrough established that the substance most likely to remain unseen until subjected to heat was fresh semen. It had to be newly produced, his instructor explained, so that a treated document would not be detected by the smell.

Little more was to be learnt in another office to which he was invited for a chat. Realising how little was known in London about the intentions of potential enemies and allies alike, Prime Minister Herbert Asquith and his cabinet decided to create an organisation that could not only find out what was going on among peoples and places that might threaten Britain's placid ways but, if necessary, do something about it. Quietly. In 1909 the Secret Service Bureau had been set up, firewalled off from the departments of state—indeed from the government itself, so that its existence could be blandly denied. How that might be done was left to a conspiracy of civil servants. After many rounds of meetings the Foreign Office was told to come up with a budget of £60,000 a year and the War Office and the Admiralty were each given the impression that they would be in charge of the new entity's operations.

The man the Admiralty thought it had appointed to run the SSB was a half-pay commander named George Mansfield Cumming, lured away from his absorbing work on boom defences—the naval equivalent of herb gardening. Secrecy being the essential requirement, he was to be known only as C. It might as easily have been S since he was born Smith. He changed that to Cumming to please his wife. The man the War Office thought it had put in charge was Vernon Kell, an army captain and thus C's junior in rank by a wide gap. Mistrustfully, neither the army or the navy did away with their own intelligence departments. A Foreign Intelligence Committee had been in existence at the Admiralty since the Crimean War but its entire staff could fit around a bridge table. It was expanded into the Naval Intelligence Service, concentrating on developments in the German navy and, above all, the ciphers it used for wireless messages. It is only a slight oversimplification to say that out of this muddle the part of the operation that Kell got hold of evolved into MI5 and Cummings's part into MI6. Confusion was compounded when the Foreign Office, which after all was paying, decided to refer to the emotive little mess as MI1c rather than the SSB. This three-cornered alphanumeric rivalry endured for two world wars and meant that Britain's intelligence services often spent more time embroiled with each other than with potential enemies.

C set up his SSB shop in a cramped office on the Embankment but, as Guy found, he was always ready to whisk visitors off to lunch at the Royal Automobile Club. He was anything but secret about his movements. The chief constable of the Metropolitan Police gave him a special number plate that let him drive his car the wrong way around Trafalgar Square. Gave him a better look at the girls on the pavements, he said.

If Guy felt temperamentally unsuited to being a sort of diplomatic supercargo, neither did he feel an especially welcome guest in Washington after his ritual reception by Secretary of State William Jennings Bryan. The occasion had to wait until the ambassador, Sir Cecil Spring Rice, returned from London to present him. He got out his dress uniform: frock coat, sword, cocked hat, the attaché's festoon of gold aiguillettes spilling from the left shoulder, but he was completely outshone by his patron's gold embroidered scarlet tunic and feathered hat. Bryan made no effort to hide his disdain for all this imperial flamboyance. An early secretary of state had decreed that the country's diplomats should dress 'in the simple clothes of an American citizen' and in accordance Bryan wore a grey morning coat to match his grey face. Bryan was a pious backwoods preacher and devout pacifist, a Democrat stalwart who had failed three times to win the presidency and eventually swung his support behind Wilson. In repayment he was made nominally responsible for foreign relations; in practice Wilson did the job for him, clacking out foreign policy memoranda on a primitive Hammond 12 typewriter. The president was self-conscious about his handwriting which was already impaired by the neurological condition he kept secret until his last days in office.

State shared the Executive Office Building next door to the White House with Army and Navy but while the secretaries of those departments conducted their activities with discretion Bryan turned his office into a public shrine, setting a bench at the open door where sightseers could sit and watch the great man at work. Since the president had taken over most of his functions what Bryan might actually have been working at was anyone's guess.

The British were no more at ease with Bryan than with Wilson. Some thought the Secretary was pro-German but he was, in fact, utterly isolationist, so opposed to the United States becoming involved in the European war that he feared contamination by anyone likely to advocate it. Wilson at least was, in cultural terms, an anglophile with an instinctive inclination towards the British viewpoint, but the two men were equally dedicated to the republican form of government. All the Allies and all the Central Powers were imperial monarchies, all of them equally decadent and undemocratic. Wilson could see no principle at stake that his conscience would allow him to support. The United States might try to show them the error of their ways but it would favour none of them over the others. Rather than help stoke the flames the United States would continue striving to quell them.

The coolness that tricked down Guy's spine like cold rain as the painful audience with Bryan stretched out also reflected the Administration's exasperation at having to put up with Sir Cecil whom Wilson found 'puzzling and incalculable'. 'Springy', poet and hymn-writer on the side, had been selected for the post before Wilson won the 1913 election and it was far from diplomatic of Britain to have confirmed him as Britain's envoy afterwards. His hitherto illustrious career had begun as a junior secretary in the Washington embassy thirty-five years earlier, an era in which the Republicans ruled. He became so close to Teddy Roosevelt, their star, that when Springy was posted back to London the future president went over to be married in St George's, Hanover Square, so that he could be best man. Springy's friends from that earlier time were now Republican grandees, flinty adversaries of Wilson's party. The Democrats assumed that he and Roosevelt, a lurking presence, still had each other's ear, particularly when Springy persisted in pressing the view he had formed in twenty years of postings all around Europe: that the Germany of Kaiser Wilhelm II was an evil empire out to dominate as much of the world as possible—especially those parts of it that belonged to Britain—and would soon attempt to undermine America's stability from within. It did not help that Springy was developing Graves' disease, a thyroid complaint that among other unpleasant symptoms caused his eyes to bulge, making the irritable outbursts for which it was also responsible, even more alarming.

There were also pragmatic reasons why the Democrats did not want to listen to him. The attempts Wilson had so far made to extend America's influence had missed their objective. The main effect of the Mexican adventure had been to make all of Latin America more suspicious than ever of *gringo* intentions and alert American voters to the cost of foreign adventures. Americans of British stock might have been ready to accept that Britain's cause was just, even if they could not explain quite why; many people in Britain had the same problem. But a similar number, especially those who qualified themselves by a hyphen—Irish-Americans, German-Americans—were ferociously opposed to any kind of support for Britain or her allies, France and Russia. Ireland was still a province of Great Britain, governed from London, but turbulent, resentful and dangerous, as were many of its people who found their way to a better life in the United States. Something like one in ten Americans had been born in Germany and at least twice that number had a German parent. Those hyphenates were all American voters and with an election due in 1916 Wilson and his

Democrats could not afford to offend any of them.

Springy was right about Germany, of course, but that was not what the president wanted to hear. Even after the war began Wilson remained convinced he could yet bring the Europeans together in peace and Springy's undiplomatic inability to keep his rabid hostility to Germany out of any discussion made him virtually *persona non grata* at the White House.

By contrast with State, Guy found dealing with Navy a pleasure once he got past its titular head. Secretary Josephus Daniels was a newspaper owner given the appointment for supporting Wilson in the 1912 election, an authoritarian bigot who caused great trouble for the Democrats by having his papers campaign for 'White Supremacy'. He had put unbridgeable blue water between himself and the uniformed ranks by banning alcohol in the fleet. Little wonder that Guy, brought up in the Royal Navy tradition of gin in the wardroom and rum on the lower deck, preferred to make his calls on Assistant Secretary Franklin Delano Roosevelt, who introduced him to the martini cocktail and was happy to talk shop. Talk ships, really. When Franklin's uncle Theodore had been president, his White Fleet project helped the persuade Congress to briefly overcome its parsimony and isolationism and authorise ten dreadnoughts. That was a start, but Britain had twenty-nine and thirteen more on the slips. Germany had eighteen and was building two more each year.

'And how many of these fearsome battlecruisers does the United States have, captain?'

'Er ... none, madame.'

Many Americans were unhappy that their country lagged so far behind in sea power; others worried about what it might be used for. When Huerta rejected Wilson's suggestion he should step down the president sent the navy to occupy Vera Cruz, Mexico's main port, effectively blockading the country. The wily old Indian was not a man to be intimidated, even with American big guns at his door. One of the many casualties of his bloody rise to power had a brother, a barber in Mexico City, who had sworn revenge. Huerta went alone every day to be shaved, baring his throat to the open razor, holding the man with that flat stare.

When the Mexicans found ways to work around the Yankee invasion Wilson embarked on a desperate courtship of Huerta's enemies. They proved no easier to manipulate, likely to take the money and fail to deliver the goods. Eventually, most of the United States Army had to be called away from keeping native Americans at bay on the westward frontiers and sent across the border in pursuit of Pancho Villa, bandit king or freedom fighter, depending on who was asked. Bryan watched these botched adventures as though from a distant shore.

Helped by his chatty and convivial ways, Guy moved ever higher up Washington's dinner tables. Invariably higher, he was pleased to note, than his rivals, the Austrian and German attachés whom he also frequently encountered in the bar of the Willard Hotel, a leatherbound snakepit between Capitol Hill and the White House brimming with cigar smoke and conspiracy. His opposite number, *Fregatten-kapitän* Karl Boy-Ed, was more congenial than the military attaché, *Kapitän* Franz von Papen, although neither had much success at ingratiating themselves with Americans who were bemused by their monocles, duelling scars and arrogant manners. Even in civilian clothes the pair came across as caricatures of the Prussian officer, though Papen was from the Rhineland and Boy-Ed was born in the Hanseatic city of Lubeck, his odd name passed down from a Turk in the family tree.

Just as Guy cultivated young Roosevelt, the real mover at Navy, he made friends with the second-in-command at State, Robert Lansing the Counsellor, who was anglophile to the point of having his shoes made in London and taking elocution lessons. Even in Springy's absence his entourage, the Counsellor and the Secretaries First and Second, could hardly tread where their leader was not welcome and Guy quickly emerged as the acceptable personification of the embassy. That made him a good deal less popular inside it. The career diplomats were nervous about the caste distinction between themselves and the attachés, always fearful that a maladroit soldier or sailor might blunder into some protocol blindspot or use the wrong fork. They had even less idea than Guy himself of what he might usefully do and all kinds of trivia that no one else knew what to do with landed on his desk. Give it to Poor Old Gaunt, the careerists would say in mock sympathy and more bureaucratic jetsam marked—as they thought amusing—POG hit his in-tray. It was no life for a sailor. No life for a Gaunt.

Tough times

1853. It takes an effort, a century and a half later, to come to terms with the life of the young Gaunts. Their earliest years were passed in a world without electricity or running water, petrol engines or railways. It took at least half a year for a letter to reach London and be answered. With no communication other than talking face-to-face or writing, no means of getting about other than horse or foot, events unreeled slowly. So little—or so it seemed to them—could be fitted into a lifetime; lives, in any case, were likely to be short. Diet was poor, accidents frequent, violence rampant, medical care more dangerous than illness. They had to get going.

Their father, William Henry Gaunt, became a civil servant soon after he reached Australia but he wondered about his choice of career when, a few months after arriving, he was nearly run over by a prospector in a buggy drawn by a high-stepping mare shod with shining gold. He would never have seen that in Leek, Staffordshire, where he was born in 1830, although he knew something of the luxury trades. His own father's fortune came from weaving and printing silk but his older brother Robert took over the business, leaving William free to choose his own way in life. Intrigued by the new wonder of steam, he had gone to work for the North Staffordshire Railway Company whose little green and black engines pottered around the Potteries at not much faster than walking pace. He rose to be manager of one of the branch lines and was wondering whether a takeover bid from the expanding London and North East Railway might move him up the executive ladder or down when the three-masted barque *Thomas Arbuthnot* reached London with a fateful cargo. On 10 September 1851 her master, George Heaton, announced that he had brought back the first shipment of gold from a vast new find in south-eastern Australia. It had not been easy. 'The colony is completely paralysed,' Captain Heaton told the *Morning Post*: 'Every man and boy who is able to lift a shovel is off, or going off, to the diggings.'

The strike was near the town of Melbourne in the Port Phillip District, a part of the continent soon to be separated from New South Wales and become the Colony of Victoria. Dozens of ships were stranded there, crews having bolted ashore to join the rush. Heaton got the *Thomas*

Arbuthnot away only by promising double wages. His account and those that gradually followed touched off a fuse that sparked its way around the British Isles, filling newspaper columns with tales of instant gratification. One good find, a single nugget the size of a plug of tobacco, could set a man up for life.

John Lees came out from the depressed cotton town of Oldham in mid-1852 and wrote home

> a week in Melbourne and started for the diggings on the monday morning, there was a mob of about 80 all met in the morning near this flag staff a motly group we were i can assure you, dress'd in colonial style blue flannel slops, belts and billy cocks, some arm'd with revolvers, in fact all arm'd up to the teeth, with revolvers, double barrel'd rifles, pistols double and single, daggers &c all looking and feeling volumes of valour, bidding defiance to, and predicting the probable fate of any bushrangers that might interrupt our progress.

Lees had to borrow half the thirty shillings he needed to stake a claim, but on 31 January 1853 he and his partners discovered the 'Canadian' Nugget, 134 pounds (41kg) and about the size of a Christmas turkey. They carried it to the assayer on a litter, breaking off bits on the way to hand out to friends. Hayes sailed away on the ship that had brought him and back in Oldham used the proceeds to put up the Ballarat Buildings in Nugget Street.

For several years the British government had been encouraging migration to the Australian colonies by subsidising fares for suitable applicants. Now people, suitable or not, scrambled to pay their own way out at premium rates. A year after Heaton's return ninety shiploads of cheerful optimists were leaving for Melbourne every month. One of the fortune-seekers, George Mundy, described his fellow passengers as

> merchants, cabmen, magistrates and convicts, amateur gentlemen… fashionable hairdressers and tailors, cooks, coachmen, lawyers' clerks and their masters, colliers, cobblers, quarrymen, doctors of physic and music, aldermen, an ADC on leave, scavengers, sailors, shorthand writers, a real live lord on his travels—all levelled by community of pursuit.

In other words—those of the historian Geoffrey Searle— 'something like a cross-section of Britain with a thin slice off the top and a thick slice off the bottom'. William Gaunt, coming from a slice somewhere in between, thought that while scrabbling for gold was unlikely to provide the kind of upright and orderly life he preferred, the newly proclaimed colony would soon need experienced administrators. He sailed from Dartmouth in the barque *Ganges* in March 1853.

Even before the lure of gold plenty of well-intentioned young men like William were attracted to Britain's possessions around the globe. Those who went to the 'colonies of settlement', nations still in the making like New Zealand, Canada, the Cape Colony on the tip of Africa and, of course, New South Wales and Van Diemen's Land, thought of themselves as merely moving within the British World. This notional space, unrelated to geography, was well understood before it fell out of fashion with historians more comfortable with later forms of globalisation and multiculturism. Later, some of them began to think of it as defined by language, which meant including the United States: the Anglo World.

But Sir Charles Dilke, an undersecretary of state, called this white lining to the Empire's cloak of many colours, 'Greater Britain'. New arrivals might find the geography a bit of a shock but they were not strangers. People already there—apart from any *indigenes*—understood what they said. Carpenters and dressmakers used the same measures as those at Home, the term for Britain that remained commonplace among those of English and Scottish, if not Irish descent, until well into the 20th Century. Cooks produced the same dull food, the doctor prescribed the same useless remedies. Children like the Gaunts, born under another capital letter— Colonials—were Britons of that Greater Britain, too, bound to their roots not just by language and the everyday values of life but by an instinctive moral code, the acceptance of law. Their feelings about this were nothing as shallow as patriotism but far more fundamental than religion—people sometimes changed that. Britishness was their natural inheritance. Self. Soul. Essence. It was also, no one had to explain to them, their natural right to go anywhere in the World, British or Anglo, that they wished to.

In the late 1840s, when a modest gold strike was reported in New South Wales, Lieutenant Governor Charles La Trobe came up with the morale-boosting wheeze of a £200 prize for finding gold within two hundred miles of Melbourne. No one could have foreseen the result of this mild attempt to stimulate economic growth. Gold seemed to appear along every dried-out creek bed and word of it travelled fast as a bushfire. The scale of the finds was staggering. La Trobe, a dilettantish travel writer and botanist who had been given his post in recognition of a little anti-slavery campaigning he had done in the West Indies, found himself in charge of the most unruly corner of the British World.

When William arrived after three months at sea Hobson's Bay, the shanty port of Melbourne, was sodden, filthy and threatening. It was his second winter of the year and the Southern Hemisphere in June was as cold and wet as Leek had been when he left. A jolting, sloshing coach ride took him through slums of teetering shacks walled with slabs of tree trunks and roofed with flattened kerosene cans. The few buildings of rough-cut stone were already grimy from the wood smoke that filled the air together with the stink of hides and sewage. The muddy tracks were deserted save for an occasional hooded figure flitting through the rain. The weight of a pistol in his pocket was reassuring. Every traveller leaving Britain had been advised to take a firearm.

As he was soon to see, gold had flipped everything out of control. Melbourne's population of 23,000, not counting aborigines, halved virtually overnight. Thousands of men streamed inland to Ballarat (then Ballar*aat*) Bendigo and other outlandishly named places, trekking through the bush, living off what they could find or steal. There was no infrastructure to deal with such upheaval, no roads and now no one to build them. There was only one flimsy jetty from which to load the ships that kept arriving stern to bowsprit in the bay, no proper warehouses for the cargos of wheat and wool which piled up because so few of the vessels set sail again.

The police had been among the first to go. Only two constables were left in Melbourne and only forty-four soldiers in the entire territory. People left behind were in daily fear of their lives and property. Time-expired convicts from Tasmania and New South Wales infiltrated the half-deserted town, cutpurses and armed robbers, violent brutes no one would want to meet in daylight, let alone in the reeking dark alleys. Bushrangers, the local version of highwaymen and hijackers, began to exploit the goldfields Some became romanticised but most were simply psychopathic misfits who would have killed many more people if their weapons had been efficient. La Trobe had warned Lord Grey, Secretary of State for War and the Colonies and son of the renowned tea fancier, that anarchy threatened. A ragtag militia of pensioned-off jailers, most of them less trustworthy than their former prisoners, had been pulled together but he pleaded to be sent a regiment that could be relied upon not to desert or mutiny. He also submitted his resignation but since it would be months before he received a reply he had to do what he could to stem the stampede for which he was inadvertently responsible.

There was only one government building and only one of its offices mattered: the Gold Fields Department. William produced his references and received a warm welcome from La Trobe—now a fully titled Governor, even though he was still waiting to hear that his resignation has been accepted—and a job as a clerk. William's attention was firmly drawn to a regulation drawn up by the Legislative Council that was serving as a stopgap until an Assembly could be elected: no mining licences would be granted to persons who have left 'public or hired service'. No job-switching, then.

Those licenses, known as a Miner's Right, had become La Trobe's second worst problem. The goldfields were not only wilder than the wildest of the American west they were far richer. In 1852 the Melbourne Town Council estimated that the average *weekly* output was more than *all* the mines in America had produced in any year of the previous half-century. In the week this was worked out the yield had been eight tons, which in 2015, would transmute into £234 million. But for all the gold that passed through its hands the government was desperate for revenue. Its only cash flow aside from customs dues—which since most new arrivals imported nothing but themselves were scanty—came from the fee charged for the Miners' Rights. Before a man could even enter a goldfield zone he had to pay thirty shillings for his licence. A repeat payment was due every month even if the holder did not stake out a 'claim', typically a 12 square foot (3.6 metre) plot, or whether or not he found gold. A year earlier thirty shillings would have bought an acre and a half of Crown land.

As well as issuing Rights, Gold Fields registered claims and organised the safe transport of gold to Melbourne and on to the London market. Prospectors who struck lucky could sell their find to a government buyer or a private operator, both of which were to be found camped by every main find alongside their scales, phials of acid for assaying and a minder with a stubby shotgun. The price was set in Melbourne every few days and advertised on posters. How much a miner actually got for his offering would depend on its purity, whether it had to be separated from quartz; in the case of a nugget rather than specks, its size.

London soon tumbled to the enormous financial benefit of Victorian gold and while it could not micro-manage the affairs of the new colony from such a distance it was evident that order must be maintained. Isambard Brunel's *Great Britain*, a huge vessel that had been the first steamship to cross the Atlantic, was put on the Australia run. On her first voyage out, a few months before William's arrival, about a third of her 750 passengers were recruits for the Victorian police or the Corps of Gold Commissioners, means by which La Trobe hoped to balance the colony's books.

The new gold commissioners were a serious force. Many had been army officers or minor functionaries in other colonies, particularly India. Swaggering and befrogged in scarlet tunics, they became a loathsome personification of stern government. They took over the issue of Rights and punishment for those who could not produce one. The penalty was £5. If a man could not pay he had to earn out the amount—plus the original fee—on roadworks at ten shillings a day. Often this was doubly unfair. The licence was crudely printed on flimsy paper that often disintegrated in a sweaty pocket and no record was kept of those issued—or of the payments.

Neither did the new constabulary bear much resemblance to the drunken and corrupt rabble of pensioners it replaced. Men of experience, many of them seasoned by strong-arming insurgents in Ireland, had been signed up as muscle to enforce the commissioners' rule. Ordinary citizens found them no help. La Trobe did not want their efforts wasted on the crime wave lapping at towns and settlements, let alone the murderous robberies that had become daily events on the goldfields. The spectacle of ragged diggers fleeing before rampaging police became so notorious that artists re-created them for newspapers. Even the distant *London Illustrated News* published the sketches. It was clear that the licence fee was nothing but a tax and a deeply unfair one. Melbourne began to hear the worrying murmur of 'No taxation without representation' that had undermined the American colonies.

After six months of dealing with goldfield matters from a comfortable distance, William was thought experienced enough to tackle his duties at the sharp end. He was appointed chief clerk of newly opened diggings at Beechworth, two hundred miles north east of Melbourne, where a find only months old had attracted several thousand prospectors. His salary was a reasonable £350 a year; in addition, he got board and lodging, forage for a horse and three candles a month. The six days in the saddle it took him to get there seemed as long as his voyage out in the *Ganges*. The track was more like the route of a retreating army than the road to riches, lined with broken-down drays and wagons, skeletons of horses and cattle and every few miles a lonely grave.

Beechworth was the archetypical goldrush town. An American, Charles Ferguson, reckoned that even in California he had never seen a place where money was thrown around so wildly. Miners played skittles with bottles of champagne. At the racetrack, an amenity as basic to a gold town as the cemetery, they ran around drunk, hands full of banknotes, placing bets on every starter. 'Such is the effect that sudden riches too often has upon those who formerly had nothing', Ferguson concluded piously.

He and several other '49-ers, veterans of the California strikes who had ended up with nothing, sailed for Sydney as soon as they heard of the Victorian strikes. When the ship berthed, men stormed up the gangway offering to buy their Colt revolvers: $250 for the jumbo-sized Navy model, $150 for the pocketable 'Baby Dragoon'. The Californians figured that if Australians wanted guns so badly they had better hang on to theirs.

The main field was in the Ovens River gorge. The claims along the riverbed and the creeks running into it were measured out along the banks. The gold was alluvial, embedded in quartz and gravel. Waist-deep in the freezing river, diggers scraped it out and sieved away the muck, hoping for the glimpse of a gleaming speck. Hundreds of them were killed by pneumonia in the winter and more would die from typhoid in the spring when sewage from their flimsy encampments seeped into the water. In the summer the streams dried out and the sieves were abandoned for 'dry blowing', the grit spread on bits of canvas, men puffing away at it like trombonists.

William's lodgings were not in Beechworth. He was given a clapboard shack at Woolshed Creek fifteen miles out, a fabled field where a man called Jonston had produced a £1 million worth of gold [at 2016 values] in a year. It was a lonely life for a young man as well as a rough one: easier to find gold than a woman to marry. There were two men for every woman in the Colony but on the goldfields it was more like fifty. Six years passed before he met Elizabeth Palmer whose father, George, had been in the merchant fleet of the old East India Company. Elizabeth was twenty-five, getting on for a bride of that time. William was thirty. They were to have ten babies altogether, although three did not survive the hazards of birth and infancy in the bush. From his big boots to the birds-nest beard he cultivated even as a young man, William Gaunt was soon a Victorian patriarch—in time as well as place—fitting the part in every respect save one: his children rarely did as he wanted them to.

Among the surprises awaiting him in the goldfields had been the number of Chinese there. Throughout Victoria there were 42,000 'Celestials', as they were scornfully called, a reference to the Celestial Kingdom against which Britain would soon unleash the Opium Wars to enforce the imperial dope trade. Almost all of them came from the Pearl River region in southern China and spoke Cantonese, in which Australia was *hsin chin-shan*—'mountain of gold'. They had their own system of trading and getting their finds out of the country. How much gold they were able to export remains a mystery now as then; informed guesswork suggests it could have surpassed even the huge amount processed through the government system and the banks.

To the European eye the Celestials were caricatures, long pigtails dangling from beneath a skullcap, shuffling around on wooden sandals, nightshirt-like shifts flapping about their shanks. *The Age* called them 'Barbarians' and—alliteration trumping geography—'miserable Mongolians'. Foam-flecked speakers in the Legislative Council accused them of cannibalism and child molesting. Another public functionary was invented: Protector of the Chinese. The intention was actually to keep the Celestials segregated. They were charged £1 for an annual 'protection ticket' that entitled them to live in an enclosed camp controlled by Chinese constables.

There was no camp around the Buckland field and two thousand Celestials to seven hundred or so whites. Many of the original prospectors, plagued by fleas and flies as well as gold commissioners, had moved to Bendigo or Ballarat but Chinese fossickers regularly turned up gold in abandoned workings, which made them even more resented. The commissioner who ran the field before William did little to encourage racial harmony. He was as much of a caricature as the Celestials, wearing the kilt and riding on a donkey. He held audiences from a bed in his tent, out of sight.

A gang of disgruntled miners waited for a day when all but one of the small force of constables were away in Beechworth and gathered at the Buckland Hotel to address 'the problem'. Provocative speeches were made, then full of rum and resentment—and led, the local newspaper reported, by Americans—a mob tore down a 'joss-house' temple then stormed along the river banks where most of the Chinese camped. Hundreds of tents and shacks were trashed, their contents scattered in the churned-up mud. Terrified Celestials bolted across the river, slipping on the logs that served as a bridge. Three, at least, drowned in the icy water.

William rode down to Buckland, rallied the constabulary, dealt firmly with the disaffected miners and did his best to persuade the Chinese to come back. It was an impressive performance which the government recognised by appointing him a Protector in addition to his other duties. He had handbills stencilled in Cantonese characters promising justice and safety for all. His proclamation ended on a splendidly florid note which, translated, raised chuckles throughout the colony. 'I am your Protector', he assured the apprehensive Celestials. 'Tremble and Obey'.

Those and other stories, told and retold by their parents, tinged the Gaunt children's memories of the police camp, a fenced-off compound on the edge of the diggings, where sunrise and sunset was marked by a crackling fusillade. The gunpowder of the time was prone to dampness so firearms were frequently discharged and reloaded to ensure it would be dry when needed. The earliest of the children were born there in a tin-roofed clapboard shack that was also William's office. The murderous confrontation between redcoats and miners at the Eureka Stockade in 1851 rattled all of Greater Britain. The role of gold commissioners was redefined and William became one of the new and responsible kind as well as a Protector and a magistrate.

Every week or so a Gold Escort formed up to take the yield to the Treasury in Melbourne. Bags of gold were packed into metal chests the size a coffin, sixty-two kilos in each, about the weight of a digger's undernourished corpse. Wooden covers were screwed on, the counter-sunk heads covered with wax into which William pressed his seal. An old-timer remembered those days as one of the cheeriest sights the goldfields could offer.

...the bounding horses, the blue and white uniforms of the guard, the sound of swords as they rattled in their steel scabbards, with the thought behind it all, 'There goes a hundred thousand pounds worth of gold.'

At their stops along the way Wlliam and the captain of the Escort would sleep on top of the precious chests, shotguns by their side.

The police were more disciplined and responsible than in earlier days, the mounted troopers especially. Smart in white cord breeches and blue jackets, they and their beautifully groomed mounts with the royal cypher VR, Victoria Regina, gleaming on the saddle flaps enthralled the young Gaunts. They knew all about the World those intertwined initials symbolised. Their schooling taught them more about Bonnie Prince Charlie and Henry the Eighth than about Sydney Cove or the South Pole; everything about the Battle of Hastings but nothing whatever about the whipping triangles in the penal colonies of Moreton Bay and Port Arthur. Their everyday life, their language, lessons, all their knowledge and striving—their future—belonged to that British World. They grew up surrounded by people talking about Home and never doubted that was where the life of roaming and adventure each of them already envisioned must begin. They were not at all discouraged by the knowledge that many of the incomers still arriving in the Colony showed no inclination to go back where they had come from. They wove together a tribal myth in which the great ship Home had run up on the rocks, its steerage class passengers brought ashore in lifeboats. The Gaunts would scramble on board the drifting hulk, find that there was plenty of steam left in the boilers and that tea was still being served in the first class saloon. Then they would begin the voyage of their restless lives. Their favourite books were by Robert Louis Stevenson. 'I travel not to go anywhere, but to go,' one would quote from this spiritual guide. Another would respond, as though in a litany, 'To travel hopefully is better than to have arrived.'

'The wander fever was in my blood,' Minnie wrote, half a century later when it was still running strong, 'and in the blood of my sisters and brothers.' Even so, the adventures that lay ahead of them never obliterated those childhood memories. The imagery of the smartly turned-out troopers, the shuffling pigtailed Celestials, the ragged miners and their scraggy, defensive women were sealed in the children's minds like the gold in the Escort's metal chests. The feel of beaten earth floors under their bare feet, the scents of sweat, lamp oil, rum, boiled mutton, billycan tea, damper loaves baked in ashes, the sulphurous whiff of reloading volleys leached into their genes. The earliest stories that Minnie wrote and her most successful books were forged from those childhood days: the colourful, dangerous life of the diggings that only a few years later were wiped away by the very riches it produced and by the electric telegraph, the railway and large stone prisons.

Brothers and sisters

Cecil the eldest son, Ernest and Guy were sent to Melbourne Church of England Grammar. Great excitement ran through the place at news that its boys, and those from the other simulacrums of English public schools, Scotch College and Geelong Grammar, were to be allowed to sit an annual examination to qualify as cadet midshipmen in the Royal Navy. Each of the Australian colonies had some kind of rudimentary maritime force to defend its main port against the French, Russians or other intruders but serious protection was the responsibility of the Royal Navy's Australia Squadron, half a dozen old men-o'-war. Not all of them were seaworthy enough to patrol the vast and scattered territories allotted them, showing the flag to frighten off 'blackbirders'—an innocuous description for the ruthless slavers of the South Seas. Much time was spent in Sydney Harbour where the officer in command enjoyed a splendid view from Admiralty House on Kirribilli Point.

The prospect inspired the younger brothers. They had all grown out of their dreams about the Good Ship Home and come to accept that there were practical difficulties to be surmounted. This was their first inkling that the wind of adventure still stirring them might somehow be funnelled through the great imperial apparatus of the World. It was only reasonable of William to expect that his sons might follow him in the law but if he was unhappy when Ernest announced that he wanted to try for the navy he was not unreasonable. Minnie remembered his capitulating words.

'If you don't get away now, you'll be miserable. And you'll only go later when I can't prevent it.'

Ernest was soon on his way to England and two years at the Royal Navy College, actually the grim old hulk HMS *Britannia* in Dartmouth. After another year under sail in a training brig was posted not to the exotic outposts of his boyhood dreams but back home to the Australia Station.

Minnie knew that to satisfy her longings; to fulfil a need that although not yet fully shaped was as compulsive as hunger, she too—and Lucy—should get away. But, she wrote in a wistful autobiographical passage, 'For us two girls there was no prospect.'

> Our world was bounded by our father's lawns and the young men who came to see us and made up picnic parties to the wildest bush round Ballarat for our amusement.

Not, Minnie was emphasising, their mother's lawns, even though Elizabeth was as impressive and capable a woman as any in the Colony. Like all the Gaunts, Cecil particularly but even the youngest, Clive and Lance, she rode every day, side-saddle as women were expected to, in broad, swinging skirts. The boys on their ponies had trouble keeping up as she led them cantering around the various properties through which William's progress moved them. Horses were inseparable from a life that, for all her yearnings, Minnie had to admit

> was not bad. Even now I acknowledge to something of the delight to be found in a box-seat of a four-in-hand, a glorious moonlight night, and four horses going at full speed; something delightful in scrambles over the ranges and a luncheon in the shade by a waterhole, with romantic stories for seasoning, and the right man with a certain admiration in his eyes to listen. It was not hard but it was not as good a life as the boys of the family were having …

She understood that her parents were merely responding to the conventions of the period in assuming that the only acceptable future for a girl was marriage. But she did not seem to be heading in that direction. The young Gaunts had always joked that money was merely 'a means of locomotion' but she had yet to discover how to get the wheels turning.

Once she did she liked to tell people she had actually grasped a central issue of feminism, financial independence, when she was only twelve. In an interview with the *Sydney Mail* in 1898 she said:

I only took to writing to make money. When we grew up and went out, my sister, who is a little younger that I am and is pretty—quite pretty, got plenty of attention, always had heaps of partners at balls and enjoyed herself everywhere but I—did not. At the age of 20 I made up my mind that I was not a social success; thought I was getting old, dreadfully old, too old to go to dances any more, and then came a terrible question—what was to become of me? And not only of me, of hundreds of other girls, too, girls of the upper middle class, who have no provision made for them in case they do not marry. I did not think then that I would ever be married, nor did I want to be. My father had always told us that we were very badly off and seeing that there was (as I thought) no chance of my being provided for in the conventional way, I determined that I would make myself independent.

Very badly off was not how most people would have seen the Gaunts but the children were a heavy liability. William held even more appointments as changing administrations fiddled with the colony's problems. For much of the time he had been studying law and eventually decided to go to the Bar. Gold had become a complex, industrialised and corporate business: expertise like his could be put to profitable use. He hoped the remaining boys would read for the law after Melbourne Grammar. But he readily paid for both girls to go to university even though he assumed they would marry. Minnie pulled off a historic first; half of one, at least, since she shared the distinction with another girl. The University of Melbourne, like most universities everywhere at the time, did not yet admit women. Nevertheless, in 1881 her English teacher at Grenville College, Ballarat, insisted she take the matriculation examination and when the doors were prised open five years later she was able to enrol for a Bachelor of Arts degree.

She was never candid about why she left after her first year. Her results had not been brilliant: she passed in only two of six subjects, but there was time in which to improve. She may have felt the decision was made for her by one of the flashes of drama that periodically illuminated the Gaunts' life. Bushfire, the lowering menace of Australia, engulfed the farmhouse in which the family was living at Potilla on the outskirts of Ballarat. There was no time to dress and only enough to grab a few possessions. It was a Sunday morning and churchgoers were treated to the sight of William in his nightshirt at the reins of a buggy, Elizabeth beside him in her dressing gown, a valuable Chinese vase in one hand, a decanter of whisky in the other. Five children—Lance was yet to come—huddled in the back seat, Lucy nursing baby Clive. Everything else had been lost, including Minnie's books and her undergraduate cap and gown: clearly a sign that her academic life had ended. Interestingly, a couple of years later Lucy enrolled for an Arts degree and sailed though her course. Then got married.

The next home was a huge jumble of a place with an ecclesiastical look to it, built by one of the early free-spending prospectors; two-storeys in the main part and a tower that rose up another two. Mullioned windows everywhere and a porch like a chapel. He and Elizabeth called it *Koonda*, after the little town where they had spent their honeymoon. It was in Sturt Street, Ballarat, near Lake Wendouree, now a wide ornamental stretch of water. In those days it was called Yuille's Swamp, after the shepherd who happened upon it and asked the aborigines if it had a name. The reply, *Wendouree*, translated roughly as 'piss off'.

Showing the flag

1882. Whether it was because of the first defector in his glamorous midshipman's uniform, back from Home with tales of wind and sea, or the contagious wanderlust that affected all the siblings, William could not persuade the sons above and below Ernest that they had a future in the law. He did not persist with Cecil, who had failed the matriculation examination three times and went from Melbourne Grammar to a mundane job in a bank, a mere means to an end. His life had come to centre on horses; a devotion bordering on obsession. Guy, still at school, began to pester his father to let him follow Ernest into the navy, which William insisted he could not afford.

Ernest had barely recovered his shore legs from the passage back to

Australia before he was bundled on board the steam frigate HMS *Emerald* which set off from Sydney on a punitive expedition. A naval schooner, HMS *Zephyr*, had been attacked in the Solomon Islands, its crewmen killed and in some cases eaten. It was an unusually dramatic introduction to the Squadron. The last spike of excitement had been registered ten years earlier when the admiral in charge was killed by poisoned arrows in the Santa Cruz Islands.

Shore parties from *Emerald* recovered the logbook and other property from the schooner and found the body of the lieutenant commanding her. Ernest joined the avenging sailors in burning down a hundred or so huts. *Emerald* then bombarded a few more villages that seemed too dangerous to enter and returned to Sydney with several suspects to be tried and duly hanged. Ernest was transferred to the squadron flagship HMS *Nelson*, a decrepit sail-steam hybrid armed with muzzle-loaders not much different from the guns used at Trafalgar three-quarters of a century earlier but sound enough still to take part in a stirring imperial sideshow.

Indifference as much as tenuous communications kept British governments largely ignorant of what was going on in such a remote place as New Guinea. The western half of the huge island had been spoken for by the Dutch years earlier but the eastern half, called Papua after its largest ethnic group, lay unclaimed by any colonising power. Gold had been found there, although deep in the jungle and hard to get at. Easier pickings were to be had by diving for pearl shell or trapping exotic birds to feather the hats of London ladies. In 1846 a Royal Navy ship ran up the flag in Port Moresby, the dingy settlement across the Coral Sea from the northernmost tip of Australia, but no one took much notice, least of all the Colonial Office. In the early 1870s Papua was bundled in with everything else that came under the authority of the Commissioner for the Western Pacific hundreds of miles away in Fiji. In reality it had been abandoned to feral prospectors, fugitives from justice and part-time cannibals.

The closest point of civilisation—to stretch the term—was the Queensland colony. For some years traders had been bringing in reports of German warships nosing around the north east sector of the island and in 1882 the chief minister, Sir Thomas McIlwraith, wrote to London expressing his concern. The new colonial secretary, Lord Derby, replied loftily that he was confident Germany had no territorial ambitions in those parts. The letter was still making its way out when McIlwraith took an executive decision and ordered a magistrate at Thursday Island, to hop over to Moresby and take possession of 'so much of the island as was not already in the occupation or possession of the Dutch'.

Derby found out about this bold act from a report in *The Times* from Berlin. He demanded that Queensland withdraw its claim. A listless exchange of views was still going on when the German Ambassador in London began to drop hints that a 'friendly understanding' might be desirable about the undeveloped north-east shore of Papua. Even as a Colonial Office delegation was sorting through its papers and maps a German warship hoisted the imperial flag over the territory in question and several adjacent islands. 'I think the German government have behaved very shabbily', bleated a British diplomat. HMS *Nelson*, Midshipman Ernest Gaunt on board, was despatched from Sydney to claim what was left of New Guinea.

Minnie felt a promising tremor of locomotion. She had sold her first piece, 'Lost in the Bush', to the Sydney *Post*. A university tutor who admired her writing was commissioned by a London publisher to edit a series of books on Australian life and invited her to contribute. A little tactical impersonation was soon afoot.

An account of the *Nelson* expedition appeared in Volume Three of *Cassell's Picturesque Australia*, published in 1888. Minnie contributed two pieces to the book that were straightforward accounts of explorations still going on to open up parts of the continent and a third that was baffling. All three articles were attributed to Mary Gaunt on the Contents page, but the one headed 'Proclaiming a Protectorate', carried no by-line. However, in the text it was clearly asserted that the writer had been one of the ship's officers and, by inescapable inference, a man.

> On a glorious sunny morning in November 1884 (such a morning as is only to be found in the tropics), we, the officers and crew of H.M.S. Nelson, found ourselves nearing the shore of that New Guinea which 'we Australians'—for I, too, belong to the sunny South Land—have made such a fuss about of late years.

Things went on to become more confusing, with the added risk of inviting bad jokes about sailors.

Taken by himself, I do not know that I hanker much after a New Guinea man; but with a dressing of [smelly cocoa-nut] oil on (and it is the only one he condescends to wear as a rule), he is a most undesirable neighbour.

A stab at bluff masculine humour did little to help the gender bending.

A pig is a far more expensive luxury than a child, or even a woman; a wife I could have bought for three sticks of trade tobacco, but a pig I could not get at any price. I did negotiate the purchase of a baby (a little brown, odorous, greasy youngster), but difficulties of packing prevented me from bringing him down south.

By the time this odd account appeared, Ernest was nineteen and a sub-lieutenant, a proper commissioned officer with a single gold ring on his cuff. If he passed his examinations he would soon get a second one and become a lieutenant which, if he was not selected for promotion to commander, he could remain for the rest of his time in the service. After eight years in the rank he would win a thin stripe between the broader two, a senior lieutenant. Naval ranks can be confusing. Three rings signifies a commander, four rings a captain—a 'post-captain', not merely the officer in command of a ship, who would be referred to as its captain no matter what rank he held. In a post-captain's ship the second-in-command would be a commander in rank, often called, to avoid confusion, the executive officer. On the next rung down stands the first lieutenant—first among several equals in rank although not in seniority; each one's place in the Navy List was fixed by the date of his promotion. Ten years would pass before Ernest was senior enough to become first lieutenant of HMS *Narcissus*, an armoured cruiser on the China Station. Among the Gaunts a lot could happen in ten years.

Windjammer

1888. Scanning a slab of type in *The Argus* of 19 May 1888, headlined 'Life on Board the Training Ship Worcester', William Gaunt came across a familiar axiom.

It has been well said that if a lad wishes to go to sea he had better be allowed to go. If he does he may repent his choice, but if he does not it will be a matter of life-long regret to him.

There followed an account of life in an old three-decker moored in the Thames Estuary off Greenhithe, otherwise known as the Thames Nautical Training College. It was attributed to 'the Captain of the Maintop Starboard', a mystifying by-line to many but the Gaunts knew it meant their Guy and that the ghostly storyteller was their Minnie. Guy was nineteen when the story appeared and third mate of a windjammer tramping the Pacific, but these were recollections of the life for which he had left home at fourteen, making a lonely passage to Britain like Ernest before him, fostered by fellow passengers.

The Maintop of the cumbersome pseudonym was one of the divisions named for a part of the ship into which the two hundred boys in *Worcester* were organised: biggest in the Foretop, smallest in the After-mizzen. They were further divided into port and starboard watches. Once readers of the article had grasped these arcane terms they were drawn into a lively, well-told story of a young man's introduction to seafaring. And there was more to come: three episodes of similar length running over consecutive weeks. It was a departure from the paper's usual content. *The Argus* ('*The Times* of the South') took itself seriously, column after broadsheet column set solid with news of commerce, politics and government business. 'Human interest' pieces like The Maintop, written in the immodest first person, were an innovation. Colonial readers seemed to enjoy them, however. They might have been even more entertained to know that the articles were not written by a young man of the sea at all but by his sister.

Worcester was the compromise William agreed to when Guy insisted on following in Ernest's wake. As the article went on to explain, the cost was a mere £100 for two years schooling. He had spent five times that to send Ernest to *Britannia*, not counting the brass-buttoned uniforms. *Worcester*'s purpose was to prepare boys for a career in the merchant service but Guy, optimist and opportunist even at that age, thought he had spotted a cut-price way to catch up with his big brother.

The *Worcester* boy who got top marks each year could become a midshipman in the Royal Navy just as though he had passed out of

Britannia. The next best half-dozen would be made midshipmen in the Royal Naval Reserve. This was a part-time force the Admiralty was keen to build up by offering merchant officers training courses and brief postings to warships. Passenger lines liked their masters and mates to have RNR after their name and wear smart mess dress at dinner. The career navy, however, kept them at arm's length, literally. The rings of rank on a RNR man's sleeve were gold but instead of being bold and straight they were wavy. Even the reservist midshipmen were marked off. They wore the same three gold buttons on their cuffs but the 'turnback' patches on their lapels were pale blue rather than the crisp white of the regulars.

At the end of two years in *Worcester* Guy had indeed become Captain of the Maintop Starboard, effectively a prefect in charge of twenty seafarers of the future. He had to see they were properly washed, dressed in the appropriate rig, and punctual at their duties. Those included much polishing of brass and scrubbing of decks but also rigorous schooling in boatwork, cargo stowage, shiphandling and other skills. The boys were fed meat and vegetables twice a day, slept in hammocks from nine at night until six in the morning. 'On Saturday night we danced, the skipper and officers joining in the fun, and no ball ashore, I am sure, ever went off with more zest....' It was common practice then for men as well as boys to dance together, one tying a ribbon around his knee to show he was the lady.

Even if he did not win a prize a *Worcester* boy was assured of a berth in the merchant service; his two years would count as four of sea time in qualifying for a third mate's certificate from the Board of Trade. To Guy's grievous disappointment he missed the top prize. A gold certificate for good conduct and the right to one of the RNR midshipman places were poor consolation. He was offered an apprenticeship by the owners of the *Carlisle Castle*, a prestigious passenger clipper on the Australia run, and William would have paid the £50 premium required. But that looked like failure to Guy and he did not want to go home with a consolation prize. Better to work his frustration out elsewhere. He signed on a three-masted barque, *Britisher*, whose skipper would not have known a midshipman's turnback from a hatchcover.

Ghost-written or not, the account of Guy's early days at sea shimmers with authenticity. 'I'm afloat, I'm afloat on the ocean sea,' he sings to himself cheerfully, waiting for someone to greet him when he and a couple of fellow apprentices board *Britisher* on a freezing December afternoon in Liverpool. The ship is ready to sail for Calcutta with a cargo of salt and a steam tug is waiting. The greeting he gets is a cuff on the ear and an order to start clearing snow off the forecastle, which none of the crewmen staggering up the gangway are sober enough to do. At the mouth of the Mersey the seas are mountainous. The towing hawser parts—twice. The tug abandons them and scuttles back to port. *Britisher* manages to make sail and clear the land but a night of horror, of swamped decks, ripped sails, helplessly drunk deckhands, shows Guy how far he has come already from the orderly routines of *Worcester* and how little he really knows about the life he has chosen.

The only food the apprentices got that night was a few cold potatoes. After keeping a watch with the second mate—during which the towline parted for the first time but was somehow retrieved—Guy was allowed below for four hours sleep in a shared bunk-hole. There had been no chance to get an oilskin from his seabag and he was wet through and frozen.

My two companions snored calmly on, but I couldn't sleep. I wasn't sick, I was utterly disgusted and very home-sick, and the wild hullabaloo of the fierce gale that howled through the rigging, the thousand and one strange and unaccustomed ship noises, kept me broad awake. I lay there and stared at the ceiling, at the dimly burning lamp that swayed to and fro with every motion of the ship, at the deck now all awash, and I reckoned how short a time was four hours, how quickly this modified bliss was slipping away from me, and then just as I had given it up as a bad job I went fast asleep, and had just had five good snores when the towing bitts went with a tremendous bang and the skipper was yelling at the top of his voice for 'all hands'. I was into my wet clothes and out into the awful night again in seconds, but once there I wasn't much good. All hands were apparently going aloft, so I went too, as I didn't like to funk on my first voyage, though I had the very vaguest idea as to what I should do when I got there. With infinite difficulty I got on the maintop, and then went up, up, up till I could go no further. I could climb like a cat on the old Worcester, but here it was quite different. All around me in the darkness was the singing, and shouting, and cursing of the reckless, drunken crew; far,

far below I could see the binnacle-light, and I knew that there the deck and safety must lie. So, finally, after much deliberation under the most trying circumstances, I concluded to make for the deck again with all speed. The first thing I fell against was a man muffled up to the eyes in sou'wester, oilskins, and sea boots—a marked contrast to me, who had only my sopping monkey jacket and dripping serge trousers.

'Hello', he said with an oath. 'Are you the new apprentice?'

'Yes, sir.'

'First voyage?'

'Yes, sir.'

'What the **** are ye goin' for to do down here, then? Awa' wi' ye aloft!'

This was Britisher's captain—'the Old Bulldog'. He kept his crew short of food and water, worked them like galley slaves but he

… made sailors of us, I'll do him that justice. He was hard as nails, careful and canny as a Scotchman behoved to be; and utterly without the milk of human kindness, but he knew how to sail a ship, and everyone who was under him had to know, too, as quickly as possible. He was a sour old man who had begun life as an ordinary seaman, and now that he was skipper held himself apart and spoke to no one but the cat and the parrot.

Minnie may have framed the words but the voice is unmistakably Guy's: artless and engaging. As he—or Minnie—go on to say after he has dried out, an apprentice who had not had experience in a training ship

would in all probability find the life unbearable for the hardships are such as the hardest-worked man in this favoured land would turn from with disgust. Yet, for myself, even after the resolutions of my first night afloat, I love the sea; I like its monotony, I like its change, I like the strange lands and the curious peoples I see, and I am fully of the opinion that the life of the captain of an Orient steamer, which I hope to be someday, can't be bettered.

It may have been true that if Guy could not get into the navy he would have wanted to command a liner. But from this and other instances in which Minnie lovingly reworked accounts of his life of sea shanties and cockroaches, stowaways and brutal bareknuckled mates, it is not hard to

see what she was yearning for, at least then. In 1906 she recalled for *Girls'
Own Weekly* her resentment that women of her generation had no option
apart from marriage or old-maidenhood.

> I longed to be like a man with a chance of being economically
> independent, so that a man might come to me and I could either accept
> or refuse without any thought that in refusing I was condemning
> myself to a life of forlorn penuriousness.

It was not just to be free of the social shackles of womanhood that she
'longed to be like a man'. Minnie would like to have gone to sea herself.
She might only have wanted to be like a man but she would love to have
been Guy. Nor was she the only sibling to covet her brother's exploits.
Years later, Lance, the baby of the brood, hijacked a couple of episodes
from Guy's life to liven up his own story.

However, Minnie's talent had been recognised and rewarded. An
important weekly, *The Australasian*, gave her an impressive fifty guineas to
serialise—under her own name—a fictional series, *The Riot at the Packhorse*.
To those who knew, Packhorse was clearly the Woolshed, William's
introduction to the goldfields. Those guineas—a pound plus a shilling—
helped persuade her that she might have a future as a writer. Professional
men like her father earned guineas rather than mere pounds. *Packhorse*
was still running in weekly instalments when she set out for London,
seventy guineas concealed about her person, on, appropriately, the SS
Ballaarat. William and Elizabeth consoled themselves that while Minnie's
misgivings about her eligibility seemed justified, Lucy had turned out to
be marriageable and the younger sons, Clive and Lance, manageable. Cecil
was another matter.

By the time he was twenty, Guy had seen enough of the sea from vertiginous
mastheads. His last voyage under sail was a year-long circumnavigation,
the five final months of which were spent battling towards Liverpool
from California via Cape Horn. He had been lucky to get away from San
Francisco in the ship he had arrived in. Excursions to the raucous redlight
quarter, the Barbary Coast, brought him to the attention of the notorious
'crimps' whose speciality was shanghaing stupefied sailors and selling them
to short-handed skippers often bound for…Shanghai. He came down to

London with his third mate's ticket and what remained of his pay after settling with the captain for working clothes and scraps of food without too many weevils in it. Ernest, now a proud lieutenant, was in London. Guy went to meet him from the only lodgings he could afford, a den in the Old Kent Road where the sign over the door read 'Good London Beds, Shilling a Night'.

Ernest was appalled at his circumstances and applied the full older brother pull-your-socks- up treatment. He warned Guy it was time to get serious about a career, reminding him of the unclaimed RNR midshipmanship he won in *Worcester*. Guy had not forgotten but disenchantment at not getting into the navy lingered. He knew Ernest was right but, the shilling a night bed notwithstanding, he was now a certificated ship's officer. 'I've no intention of going in as a midshipman.' Leave it to me, said big brother.

In Nelson's time it was called 'interest'. Influence. Usually it stemmed from a family connection or the patronage of someone in the Admiralty and such things still counted. The Gaunts had no powerful friends in Britain but all of them had a natural gift for hitching a tow. On the way over to join *Worcester*, Guy cultivated a young fellow passenger whose family, the Horsfalls of Liverpool, made their fortune in the African slave trade and just happened to own the steamer they were travelling in, the SS *Chimborazo*. He had been welcome at the Horsfall home whenever he had leave from *Worcester* and it had been they who got him the offer of an apprenticeship in the *Carlisle Castle*. They had not been pleased when he turned it down but they remained friends.

Ernest had quickly found that while naval officers were divided vertically by rank there were also horizontal links when, as with freemasonry or a gentlemen's club, the crucial factor might be a shared interest like hunting or a distinguished acquaintance in common. Within weeks Guy was a sub-lieutenant in the RNR, signed on for a year's training at five shillings a day, more than he had ever earned. Even so, Guy jibbed at the last hurdle. 'What about the gear?' he asked Ernest, thinking of the couple of hundred pounds worth of uniforms he would need. 'Father will stump up.' And of course poor old William did.

There was still a way to go before Guy could hope to catch up with Ernest in fulfilling his boyhood ambition. Feeling his way through the unmarked channels of life in the junior wardroom of HMS *Northumberland*, an old hybrid ironclad, showed him that a Reserve man was *of* the Royal Navy rather than *in* it. The compensation for being genially despised by straight-ring oafs from *Britannia* was in discovering that he was a far better seaman than any of the officers, indeed of the entire ship's company. When the screw had been hoisted inboard and the funnel wound down bluejackets struggled to shake out the unfamiliar sails. He longed to scramble aloft with them as he had in the short-handed merchant ships and show how things ought to be done.

Most of the junior officers' amenities were handed down from the senior wardroom, leftover food and sour wine. Smoothing out a crumpled copy of *The Times* only three weeks old, he read that the newly appointed Second Naval Lord, the Admiralty honcho in control of appointments, was someone who had once enjoyed his father's hospitality in Ballarat. Admiral Henry Fairfax had been in command of the Australia Station in 1887 and while touring Victoria called on William, the obvious man to come to for anyone who wanted to know about gold. He had taken a Cobb and Co coach up the road from Melbourne. Minnie put on her dustcoat and took him down a mine. Interesting, Guy thought. Interest, actually.

At the end of his training voyage Guy went to see Admiral Fairfax, reminded him of the visit to Ballarat and cheekily volunteered for a mission he had heard discussed in the wardroom. A pair of torpedo boats were being sent over to Halifax, Nova Scotia, an important Royal Navy outpost. Fairfax gave him a polite if bemused reception. Even permanent service officers of junior rank did not simply bowl up and ask for a berth. But effrontery triumphed. Guy was appointed second-in-command of Torpedo Boat No. 62. These tiny craft were in vogue. Even before the first dreadnought—or the first effective submarine—had been built it was being argued in radical circles that large, expensive battleships would be at the mercy of the newest wonder weapon, the automobile torpedo, fired from vessels a fraction of their size.

The two boats being handed over to the Canadians were perfectly suitable for their intended role of guarding a harbour against marauders. They were never intended to cross the Atlantic, even in mid-summer; even escorted by a troopship that would coal them en route and, if they broke down, take them in tow. They sailed from Chatham in mid-July and well before they cleared the Channel, No. 62 was so swamped and battered that the skipper, Lieutenant Brian Barttelot RN, was ready to give up. It dawned on Guy that he might have got the appointment because no other officer could be found to take it.

'ACROSS THE NORTH ATLANTIC IN A TORPEDO BOAT by An Officer On Board', appeared in *The English Illustrated Magazine* of February 1891. Once again Minnie's spectral typewriter had been at work but it produced pure, heartfelt 18-carat Guy.

Of all the craft that ever I sailed in, the torpedo boat is the worst, the very worst without exception....

TB 62 was 125 feet long and only thirteen feet across at her broadest. The feet of a man on deck were less than a metre above the waterline. There was really no deck in the usual sense. Anticipating that such a craft would spend as much time diving under waves as riding them, her designers created a long cambered 'whaleback' to let the seas run off. Most of her topsides were taken up by three torpedo firing mounts, a pair of funnels and a dinghy in chocks, together with a conning tower into which the helmsman and another man other could squeeze if they were skinny and not averse to intimate contact. Below decks the aftermost two-thirds of the hull were filled by the twin steam engines, boilers and twenty tons of coal. The space that was left was comparable to the lower deck of a London bus but with less headroom. There all the ship's equipment was stowed and three officers and thirteen crew slept and ate. When they could.

The account by An Officer on Board began with a typical Guy story of trying to get something to eat in the middle of a gale. Most of the crew were immobilised by seasickness, including the signalman who was supposed to double as the officers' servant. Guy and the skipper escaped the foul messdeck and spent the night huddled in the only shelter available, the dinghy. Wanting breakfast, Guy struggled below and discovered a large ham by treading on it with his seaboot. Ham, like boot, was coated in coal dust but he hacked off a few slices and clambered back to share his find with Barttelot.

The boat gave a sharp lurch and in a moment we were both flung out of the dinghy. The skipper scrambled to his feet but I was not so lucky for I hit the slightly convex deck as I fell and in another second was overboard. There are no bulwarks, of course, to a torpedo boat, only stanchions supporting at intervals a wire rope and between these I slipped. As I did so, however, I flung my hands up instinctively and caught the rope as I passed under it. Down went the little ship, down, down until the sea bubbled around my shoulders and I wondered if I could hold on if the water came over my head. By the strain on my hands then I knew it was not possible but luckily the boat rolled back again and the skipper and the man at the wheel hauled me on board.... The only damage was to our breakfast which had completely disappeared.

They were at sea for three weeks with barely a day of tolerable weather. They lost sight of their escort and No. 61 in fog for days at a time and when the troopship did reappear she had to pour oil on the severely troubled waters before No. 62 could get alongside to coal. Off Nova Scotia they emerged from the mist into the middle of an icefield, bergs towering over the little craft on all sides. By the time they made Halifax she was leaking dangerously, everything swept off her uppers save the conning tower. It is not in Minnie's version but Guy recalled a Glasgow merchant skipper coming on board to look over the damage. 'I dinna ken whether ye're heroes or fules,' said the old Scot as he departed. 'But I think you're fules.' So did Guy. Compensation for ruined uniforms was covered by the standard Admiralty 'hard-lying' allowance of a shilling a day while at sea.

London Life

1890. Rich Americans went to Paris; wealthy Australians to London. The inertia of an earlier generation—to which the young Gaunts were such an exception—had been overcome by money. Those who had done well from gold or grazing began to arrive in herds, out to show off to relatives, throw money around and find ways to make some more. Landladies competed to accommodate the waves of arrivals, advertising premises with showers at sixpence a time. The plumbing fixtures, hitherto unknown in Britain, were imported from America. Some of the visitors brought sons and daughters along to scout for socially uplifting marriages but it was the stream of footloose young women who soon formed a conspicuous subset of London's tribal map, screeching, bright-hued flocks of them perching in the aviaries of Bloomsbury and Kensington at thirty shillings a week, bed-and-breakfast.

The visitors were also catered to by the *British-Australasian*, launched in 1884 as 'A Newspaper for Merchants, Shareholders, Land Selectors, and Emigrants, And all interested in the Magnitude and Growth of British Interests in Australia, New Zealand, Tasmania and the Western Pacific'. At the paper's office in High Holborn, a stroll away from the Strand, travellers could meet, pick up mail, invert the space-time disparity by reading Australian papers a few weeks old, and even use a telephone if they know anyone else with access to one. These were not tourists. They belonged. Their displacement was merely physical. They had moved thousands of miles but merely shifted from one part of their World to another. Even Colonials were perfectly at ease in their Home away from home, much as those who went the other way had felt when they arrived in Australia.

But if the British World lacked borders it had barriers. London could be dispiriting for the ambitious. Minnie was in her late twenties, too old for the twittering of her younger fellow countrywomen. She did her best to escape them in the more staid Australian gathering spots, particularly, the Austral Club in Dover Street, Mayfair, but she had not achieved enough to make herself stand out from the small horde of Australian women writers also on the creative make. She was not, though, of the same literary ilk. Her contemporaries tried to emulate their English counterparts with the kind of romantic fiction that was in fashion, delicate feasts of the spirit. Minnie preferred to put together a good story but she found she could only write successfully about things she had actually seen and, eventually, that she did. Or that someone she knew did. Even if she could not write convincingly about British life, though, she was even less likely than most authors to let an experience go to waste. As well as being a skilful literary impersonator she was an accomplished time-shifter and in a later autobiographical period those unhappy London days would be reprocessed and repositioned.

The editor of *Illustrated*, a genteel literary hustler, Clement Kinloch-Cooke, accepted the vividly told story of No. 62 as soon as he read it. Only when he wrote asking the author to clear up some details did he discover who had actually written it. He was vastly amused. By one of the strokes of good fortune that seemed to be a Gaunt birthright, Kinloch-Cooke had been a civil servant in the office of the Colonial Secretary and thus knew something of Victoria. It was an important breakthrough. *Illustrated* was a prestigious showcase; among its contributors Thomas Hardy, G B Shaw, Oscar Wilde, Frank Harris, Wilkie Collins, Stephen Crane, Rudyard Kipling, H G Wells. As well as taking more pieces from Minnie, Kinloch-Cooke had some good advice. The literary agent was becoming an influence in publishing. He recommended her to Alexander Pollock Watt, who represented, among others, the eminent Mr Hardy.

Guy's resentment at having to shell out for a new wardrobe evaporated when Admiral Fairfax informed him that the seamanlike manner in which he conducted himself in No. 62 had qualified him for a place in the regular navy. Of course, it would mean remaining in his present one-ring rank until he passed the five examinations for lieutenant that regular officers would have been preparing for since they left *Britannia*. Undimmed as his ambition was to become a fully fashioned Royal Navy man, this was a problem. Actually, said Guy, who had innocently imagined he would not need any qualification beyond his Board of Trade certificate, I'm not very good at examinations. In that case, said Fairfax, it might be best if you look elsewhere for an appointment. Little navies were being launched across the empire: the India Marine, the Hooghly River Pilot Service, the Oil Rivers Fleet in Nigeria as well as in some 'white' colonies. The Admiralty was happy to help with 'Imperial' officers to run them. Superannuated captains and admirals could be cleared off the payroll and reservists get their sea time in at another government's expense. Why not try back home? Fairfax suggested. The Royal Victorian Navy.

Marvellous Melbourne

1892. Guy did not know much about what had been happening in his native colony in the years he had been away. Easy money from mines and pastures made Melbourne the richest city in the world for a while, bigger in size and population than any in the Empire apart from London. Bigger than any European capital for that matter, or anywhere in the Americas other than New York and Chicago. Visitors were awed by the flourishing city at the bottom of the globe that a London journalist, George Sala, labelled 'Marvellous Melbourne'. There were nine-storey buildings served by hydraulic elevators, a telephone system, trams hauled along by cables beneath the tarred roads. Cables of a different kind provided a miraculous link with London, reducing weeks of waiting for news to hours. There were sumptuous hotels, the largest built by temperance societies in which no liquor was sold, and a glittering arcade of shops lit by electric light.

Adding to its prestige, Victoria put together a miniature armada that far outweighed the token forces of the other capitals: its supporters dreamed of a Gibraltar of the South. Earlier in the century there had been some newspaper scaremongering when a couple of Russian ships made unexpected visits to Port Phillip. More recently Japanese whalers appearing off the coast, had the Legislative Council worried. But if things ever became serious Port Phillip could be defended by HMVS *Cerberus*, a lumbering steam-powered wonder mounting a pair of ten-inch muzzle-loaders at each end, a brace of torpedo craft and Ernest's old *Nelson*, which the Royal Navy had donated to save the trouble of taking her home to be scrapped. In addition there was a landbound Naval Brigade, a volunteer militia trained to impress the populace with drill displays. Gilbert and Sullivan would not have needed to do much, except set it to music and find a few rhymes to fit the outburst of provincial petulance caused by Guy's appointment.

The little fleet had vacancies for two sub-lieutenants to bring its officer strength up to ten, the senior six of whom were, of course, 'Imperial men'. The lucky other was also an RNR sub who had failed to get into Royal Navy through the main hatchway, Algernon Buck. He was a product of the school ship *Conway*, a counterpart to *Worcester* moored in the River Mersey, and as English as a toast-rack. He could hardly wait to let his old classmates know that 'this is a very good thing, plenty of leave on duty one Sunday out of four and one night aboard out of four ...'. The pay was £200 a year—twice the RNR rate—and £250-£300 for a lieutenant. There might soon be more jobs going, said Buck. Two years RNR service and a second mate's ticket would qualify an applicant if he met the requirement of one other little Regulation—an unwritten one that cannot well be added, but is none the less desirable— 'All candidates must be gentlemen.'

Buck did not mention the sour protests his appointment provoked from officers of the Naval Brigade who had understood that their unpaid service would be a step towards a place in the floating—and salaried—half of the service. They complained that Buck had no connection with the colony. They would have been even more unhappy if they had known what he told the *Conway* chaps about landlubbers like them.

These are men drawn from all classes ashore and, though very fine as men, are no use for anything but ornamental purposes. The drawback is that they cannot see this, and being backed up by a rotten press and patted on the back by the mob, before whom they occasionally march past, or perform cutlass exercise at a shilling a head, they fancy themselves the most smart, well-drilled and best officered force "south of the Line".

A Brigade sub, Arthur Ray, was foolish enough to bring up the matter of interest. He should have had preference over Mr Gaunt, he said, because his father was a retired RN captain. Besides, no other candidate had been considered, as the rules required. Also, Guy did not have two full years of RNR time. He held a third mate's ticket, not a second. The regulations 'had been especially altered' to allow his appointment. Of course they had. William Gaunt was by then a District Court judge and a friend of the Secretary for Defence, Sir Frederick Sargood, who had been a miner and now sat in the Legislative Council. Blatantly, even as Ray was arguing his case, Guy was confirmed in the rank of lieutenant after only eight months of probation instead of the statutory twelve. The wrangle entertained the colony for months but poor Ray was hopelessly outgunned.

Whether or not Guy deserved the job he did it well. In 1937 an old timer of the little navy, George Prideaux, remembered him as

one of the most popular officers that Victoria ever had, as well as being a very efficient one. He could always get the best out of the men. If on shore to a theatre the night boat crew never went to their hammocks after bringing him off to the ship without being taken to his cabin for a stiff whisky.

Even while the overwrought pieces Sala had written for the *Daily Telegraph* in London were running the golden bubble burst in a splatter of bankruptcies and foreclosures and Melbourne was soon a good deal less marvellous. Still, Guy managed, as he usually did, to enjoy himself. He went riding with his brothers, especially Lance. Neither of them was as good or fanatical a horseman as Cecil but both were fearless steeplechasers, well worth a bet at the amateur meets they rode in at Flemington racecourse. The starter's gun loosed off Guy's essential spirit. Light and wiry, he was as confident in the saddle as on a heaving deck with a quick eye for an opening in a crowded field and the nerve to go for it at full gallop.

The opera and theatres that showed serious plays were emptied out by the depression but light-hearted imports, English variety and American vaudeville shows, packed in everyone who could still afford a ticket. The theme of an American show called *Tuxedo* became a big party hit. Whenever young people got together out of sight of their elders someone was certain to launch into

A sweet tuxedo girl you see
A queen of swell society
Fond of fun as fond can be
When it's on the strict QT
I'm not too young, I'm not too old
Not too timid, not too bold
Just the kind you'd like to hold
Just the kind for sport I'm told

Daringly, couples bumped their hips together to the chorus.

Ta-ra-ra Boom-de-re!

Whatever Guy got up to on the strict QT he had to pay some attention to duty. The two larger ships, *Cerberus* and *Nelson* were moored in Hobsons Bay. A couple of times a year they got up steam, took the cutlass-twirling Naval Brigade on board and set out on an exercise. These began as gala events but were taken more seriously after an experimental mine exploded, blowing a boat and its crew of five to pieces. On another occasion the captain of *Cerberus* ordered a broadside—firing all four giant guns at once. The shock damaged the ship so badly that she was never to fire another shot. *Nelson* on the other hand loosed off a shell by accident that took out a coach house in St. Kilda across the bay.

It took Guy four years to conclude that Melbourne was never going to be marvellous in career terms, which coincided with the Royal Victorian Navy deciding it could no longer afford him. The colony's budget was squeezed. Businesses were closing every day, the temperance hotels so short of customers that they applied for liquor licences. Although he had already decided it was time to move on Guy took offence at being declared redundant. The new premier, George Turner, was also Secretary of Defence. Guy paid him a visit to ask why he was being made to walk the plank. 'You are impertinent,' says Turner. 'You've got to go and it's no use arguing.' Guy threatened to take a story of the navy's shortcomings to the editor of *The Age* whom he knew from the racecourses. The following day he was offered a year's pay—but he still had to go. Quintessential Guymanship. In his pocket was a cable inviting him to apply for one of a hundred new places the Royal Navy had created for lieutenants. *Ta-ra-ra* Boom-*de-re!*

The belated bride

Before parting from the Victorian Navy, Guy had the pleasure of going to Minnie's wedding. The family had come to share her own doubts that at the seriously advanced age of thirty-three such an event would ever take place but it did, in the parish church at Malvern with her sister and three of her brothers in attendance. Lucy had already produced a child but was to about to conform to family rule by going off to the Malay jungle with her husband, a mining engineer named Archer.

Back from two frustrating years in London Minnie settled down to make use of the background she knew best. She sent A P Watt. the manuscript of a novel called *Dave's Sweetheart*, a vivid evocation of the sex-starved, hair-trigger goldfields. In 1894 he placed it with the firm of Edward Arnold and, in true romantic fashion, it became a blockbuster. Ballarat and beyond was undiscovered territory to British readers and they were enthralled. The sweetheart in question, Jenny, a shanty publican's daughter, paid the harsh price expected at the time for trying to break out of an oppressive marriage. But much of the book's appeal lay in an unsentimental restatement of Minnie's personal theme: the few options convention allowed a woman in such a plight.

With Mr Watt playing off London publishers as astutely as Minnie followed her literary mother lode, three novels soon made it into print. *The Moving Finger* was brought out by Methuen the following year, *Kirkham's Find* in 1897 and in 1888 *Deadman's*. All were published in the United States as well. The books reflected something of Minnie's own life and feelings, *Kirkham's* most of all. The heroine, Phoebe Marsden, was tall and bony, the eldest child of a large family dominated by a stern father. Apart from the obvious discrepancy of Minnie being short and 'stout', the story was shamelessly autobiographical. Phoebe had a pretty sister and other siblings, the younger of whom '... looked on her as quite an old maid, and she herself felt her life, as far as any happiness or pleasure to herself went, was nearly over.' Minnie was getting her own back for her chastening first experience back Home. Despite ever more enthusiastic reviews Minnie stopped writing.

I met a tall, good-looking young doctor and—what were literary aspirations to me? Though critics in London were putting it on record that they considered me distinctly promising, I was content and more than content, to make a home for one man in the little town of Warrnambool, away on the south coast of Australia.

The young doctor, Hubert Lindsay Miller, was a widower of thirty-seven. He had been medical superintendent of the Royal Melbourne Hospital but resigned after discovering it to be a pit of contagion and incompetence. A coroner reckoned its shocking death rate could be halved if its doctors stayed home. Minnie became the receptionist at the surgery attached to the comfortable iron-roofed house they moved to in Warrnambool, a growing port three hundred kilometres away. She bought a bicycle when it was still quite daring for a woman to ride one and was soon a familiar sight, wobbling around town. Sending off the proofs of Kirkham's she added the dedication

To my husband in loving acknowledgement of the tenderness and sympathy

which makes these first days of our married life so happy.

Happy as she was, Minnie still brooded about economic independence. She wrote a series on 'Little Industries for Women' in a local magazine that offered practical advice on making money by breeding chickens and selling eggs, cultivating silkworms, growing asparagus and bee-keeping. Despite A P Watts's energetic marketing the Millers were far from rich but her otherwise indulgent husband refused to let her damage their standing in the community by doing any of those things herself, at least for profit. In Victorian Victoria a doctor's wife could not be seen peddling eggs and vegetables.

Who's this chap?

1895. The intake of officers that included Guy went into the annals of the Royal Navy as the Hungry Hundred. Need for them was created by the new generation of battleships Britain was building, monster vessels, heavily armed and armoured, but still driven by clanking piston engines and coal-burning boilers. Some of them were still on the slips when their design was rendered obsolete by HMS *Dreadnought* sliding out of a secret dockyard, ready to flash up her oil-powered steam turbines. Overnight the earlier ships became pre-dreadnoughts. Nevertheless, both new and prematurely outmoded vessels were complicated machines that needed a lot of bright young men to work them.

Since the Admiralty did not want to upset the career progress of established officers, the Hundred, most of them from one of the peripheral naval services, had to agree to remain lieutenants for a ten-year engagement after which they would have to retire on a pension of £500 a year. It was not what most of them had hoped for but at least they were in the straight-ring Royal Navy. Also, the shrewder of them thought there might be a way around the rules. The navy had shown itself ready to reward outstanding service or a deed of valour. Guy imagined someone in the Admiralty looking down a list and saying, 'Hello there, who's this chap with the Distinguished Service Order?'

To his relief there were no exams but the Hundred was only one rung up from the bottom; in Guy's case the bottom of his first ship, HMS *Swift*. She was a sloop not much bigger than a Thames barge, and the bottom was flat, enabling her to chase pirates up the great rivers of China with a pair of seven-inch muzzle loaders. Guy joined her in Hong Kong after a leisurely passage out in the company of the new Minister Plenipotentiary to the Manchu court, Sir Claude Macdonald, a fine figure of a British diplomat whose waxed moustaches stood out beyond his jowls like daggers.

Applying some diplomatic skills of his own, Guy was accepted as a sort of *aide-de-camp* to Sir Claude for the duration of the voyage. He also managed a cabin upgrade and a seat higher up the captain's table than he could otherwise have expected. Recollections of that first-class luxury often surfaced as he lay in his squalid bunk in *Swift*. The waste pipe from the captain's lavatory cleared his nose by inches and the starboard propeller shaft ran beneath his bedboards, its vibration the lesser hazard since it was less frequently used. The sails on *Swift*'s three stubby masts were more dependable than her ancient engines.

It took some time for the old hulk to be made ready for her next voyage. Guy spent much of the wait taking horses over the jumps at the rough-and-ready Hong Kong racecourse, Happy Valley. Many of his mounts belonged to *taipans*, the avaricious British merchants of the colony. He often won but a gentleman jockey could never take an owner's money. Sometimes he would be rewarded by the attentions of a playful wife or—far more riskily—daughter. The amatory encounters of a bachelor officer were of necessity inadvertent. Marriage would be out of the question until he was either promoted commander or, resigned to a life of lieutenancy, turned thirty-five. Meanwhile, he had to live cautiously. The service was forbearing about fleshly lapses so long as they were discreet and, preferably, brief; the slightest cluck of public scandal could ruin a career faster than a shipwreck. Mostly, he collected invitations, letters of introduction to help over the social hurdles at new ports of call;

The Admiralty decided that if *Swift* could frighten pirates in the Pearl or the Yangtze she would be just as well suited to going after another brand of marauder that Russia, the United States, Japan and Britain had found rare common ground in condemning: the seal-poachers of the Bering Sea. A century later popular newspapers could stir up popular indignation with reports of new-born seal pups being clubbed to death for their pelts. In the 1890s there was more concern about the fate of legitimate British and American sealers who, if they escaped the poachers, might be dumped by the Russians into some icy Siberian sinkhole from which they would never emerge. An International Commission agreed that the poaching was illegal and ought to be suppressed, if only in the interest of avoiding trouble. *Swift* was assigned to keep the predators away.

Guy encountered his first poachers in Hakodate, the largest of the Treaty Ports that the Japanese opened to foreign ships after Commodore Perry shouldered his way in to the isolated nation forty year earlier. *Swift* had been pottering around, waiting for the weather to get warm enough for her to make it to the Kamchatka Peninsula. One of the ship's company was stabbed in a drinking den called the Black Diamond. Guy took a party of bluejackets ashore to investigate, searching for the place among earthquake-ready hovels made of old sails and paper, boulders weighting down the roof against gales. The clientele of the Diamond looked even more depraved and dangerous than the crimps of the Barbary Coast. He was wondering how a naval officer might remonstrate with them without loss of dignity or worse when a Japanese police captain borrowed a box of matches from him and simply set the flimsy structure alight, leaving the snarling grog-soaked desperados to save themselves. The effectiveness of this straightforward solution made a deep impression on Guy.

The long stays in harbour enforced by *Swift*'s sorry condition often left him free to do as he liked. He cycled inland and put up at a village tea-house where the guests bathed together 'in the garb they wore in the Garden of Eden'. Fascinated by life beneath the kimono he joined in. The police there were less helpful. After he had enjoyed a few sessions in the communal bath a constable politely invited him to leave town. 'Whether the Japanese were not elated with my physical proportions I am unable to say.' Something must have impressed the little chambermaid who unrolled his bed on the floor each evening, warming it with a pan of hot coals. On the second night she popped under the covers herself, giggling. She was a chubby, stubby little thing but full of tricks. The shadows their limbs threw on the paper walls were far more interesting than he and his siblings had made with their hands in front of a candle: the perfect hemisphere of a breast in profile, her little feet flicking about his ears.

For the rest of his adventures in *Swift* Guy needed to be very fully clothed indeed: boots, sheepskin, woolly mittens. Among the freezing Kurile islands there were encounters with the sealers' sinister blood-blackened schooners but the sight of *Swift's* great cannons discouraged them. Ashore, he toted a Winchester rifle with a cartridge ready beneath the hammer. Sea-lions and brown bears both moved faster than a lot of dead men had thought possible. He shot an aggressive bear, not realising she had cubs. Filled with remorse, he took one on board as a pet: thus the yarn for dinner-tables to come. Out of touch with civilisation for months on end, a certain moral slippage set in. The officers made a gut-rot concoction from wardroom liquor dregs and bartered it with trappers for precious pelts: ermine, sable and arctic fox. They could be sure of a warm welcome if they ever saw civilisation again. This rawboned life, the hangfire tension of every day on those wild, treacherous seas and shores, the unforeseeable tomorrows, the racing pulse, churning, hungry guts, explosive rum-powered release—this was *adventure;* the dream of distant childhood, the end to which the navy was merely the means. Guy could not have been happier.

Gaunt's Brigade

In Hong Kong, Yokohama and Manila those letters of introduction always did their stuff: tickets to ride on the cosmopolitan social roundabout. Back in London two years later things were different. Guy had a rich collection of stories, some hilarious, some hair-raising, but none likely to impress the Second Lord and get him a desirable berth. He was put on half-pay, the fate of an officer without a ship. Wandering up Lower Regent Street after a fruitless call at the Admiralty he recognised a man approaching on the opposite tack: Admiral Sir Alexander Buller who had been commander-in-chief of the China Station. They were both in civilian clothes so Guy raised his hat, the prescribed courtesy. Buller stopped and looked him over. 'Aren't you that boy who used to ride races? Come and have a drink with me.'

At the Travellers' Club, Guy mentioned that the only berth on offer was for a navigating lieutenant in HMS *Porpoise*, victualling for the Australia

Station under Commander Frederick Doveton Sturdee. Why not apply for that? asked Buller. Sturdee was a good man. 'Good heavens, sir. I couldn't pilot a cow down a lane.'

That, at any rate, is what Guy always said that he said. It seems improbable. As does the reply he attributed to Buller: 'Don't talk damned rot! Look at the fools who do take it on and get away with it.' A typical bit of entertaining self-effacement on Guy's part, most likely, as is his explanation for being a poor fit for a navigator's berth. 'Admitting that the navy of forty years ago was infinitely slacker than it is now', he wrote.

There still remained the disquieting knowledge that the only examination I had ever passed was eight years before, and that as master in the Merchant Service, which any educated child could have done.

At the time, however, Lieutenant Guy of the Hungry Hundred was right to realise that despite being a far more experienced sea officer than most of his contemporaries he was underqualified to take a Royal Navy vessel half-way around the world. The Victorians had given him a second ring without even asking if he could find his way from one side of Port Phillip Bay to the other and in *Swift* he had been happy to leave it to the captain to establish their whereabouts. His third mate's ticket, a Board of Trade Certificate of Competence, recognised a grasp of practical matters: cargo stowage, shiphandling, chartwork and pilotage—conning a ship by buoys, lights or bearings taken on landmarks. Its navigational requirements did not extend beyond using a sextant to 'shoot' the sun and working out a position with a chronometer and a book of tables. A master's ticket took matters to a far higher plane, observations of stars and planets: spherical trigonometry. Whatever Guy really said in the Travellers', Buller did not take his protestations seriously. He was due at the Admiralty himself, the old boy declared, and he would see what was to be done.

Full gallop

Before newsreels, film and television people could get some idea—a highly formularised one, obviously—from re-enactments or historical tableaux staged by costumed actors: *The Death of Nelson, Storming the*

Bastille, The Charge of the Light Brigade (noises off). Guy took a young lady to an intimate little music hall, the Coal Hole in the Strand, which was presenting *Treachery at the Malakand Fort,* a fanciful tableau of fighting in Afghanistan. He wanted to catch up with what Cecil had been doing.

Cecil's decision was really the boldest taken by any of the young Gaunts. Between eighteen and twenty-three he followed the undemanding routines of a Melbourne bank clerk, living at home with his parents, going to pubs and theatres with friends, riding at weekends; he was easily the most skilled and courageous Gaunt horseman. When he left for Britain in 1887 William and Elizabeth believed he was merely off on the kind of global walkabout young Australians had begun to make. But that autumn, he presented himself at the barracks of the Thirteenth Hussars in Canterbury to sign on as a trooper.

Whatever talent or motivation drove Cecil, his upward mobility was impressive. Ten years earlier he could have bought his way in as an officer: a mere £840 for the starter rank of cornet. But the purchase of commissions had been abolished and since appointments were now supposed to be based on merit, i.e. ability, the British army was short of officers. Few recruits could see themselves jumping to commissioned rank over the hurdles of class. Also, it took private means to live the life of a gentleman.

So there was no escape for Cecil from the early character-building experience that confronted a recruit: grooming, mucking out, endless drills, sleeping quarters less clean and comfortable than the stables. But he was enthralled by the stomping, snorting drill assemblies, mounting and dismounting in unison, the crescendent jangles and creaks as a hundred horses quickened to the trumpet calls: trot...canter...wheel. There was sport, too, games brought back from wilder parts: polo and pigsticking, although in England the vicious wild boar was a sack stuffed with old saddle bits. Within three years of joining up Cecil was promoted to sergeant, a step that took many men a decade to achieve. Four years later, in 1891, a vacancy for second lieutenant came up in another regiment that had Balaclava on its battle honours, the Fourth Dragoons. By then the dearth of officer material had made it less rare for a non-commissioned officer to break out of the ranks. The Fourth were about to take their turn in India and out there a junior subaltern stood a chance of living on his pay. Besides, India was horse heaven and there were real wild pigs.

The Fourth's new home was at Muttra, an ancient city of white stone temples and bathing-stairs along the bank of the Jumna River in the northwestern province of Uttar Pradesh. Most of the people were Hindu, although down the years the place had been captured and plundered several times by Muslims, especially bloodthirsty raiders from Afghanistan. It was the outer limit of the World. In the genteel life of the cantonments and the regimental mess life went on as though the parched surroundings were Surrey. The year comprised seven months of training and manoeuvres and five months of leave, during which officers were free to travel the country, play polo, stick pigs and try their luck with fretful wives in the hill stations.

Cecil was a captain and already a veteran of long months of skirmishing on the North West Frontier when a coalition of Afghan tribesmen marked the queen's Diamond Jubilee by surging out of the hills and ravaging frontier posts around the Khyber Pass. The British put together the largest response to local misbehaviour since the quelling of the Mutiny, the Malakand Field Force. Cecil was appointed the Force's orderly officer, responsible for managing an exotic mix of Bengal Lancers, Sikhs, Punjabis and Scots. There had been weeks of rough, tough and dangerous soldiering against an enemy who rarely stood still to be shot at.

The London evening papers ran off editions well into the night, distinguished by different coloured newsprint: green, yellow, pink. When Guy and his lady friend emerged from the Coal Hole he took the latest *Evening News* from a street seller and found that Admiral Buller had meant what he said. There it was in the Naval and Military announcements: Lieutenant G. R. Gaunt to HMS *Porpoise* for navigating duties.

The only thing for it, Guy thought, was to call on Commander Sturdee and own up to his deficiency. But Sturdee nipped in first with a telegram inviting him to lunch. They got on well, reassuringly connected in that wide British World: Sturdee's brother was a dentist in Bendigo. Guy could not bring himself to confess. 'I found him so charming, and he treated me to such a nice lunch, that my courage failed me.' His steeplechaser's instinct to go squarely at a hurdle did not.

Yachting had become a fashionable pastime and a master mariner set up a school near the Tower of London offering tuition to amateur sailors. Dressed as little like an officer as he could contrive, and giving his name as 'Grant...George Grant', Guy presented himself as a moneyed young chap who had bought a boat and wanted to take it on a long voyage. Every evening for weeks while *Porpoise* was fitting out at Chatham, he headed eastwards to swot. The luck, or more aptly the cheek, of the Gaunts held up and her navigating officer duly guided his new ship through the Mediterranean and the Suez Canal, around the Dutch East Indies and down through the Great Barrier Reef to Sydney and Melbourne.

1898. William was keeping the two younger sons on track to follow him into the law. Lance had nearly finished his university studies despite the distractions of a vivid social life and the amount of time he devoted to the Victorian Horse Artillery, particularly the half of it known as the Rupertswood Battery. Rupertswood, a breathtakingly pretentious estate outside Melbourne, had been built by Sir William Clarke, heir to a £1.5 million squatter fortune. The railway line to the town of Sunbury ran through the property and a station had been built there for guests coming to balls and hunts. When it was feared that the Russians were coming Sir William raised a volunteer half-battery of militia in the spirit of the exhibitionist naval brigades, a private army that offered enormous fun for young men who wanted to add zest to their riding experience. Decked out in pillbox hats and gold-frogged tunics they galloped around at every ceremonial occasion in Melbourne, an ancient cannon and a couple of prehistoric Nordenfelt machine guns in tow. Lance managed to hide the itch created by these events from his parents but while *Porpoise* was getting ready to show the flag around the South Seas he confided to Guy, 'I'd give anything to be in a real scrap'. Neither of them could have predicted the adventure and excitement they would soon be sharing, let alone the feud that would result.

1897. Anchoring in Suva, the main harbour of Fiji, a few weeks later *Porpoise* found the German cruiser SMS *Falke* already there. A couple of days later *Falke* was nowhere to be seen. 'Cleared off at first light,' said the officer of the day. 'No fare-thee-well, nothing. Must have got steam up through the night.'

Commander Sturdee did not like the look of that; the Germans were meticulous observers of the courtesies. He went off and spent the morning with the Commissioner for the Western Pacific. 'Germans up to mischief again,' he told the officers when he returned. In Samoa, the island group 600 miles to the east, King Malietoa Laupepa was dying and the Germans were conspiring to plant a successor on the throne.

Samoa had been producing threatening rumbles for years. By the time Germany made her belated bid to become a colonial power, the United States, which had its own interests in the eastern Pacific, was not encouraging Europeans to go sniffing around. In order to develop the New Guinea acquisitions or the concessions they had been able to grab in China the Germans needed secure coaling stations en route. In the chain of toeholds the Germans had bought up or annexed, Samoa was the weak link. Britain and the United States also claimed some of the islands in the group.

There were years of friction between the colonising powers before they agreed to exercise authority via diplomatic representation from each: the rule of Three Consuls. The imperial triumvirate allowed the Samoans to elect a king whose role was supposed to be symbolic but their most recent choice, Tupua Malietoa To'oa Mata'afa Iosefo, had encouraged resistance against the Germans, the largest settler community. Weeks earlier, without consulting his British and American colleagues, the German consul banished Mata'afa to the all-German Marshall Islands. In response to this effrontery America and Britain persuaded the Samoans to accept their nominee, Malietoa, as the new king. But now that Malietoa was on the way out, it seemed that the exiled Mata'afa was ready to make a comeback.

Under the Consuls everyday executive power was exercised from Apia, on the main island Upolu, by a Supervisory Committee whose Chief Executive was a former judge from Alabama, William Chambers. He was also the Chief Justice and in that capacity he ruled that the throne should go to the Malietoa's son, Malietoa Tanu, a seventeen-year-old just returned to the islands from school in New Zealand. The German colonists, mainly copra planters, refused to accept the ruling. Supported by local Mata'afists, they acclaimed the German consul as head of a government and refused to recognise the other two. German officials took over the courtroom and locked Judge Chambers out. *Falke* was sent to bring Mata'afa home.

There was no time to wait for orders from the admiral in Sydney to reach Fiji. Guy got out his sextant, Sturdee clapped on full sail or full steam as appropriate, and when *Falke* arrived in Apia just before Christmas

1898 with the pretender on board, *Porpoise* was waiting for her. On the way, Guy had written a letter to Lance: Before sending it off to the mail steamer about to leave for Auckland he scribbled a postscript: 'If you want a scrap you had better shove off at once. We'll get going here very shortly.' It was a joke, really. The last thing he expected was that Lance would take him seriously.

The scrap he foretold was soon raging in the dusty streets. Samoans, some with firearms but most with spears and fearfully sharp swords they called *nifs*, split into equally bloodthirsty and unruly hordes, those loyal to Mata'afa adopting a white head-dress; the faction favouring Tanu a red one.

The mail steamer also took away despatches from all of the Consuls to be cabled onwards to London, Washington and Berlin where their arrival set off loud alarms. The powers concerned were on relatively good terms and all immediately saw that anarchy in their distant possession could easily spark a lot of trouble that *Falke* and *Porpoise* would not be able to contain.

Sturdee was not having anarchy. He sent Guy ashore with a landing party and orders to get the courthouse reopened and the young pretender under British protection. Guy marched his bluejackets off to the American consulate, collected Justice Chambers in a *gharri* and escorted him back downtown. There were plenty of undesirables waving *nifs* around in the streets and some whites snarling at him in German. He spotted a couple of bloody bundles in the dust, red-top Malietoans who had found themselves in the wrong place. He ordered the seamen to fix bayonets, a show of white man's *nifs*. Beside him *Porpoise*'s chief shipwright towed a handcart full of tools. It took only a few minutes to knock the locks off the courthouse doors. Guy wondered if he should get his men to keep the mob out in the street but decided it was better to show them who was in charge. When a smelly mix of Samoans and Germans filled the courtroom he slipped out his revolver and put it in the drawer in front of Chambers. The judge kept a hand on the gun as he declared the court in session and, order formally restored, adjourned the proceedings.

In the chaos that followed stereotypes ruled. The natives were untrustworthy and barbarous, even the redtops, prone to offer their European friends the tribute of a severed head or a string of freshly *nifi-*

ed ears. Germans were bombastic: the leader of the settlers challenged Sturdee to a duel for refusing to speak to him in the street. Americans were gung-ho and trigger-happy. The British ... well, the Royal Navy at least, seemed to epitomise coolness and courage.

Guy was to rack up many admirable achievements in Samoa, the first of which was to ensure that young Tanu's head stayed on his shoulders. At the Mission Society where the boy had been taken there were—apart from a few bemused missionaries—twenty-five bluejackets and Guy. Outside the fence Mata'afan warriors in white turbans and warpaint milled around, more numerous and aggressive by the hour. They wanted the young king handed over and became increasingly aggressive about it. Guy warned their leader—'a half-breed German'—that if they tried to enter the compound his men would shoot. A messenger from *Porpoise* brought a note from Sturdee apologising for not being able to help. The ship had been warped away from the wharf to keep her safe. So many seamen had been sent ashore to protect Europeans that the guns were manned by stokers. Guy considered the situation in the assertive spirit of the Japanese policeman and his matches.

Get the king out of the Mission grounds I must. The lucky thought came to me that he might be unknown by sight to the howling enemy outside, as he had spent much of his boyhood days in New Zealand. He spoke English well, and when I told him to take off his smart white jacket and just wear a ragged lap-lap he understood the situation perfectly.

Guy waited until a cloud hid the moon then pushed the boy through the fence at the back of the mission. The two of them dived into the bush and bolted for the foreshore where *Porpoise* now lay at anchor only a hundred yards off. He dared not hail her to send a boat. A pair of startled British settlers were getting ready to go fishing. He commandeered their leaky dinghy. With Tanu safe in *Porpoise* he sneaked back into the compound and invited the Mata'afist ringleader in to look around. King? What king?

The peace lasted until 13 March, when the American cruiser *Philadelphia* arrived with Rear Admiral Albert Kautz, followed a few days later by the Australia Squadron flagship, HMS *Tauranga*. Meanwhile, Guy was free to explore the pleasures of Samoan life, including a visit to Robert Louis

Stevenson's house, Vailima, on the slope of Mount Vaea not far out of Apia where the young Gaunts' childhood adventure hero had been buried only four years earlier. Minnie would treasure a description of the place to remind her of their goldfield hours with *Treasure Island* and *Kidnapped*.

Guy's personal treasure was a girl called Tulia. She and a couple of friends materialised out of the leafy jungle one afternoon when Guy and some other officers were cooling off in a little clearing they had been directed to by locals. It was marvellously clean and cool by contrast with the baking town. A stream from Mount Vaea splashed down into a pool as clear as London gin. The men, caught sitting on the rocks in their drawers, were embarrassed. But the girls just giggled and jumped straight into the pool in the bright sort of gown they all wore, the *lava-lava*. When they came out, wet cloth clung to every curve and cranny; they might as well not have worn anything, Soon they did not. The *lava-lava* was a miraculous garment, sticking like a coat of paint when the wearer swam or climbed a palm tree but a tug at some secret twist of fabric and in a split second it was on the ground.

'Man at the gangway asking for you, sir,' said the quartermaster. *Porpoise* was alongside again and visitors were frequent. Guy got up to the well-deck and there was Commander Sturdee, telescope under his arm, chatting to Lance. 'Looks as though we've got a newspaper writer with us,' said Sturdee.

Guy's light-hearted line in the letter had caught Lance at a moment his spirits needed a boost. He was recuperating from a serious fall in a steeplechase at Flemington and grabbed at the chance to do something positive. 'Went to see the editor of *The Age*,' he told Guy. 'You remember him from the races?' As indeed Guy did. 'Told him you thought things were warming up out here. There's a lot of interest in the situation, you know. He said they'd take any stories I cared to send about what was happening. Pay for it, too. So I jumped on the first steamer to Auckland then took the mail boat on.'

Guy could only embrace the unexpected arrival but he was far from pleased to see him. Lance, on the other hand, glowed with achievement. 'Mr Sturdee says I can mess on your account. I'll pay you back once I get the cheque from *The Age*. He also said I could share your cabin.' That was pure mischief on Sturdee's part. Guy's cabin was so small he had to step outside to pull on a jacket.

For his first attempt at combat reporting Lance attached himself to Admiral Kautz's flag lieutenant and, together with the British consul, they rode out to see what the Mata'afans were up to. Lance became part of the story when hostile warriors surrounded them and they had to draw their six-shooters to break through the mob. *The Age* carried a colourful account of this incident involving 'the brother of Lieutenant Gaunt'.

> ...an armed rebel covered the flag lieutenant with his rifle, when the consul and Mr Gaunt drew their revolvers and closed with their assailants. All three displayed great bravery.

Kautz had been authorised by the State Department to settle the dispute America's way. He did so by upholding Judge Chambers's decision declaring Tanu the rightful king. Stirred up by the German faction, thousands of Mata'afans surged through the streets of Apia once again, shooting their opponents or chopping them up. Guy and a couple of dozen sailors went ashore to guard the British Consulate. This time Guy asked for a machine gun, the preferred method of colonial crowd control in accordance with the English poet Hilaire Belloc's celebrated Maxim maxim.

> *Whatever happens, we have got*
> *The Maxim Gun, and they have not.*

The two Maxims that *Porpoise* carried were already deployed, so Kautz lent Guy a Gatling gun, a clumsy crank-operated weapon of mass destruction from the Civil War. Six sweating American seamen hauled it over to the consulate on its wheeled carriage but refused to let the British touch it. 'You give the orders, lieutenant,' said the petty officer in charge. 'We'll do the shooting.' Guy did and they did, thus providing him with the entertaining dinner party claim of years later. At the American consulate marines from *Philadelphia* set up Colt guns, automatic weapons not much bigger that a rifle, that the British had only heard of. They had also heard that once a Colt began to fire it could be difficult to stop.

During the night the Mata'afans attacked both consulates. At the American buildings several marines were killed. Guy lost a young rating and another was wounded. The Gatling, cranked until the handle was too hot to touch, drove off the attackers. Suddenly a dreadful whirring filled the air and a blast peppered the walls of the consulate with shrapnel. 'God-damn!' yelled one of the Americans. '*Philly*'s loosing off with the six-inchers.'

The defenders were still recovering from their introduction to the American penchant for friendly fire when the first lieutenant of HMS *Tauranga*, a man senior to Guy, scuttled in to the consulate. 'Sorry old chap,' he said. 'I've come to take command here. You can't hog all the fun.' Guy gave way resentfully. 'You know what it's like,' said the intruder, 'My promotion could depend on it. You're much too young to be here anyway.'

By then though the shooting had stopped. On April Fools' Day the bumptious *Tauranga* officer and his counterpart from *Philadelphia*, Lance's earlier companion in arms, led a force of about 120 sailors and marines from both ships into a German plantation. The column was ambushed by Mata'afans and both lieutenants *nifi*-ed to bits. Pinned down, the remaining Americans placed their faith in a Colt gun. Rather than refusing to stop firing, the new-fangled weapon spat out a few rounds and jammed. Heroic efforts to clear it under Mata'afan fire failed and the gun had to be abandoned.

Kautz, the senior officer, took command. Sturdee was put in charge of land operations and decided to keep all the marines and seamen in Apia to safeguard civilians—including Germans, since the captain of *Falke* declined to put any of his men ashore. For days on end the British and American ships made sorties along the coast to shell villages and plantations where Mata'afans assembled. But out among the plantations and in the jungle, where at least three thousand Samoans would die in vicious fighting, the campaign was left to Guy. The young king had come to trust him and therefore the pro-Tanu tribes accepted his leadership. A couple of hundred Enfield rifles were shipped in from Fiji and the redtop warriors trained to use them, or at least to point them at the enemy before firing. Within weeks this ragtag army, led by Guy on a pony, was famous far beyond Samoa as Gaunt's Brigade.

There were some five thousand redtops including a couple of hundred girls, the marvellous Tulia among them. 'It is our custom to allow women to come into the battle with us,' Tanu explained. 'If they are there the men will be ashamed to run away. They bring food and water, too. Killing makes thirst.' Guy's redtops never showed any sign of running. They took it in turns with the Enfields and the rest of the time used their *nifis*. As they were slashing away or shooting, the women would pop up like mad marionettes, yelling encouragement. 'They are saying, "Kill!", Tanu explained, rather un-necessarily. 'Kill! Stab! Cut!' After each battle he was offered a disgusting pile of tributes; strings of ears and other human parts. When an encampment was over-run the only captives taken were the pigs, which the women cooked in a pit. At least they told Guy it was pig.

Every few weeks he rode into Apia where passengers from visiting cruise ships would come across him on the verandah of the Tivoli Hotel, dressed in ragged once-white trousers and a red turban.

I had been living for weeks on end on coco-nuts and bananas, so that when someone asked me to dinner, I jumped at the chance of a decent meal. I daresay I was a comical-looking British officer, resembling an Australian bushwacker more than anything else.

After a heavy evening he headed back to the Brigade camp in the moonlight, 'in pot valiant state' and was ambushed.

A native suddenly jumped from behind a coco-nut tree, crossed about five-feet in front of my pony, 'Sammy' and fired at me. Why he didn't let fly from his ambush goodness only knows: he must have killed me stone dead. As it was, he blasted off in a panic, doing no more damage than covering the pony and me with the fumes of powder.

'Sammy' had more sense than his rider. He didn't rear up, he just sat down. I slid off and fell into the ditch. Nothing happened for a few minutes, then I pulled myself along a bit on my stomach, revolver in hand, waiting for a shot.

Presently I heard a movement; the fellow must have jumped back among the trees after firing. Cautiously he made for the ditch, looking for my body, parting the reeds with the muzzle of his rifle. Then I let him have it, right in the middle.

Mata'afa made his last stand at Vailima. The hill was out of *Porpoise's* range and *Philadelphia* had expended most of her ammunition on plantations and uninhabited jungle. Once again there were no more sailors or marines to spare from protecting the Europeans in Apia. Guy got written orders from Sturdee with a paragraph underlined. 'Admiral Kautz asked me to instruct you that once the rebel stronghold has been cleared the Stevenson house is to be destroyed with charges in order to prevent the insurgents returning to it.'

Guy was within sniping distance of Vailima when he read this. The whitetops had thrown up a rampart over which the imperial German flag had been hoisted. He wondered if some diplomatic ramification meant that he might be about to declare war on a major Power. He had some dynamite, which Tanu had often wanted to use but it would have been wasted on most of their targets. He made up bundles of explosives and stowed them in a satchel but kept the fuses in his pocket. He told the redtops to sharpen their *nifis*.

The brigade went in at dawn. It was all over in a few volleys and a flurry of *nifis*. Guy tumbled over the rampart, intent on pulling down the flag. Suddenly he was flat on his face, forced into the clay by a soft presence emitting excited shrieks. Tulia had saved him from a bullet in the ribs. He had not seen a couple of Mata'afan defenders crouched at the foot of the flagpole with rifles. They were hacked down by the warriors who followed her scrambling charge.

The house seemed empty. He had no inclination to use the dynamite. Virtually within sight RLS lay under the wide and starry sky specified in his poetic epitaph. What could Guy possibly say to Minnie if he blew the place up under their hero's mummified nose?

Samoa was the making of Guy. Reports by the senior officers of both the British and American navies ensured that his feats received generous recognition. A letter in the *Sydney Morning Herald* suggested that he deserved to be acclaimed as Australia's first distinguished *soldier*. The Admiralty confirmed him on the permanent list and he was promoted to commander, although he had to ask if the signal informing him was correct. It referred to Grant, as he had called himself at the sailing school. Had he been found out? But only a misplaced dot or two of Morse code separated the names and it was indeed Gaunt. He began to think that there might be something auspicious and protective about that other identity. He wrote Kautz a note apologising for not having carried out his order. The admiral seemed relieved; destroying a literary shrine might have spoiled the glowing impression created by reports of the campaign that were being published back in the United States.

Sturdee told Guy that a Distinguished Service Order was in the works but it was never to materialise. The Admiralty obviously thought enough was enough. The Foreign Office offered to have him made a Companion of the Order of St Michael and St George 'for services to the Crown in relation to the foreign affairs of the Empire' but, irked by not being put up for a DSO, he declined. No one was going to look down a list and say, 'Hello there, who's this chap with the CMG?'.

When *Porpoise* returned to Sydney his fellow officers were interviewed by the *Daily Telegraph*.

> two names will stand out as the hero and heroine in the unhappy conflict, Lieutenant Gaunt of HMS Porpoise is undoubtedly the hero of the campaign; while the value of Tulia, described as 'one of the most sweetly pretty girls in Samoa,' is certain to remain green in the memories alike of the English and American seamen who witnessed her brave acts and were recipients of her kindness. It is the custom in Samoa for certain girls to accompany the fighting men. Tulia placed herself at the head of Lieutenant Gaunt's famous native brigade, in which he was the leading chief, and nerved them on to victory. In the jungle, when the men could scarcely see each other, much less their enemies, and with bullets flying all around, Tulia would suddenly show herself, and shout out to the dusky warriors, 'Fight, fight!' in tones of earnest encouragement. 'She is as plucky as they are made,' is the testimony of more than one eye-witness of the girl's bravery.

Guy himself remained tantalisingly discreet. He described Tulia with the French word *vivandière*, a sort of victualler, while explaining how—'flatly disregarding my orders'—she stuck to his heels in the final attack. Native girls were all very well in their place but now he had a reputation to consider.

A Sydney photographer, Charles Kelly, made postcards of *Tulia the Samoan Girl* for sale to cruise ship passengers. In one of them, a *nifi*-sharp image from a big glass negative, her springy mass of hair is piled high and decked with hibiscus flowers. A bodice of missionary proportions encases her bosom but below it her midriff is bare. Her neck is ringed with necklaces of shells and boars' teeth. She looks off-camera with bold intelligent eyes and an amused, almost defiant, expression on her slightly broad face. Some *vivandière*.

Lance did not try to make a career switch into journalism. It is hard to tell how much of his reporting was published, if any. When he put together a kind of life story for his family he ended this sequence with 'My Age story not found.' Story, singular.

When *Porpoise* got orders to return to Sydney, Lance was left to get home as best he could, falling foul of card sharps on the mail steamer and having to sell extracts from his diary to New Zealand papers to pay for the final stretch. Lance was no simpleton but like Forrest Gump the movie Everyman he seemed destined to make walk-on appearances in events with which he had no part to play. He also seemed, like Leonard Zelig, Woody Alan's earlier creation, to adopt the experiences of others as his own. Minnie remembered that Guy had told her the story of the slaughter in the plantation. Ever hungry for details of the boys' doings, she dramatised the incident in a short story, *When the Colt Jammed*, studded with expository dialogue. 'Why ain't it got a water-jacket like the Britishers' Maxims?' She would have been surprised to read in Lance's memoir that *he* had been the source of the Colt gun story. Lance also described striding alongside Commander Sturdee as he led detachments of sailors and marines ashore and of helping to defend the British Consulate under fire. Psychologists had just begun to speak of the ego defence mechanism of 'introjection', by which a person unconsciously incorporated the qualities of another— usually a significant other—into their own personality. They linked it with 'cryptomnesia' or false memory syndrome. Something a person had been told would later be recollected as their own experience. This made it a much more intriguing proposition than 'pseudologica fantastica', a condition in which the compulsive liar knew he was not telling the truth but could not help himself. No knowing if any of these conditions caused Lance to appropriate various incidents in Guy's life or whether he was simply trying to make himself seem more interesting.

Whatever the case, some form of sibling rivalry or resentment had begun to corrode the fraternal bond. Apart from a reference to the letter that inspired his dash to Samoa, Lance's later account of the time makes no mention of Guy at all. Nor does Guy make any reference to Lance being in Apia. Indeed, there is not a single mention of Lance anywhere in his autobiography, *The Yield of the Years*. But all Guy's recollections were brusquely selective. He owed a great deal to Minnie for her encouragement in their early days but even she did not find a place in his memoirs. A few years later he was to marry a wealthy widow, thus consolidating the lifestyle suitable for a promising officer. No mention of her, either.

Catching up

1901. Minnie, too, left many a gap in jigsaw accounts of her life. The marriage in which she had unexpectedly been so content came to a grim end in 1899. Lindsay Miller began behaving erratically and died within a year. Although neither Minnie nor any other member of the family left any reference to the events, a literary scholar, Bronwen Hickman, mined the files of Melbourne's uncompromisingly named Kew Lunatic Asylum that recorded Miller's manic behaviour and distressing symptoms. 'Mary sat with him daily,' she reported, 'watching the ghastly downhill slide towards dribbling incoherence and physical decay.'

The Asylum casebook recorded death due to 'disease of the brain'. Hickman showed the notes to medical authorities who thought the symptoms suggested tertiary syphilis. The disease was widespread in those days and one of its pernicious aspects was that early symptoms disappeared. The condition ceased to be contagious but emerged later in the devastating form described. This may go some way towards explaining why Minnie remained childless for the six years of her quiet domesticity, although there is no reason to suppose she experienced anything other than the usual forbearing sex life of the time.

Miller's finances were also in a terminal state. He had been 'involved' in the bank failures that brought down the curtain on Marvellous Melbourne. Minnie was left with £1,000 and £30 a year from some emaciated investments. Sorrowful but realistic, she sized up the situation. Her parents were willing to take her in but there was no family fortune. When they died she would be just as badly off and so much older. Royalties from her earlier triumphs were dwindling. A few publishing houses had set up in Australia but there was no market to compare with the one in which her name still meant something and where the energetic Mr Watt was there to push it. There was only one solution. Go back to London and begin again at forty. She gave £900 of her derisory inheritance to Miller's mother and used the remaining £100 for her journey Home.

The London to which she returned in 1901 was subdued by mourning for Queen Victoria and shaken by events in South Africa. Australians were more welcome than ever, people often taking the trouble to thank them 'for your help in the war'. They meant the war within the World.

On Minnie's first trip her ship had gone through the Suez Canal. This time she travelled the longer route via Cape of Good Hope. Had she known that Cecil was ranging the veldt only a few hundred miles away she would have stopped off and gone to find him. The South African territories, the strategically and commercially valuable Cape Colony at the southern tip and Natal around to the east, had been important waystations to and from Australia until the Canal siphoned off much of the ship traffic. Australians thought of those parts of the World as smaller variants of their own country but with more troublesome natives and strange neighbours. When the Boers, mainly Dutch settlers diluted by a few French, lost out to the British over who was to dominate the Cape they trekked inland and founded the republics of Transvaal and the Orange Free State. The British were happy to see them go—until the Transvaal turned out to be a new Eldorado, glinting with diamonds as well as gold. The familiar rush ensued with many Australians coming over to join in. At first the Boers, who were mainly farmers, welcomed these *uitlanders* for their mining know-how and energy but came to see them as a subversive British influence. Stimulated by financial opportunists, the imperial government in London began to provoke the Boers. A short, victorious war would deliver control of the mines to Britain. In October 1899 the Boers helped matters along, raiding into the neighbouring territories. Britain shipped out an army.

Disappointed to find that the Fourth Hussars was not one of the regiments in India ordered to sharpen—as the cavalry liked to say—for the event and fearful of missing the chance of a bit of extreme horsemanship, Cecil applied for a vacancy in the Fifth Dragoon Guards who *were* sharpening. Within days, the Fifth shipped out, bound for the town of Ladysmith in Natal which was already under threat from the Boers. He was made second-in-command of its C Squadron, a hundred and twenty horse led by Major St. John Gore.

In December came 'Black Week' when the Boer army of pious, sharpshooting farmers inflicted a series of embarrassing defeats on British regulars. The Boer cavalry were mounted on tough little ponies that took them from one ambush point to another, outshooting British infantry with Mauser rifles bought from Germany. They would often outride conventional cavalry. But the regiments from India, hardened in the asymmetric warfare of the Khyber, were a match for them. Cecil and his men would hurtle around hills at full gallop, taking Boer formations by surprise, riding them down when they tried to flee, hooves pounding, freshly sharpened sabres slashing as they caught up.

It was high summer in the southern hemisphere and the veldt was baking. Ladysmith was a hot spot, less because of the sun than of the large artillery pieces the Boers had quietly imported from Germany, six-inch Krupp guns on wheeled carriages and eight-inch howitzers that could lob high-explosive shells over the encircling hilltops. They also had a new Nordenfelt model called a 'pom-pom' that pumped out salvos of one-pound shells which could tear a horse apart, to say nothing of the rider. Major Gore made a vivid record of the earliest actions in reports to headquarters and in his diary. An account of 8 December told of Cecil's double escape from an unpleasant end. A cavalry detachment

> had made a most gallant night attack on the guns on Lombard's Kop (Gun Hill, to be exact). This attack was completely successful, and 'Long Tom', a six-inch gun which had annoyed Green Horse Valley more than any other, together with a howitzer, were blown up with gun cotton, and lost to the enemy. The Boers were evidently very much upset this morning! Lombard's Kop could not fire on us for obvious reasons, and the big gun on Bulwana did not open fire until we had moved under cover of Observation Hill. Many eye-witnesses of this short but very sharp bombardment to which the 5th Dragoon Guards were exposed at this time, expressed their wonder at the marvellous escapes that must have occurred, as the shells came absolutely into the middle of the regiment as it stood still on the road.

Three six-inch shells, each ninety-six pounds of devastation, exploded among the mounted men. A horse was killed and three wounded. Cecil took a steel splinter in his right leg. The regimental doctor, a Major Hilliard, treated him at the roadside. The two men were no more than eighteen inches apart when a Nordenfelt shell hurtled between them and blew apart a pile of saddlery. Neither Cecil nor Hilliard was hurt but each had a fleeting, indelible glimpse of the lethal little pointed cylinder as it zipped past and a whiff of the hot breath it left. The luck of the Gaunts was holding.

The British pushed the Boers back into their republics and captured the mines. Their commander, Lord Roberts, declared victory and went home. The Boers made a comeback with 'commandos', small mobile formations that harassed the unwieldy conventional forces. Lord Kitchener, who took over, integrated the Australians and other Colonials into fearsome mounted columns with which he set out to ravage the Boer countryside, burning farms, herding women and children into concentration camps. His methods raised protests around the world but they worked. The war over, the Transvaal and Orange Free State became partners in a new British dominion. The Boers were assured that the imperial government would never do what both white tribes feared most: extend equality to any other colour. That was the way of the World.

Even while a treaty was under discussion, Boers continued to mount raids and a figure who had become famous by staying out of the fighting emerged: Lieutenant-Colonel Robert Baden-Powell. He was actually the Fifth Dragoon's commanding officer but when the Boers had first became restive he went over to South Africa from India to organise volunteer militias and trotted into a Boer trap. Soon after fighting started he and the force he took over were besieged in the township of Mafeking, where he remained for most of the time his regiment was in action elsewhere, working up the Boy Scout concept. Deft public relations presented his embarrassing predicament as a triumph and when finally sprung he was hailed as a hero. Now he was organising a peace-keeping force called the South African Constabulary, soon to be known as Byng's Burglars after its leader, Lord 'Bungo' Byng and its penchant for looting Boer farms. Regular cavalry officers were invited to enlist for a two-year stretch. The pay was good and the time would count towards promotion when they returned to their regiments. Ready for anything that would keep him in the saddle, Cecil signed up and was sent to see order maintained in the Orange Free State, where the capital, Bloemfontein, had been the scene of a dubious British victory on the lines of Balaclava: eighty-two dead for a hundred Boers.

Roaming around, Cecil came upon the grave of Lieutenant-Colonel Charles Umphelby, the most senior Australian of the 600 who died in South Africa. It was not a heroic end. 'Uncle' Umphelby was a middle-aged officer of Victoria's garrison artillery who had come over as an observer.

Making himself useful as a British staff messenger, he had been picked off by a sniper and buried near a field hospital that had soon moved on. It is doubtful Cecil had ever heard of Umphelby but he read the crude inscription branded on a piece of ammunition box and thought it deserved to be improved upon. As he wrote to *The Argus* in a letter which took three months to reach Melbourne

> I carved a headstone and put the grave in order. The carving is rough, for I am not an expert, and I made my chisel out of a table knife.

This respectful gesture to a compatriot could have been wasted effort. Poor old Uncle's body might already have been disinterred by the army's undertakers. The records are contradictory: Cecil's hand-made tombstone was rediscovered in 1996.

African shores

On her first visit to England Minnie had been able to see Ceylon, India and Egypt en route. On her second trip, steaming up the west coast of Africa, she had been haunted by a wispy memory from one of her childhood story books of a young castaway, a kind of junior Robinson Crusoe, although black, stranded somewhere on that mysterious wild shore. That re-awakened memory was the beginning of an enthrallment with Africa that would rebuild her life and livelihood.

In London she felt a general sense of renewal and progress. The beamy bottom of King Edward VII, Herring's father, had replaced Queen Victoria's on the imperial throne. Elsewhere, change had been less orderly. In the United States an assassin had made a sloppy job of bringing William McKinley's presidency to an end in 1901 and the successor, Theodore Roosevelt, was asserting himself with the image of a Big Stick that America might have to use to keep the world in line. There was no one to meet her when she landed; both Guy and Ernest were in China and it would be a couple of years before they showed up. When they did, Ernest was in a wheelchair.

Ernest's steady progress set the pace for his brothers. On the China

Station in 1896 he had shown his worth as first lieutenant of HMS *Narcissus* when the captain drowned in a boat accident and he went to the rescue of those who survived. That boldness ensured his promotion to commander soon afterwards and in the years to follow he became, in effect, governor of the island of Wei-Hai-Wei, a strategically valuable spot Britain had snapped up while the Chinese owners were distracted by a squabble with their Russian neighbours. Characteristic Gaunt assertiveness saved the lives of hundreds of missionaries who fled from the fighting and threw themselves on his mercy. Ernest shook down the local banks for all the money they had, commandeered accommodation, requisitioned food. Job done, he went down to Hong Kong and got married to Louise Geraldine Martyn of County Clare.

'Gerry' had come out with the 'fishing fleet', the hundreds of genteel, nubile hopefuls who set out each year to cast their net in compatible gene pools around the British World: Malta, Egypt, India, Hong Kong. In the main, the deal on offer was quite fair. Naval officers, even those from wealthy families, were usually younger sons, their expectations limited by the iron rule of primogeniture. Certainly none of the Gaunts had any prospect of inheritance. But there was clear social standing attached to commissioned rank and a wife would share in the graduated uplifts that came with promotion. In turn, the bride's dowry might bring her husband a house as well as a hostess; assure the children's education. Having reached the rank at which they were allowed—expected—to marry, both naval brothers were scanning the horizon for a bride ready to trade her dowry for their status. Marrying Geraldine—Gerry—though, was a risky career move; Irish intransigence was a constant worry for the British government. Also, she was a Roman Catholic and the navy was firmly Anglican. But she was beautiful. And bountiful. Her family owned the most dependable source of wealth in Ireland, short of a gold strike: a brewery.

In 1903, five years after the wedding, their time in the East was up. Gerry set off to find a suitable London house. Ernest was given an outmoded 'torpedo cruiser' to take home for scrapping, HMS *Mohawk*. After that undemanding command he would, at the turn of the year, ascend to his post-captaincy and, no doubt, a ship suitable for a modern naval officer. He sailed from Hong Kong without ever having heard of Mohammed Abdullah Hassan, the original Mad Mullah.

The Mad Mullah of Somaliland was the Osama bin Laden of his time, although he did his stuff in a different corner of the globe, one that like Afghanistan remained a risky place for Europeans a century later. Hassan was a Muslim ascetic reputed to have memorised the Koran by the age of eleven; a *Daraawiish*. 'Dervish' to the British evoked the 1884 uprising in the adjacent Sudan, shrieking, scimitar-waving, white-robed hordes, the slaughter of General Charles Gordon, the glorious relief of Khartoum. Thus Hassan was assured of notoriety from the moment he emerged as leader of resistance to British annexation of northern Somaliland, across the Red Sea from Aden on the lower corner of the Arabian peninsula. The unhappy experience of the Boer Wars had curbed Britain's appetite for chunks of Africa. Still, she needed to control both ends of the main highway to India and the wider world beyond, including Australia, on which Britain increasingly depended for food and commerce.

Even more provocative to Hassan, Italy, a latecomer in the colonial scramble, set out to seize all Abyssinia, of which Ethiopia was part. The invading Italian army was soundly defeated, the first such failure for European expansion. The Italians withdrew to the coastal province of Eritrea, then laid claim to the strip of Somaliland on the far side of the British enclave. The Mullah switched his *jihad* over there. In several years of harassing his neighbours he had learnt a few things beyond the Koranic Verses. His followers were well-organised and plentifully provided with rifles; as skilful at unconventional tactics as the Boers.

Despite their own inadequacies the British felt obliged to come to the aid of their fellow colonists. The Admiralty provided port facilities at Aden but in keeping with the policy the Italian navy was to pursue for most of the century the cruiser stationed there spent most of the time safe in harbour. Dangerous work was left to junior officers who followed the British in using armed *dhows* to patrol the many small harbours, local sailing vessels with a single three-pounder gun bolted to the deck. The Italian word for these graceful but flimsy craft was *sambuco*, the elder tree whose bark flavours the liqueur.

When Ernest brought *Mohawk* into Aden for coal in December, the dervishes were sitting tight in the Somaliland badlands along the Indian Ocean. Nothing had been heard from the African side for some time and the Senior Naval Officer asked Ernest if he would mind steaming over to take a look around. Just for a few days, old man. You'll still get home for Christmas.

At his first landfall Ernest found an Italian petty officer in serious trouble, the boatswain of a *sambuco* that he had just brought back around the Horn with its skipper, Lieutenant Carlo Grabau, dead and four crewmen wounded. *Tenente* Grabau had spotted a dervish flag flying over the coastal village of Durbo and gone ashore to demand that it be replaced by the Italian colours. When the headmen refused he shelled the place with his feeble cannon. As the *sambuco* hauled around to sail out of the harbour, a volley of rifle fire felled most of the Italians on deck.

It never seemed to occur to Ernest that this might not be Britain's fight, let alone his. He had been raised and shaped in the spirit of white dominance, faith in which had been reinforced by his time in the Far East. Natives had attacked a white man, a fellow naval officer at that. The offence must be punished. He had no doubt that he was entitled to act on behalf of the Admiralty, the British government, the king himself. Even the king of Italy. There was something more. Ernest was not exactly jealous of Guy and the acclaim his swashbuckling exploits in Samoa had attracted, nor was he envious of Cecil with his honourable wound, but it did rankle that those brothers had seen vivid action while he had not heard a shot fired in anger since his midshipman days. As he later told Minnie, he needed to know what was it like to be in combat; whether or not he would feel fear and if so how he would deal with it. Here was his chance and there was no time to lose. He steamed around into the Indian Ocean. The offending village awoke next morning under *Mohawk*'s six-inch guns.

If John Ford, the director of classic Westerns, had ever made an Eastern, the script could easily have been built around the events that now unreeled—John Wayne playing Ernest, of course. The Royal Navy had seen little action at sea for the better part of a century but plenty on distant shores. Leaving seventy armed sailors and marines deployed along the tideline, a Maxim gun out in front and another two in boats that hauled off to wait beyond the surf line. Ernest and a small escort went forward to parlay with the village elders. A local trader was enlisted as interpreter.

Four tribesmen hung with pistols and daggers received the British party. Ernest explained that he was a friend of the Italians who had been so ignominiously attacked. Such a lawless act could not go unpunished. Two of the chiefs must come back to Aden and surrender to the Italians. The village was also to run up the Italian flag he had thoughtfully brought with him. This discussion, Ernest assured his daughter Yvonne years later, was conducted with civility and good humour, rather as though he had been buying a camel. 'Neither side showed the slightest animosity,' he recalled. 'It was extremely polite and civilised. We understood each other implicitly.'

Negotiations remained civil even when the elders told Ernest they would have to refer his request upwards. They should have an answer for him in about a week. At Ernest's back the landing party had been exchanging semaphore signals with *Mohawk* from which telescopes were scanning the village. A signalman whispered that women could be seen leaving the houses; men were digging foxholes. I'm afraid that I cannot wait, Ernest told the Somalis, his smile a little tight. 'I will now fire a big gun over your village as a warning. If you then offer no terms, I shall fire six three-pounder cannon shells *into* your village and advance and burn it....' With this calibrated reprisal plan spelt out, Ernest withdrew to the foreshore. *Mohawk* was signalled to fire the demonstration round. The six-inch projectile howled overhead and exploded in the desert beyond. There was no response from the village, so more signals flicked across the water and the lighter guns dropped the promised half-dozen shells among the clay-brick houses. The Somalis immediately opened fire on the landing party.

Ernest drew his sword and ordered his men to advance. All too soon he discovered what it was like to be in action. The next Somali volley cut him down. He was carried to the rear. *Mohawk*'s first lieutenant, Frank Powell, took command. The seamen and marines set the nearest houses alight and withdrew with the body of a young marine shot in the head. Heavy surf made it difficult to get back into the boats, especially with Ernest, his leg strapped to an oar.

It was a frightful wound. The bullet smashed Ernest's tibia, leaving a section of bone protruding. A few years earlier it would have been fatal but much had been learnt about treatment in the Boer Wars. Nevertheless, it took six months in the European General Hospital at Aden before Ernest was fit to be sent home. The cable confirming his fourth gold ring reached him on New Year's Eve. Ten months later he went to Rome to receive the

Silver Cross, a high Italian honour. No one questioned the wisdom of his intervention. The SNO who had sent him believed that

the effect upon the natives along the entire coast will be a good one, impressing upon them the reality of British and Italian co-operation in the present campaign against the Mullah.

Mohawk was not to make it home for Christmas. Lieutenant Powell remained in command and in March he took her, together with two other British warships, to land a large force at a place called Illig for a confrontation in which the Mad Mullah was routed, at least for a time. Perhaps it should have been John Wayne for Powell; Ronald Reagan for Ernest.

Time Tricks

Minnie folded much of her personal story into the accounts of her travels, rather as though with these new styles of book she was resetting her life to a fresh starting point. Most of it is undoubtedly—and touchingly— believable but parts are thoroughly disingenuous. A favourite passage among admirers, especially scholars who acclaimed her as a pioneer literary feminist, was framed as a lament to her second London period, one that in reality had been happy and fulfilling.

Oh the dreariness and weariness of life for a woman poor and unknown in London! I lodged in two rooms in a dull and stony street. I had no one to speak to from morning to night, and I write and wrote stories that all came back to me, and I am bound to say the editors who sent them back were quite right. They were poor stuff, but how could anyone do good work who was sick and miserable, cold and lonely, with all the life crushed out of her by the grey skies and the drizzling rain? I found London a terrible place in those days; I longed for all my heart for my own country, my own little home in Warrnambool where the sun always shone (...). I did not go back to my father, because my pride would not allow me to own myself a failure and because all the traditions of my family were against giving in. But I was very near to

72

it, very near it indeed.

This is undoubtedly heartfelt and, in the early days, understandable. But in a writerly trick with timelines she was re-arranging past events to fit another purpose. The 'dull and stony street' period encompassed some seven years during which she produced her most profitable novels. She was using the frustrations of her first visit to Britain years before to accentuate the later sorrow of her widowhood.

The street she evoked so plausibly was Finborough Road SW10, which runs along the side of Brompton Cemetery. Not a fashionable part of London then or now but hardly a slum. Alice Rosman, who interviewed her for *Everylady's Journal*, found everything there

> ... cosy and delightful ... an ideal sanctum ... a bright fire ... plenty of easy chairs, well-filled bookcases, a business-like writing desk, a table with typewriter and paper, and on the mantelpiece a beautiful grinning blue deity, looted from some Chinese temple or another.

As for 'the traditions of my family', a single generation was hardly long enough for any to develop. There were the shared characteristics of compulsive wanderlust and the young Gaunts' adamantine resolve to finish whatever they set out to achieve. But what they shared above all was that glinting stratum of good luck, although any old goldfield fossicker could have told them that no lode ever ran far without a break.

Nor was Minnie particularly lonely. The Australian colony were forever organising banquets and dinners. Ernest was in Britain recovering from his wound and would squire her around. Guy came back from China, fell off a horse and had to spend many months on half-pay recovering. He and Minnie passed most of one autumn in Brittany where oysters and the sancerre were cheap. Both Clive and Lance turned up, feeling their way along yet another strand of the network from which the Gaunts swung around the World like trapeze artists—the Law. Clive had no sooner fulfilled his father's wishes by getting called to the Bar in Melbourne than he was off to explore the endless career openings under the Raj—for a member of the *English* Bar. It took a while but he could now afford the pupillage in London that would provide his *entrée*.

Lance had been taken on as a clerk by Mr Justice Higgins, whose reputation as a hanging judge he was ready to overlook for £300 a year 'and perquisites'. He qualified as a barrister but times were still hard in Melbourne and the congenital inability to stay home soon kicked in. An old friend from the Rupertswood Battery was shipping four hundred horses to Calcutta. Lance signed on to escort them for £1.50 a week and a return ticket. His parting from a tearful but resigned William was fateful. The old man died a year from that day without seeing any of his children again.

Rather than go back to Australia, Lance made for Singapore where he bowled up to a law firm with one of those helpful letters of introduction people in Melbourne had given him. He was offered not just a job but the means of accepting it. Courts of the Straits Settlements would not recognise his Australian credentials but the law firm William sent him to paid for him to go to London and qualify. Twelve months of legal skivvying and eating ritual dinners among their professional betters at the Inns of Court and the two youngest Gaunts would be able to plead, prosecute and respectfully submit their bills anywhere in the British World.

A more genuine concern for Minnie than playing the lonely widow was that she had run out of material. As before, she found that

> ... it was simply hopeless for me to think of writing stories about English life. The regular conventional life did not appeal to me; I could only write adventure stories, and the scene of adventure stories was best laid in savage lands (...) I sought for information about West Africa and I found it, not easily; every story I wrote cost me a world of trouble and research and anxiety ...

That hazy glimpse of the African coastline from her passing ship and the reawakened memory of the childhood story of the little black Crusoe came to replace the goldfields as the mainland of her imagination. Lack of knowledge was easily remedied. Since the Stanley and Livingstone saga of the early 1870s the Dark Continent had loomed large in the European mind. Explorers swarmed all over it, sizing up territory to snitch, searching for the source of the Nile, bartering for ivory and gold, pursuing large animals to shoot and souls to collect for Christianity. Some of the bodies housing the souls were in poor shape and modern missionaries made it a priority to keep the owners alive long enough to be converted. Christian heroes returned to London from jungles and deserts to entrance packed lecture halls with stories of their experiences. Prominent among them was Dr Thomas Jobling Tonkin who had accompanied an expedition to the Sudan where he met everything

… from poisoned fish to fiery dragons—to say nothing of the sneaking road-thieves, predatory slaving bands, professional robbers, naked savages, and man-eating cannibals.

This was music to Minnie; a new vision of the exotic. Tonkin was the very model of a modern adventurer, posing for photographs in expeditionary kit: stout boots and leather gaiters, riding breeches, unbuttoned shirt and across his shoulder a double-barrelled .450 express rifle, the elephant gun that was central to stories by Rider Haggard and other writers who had picked up on the vogue for tall tales of Africa. In Minnie's forthright way she simply wrote to Tonkin with a proposition: books about Africa are selling. You provide the knowledge, I'll do the writing.

Tonkin did not hesitate, although he insisted on hiding his professional identity behind the *nom-de-plume* of John Ridgwell Essex, presumably lifted from the town of that name in that county. He may even have contributed some of the prose in the novels that were to appear under their joint names. Writing insightful papers on the treatment of leprosy his style was scholarly and restrained. Elsewhere, he let rip. Describing a scene for *Wide World* magazine in which he and some companions were confronted by a 'dense armed crowd' of Africans bearing a threatening array of fetish items, he wrote

The priests were made horrid with feathers and bones and chalk, as in the manner of the devil dancers of the country. As they danced they yelled and screamed and pointed in our direction. The people howled in concert. It was deafening. The pole swayed, the brasses clattered, the captive vultures screamed and fought and struggled. Behind it all there streamed up into the sky from a blackly forbidding range of hills that lay across the valley the fiery bands of a dying sunset like blood-red flames from the mouth of the pit. It was a picture worthy of the pen of a Dante, but we had no time to devote to artistic possibilities. It was what you call an acute situation.

The situation became less acute when the Africans sized up the white men's arsenal and Dr Tonkin lived to recycle variations of that and other exotic tales.

Tonkin/Essex was five years younger than Minnie. Like her lamented Dr Miller he had taken his medical degree in Edinburgh. Whether the collaboration, which lasted several years, went beyond the literary is impossible to say. A diary unearthed by Bronwen Hickman showed that Minnie spent lengthy periods with or near Tonkin in parts of Britain that she would not normally care to visit—Sheffield, Stoke on Trent—but neither in that or in anything else she wrote about herself was there any suggestion that she wished for a man to share her life. He was married and at least nominally a Christian, although neither factor eliminates the possibility. She enjoyed the discreet freedom that Edwardian society allowed a widow. Both in creating her principal female characters and when writing about herself, Minnie was sympathetic to the usual human needs and weaknesses. She was quite aware there were 'passions' to be accommodated but never hinted of an interest in assuaging them. The collaboration with Tonkin/Essex petered out after three years with Minnie's mating inclinations a mystery but whatever else may have happened it produced three novels, *The Arm of the Leopard*, *Fools Rush In* and *The Silent Ones* and contributed to a weird but highly successful pot-boiler, *The Mummy Moves*.

1910. Minnie needed a new book badly and yet again Africa would provide it. At the beginning of the Twentieth Century writers worked in much the same way as they did at its end. For an account of adventurous travel the idea was to find a sponsor, or at least a publisher who would offer an advance on royalty payments to cover the cost of research. The house of T Werner Laurie, the tenth publisher to handle Minnie's work, had just accepted *The Silent Ones*, third and last of the African titles with Tonkin/Essex. Her industrious agent A P Watt persuaded them to cough up. A wily author would also try to reduce the outlay by wangling a freebie, as it was not yet known. Minnie got out her address book.

Sir Charles Lucas, head of the Dominions department of the Colonial Office, had just been out to Australia to see what he had to deal with. He mentioned to Minnie that the governor of the Gambia colony in West Africa, Sir George Denton, was about to go back there from leave in a steamer of the Elder Dempster line. What a coincidence! The shipowners were friends of the Horsfalls, the Liverpool family who had been so kind to Guy in his cadet days; Minnie had come to know them well. Elder Dempster were persuaded to provide her with a free passage on the SS *Gando* the ship Sir George was taking. Rustling through her acquaintances Minnie soon had an impressive list of friends of friends and an entire folio of crisp letters of introduction that were as good as hotel vouchers. Though she was past fifty, she was more excited at the prospect of the expedition she had organised than by any other experience that had so far come her way. Boarding *Gando* on a cold grey Liverpool morning brought back all her vicarious love of the sea and adventure in far-off places.

The book for which Mr Watt negotiated a reassuring advance was to have been an illustrated study of the string of picturesque ruined fortresses left down the coast of the Gambia by early Portuguese explorers and slave traders. Minnie would take the photographs herself; the heaviest items in her kit were a huge camera and tripod and several wooden boxes with racks for the negatives, heavy glass plates coated with silver nitrate.

The book that Werner Laurie actually got was far better. *Alone in West Africa*, which Minnie turned out within a couple of months of her return, scored a timely hit: stirring, real-life adventure by a real-life *woman*. A couple of intrepid spinsters had already titillated the reading classes with accounts of their desert journeys but publishing had never seen anything like this, written with all the disarming candour and deft reconstitution of events that came naturally to a Gaunt, of a lone female bestriding the African jungle and living to tell her colourful tale. The praise for Minnie's daring was so clamorous that hardly anyone noticed she had not really *stridden* anywhere: she had been lugged around in a hammock. Nor, despite the book's bold title, was she *Alone* unless, as Guy teased, her entourage of a couple of dozen native bearers was overlooked. But even people who picked up on these discrepancies would not have considered them remarkable. That was the way things were in white man's Africa. The transfixing element of the book was that the intrepid traveller was not a man.

Nor did anyone seem to notice another of Minnie's time-shifting feats, a tantalising bit of literary trickery. Some of the power of *Alone* came from the idea that she was writing about her first encounter with Africa, her impressions fresh and vivid. In fact she had already visited the West Coast—in April to September 1908, a time when her collaboration with Tonkin seemed most fruitful; a journey that remains a tantalising puzzle. In the same way that she synthesised episodes of her London life, many of her experiences from that intriguing earlier trip to Africa were streamed in, not altogether seamlessly, with events of the *Alone* journey of 1910.

The *Alone* expedition certainly began as she described it; she appears on the *Gando* passenger list, as does Sir George Denton, whose help she was out to ensure. But how she got out to West Africa on that earlier occasion remains as baffling as why she went and whether anyone else—Tonkin, perhaps—went with her. Remaining constructively vague in *Alone* about dates, distances and the sequence of events, she wrote about Accra, where she had actually been on that first trip.

In the Gambia, Sir George could not have done other than put her up at Government House in Bathurst, the tin-roof capital, while she organised her expedition. Job interviews for a personal servant began immediately and the successful applicant was called Ansumanah ... Grant. Minnie may have known that Guy had adopted Grant as an occasional alias and thought it a happy omen but in any case she was never to regret her choice. Grant was a twenty-three-year-old Muslim, partially reformatted by Wesleyan missionaries. Minnie took the process a stage further by getting him out of the rig in which he had turned up for his job interview— pink pyjama jacket, old breeches and red carpet slippers—and into khaki knickerbockers, white shirt and red cummerbund. She did not think he really needed shoes, a view that had been formed on that earlier visit. Accra had a large European population and as a result many Africans had gone native in reverse and to Minnie's mind:

> There is something in the tight-fitting clothes of civilisation that is utterly unsuited to these sons and daughters of the Tropics, and the man who is a splendid specimen of manhood when he is stark but for a loincloth, who is dignified in his flowing robe, sinks into commonplaceness when he parts his wool and comes out in a coat and high white collar.

No matter where they ended up in her haphazard wanderings, Grant managed to get together her morning and afternoon tea and the few meals she had to arrange for herself. More often than not she contrived to end the day at a government residence, the outpost of some lonely official or at least a mission

Minnie covered nearly seven hundred miles slung between the shoulders of her bearers and spent three months doing it. It is an extraordinary vision, an amalgam of Sanders of the River and Mr Magoo, this pint-sized matronly chancer being lugged along jungle tracks in her canvas cocoon. Although she enjoyed comfort and safety whenever she could, in many of the places she insisted on going to she was the only white woman ever seen; in some cases the only white person. Where whites were numerous, she was spooked by lnative functionaries who

had lost all awe of a white face, and, I felt, were inclined to be presuming. What could I have done if they had forgotten their thin veneer of civilisation, and gone back to pure savagery? I wondered if my canoe-men, who were very decent, respectable savages, would come to my help. I wonder still ... I was quite powerless. I wondered if a Savage, on these occasions one spells Savage with a very large "S", did come into my bedroom what should I do ... But I never thought of going back ... in any case it is against family tradition.

That family tradition again. In this case she shared with Guy an admirable readiness to overlook conventions if they got in the way, as well as her cheerful tendency towards sleight-of fact. Also like Guy, she was capable—in instances like this—of courage to the point of folly. The truly remarkable aspect of Minnie's trek was her steel-nerved ability to bend shambolic teams of half-savage tribesmen and women to her will for a silver threepenny bit each per day and finish the long haul in one piece.

In stirring the first secretive trip—her real introduction to Africa,—into the later one Minnie may have simply been exercising a little literary licence. It could also be that if she and Dr Tonkin were already drifting apart she was running low on local colour. In *The Arm of the Leopard* she and Essex created an 'educated nigger', Dr James Craven, to personify the colour and sexual prejudices on which her stories frequently depended. When *The Silent Ones*, which she had researched in 1908, appeared under her solo byline there he was again.

Race relations had been such a recurring issue in Gaunt/Essex fiction that when she turned to factual writing in *Alone* a policy statement seemed appropriate.

It is no good trying to hide the fact: between the white man and the black lies not only the culture of the west—that gulf might be, and sometimes is, bridged—but that other great bar, the barrier of sex. Tall, stalwart and handsome as is many a negro, no white woman may take a black man for her husband and be respected by her own people; no white man may take a black girl, though her dark eyes be soft and tender, though her skin be as satin and her figure like that of the Venus de Milo and hope to introduce her among his friends as his wife. Even the missionaries who preach that the black man is a brother decline emphatically to receive him as a brother-in-law.

Only when nearly at the end of her epic trek was Minnie prepared to modify her stern views about race. She had reached a sorry-sounding place called Peki Blengo where she encountered Mr Olympia from French Dahomey and 'I felt like apologising to all the African peoples for anything I may have said against them'.

He was extremely good-looking, and had polished, courteous manners such as one dreams of in the Spanish hidalgos of old. If you searched the wide world over I do not think you could wish to find a more charming man. ... I only met him casually, as I met other black men, men outside the pale for me, a white woman, but I felt when I looked at him that there might be possibilities in the African race: when I think of their enormous strength and their wonderful vigour, immense possibilities.

Although Minnie had plenty of unnerving experiences, getting away from the Volta was the most truly dangerous and she put all her novelist's powers into recalling it; less a show of narrative than a full-blown stampede of description. She was standing next to the captain on the bridge of the little steamer taking her out to a ship waiting offshore. Crossing the sandbar at the river mouth they were nearly swamped, great Atlantic breakers sweeping the length of the vessel.

Crash, crash, crash came the tons of water; there was a ripping of broken wood, and a human wail told me that crew and black passengers had realised their danger And then I looked around me to see the havoc...the bulwarks were swept away, the boats were smashed, the great crane for working cargo was smashed and useless, the galley was swept overboard, the top of the engine-house was broken in, and, transformation scene, every solitary creature on board that little ship, with the exception of the captain and me was stark naked. Custom-house officers had stripped off their uniforms, clerks who had come to tally cargo in all the glory of immaculate shirts and high collars were nude. Everyone had got ready to face the surf. 'Much good it would have done 'em,' opined the captain; 'no living thing could have got ashore in that sea.'

Grant appeared, sodden but clothed. 'All gone, Ma.' Most of her possessions—Cecil's splendid medicine chest and campaign bed, pots, pans, food and drink and all her boots—had gone over the side. The greatest loss was her typewriter, soaked and beyond repair. She got back to London with only half the amount of gear she had started out with, but all the notes and photographs she needed to produce *Alone*, to find herself the beneficiary of the greatest piece of good fortune a writer can hope for: one of her books had been banned.

This was *The Uncounted Cost*, which had been written between that sneaky trip to Africa and the one she was about to describe in *Alone*. In it, a young woman had been persuaded to set up house with a naval lieutenant—what else?—who promised to marry her as soon as he could afford to. Uncomfortable in such a relationship she broke it off. The illicit romance was over when the story proper began, referred to only in a letter written by the heroine. In the main narrative she contracted a case of true love with a worthy chap but that besmirched past made her too ashamed to accept his proposal.

Most readers accepted *Cost* as the morality tale Minnie had intended but the powerful organisations on which sales and readership relied found the idea of a couple living together outside matrimony, even at a remove from the main story, too much. W H Smith, Mudie's Circulating Library and *The Times* Book Club united in refusing to handle the book. The result, of course, was that sales elsewhere soared. Novels, though, were things of the past for Minnie. She was hooked on real-life travel and adventure and had the money to pursue them. As soon as she turned in the manuscript of *Alone* she was planning to head for territory even more promising for a solo appearance: China.

PART TWO

Disaster

1912. All Guy could think of were his feet. They seemed frozen solid. He got them out of the seaboots they had been packaged in for nearly twenty-four hours and wrapped a towel around them but the cramped steel cabin in which he was huddled on the edge of a bunk had no heating, nothing as luxurious as hot water. It was the captain's sea cabin of HMS *Centurion*, the new super-dreadnought being readied to join the great armada Britain was building to keep ahead of Germany in the Great Twentieth Century Naval Race. Strictly speaking, she was not yet a British warship although she certainly looked like one: nearly six hundred feet long, 25,000 tons displacement, ten 13.5-inch guns. Also, Guy was in command only for the series of sea trials the Admiralty demands before accepting her from the builders. But once those were complete she would be the latest and largest battleship in the fleet and he, undoubtedly, would be confirmed as her captain. At last he would have a command worthy of him. Until then he could only dream of the main quarters aft as he had seen them in the designers' sketches: mahogany tables and bookshelves, leather armchairs and a cosy coal fire. He would make damn sure there is also serious heating for this horrible little iron box high up in the superstructure where he has to sleep whenever he might need to reach the bridge in seconds.

The inert radiator on the unpainted bulkhead was only one of many things that remained to be done: the list was as long as the ship. But *Centurion* had been hustled out of Devonport dockyard the previous morning, 9 December, because a vital requirement had to be completed before Christmas got in the way: the first real test of the turbines that drove her four propellers. A dreadnought was built around these mighty marvels, their beds installed as soon as a keel was laid. They were a world apart from the old triple expansion engines that made a ship rumble like a railway bridge from stem to stern, thumping, rattling, spewing steam and water. Two of the monsters ran the length of the main engine room, tapering humps of casing inside which jets of superheated steam spun the turbine blades like waterwheels. Each of the remaining two had its own compartment on either side. For cruising speed, the everyday requirement, only the inner pair of shafts was used but the Admiralty test required *Centurion* to steam on all four for thirty hours without a break, making eighteen knots—three-quarters of her full speed. A man in brown dustcoat and bowler hat, Mr Spinks, foreman engineer from Parsons, the firm that built the turbines, was in charge of them. 'Once we've got the revolutions up for the three-quarter mark,' he told Guy. 'they mustn't lose a turn. Don't let anything stop us, captain, before the day after tomorrow.' Guy knew he would be stuck on the bridge with only an hour or two off for a snooze until he brought her back to Devonport.

In commission, *Centurion* would have a complement of some eight hundred men but she has had to leave harbour with only a skeleton crew of officers and ratings, three hundred men from Parsons and the other shipbuilders crawling over her. There were a full four watches of boiler-room hands to provide Mr Spinks with steam—civilians couldn't be expected to trim coal and shovel it into the fireboxes—but only a couple of stewards to look to the officers' needs, such as dry clothes and footbaths. There was a wardroom galley but no steam or electric power for it so nothing hot to eat or drink.

The bridge, an upstairs-downstairs arrangement of open compass platform, enclosed wheelhouse and the 'plot' where charts were laid out, was as unfinished as everything else. Shown it for the first time a few days earlier Guy had immediately seen it was not even weatherproof. 'Look at those gaps,' he said to the lieutenant shipwright in charge, sticking fingers in the space left between deckhead and bulkhead. 'Rain will drive in there like a sailor pissing down a windscuttle.'

Guy knew little about the half-dozen deck officers he had been assigned; even less about the engineers who, in any case, were only bystanders while Mr Spinks's team was on board. The officers would not know much about him either, apart from the legend of Gaunt's Brigade, aspects of which suggested that he had steered a rather unusual course through the ranks, and that he had an older brother who was within reach of his rear-admiral's flag; and that he was a Colonial. They would be out to impress him, though. Once confirmed in command of *Centurion* he would be able to choose pretty much who he wanted to help him run her and they would all be keen to join a ship of such distinction.

It was more than two years since Guy had had a command. He had been confident something would come up eventually but *Centurion* was a richer prize than he had expected. He had done everything he could to make himself known to the new demigods at the Admiralty. At the beginning of the year Winston Churchill had become First Lord, and his Naval Secretary, the man in uniform at his side, was Rear Admiral David Beatty. Guy had spotted Beatty as a man who might one day throw out a towline and, to pull close alongside him, joined the Quorn, the aristocratic hunt around Leicester with which the navy rode. A firm seat and an eye for a jump could do as much for a chap as knowing how to push a man o'war around.

He got in plenty of hints and bootlicking while managing to give Beatty's mad American wife Ethel a wide berth. She was as rich as she was barmy, heiress to the Marshall Field department store fortune. Out in Malta Beatty had damaged a cruiser and was looking at a court-martial. Ethel shrugged an elegant shoulder. 'I'll buy them a new ship,' she said in her harsh Chicago accent. She had hauled the trousers off most of her husband's friends but she frightened hell out of Guy, although he had begun to wonder if it might have been better tactics to cultivate her favours instead of her complaisant old man's. He had put in nearly two years in Devonport signing off repairs and inflicting minor punishments on defaulters when, out of nowhere, he got orders for *Centurion* and a note in Beatty's atrocious handwriting: 'Once over the jumps and she's yours!' He took that as a reference to the ship rather than Ethel.

'There's also the seaboat davits,' said Commander Bernhard Pratt-Barlow, who as executive officer saw to the state of the ship. He had noticed something Guy had not yet got around to. There *were* no seaboat davits. *Centurion* was not short of boats. A large steam crane aft of her two great funnels was surrounded by them, stacked neatly inside one another. Boats for all purposes: great galleys and jumbos to land marines and ferry provisions, a smart sailing gig for the captain—although Guy would prefer a steam pinnace—workaday whalers and cutters. These were the boom boats; at anchor, the crane would put them over the side. None could serve as a seaboat, the essential emergency craft ready to be sent away on any task: man overboard, lady's hat blown off, tow a line off to a tug, take a peek at that funny looking vessel over there.

In commission there would be two: a twelve-oar cutter hung in davits on each side of the quarterdeck. If a bosun's mate piped 'Away seaboat's crew' one would be in the water within seconds, its crew sliding down ropes to reach their place as the boat was lowered away beneath. When it reached the water, the coxswain would strike off the falls on a rising wave and let the cutter slide into the water at the same speed as the ship. 'We'll see what they can do,' said the shipwright, embarrassed.

Clear of harbour, Guy set the usual cruising watches. The most junior lieutenant, Hector Boyce, took first turn as officer of the watch, nominally in charge. The navigating officer, Lieutenant Alfred Coplestone-Boughey, laid a course down-Channel, past the Scillies into the Atlantic. Doing as Guy had been ordered meant ploughing outwards some 250 miles and a similar distance back. The rest of the thirty hours required of the engines would be taken up getting back into Plymouth. Boughey showed every sign of knowing his job. He stuck to the plot for most of the day, keeping his log, trying to make sense of cryptic weather messages received on the Marconi set.

Pratt-Barlow—why did they all have such silly names, Guy wondered— was thundering up and down the main deck with the warrant boatswain and a rigging party, making things Bristol fashion where they could and listing everything that remained to be done. Looking down, Guy saw them peering at the strange arrangement the dockyard had come up with for the seaboats. A cutter sat in chocks on either side of the foredeck, a low wooden derrick beside it stretching out over the ship's side. If a boat was needed it was to be swung out and lowered on a wire by one of the mooring winches. The commander came up, jerked his head towards the bow and said, 'It'll get a boat in the water, all right. Never get it back out.'

The watch changed at noon and again at 1600 by which time it was already dark, sea and wind rising, gobbets of wet snow slapping on the wheelhouse glass. In better weather *Centurion's* unfinished state might not have mattered but in the open Atlantic heavy seas surged along the foredeck, sending freezing spray as high as the compass platform. Temporary baffles that had been built to protect the bridge were useless.

Water spurted through cracks in the joints as though a hose were being played on them. Even in the sheltered plot everything was drenched; charts, logs, the navigator's notes reduced to pulp. Everyone was in oilskins but soon the uniforms beneath were soaked. When the earlier watches changed they had been able to change clothes but the steam pipes in the drying rooms, like the radiator in the sea cabin, were iron-cold. They had no more dry kit to shift into.

Nor did Guy. He took a few stiff paces around the wheelhouse. Sized up its sodden, freezing denizens. Tried to detect some sensation in his feet but could not. A sort of periscope coming down through the wheelhouse deckhead caused most trouble. It was meant to allow the steering compass in front of the helmsman to be read from the platform above but it kept filling with watery snow that cascaded down it, flooding the compass binnacle and drenching the man at the wheel. 'Hard to make out the heading, sir,' complained the third helmsman to end his trick at the wheel sodden from the waist down, hands blue from sweeping away the wet flakes.

'What about the conning tower?' asked the officer of the watch, by then the first lieutenant. This was a curiosity from earlier days of sea warfare that designers persisted in carrying over to modern ships, a little pillar box of thick armour plate just big enough to shelter the captain, navigator and a helmsman from enemy fire. In *Centurion* this ludicrous last redoubt stood on the lower part of the superstructure, three levels down from the wheelhouse. Whether it might resist enemy shot and shell, Guy never expected to discover but it was weatherproof. The ship could be steered from there, helm orders shouted down one of the voicepipes that sprouted along the fore bulkhead of the wheelhouse like brass lilies. 'Very good,' said Guy. 'Two helmsmen down there. Make sure everything gets tested.'

The engineer commander came up, a watchcoat over his white overalls, to report that all was going well below. Guy could tell he might actually have preferred it otherwise, his territory invaded by disrespectful landsmen. 'All sitting around drinking tea and reading the *Daily Mirror*,' he grumbled.

'Lucky for them,' said the commander, propelled into the wheelhouse by a blast that swept away what little warming fug the swaddled bodies there had managed to generate. The engineer looked around, suddenly aware of what a different world he had entered. The compass lighting had been short-circuited by slush pouring on to the binnacle; the officer of the watch needed an electric torch to check the ship's head. The navigator was trying to smooth out his charts, which had dried into crinkled *papier-maché* models of the sea floor. The unmanned wheel was still linked to the steering system; its spokes moved one way then the other with ghostly hydraulic sighs as the helmsman in the conning tower kept his course. The chief checked the turbine indicators, one for each shaft, and as soon as he decently could scuttled back to the warmth below.

Despite the miseries suffered by the ship's company, *Centurion* was performing like a thoroughbred, barely rolling as she sliced through the big seas. But Pratt-Barlow had found plenty to worry about. Below decks water was finding its way into scores of places. The ovens in the main galley could not be fired up: no hot food either for the sailors or civilians, although most of the dockyard hands were too seasick to do whatever they had come on board for. He did not have enough seamen to keep the upper deck secure. Some of the boom boats have shifted in their chocks. Topmast stays have parted; the Marconi aerial could be blown away.

If Guy could order some speed taken off everyone would be more comfortable but that would mean aborting the trial. It would have to begin all over again perilously close to the Christmas season for which Guy had firm plans. Also, with the trials completed and an offer of command practically assured he was impatient to move his temporary household back to the house that had turned a boy from the bush into an English county squire. There were horses to be floated up, his pack of hounds, his Rolls Royce.

'That's enough, pilot', he said to Coplestone-Boughey. 'Mr Spinks's spinning tops seem to be doing what's expected of them and there's no need to make us all suffer more. We'll do the rest of the run all the way up the Channel and down again.'

Guy could see the navigator was in two minds over the prospect. The reason they were out in the open seas in the first place was for the ship to have an unobstructed run. Sheltered Channel waters would make for easier going but at the prescribed rate of knots they would be barging along busy shipping lanes in the dark a little faster than was prudent. But the navigator did not want to spend more time out there than anyone else and they would not be hazarding the ship. Without seas breaking over her all the time they would have clear visibility. All the officers—except Guy—had spent half their seagoing lives trolling up and down the Channel; they knew every light and buoy.

'What we want now', Guy told the navigator, 'is a nice wide 180-degree turn so as not to break the crockery—if there's any on board—and a course for the Eddystone Light. Then up to the Isle of Wight, put about and back down to Devonport. We'll be alongside for breakfast. A couple of days for our write-ups and we'll all be off home in good time for Christmas.' In his case a Colonial Christmas, a rare gathering of Gaunts.

Five out of seven anyway, more Gaunts than had been together since Ernest sailed from Melbourne at thirteen. He and Gerry would be there but two brothers would not. Cecil was out in Bangalore, back in the Fourth Hussars as a major. He too had made an advantageous match. Helen, the colonel's daughter he hitched up with, shared his obsession with horses and was well-shod financially. They would soon be retiring to enjoy the comforts the darker parts of the British World offered its fair-skinned defenders. Clive was in Rangoon, laying down the white man's law to unruly Burmese and stringing up those who would not heed. Lancelot was over from Singapore with a wife, another link with the World. The footloose young barrister had evolved into a prosperous legal nabob of the Straits Settlements—Singapore Island and several other territories scattered around. He sat on the board of trustees of the Anglican cathedral and the committee of the Singapore Racing Association and went home to a life of tropical ease in a cool and roomy fretworked mansion with a punka-wallah nodding on the verandah, tiffin at Raffles or the Hotel de l'Europe, tennis, golf, shooting.

Lucy, too, had arrived in England with her daughter, Ellinor. She was now a widow and Warden of Melbourne University's first college for women. Minnie had been powerfully impressed to hear that her sister had responded in the true Gaunt spirit when she had found the place besieged at the ten o'clock bed-time by a crowd of men students who were 'joyful and excited'—meaning drunk—wanting to serenade her charges. Rather than order them away, Lucy invited them in, unlocked the pantry and girls and boys sat down together to a midnight feast. After a rousing chorus of 'For She's a Jolly Good Fellow' the boys, libidos defused, went quietly off to their own dormitories. The acclaim that followed Lucy's deft handling of the event gave Minnie the theme for an article on gender equality. How were young women to develop into sound citizens, she asked in the *Daily Chronicle*,

> if they are taught in their most impressionable years that a man is a dangerous animal, that he cannot be looked upon as a good comrade and a useful friend, but must always be kept at a distance and his sex remembered?

Lucy and Ellinor would be meeting Guy's wife, Margaret, for the first time. The promotion Gaunt's Brigade had won him could not be put to its full use until he had recovered from that fall from the saddle that put him on half-pay for months. In 1905, bones knitted, he was posted to the China Station as executive officer of HMS *Vengeance*, a pre-dreadnought based on Hong Kong to keep an eye on the Japanese, who were about to go to war with Russia. Most of Japan's modern warships had been built in British dockyards and the Admiralty was interested in knowing how they would perform. There was no convenient sailing so he was given a ticket for the Trans Siberian Express. After a series of characteristic episodes involving a horse sleigh, a pretty brunette and the French Minister to Korea he arrived in Peking, where he looked up George 'Chinese' Morrison, the celebrated correspondent of *The Times*, who in an earlier career had been a doctor in Ballarat. In keeping with the Gaunts' gift for making useful connections it was to be expected there should be a family link. Lance had married one of George's sisters, Violet. Soon Clive would marry the other, Evelyn.

Morrison was not hard to find. Every rickshaw boy in the city knew the way to his headquarters in Wangfujing, the street alongside the Legation Quarter. The colonial powers had divided up most of Asia and Africa between them but China was too large and populous for any of them to take on. They bullied the Chinese into granting them 'concessions' as trading posts in different parts of the country, enclaves governed by the foreign government's own law, from which Chinese were excluded except as servants and labourers. The Morrison establishment was more hamlet than house, thirty or so rooms and linked courtyards teeming with guests and servants, animals and spies. Apart from the housemaids, whose duties seemed comprehensive, Guy was pleased to find that there was often a spare European female or two. Morrison's accounts of his adventures attracted many admirers, lady travellers doing the Far East on cruise liners, under-occupied diplomatic wives.

Born in Geelong, Morrison had surfed the colonial countercurrent as enthusiastically as the Gaunts. He made a debut in journalism while still a student, dashing off to New Guinea to investigate blackbirding for the *Sydney Morning Herald* and *The Age*. Even after graduating he continued to write about events in Spain and Morocco where he went to practice medicine. *The Times* signed him on in Peking, just in time for the Boxer uprising in 1900 when the foreign legations were besieged and largely cut off. Or, as *The Times* had it, 'the last heroic remnants of Western civilisation in the doomed city were engulfed beneath the overwhelming flood of Asiatic barbarism'.

Morrison and other distinguished foreigners, The *Daily Mail* reported, had been killed. In Geelong flags were flown at half-mast but weeks later Morrison had the elusory pleasure of reading his own obituary, probably the most fulsome ever carried by *The Times*.

No newspaper anxious to serve the best interests of the country has ever had a more devoted, a more fearless and a more able servant than Morrison. An Australian by birth, he brought to the service of *The Times* and to the furtherance of British interests in the Far East the deep and sustained enthusiasm for the greatness of the Empire which has so conspicuously distinguished our great self-governing colonies. Of the singular ability with which he discharged his responsible duties during a period of constant stress, the daily evidence furnished in these columns by our Peking Correspondent's messages is still too fresh in the memory of our readers to need expatiating upon. It is not too much to say that throughout the last three critical years in China it is to Dr Morrison that the British public has looked from day to day for the earliest and most accurate intelligence concerning events in which the interests of the country have so largely and often, we fear, prejudicially involved. With extraordinary judgement, amounting almost to intuition, in an atmosphere which he used himself to describe as 'saturated with lies' he discriminated with unfailing accuracy between what was true and what was false. With never a penny of 'secret service' money at his command, his own shrewdness and resourcefulness, his untiring industry, his infinite capacity for taking pains enabled him time and again to transmit important information of which the official confirmation used only to limp in with halting steps two or three days later.

Heady stuff. And *The Times* saw no reason to take back a word when its next despatch from the region began by admitting that it was 'in some respects at variance with earlier information received …'. Morrison and the other distinguished Britons were not dead after all, although he had been wounded. The *Mail* story had been filed from Shanghai by a rogue American reporter, Fred Sutterlee, out to make a quick buck.

Vengeance was not able to observe the Japanese victory over the Russian navy at the battle of Tsushima, the only decisive shoot-out, had anyone known it, there was ever to be between the great battlefleets that were being built. Her best seagoing days lay well astern and she spent most of the time in Kowloon Number One dry dock. Guy was sorry not to have seen the devastating spectacle at close hand but Hong Kong was familiar territory and he was pleased to have time to spend with friends old and new. Even to get married.

Margaret Worthington, as she was when they met in Hong Kong, had not gone out as a typical fisherwoman. She was thirty-five, the same age as Guy, a widow of three years with a small son—another Lancelot. She had been married at twenty to Major Philip Jukes Worthington, fifteen years her senior, who had been stationed in the Colony. Guy met her out at Happy Valley where he was wandering about in his silks after going over the jumps; she took a while to recognise him when she saw him in Kowloon a few days later all starched whites and gold braid. She was impressed by both turnouts and by the way everyone seemed to know him. What took Guy's interest about Margaret was her connection with Staffordshire. When he worked out who her family was it dawned on him that she stood to benefit from one of the more intriguing fortunes in Britain. His eye for an opening in a crowded field took him through on the rails at full gallop.

All the Gaunts who visited England paid a duty visit to Leek where cramped stone buildings and cobbled streets gave them a salutary glimpse of what their lives might have been like if William had not left home. Elizabeth's father, Sir Thomas Wardle, had made far more money than any of the silk trade Gaunts by refining an Indian method of printing on silk at just the time that William Morris and other designers created a huge demand for decorative fabrics. And in another of the overlaps that linked the shakers of the World, he was a director of the North Staffordshire Railway which had given William Gaunt his first job. Like her mother, another Elizabeth, Margaret played an important part in building up the Wardle business. Both of them were inspired needlewomen, adept at finding ways to shape the delicate fabrics. In the 1880s Elizabeth had set members of the Leek Embroidery Society stitching away at a copy of the Bayeux Tapestry that, after being exhibited around Britain, was installed in Reading Museum where it can still be seen.

The wedding took place in Hong Kong, where Ernest and Geraldine had married only the year before. The couple went to England as soon as they could, partly so that Guy could be presented to his father-in-law but also because in order to live up to his part of the deal he was going to have to apply himself to his career. The navy was changing. It needed captains whose abilities went beyond subduing savages. Admiral Jackie Fisher who had become First Naval Lord—and, tellingly had the dignitaries' titles changed to Sea Lords—told them how. It was no longer enough 'to possess that peculiar knowledge which only wind and sea, dark nights and mists can give'. The present day officer lived in a vast machine. He must learn its workings. To get a fourth ring on his cuff Guy would have to face up to demanding courses in torpedoes, gunnery and signals. Examinations.

Margaret took her new husband to the weird but sumptuous Wardle house at Manifold Valley in the Staffordshire moorlands. Less a stately home than a monument to Victorian commercial exuberance, Swainsley Hall had been built as a country retreat by a London solicitor. To begin with it had been vaguely Queen Anne in style but Sir Thomas added a wing that wiped away its Anne-ish symmetry. He wanted space to show off the treasures brought back from his trips to India, including a stuffed Bengal tiger that reared over the entry hall.

The rich mix of Eastern exotica, ethereal paintings by Dante Gabriel Rossetti and other pre-Raphaelites he admired, together with draperies in the delicate Arts and Crafts designs that had paid for it all was overwhelming enough but the mightiest folly was a pipe organ in the main saloon powered by water from a tributary of the Manifold. Sir Thomas was just as eclectic a collector of personalities. The visitors' book recorded, among many others, Mark Twain and Colonel Baden-Powell by then in full Boy Scout mode, assuring himself of attention by such calculated eccentricities as going about in short trousers and never sleeping indoors. When he came to stay he brought a little tent to put up on the front lawn. From there he could admire the splendid moorland views old Thomas had preserved by insisting that a new branch line be sunk out of sight in a culvert.

Guy and Margaret were soon back in Hong Kong. He had that fourth gold ring and a respectable command, the cruiser HMS *Andromeda*. She was only ten years old but already dated, although Guy made her look good, especially in contrast to the American men o'war that became regular visitors to the Colony. Taking over the Philippines from Spain made the United States a major player in the western Pacific, more so when Admiral Togo's British-built fleet upped the ante in Tsushima Strait. If the orientals were likely to go on behaving like that the US Navy had some catching up to do. President Theodore Roosevelt had sent his Great White Fleet around the world in a show of muscle but what it had mainly showed was how far America lagged behind in warship development. American ships on the China Station were particularly antiquated and so were their officers. To Guy's grizzled American counterparts a captain of only forty was a painful sight. He was delighted when a senior American naval wife who watched him pull off a neat manoeuvre in the crowded harbour asked, 'Are *you* the captain of that four-stack cruiser? You ought to be in the kindergarten!'

The Admiralty however, thought Guy mature enough—perhaps Australian enough—for a delicate mission. Before Federation in 1901 the colonies had no choice but to accept Britain's assurances that, should danger threaten, their shores would be protected by the Royal Navy. With the Japanese showing off as they had, not everyone was convinced that the Australia Squadron might be up to the job. Australian misgivings went up a notch when the Admiralty, mesmerised by Germany's challenge to its dominance, let it be known that it would not be able to spare any powerful ships for Australian waters. Britain put together an agreement with Japan by which Australia's maritime bodyguard would be...the Japanese navy. Since Japan was now the trespasser that Australia feared most, this decision caused some puzzlement. As the Melbourne *Punch* put it: 'To offer us Japanese protection is very like telling Mary's little lamb—Have no fear, small and tender sheep, you are excellently provided for. We have set the wolf to watch over you!' A desultory argument over whether Australia ought to have a navy of its own shifted into one about the kind of a navy it needed to be and how soon one could be created.

Australia's plans were short on detail. The Admiralty offered the services of a recently retired admiral, Sir Richard Henderson, aged fifty-four, to advise. He arrived in Australia in September 1910 to find Guy waiting to show him around.

HMS *Challenger*, Guy's command for the sensitive mission, was a sea-kindly and smart little colonial cruiser. Normally her accommodation seemed airy and spacious but Henderson had a staff of three and a couple of Australian quasi-admirals insisted on coming along. In steamy northern waters he did his best to make the guests comfortable, giving them dinner on the quarterdeck under the stars: wine from South Africa and prawns the size of cucumbers. Nevertheless, when they got to Port Darwin the admiral and his entourage bolted for the Government Residence.

Challenger's band set up on the lawn to entertain local dignitaries who were anxious to let the visitors know what they thought. Henderson did not need much telling. The vast unpeopled reaches of the west and north around which Guy took him had been a revelation: fleets of Japanese pearlers and fishing boats nibbling away at the outer fringe of the continent, vast unprotected inlets where an army could land and live for months before anyone knew it was there.

Whether Henderson's views were shaped by the territory or by Guy's unrelenting hospitality, the concept he came up with in March 1911 was impossibly grandiose, far more ambitious than anyone in Melbourne or London had been ready for. He proposed a vast fleet: fifty-two ships, fifteen thousand men and nearly twenty bases. Out of all proportion to the country's needs and resources, most of the Henderson Recommendations were quietly shelved and attention returned to a handful of ships being built in British yards. There would be an Australian fleet within a couple of years, a modest and rather mismatched one to begin with, but a fleet nevertheless, an interesting opportunity, Guy thought, for someone ready to start at the top.

Challenger was sent island-hopping all the way across the Pacific to the Americas before being ordered back to Britain. Guy paid a farewell call on the last commander of the Australia Squadron, Admiral Sir George

King-Hall, at Admiralty House. King-Hall was an amiable old buffer who had been hauled off the half-pay list. He was an evangelical Christian with a taste for salacious gossip, of which Sydney provided plenty, and a shifty interest in reports about young women who walked out with sailors and 'frequented chemist's shops'. He had been enthralled by a letter Guy wrote him after *Challenger* visited Pitcairn Island, relating the strange goings-on there, including a man found *in flagrante* with a pig.

This time Guy had something more serious to put to him. For all his foolish ways, King-Hall was in favour of an independent Australian navy—as long as the key decisions governing it were taken in London. He was well-connected at the Admiralty and his advice on who was to be given seagoing command of the new fleet would carry weight. After the chat with Guy he noted in his diary:

> He thought he would have been the person to be Commodore of the Australian Unit. I told him that I did not think so, etc. He being an Australian was too much in with the politicians and people and that an Admiral was required ready to stand up against them, especially in the incipient stages of the RAN and he would have found it very difficult to do this.

Of course an admiral was required. Exactly the career uplift Guy had in mind.

Any disappointment over negative signals from King-Hall was dissipated by his promising reception back in England. Sir Thomas died in 1909. The main heir was his son, a solicitor, but Margaret was left an impressive income and the tenancy of Swainsley. At that time a wife's property was, in effect, her husband's but the house had been put in trust for her son. Nevertheless, it was renamed Gaunts Wood. He became a country squire, keeping a stable of horses and riding to hounds with the local South Staffs hunt if the Beattys were not turning out with the Quorn. Posted to the reserve fleet in far-off Devonport he ransacked the attics for furniture and took along his horses and dogs to harass the Dartmoor foxes. But now there was *Centurion*, her firepower greater than the entire Australian fleet, a gleaming jewel in the world's most powerful navy. At least she would be once Guy had licked her into shape.

The tremor might have been no more than the impact of a large wave, hardly enough to raise a ripple on a glass of whisky, something Guy could readily have done with. But a captain's senses are sharp as a mother with a child asleep in a distant room. He had only just got his seaboots off but he pulled them back over his numb feet and shrugged back into his oilskin. As he reached the sea cabin door one of the bridge lookouts banged on it from the other side. 'Ship in collision, sir.'

It was only a few steps up to the bridge. The officer of the watch, Boyes, turned, face pale, eyes wide in shock. 'Collided with a steamer, sir. She had no overtaking light.'

The enveloping night was still wet and windswept, moonless and dark except for a lighthouse beam to starboard: Anvil Point, on the Dorset coast. Guy glanced at the turbine indicators. All four were showing Full Astern. Good for Boyes. Down in the humming, brightly lit engine room Mr Spinks and his men must have responded instantly to the alarming clang of the telegraphs but stopping a ship this size would take time.

'As soon as the way comes off her', Guy told Boyes, 'ring down Stop Engines. Call away both seaboat crews.' He remembered the makeshift mess on the foredeck. 'Belay that. Call the crews to muster at the boats and wait.'

In the time it might take to smoke a cigarette everything had changed. Out of the black night some cosmic elbow had nudged Guy's life sharply off course, his luck spinning in reverse like the great machinery below the waterline. He could hardly believe it was less that ten minutes since he took a final look around and went to the sea-cabin, saying to Boyes, as he said to each officer of the watch whenever he had left the bridge for a few minutes: 'Give all traffic plenty of room.'

There had been nothing in sight other than the Anvil Point light. A quarter of an hour before they had seen navigation lights over towards the coast, statutory white over white steaming lights, indicating a ship well clear of them headed up-Channel on an opposite course. 'What about those two whites?' 'Lost them, sir.' Or bloody well found them.

The faint shrill of bosun's calls piping 'Collision Stations' drifted up. Throughout the ship men would be winding watertight doors closed, hauling out baulks of wood to reinforce bulkheads, tar and canvas for patches. Striding out on the starboard wing Guy saw a small steamer surging along with *Centurion*, hugging the battleship's side slightly aft of the funnels. He slithered down a ladder on the superstructure to get closer. He wanted to make the skipper of the stricken ship try to keep her alongside. 'I will lower boats!' he shouted. But the steamer peeled away, bow swinging landwards. Guy glimpsed two white lights, one above the other, on her foremast.

A great blast overhead drowned out his voice and every other sound. With *Centurion*'s engines stopped pressure bottled up in the boilers forced open the safety valves, spurting out a geyser of steam. Then, as the ship slowed, the vast plume of funnel smoke trailing astern of her caught up and settled along her length. Guy caught a last glimpse of the smaller ship's stern as she peeled away. Back on the bridge, he said to Boyes, 'You are right. She had no overtaking light.'

'She must have been those two whites we saw before you turned in, sir,' Guy wanted to say that he hadn't damned well turned in, just wanted to get his boots off for a few minutes. Boyes was already on the defensive. And with reason. This could end his career. Guy's, too. The ship had been in Boyes's charge, although the ultimate responsibility would come to rest, like the black cloud of funnel smoke, on the shoulders of the captain whether he was drunk or sober at the time, deep asleep or just having a pee.

Coplestone-Boughey was on the bridge, trying to smooth out the ruined charts to mark the ships' positions. Damage control was the executive officer's responsibility and Pratt-Barlow had gone directly to the forecastle. Within minutes he arrived to report that the upper section of *Centurion*'s bow was twisted out of shape and there was an open gash in the starboard side running back nearly a hundred feet. 'Well above the waterline, fortunately. The carpenter's party is patching it as best they can.'

Wherever blame might eventually settle, the imperatives were, as always at sea: save life and preserve the ship. Guy gave helm and engine orders to get under way again and turn in the direction the steamer disappeared. The civilians on board were working as competently as the overstretched ship's company. The dockyard electricians soon got the huge searchlights that were among the ship's impressive assets working; their beams swept the dark waters. He set *Centurion* steaming in slow circles, lookouts straining their eyes in the glare for wreckage or survivors. Trying to piece events together, Guy asked one of the bridge lookouts, an able seaman named

Pearce, what he had seen. 'Just a big black patch, sir, then bang!'

The makeshift seaboats were ready but there was no point in putting them in the water until something was sighted, particularly since it might be difficult to recover them. A seaman from the working party on the foredeck arrived on the bridge with an object prised from the twisted steel plating: a large metal oil lamp, its glass encrusted with soot but unmistakeably red: the steamer's navigation light from her port—left— side. The wick inside it was still burning weakly. Guy peered at it glumly, biting his lip. 'That's bloody well torn it.'.

The find showed that whatever else might be taken into consideration the steamer had right of way. *Centurion* had evidently struck it from behind with the starboard edge of her huge stem. Under the rules of the road at sea a vessel had an ironbound obligation to keep clear of another she was overtaking. The only possible defence might be that the steamer had not been showing that single white light on her stern that would warn off a ship coming up astern.

The officers ran through the probabilities. Navigation lights on modern vessels were electric but oil lamps like the one that had been catapulted on board by the force of the collision were still common on older ships. Hoisted up the steamer's mast, those two whites might not have stayed firmly in place. Swaying around on their halyard they could have been seen from further aft than they should have been visible and thus suggested the ship was heading towards *Centurion* when the battleship was actually overhauling her. As to the absence of an overtaking light: sometimes oil lamps simply blew out.

But how badly had the little steamer been damaged? And what ship was she? There was no point in trying to reach her with the Marconi. A vessel without electric power was unlikely to have a wireless. Guy was not inclined to send a signal anyway. It could be read by any receiving station afloat or ashore and he thought it best not to advertise the misfortune that had befallen one of His Majesty's finest warships. At dawn there was no wreckage or flotsam. 'I reckon she made straight for land,' he said, hoping that would turn out to be true. 'Let's hope she got there.'

All the deck officers had crowded into the wheelhouse, apart from Number One who was on the foredeck in case the cutters had to be lowered. Guy scanned the drawn faces, shadowed like his own with overnight bristle. 'What do you think, gentlemen? Have we done all we can out here?' The officers would rather have been told than asked. Nevertheless, Guy wanted to draw them in to the decision; tell him he was right. Each of them nodded in turn and he told the pilot to set a course for Devonport and whatever consequences awaited. At the dockyard, *Centurion's* battered bow was the first sign anyone there had seen of what happened. There had been no report of a collision. No one had any idea what ship *Centurion* might have hit. Twenty-four hours went by before a lifeboat containing a body with a broken neck drifted ashore on the Isle of Wight and it became evident that she had sunk the Italian tramp steamer *Punch* with thirty-five other men on board, none of whom was ever seen again.

Back in Devonport everyone seemed understanding. There was a lot of wardroom talk about the negligence of the dockyard in sending an important vessel out so ill-prepared for sea. Most officers of experience could easily see themselves in Guy's place, understand how events had unfolded. But Guy could tell from the way glances flickered around and smiles stiffened at his approach that there were doubts. Where had the captain been when the collision happened? Why was an acceptance trial taking place in mid-Channel?

Within a few days Guy and Lieutenant Boyes were summoned to the Isle of Wight as witnesses at an inquest. The body turned out to be that of *Derna's* boatswain, Anseldo Schiaffino, who apparently dived into the boat and suffered a broken neck. Any inclination Guy might have felt to treat the matter lightly faded when the coroner instructed the jury that if it found there had been negligence by anyone in *Centurion*, a charge of manslaughter would almost certainly follow.

The jurors, however, found both officers blameless and the cloud over Christmas lifted only to return and overshadow the New Year. On 27 December, a naval board of enquiry at Devonport begged to differ with the Wight jurors. It concluded that Lieutenant Boyes appeared to have been at fault and that Captain Gaunt should have made a greater effort to look for survivors 'although there is no evidence to show that any life would have been saved by a longer search'. The report went to the Fourth Sea Lord, who was responsible for the care and maintenance of His Majesty's ships. He could see that irrespective of what any enquiry might say there would be mutterings and rumours. The minute he scribbled on the report noted the inquest finding but added, 'It would probably be more satisfactory to everybody if the point were authoritatively set at rest by the decision of a court martial.' He was William Pakenham, who had been the Royal Navy's observer in the Japanese flagship when the Russian Fleet was decimated. He knew Guy from the China Station and was offering him the chance to clear his name.

A naval court martial of the time was very different from an ordinary trial: no lawyers, no jurors in the usual sense. Verdict and penalty rested in the hands of half a dozen officers of the accused's own rank. Another was appointed prosecutor and one as Judge Advocate, who had to see that the King's Regulations and Admiralty Instructions were adhered to. Thus the man on trial and those trying him were of the same ilk, with an implicit understanding of everything to be said—and what did not need to be said. Proceedings were orchestrated by the president, an officer senior to the rest, in this case another who had been at Tsushima, Rear Admiral John de Mestre Hutchison. There was little ritual, just a solemn moment when the officers facing charges unsheathed the swords they wore with full dress uniform and placed them on a table where they would lie throughout the proceedings. Even today the custom prevails. When an accused officer is called in to hear the court's verdict the first thing he looks for is his sword. Its point turned towards him signifies that he has been found guilty.

Nearly six months had passed since the collision when this court assembled on board the cruiser HMS *Amphitrite* in Devonport. Guy was charged with hazarding his ship and of negligence in that after colliding with *Derna* 'he did not take every step possible to afford aid to that vessel, or to save life'. Boyes was accused of negligence in failing to appreciate the significance of the white lights he had seen.

The prosecutor was the Honourable Horace Hood, a captain of about Guy's age with a long naval pedigree: an old battleship in the dockyard bore the name of an ancestor who had been Nelson's sea-daddy. On his chest gleamed the white enamel cross of the Distinguished Service Order, towards which Guy flicked an occasional surly glance. The Honourable Horace had won it at Illig in the decisive battle against the dervishes whom Ernest had so spectacularly stirred up.

Most of the evidence was on record from the earlier enquiry and the inquest. Only a few witnesses were called, among them the seaman who found *Derna's* red navigation light, whose embarrassment at having to repeat Guy's exact words on seeing it raised a laugh. Lieutenant Coplestone-Boughey produced the charts that had been turned to pulp on the flooded bridge and testified to the difficulties of conning the ship in her unfinished state. No grounds seem apparent on which to challenge Guy's behaviour before the collision so Hood zeroed in on the suggestion made by the initial enquiry that the search for survivors ought to have been longer and more thorough. He pressed his case with rather more zeal than the *Centurion* officers thought necessary but got nowhere.

Another distinctive aspect of court martial proceedings was that the accused himself could cross-examine witnesses, indeed was expected to. Guy was happy to take on the Honorable Horace. Whenever an unfavourable admission had been extracted from a *Centurion* man he coolly stepped in to put the narrative back on course. Only at the end of his statement in defence did he allow his feelings to show. 'I have been at sea almost continuously since 1887', he told the officers sitting in judgement, 'in almost all descriptions of vessels in His Majesty's Fleet and in all parts of the world, and I have never been connected with any accident whatever. I feel keenly this position in which I find myself, through I am certain, no fault of my own, and I therefore ask this honourable Court to fully acquit me of the charges on which I am being tried.'

The court obliged. It took only twenty-five minutes of deliberation for him to be given back his sword. Boyes was found guilty of hazarding the ship by default—rather than negligence—and merely reprimanded. The members of the court would have remembered Jackie Fisher's reminder about the peculiar knowledge that only wind and sea, dark nights and mists could give. They knew what it must have been like on *Centurion's* bridge.

A question never explored was whether it might have been entirely wise in such foul weather to take *Centurion* up and down the world's most congested waterway at high speed. Coplestone-Boughey had to admit under oath that he had not been comfortable with the decision. Guy merely attested that he had been under orders to run the turbines at the rate required and for the prescribed period. By implication, if they had stayed in the raging open waters the condition of the ship might have made it impossible to complete the acceptance trial. The further implication, that it might have had to be repeated a few days later thus preventing him from getting up to Gaunts Wood for Christmas occurred to no one.

Guy was swamped with congratulations, including a cheering note from Beatty. But relieved as he was, a brand new ship had suffered an expensive dent while in his hands—the thirty-six dead Italians were a secondary consideration—and it might be a long time before the Admiralty entrusted him with another. He was agreeably surprised to be given the super-dreadnought *Thunderer* almost immediately; less so to be called off her after only two months and asked—firmly—if he would like to be the naval attaché in Washington.

This was a strange change of course on the Admiralty's part, for which no explanation is evident in either the archives or Guy's own account. Such slots were usually filled by officers treading water between serious appointments. But HMS *Thunderer*, only two years older than *Centurion*, was an important element of the battle fleet. He took her over smoothly and, however briefly, commanded her efficiently. With the navy convinced there would soon be war experienced captains were in short supply; it seems perverse to have stranded one in a career backwater. Continuing embarrassment over the *Derna* death toll seems the most likely reason. English newspapers—and of course Italian ones—had reported the drowning of the *Derna*'s crew in colourful terms, reviving the story every time some piece of flotsam from the lost ship came ashore. Ernest and other sources of interest might have advised that he drop out of sight for a while. It is also possible that someone along the shadowy corridors of Whitehall got around to reading the court-martial transcripts and decided that since Ernest was about to be given his admiral's flag, one brash Colonial in the fleet was enough. Guy could only hope that *Der Tag* would be held off for a while and remember some other attributes Jackie Fisher thought necessary in the modern naval officer.

In distant parts of the globe he has to represent his nation, and is often called on to exhibit considerable diplomatic and social qualities.

Ta-ra-ra....

Guy's first inkling that the situation in Europe had become sensitive was that hostesses begin to seat him apart from Countess Dumba, the flirtatious Russian wife of the Austrian ambassador, who until then had been his favourite dinner table companion. At first he thought their occasional *frottage sous table* must have been noticed. Living with the enemy on neutral ground, he saw, would be delicate beyond diplomacy. He remained on cheery speaking terms with the German attachés right up until the eve of war. After that it was silent, severe nods exchanged through the Willard smoke.

When Britain declared war on 4 August the effects on the far side of the Atlantic were as sudden as they were unforeseen. The great German and British battle fleets stayed in harbour, frozen in a stand-off of mutually assured destruction. The belligerents turned to the same secondary strategy: blockade. Each side reckoned that cutting off imports of food, munitions and the raw materials of war from the other would end hostilities in a few months. The Royal Navy had scores of fast, powerful cruisers able to intercept freighters. Without risking a single dreadnought Britain could prevent cargoes reaching German ports. Germany had only a few such versatile warships with which to threaten the approaches to Britain but the fast freighters and passenger liners of the German merchant fleet could easily be armed as auxiliary warships.

But the war came too suddenly and the Royal Navy moved too swiftly. German merchant vessels were trapped in foreign ports around the world. Those in neutral harbours, often with a British or French cruiser waiting offshore like a cat at a mousehole, were instructed to let themselves be interned. At least they would not be sunk. International law obliged neutral governments to shelter them as long as they were immobilised, their wireless gear removed or sealed.

Around America, some ninety German freighters and passenger ships cluttered the waterfront, plunging port authorities into confusion. In Hoboken, New Jersey, across the Hudson River from Manhattan, half a dozen liners settled into the North German Lloyd and Hamburg-Amerika piers, among them the 54,000-ton *Vaterland* and, embarrassingly, the *Kaiser Wilhelm II*. More than five thousand officers and men are laid up with them. The law also allowed merchant crewmen to be repatriated on neutral ships but many of the Germans were naval reservists and the Allies wanted them kept where they were.

One of the liners, the *Kronprinz Wilhelm*, had already got away from New York by the time Guy realised what was going on. And, as he later discovered, *Kapitän* Boy-Ed had sent off several chartered freighters full of coal for German warships and passenger vessels at sea. He turned first to Bryan. Seeing that the Secretary was not likely to be helpful, he tried next door at Navy. Assistant Secretary Roosevelt immediately saw what needed to be done and promised to alert the New York authorities. He advised Guy to get up there on the next train to monitor the situation.

Drama! Action! The Congressional Limited was due to pull out within minutes. Guy bolted into Pennsylvania Avenue and jumped in front of '… a dashing young fellow … in a big two-seater touring car'.

I held up my hand and as he slowed down to save my life, shouted out: 'My country is at war. I belong to the British Embassy and it is imperative that I catch the Congressional. For Heaven's sake, help me …'. The boy was a first class sport; he pulled me inside, 'stepped on it' and whizzed me down to the depot with three minutes to spare.

'Anything else?' asked the obliging driver. 'I'm neutral in this show and I don't care a damn who kills the Kaiser.' 'Since you offer', said Guy, scribbling down his address, 'would you mind asking my valet to pack some bags and get on the next train with them.'

Wodehouse could not have improved on that.

Roosevelt did his stuff and all the German ships were instructed to empty their bunkers, keeping only enough coal for light and heat. Guy hired a launch and went across to New Jersey to look over the principal suspects. Most of the big liners lay bow to shore, able to leave their berths only by conspicuous manoeuvring and the aid of tugs. But on the outermost pier of the facility the 11,000-ton *Prinzessin Irene*, named for Queen Victoria's haemophiliac grand-daughter who married to the Kaiser's middle son, had her bows pointed towards the open Atlantic. Such a speedy ship, fitted with heavy guns the Germans must have available somewhere, would make a dangerous raider. Guy ached to get on board her but he had been warned at the Port Authority that the State Department would probably consider the vessels as German territory. He needed to be careful. The diplomatic immunity that allowed both him and his country's enemies to move freely around in their host country carried obligations. Anything that might be interpreted as a warlike act could endanger that precious privilege. Also, he saw that the Germans had posted armed guards on the pierheads. On *Irene's* main deck a group of uniformed men were looking out at him. One seemed familiar. *Kapitän* Boy-Ed. Nod. Nod.

When Springy got back to Washington his first challenge was shipping. The pressing question was whether neutral America would permit the sale and export of war materials to any of the various belligerents, all of whom were in the market for something. Wilson was taking a moral rather than a legal stand—and morality was the last factor Britain wanted brought into play. He would have liked to prevent the warmakers from obtaining weapons and munitions but there was no international or American law he could invoke to prevent it. He could and did decree that the federal government would not provide such goods and set lawyers to draft a bill to try to stop private American industry from doing so.

This was of no great immediate concern to Germany. British warships were already diverting neutral ships carrying any but the most anodyne cargoes. But the Allies wanted everything America could produce, short of active participation. To the relatively small number of forward thinkers on all sides it seemed likely that if the war went on for long the United States might eventually be drawn in and none of them thought that desirable. Most Americans would not want it and none of the imperial regimes fighting each other would care to see a democratic Power shouldering its way into Europe. For the moment, though, being cut off from the American market would not be a crippling disadvantage. Britain's mighty navy, France's great army and Russia's endless supply of gunfodder would soon see off the Germans, Austrians and foolish Italians. Asquith's cabinet convinced itself that the war would be over by Christmas.

Lord Kitchener, scourge of the Boers and now Secretary of State for War, did not agree. He foresaw a winter campaign on the Continent for which no real preparation had been made. The recruits who responded to his imperative finger pointing from a thousand posters would be short of everything: boots, clothes, arms and ammunition, food. He was not ready to wait for British factories to catch up with his requirements. The government *must* go shopping in America.

Fortunately for Britain, leaking out of Congress, welling up in the nation's mines, mills and markets, old-fashioned American greed came to the rescue. The shopping lists being sent over from London promised a bonanza the like of which had never been imagined. There seemed to be nothing the Allies did not need. Atavistic, innovative American business persuaded Wilson to backtrack. None of the warring governments would be allowed to buy war goods in the United States but deals between individual traders would be tolerated. What was done with whatever they could buy in America and how they got it home would be up to them. Nimble minds on both sides of the Atlantic went to work on ways to fool the American government about who would really be paying the bills.

Guy took another little sea trip: a steamer down the Potomac River and across to Delaware and the smokestacks of the Du Pont Nemours chemical factory. The Royal Navy planned to ring German harbours with mines and the British products were useless, prone to blow holes in the ship laying them but failing to explode when an enemy vessel ran into one. Du Pont had patented a type of guncotton—slabs of fibre impregnated with nitro-glycerine—that would explode only when it was supposed to. Was there a thousand tons of the stuff available? Sure, captain, much as you want.

One of the legion of Americans who scented opportunity, an archetypical carpetbagger named Alfred Fraser, crossed the Atlantic and turned up at the War Office with samples of a sheepskin coat that would keep soldiers warm on the battlefield. He had no difficulty getting a passage on the *Lusitania* of the Cunard Line. U-boats had begun sinking British freighters but shipping lines reasoned that the speed of the 'towns of painted steel', as J B Priestley called the great mail steamers, keep them safe. Even if a slow and unwieldy submarine could catch up with one, it would never dare risk drowning Americans, who dominated the passenger lists. The loss of the *Titanic* two years earlier had not frightened them off the Atlantic crossing, nor would a war that had nothing to do with America. Confident in their neutrality, they assumed a right that was all but constitutional to go on travelling to and from Europe. They were reassured by an edict the government was able to impose to impede the flow of material it disapproved of: no passenger vessel of any nationality could leave a United States port carrying anything that was 'likely to endanger the health or lives of the passengers or the safety of the vessel'.

Fraser got an order for 100,000 of his sheepskins at £1.8.0 each. With five dollars to £1 Sterling it was a million-dollar sale in a year that one of Henry Ford's all-black Model T runabouts cost $450 and—as Guy had been pleased to find—dinner for two with a bottle of champagne at Rector's Lobster Palace in New York, only $15. The conspirators at the War Office were ready to pay Fraser's price but only if they could be certain of delivery. Laundering British government payments to American merchants and manufacturers turned out to be relatively straightforward. George Booth, a Liverpool banker whose brother Alfred was chairman of the Cunard, was ready to do it for both the Fraser deal and Du Pont. The real challenge was delivery. A few sheepskins might slip through the American rules but not a warehouse-full. And it was hard to see how a mountain of acrid guncotton could be made to look peaceful.

The Du Pont purchase was straightforward: cash on the nail, take it or leave it, but Guy, making discreet enquiries into how goods might be passed off, found that Fraser was charging five times what he was paying the manufacturer in Boston. When Booth arrived Guy suggested that the sheepskin peddler be left to him. He went to their first meeting in uniform but Fraser soon found he was not dealing with some brass-buttoned dummy but a hard-eyed bargainer who had traded pelts with ruthless seal hunters, faced down the pimps and crimps of the Barbary Coast. At the end of the discussion Guy had restructured the contract, giving the War Office the coats for a fraction of the original price. He also enrolled an accomplice of his own. Export records from New York for 1914 and 1915 showed that the petty crook Fraser became 'one of the largest traders in North America, when in fact he was an undischarged bankrupt, living off the combined wits of himself and Captain Gaunt'.

Voska and daughter

A few mornings into the war, the foreign editor of *The Times*, Henry Wickham Steed, came out of his house in Belgravia to go to his office. On the front steps a rumpled figure awaited. Voska apologised for his appearance and explained, 'The Professor sent me.' He was referring to Thomas Masaryk whom Steed knew well. Masaryk was a token member of the Austrian Parliament but his real purpose in life was running a secret organisation dedicated to independence for the Czech nation and adjoining Slovakia. Although Steed was an unpleasant character in some ways—a profound anti-semite, among other failings—he was an effective journalist. As a correspondent covering Central Europe his sympathy with opponents of Austro-Hungarian hegemony had been evident. The Professor had been one of his key sources.

Voska explained that he had made a circumspect visit to Prague, Masaryk's home and political base, covering his movements by taking his sixteen-year-old daughter Villa along. The Czech nationalists believed that if Austria was going to be preoccupied by war the time had come for them to revolt. Masaryk wanted guidance. He needed to know if a breakout bid would have the backing of Russia, the Slav motherland, and if the war was likely to be lengthy. As a gesture of good faith he put together a dossier of economic and military information and asked Voska to take it to London. The data was transcribed on to tissue paper not all of which could be stuffed into the hollowed soles of Voska's heavy boots. Villa took the stays out of the corsets that even a young girl in those days had to wear and replaced them with the rolled-up sheets. The Voskas had to endure five gruelling days in packed trains and a ferry to get to London. They could not have removed either boots or corset even if they had wanted to.

Steed got his visitor cleaned up and took him along to the Foreign Office. There was no question of *The Times* reporting Voska's intrepid feat or the valuable information he delivered. The paper was as much part of the imperial apparatus as any government department and it knew when to keep quiet. Steed did call in the paper's proprietor, Lord Northcliffe, who immediately picked up his telephone. An appointment with Lord Kitchener was arranged for the following day, another with the Russian Ambassador. Kitchener was delighted to air his view that the Allies were in for the long haul. The Russians, suspecting a plot, declined to commit themselves.

Scotland Yard was less impressed by the Voskas. When they returned to their hotel detectives were waiting to question Voska about a sharp knife and the remains of a pair of boots found under his bed. With a conspirator's unerring instinct, Voska had put up at the Three Nuns Hotel in Aldgate High Street, where Jack the Ripper picked out some of his victims. The chambermaids were nervous about *nifs*.

When Voska was ready to leave for America, Steed told him that if anything else interesting came his way *The Times* man in Washington, Arthur Willert, would know how to handle it. Something soon did: a list of German naval reservists from laid-up ships around America who were preparing to sail for home using passports bought from neutral Dutch or Scandinavian seamen. Once again, there was no story in *The Times*; Willert simply handed the list over to the embassy. 'Springy', seeing that it was something about sailors, sent it around to the naval attaché: POG.

Had Guy been a religious man he could not have been blessed with a better response to his prayers for something worthwhile to do than the Voska list. It showed the names of dozens of original passport holders and of the Germans and Austrian reservists who had bought their documents. Guy cabled the list to the Admiralty and the masqueraders were lifted off the neutral ships carrying them, mostly at the first landfall in France. Willert had no way of keeping in touch with Voska so Guy launched discreet enquiries on the attaché circuit that led to someone at the Serbian embassy he knew slightly, a Colonel Gruich. It might help Guy's work, this amiable colleague suggested, if he was able to spend more time in New York. Good apartments were not easy to find but he happened to know of one in a quiet part of the West Side.

The Little People

Guy and Victor Voska were enchanted by one another. After the preliminaries of their West Side meeting they talked for hours, and by the time they parted each had a new perspective on the war. Until then, Guy's had been almost entirely maritime but he came to see that the outcome was as likely to be settled by the landbound mass populations of the European continent as on the high seas. He was fascinated by Voska's explanation of the surly nationalist resentments that underlay the patchwork Empire of Austria-Hungary, astonished to learn that thousands of former subjects of the Dual Monarchy had, like Voska, migrated to the United States: Czech-speakers from Bohemia and Moravia, others from Slovakia and Slovenia.

Many, though, had grown up speaking German as a second language, if not their first. Lumped together as 'Bohunks', they settled easily into the German communities. As proud American citizens they would do nothing to damage the interests of their new homeland but plenty of them, Voska assured Guy, still loathed their former overlords whose double-jointed regime was now aligned with Germany. The atavistic grudge locked in the hearts of these *malí lidé*, the Bohunk 'Little People', could be harnessed to counter the German propaganda campaign being cranked up to discourage Americans from supporting Britain and her Allies in their war. His organisation, the Bohemian National Alliance, was at work across America. rousing his compatriots by fiery messages in its Czech language newspaper, *Hlas Lidu*, the *Voice of the People*.

They certainly seemed to have the means. That list of false passports had been supplied by a Czech working in the mailroom at the Austrian Consulate in New York. The German Ambassador's chauffeur was one of one of Voska's men. He reported in whenever Count Johann Heinrich Bernstorff, a well-corseted career diplomat, came up to visit one or all of the three mistresses he kept in Manhattan. There were other Voska operatives, it seemed, in the Hamburg-Amerika office; even in the wireless station at Sayville, Long Island, that sent and received German diplomatic messages.

Knowing that most of the global submarine cable network was British-owned and thus likely to be unavailable to them when they needed it most, the Germans had developed a powerful short-wave wireless system centred on the Telefunken company's 250 metre-high antenna at Nauen, near Berlin. They had been wise to do so. Within hours of war being declared the Royal Navy had fished up all the cables off the German coast and sawed through them. For good measure the British tapped a connection into another cable belonging to neutral Holland, ensuring that everything the Germans sent that way was monitored. Apart from a cable across the Baltic to Sweden, another neutral which allowed the Germans only limited access, all their communications now depended on Telefunken. The disadvantage, of course, was that anyone could intercept wireless signals; messages could be kept secret only by ingenious cyphering.

All told, Voska controlled about eighty more-or-less full-time operatives and was assured of limitless help from the *malí lidé*.

If we wanted an expert in safe construction, telegraphy, telephone wiring, chemistry, handwriting, police work, a dozen other specialities, I had only to give the word and he bobbed up, sometimes within an hour.

Even Villa Voska got a job as a stenographer with the American Import and Export Company at Number One Broadway. Her boss, Dr Heinrich Albert, was the German commercial attaché and—as soon became embarrassingly clear in an episode that could have been scripted for the Keystone Cops—paymaster for a lot of highly undiplomatic activities.

Guy could see that he had stumbled into an Eldorado of subversion, confusion and deceit. Not only could Voska's organisation be a huge weapon to turn against Britain's enemies it could change his own role in the war from clown to ringmaster. But who could he trust to assay this whopping great Canadian Nugget of espionage? Remembering the chaos and eccentricities of the emerging intelligence community, he felt it would be best to say as little as possible to anyone in London about Voska and the new Gaunt's Brigade of *mitteleuropa* subversives in the offing until he could find someone dependable to report to. Nevertheless, he bought in on the spot. If he knew nothing else about spying he knew there would have to be code names. Voska, rather unoriginally, became Victor, the mailroom source Zeno, after the Greek philosopher who bit off his tongue rather than inform under torture. Guy himself was to be No.1. Far preferable to POG, although he would have to go on strutting his attaché stuff.

1914. Guy was thundering down the Hudson River at the helm of a shiny new speedboat. It was December. Ice was forming on the water and ashore New Yorkers had got out their fur coats. He had picked up word that his nervousness over the German liners was justified. The coal ration delivered to the ships tied up in Hoboken was being pooled in *Prinzessin Alice*, enough of it perhaps to get her out of the harbour and into international waters where she could top up from one of Boy-Ed's freighters. A friendly tug skipper had run him past the Hamburg-Amerika piers but the sight of guards spaced around the main deck made them cautious. He needed to get closer to see if anything suggested that Alice might be preparing a getaway.

Back from the tug trip he poured out his frustration in the bar of the New York Yacht Club on West 44th Street, his favourite among several desirable oases in the city to which Franklin Roosevelt introduced him. The dining room was a facsimile of the after-cabin of a windjammer. Guy in his uniform was a welcome curiosity, especially when he told his tales of what he had been given to eat in the real thing. He got a particularly warm reception from 'Jack' Pierpont Morgan, heir to the firm of J P Morgan which had become Britain's financial agent in the United States, and his partner Edward Stettinius. Between martinis he soon came to see that any intelligence operation he could patch together would be hard put to equal the information exchange operated by the heavy movers who gathered in such places: staid and secretive bankers who for generations had underwritten kingdoms and empires, wars and revolutions.

One of the more sprightly members listening to Guy pour out his longing to find out what was going on with *Prinzessin Alice* offered to take him back to Hoboken in his new motor-launch. Guy was thrilled but warned: 'You might easily get yourself killed... the prospect only seemed to make the bold young chap keener.'

With Guy at the helm and his adventurous benefactor working the controls of the twin engines, they zoomed down the river at dusk. Lights sprinkled the Jersey shore. Against their loom the great darkened hulls of the laid-up liners stood out like a mountain range. There was plenty of river traffic in the dusk: ferries, tugs hauling barges. Guy yelled orders and the owner throttled back. As the boat's wash settled he swung the bow towards the piers. A quick look around showed the blue lights of a police launch at the far end of the Hamburg-Amerika terminal, too far away to hear their engines.

Guy had planned to run right up alongside the *Alice* looking for clues like singled-up mooring lines, the general feel of a ship being readied for sea. If a guard spotted them, he told his companion, he will call for full ahead both engines, put the wheel hard over and scoot back into the river. Engines muttering, the boat, still with plenty of way on, glided under *Alice*'s elegant stern. There was a splintering crash and the floorboards heaved upwards beneath the men's boots. A huge baulk of timber had been moored between the piers, floating awash to block the opening. In minutes the beautiful boat sank under them.

Without lifebelts and hampered by heavy clothes the pair would have drowned had the police launch not reached the end of its beat and turned back. Guy left the talking to the speedboat's owner who was clearly accustomed to dealing with cops. The cops in turn were used to the antics of the irresponsible rich. Back on the Manhattan side a sodden wad of bucks changed hands. Dry dungarees appeared. So did a cab to take them uptown. Guy, mortified, poured out his embarrassment. 'Forget it', said the American. 'Great stunt. Wouldn't have missed it for worlds.'

'But the boat... ?'

'The b'at didn't count a row of beans!'

Everyone in the Yacht Club soon knew what had happened but the great stunt never reached the newspapers. It may, in fact, have spooked the Germans. The *Alice* and all the other ships stayed where they were.

By that time, Guy was reporting—rather cautiously—to the new Director of Naval Intelligence, 'Blinker' Hall. Captain Reginald Hall was several years senior to Guy. The two had never met, although they knew of each other from the fleet: Hall's nickname came from a disconcerting tic that was likened to a signal lamp. Guy's deals in guncotton and sheepskins impressed him but not as much as that reckless run down the Hudson. A few years before the war Blinker had pulled off a similar stunt himself in the German harbour of Kiel, borrowing a launch and faking a breakdown in order to photograph some lock gates. Captain Gaunt looked like a man after his own incautious heart; the kind of chap the navy needed to stay ahead in the rivalry between the nation's intelligence brokers.

Guy imagined that he was doing the manipulating when he began to hint that Washington was no longer the best place for a naval attaché to be. He understood all too well Springy's frustration of not being able to get on with what he was supposed to be there for but he knew that even if the ambassador was, diplomatically speaking, merely spinning his wheels he would not want to be told too much about the shady parallel world his naval attaché was being drawn into. He did take Voska down to Washington and discreetly introduced him. Afterwards, Springy conceded that it might be necessary in such uncertain times to turn to such people but the less anyone in the embassy knew about it the better. With professional blandness he accepted that Guy would need to spend more time in New

York, the shipping hub, and with professional sleight of purpose made a move of his own. Not only did Springy have no one in Washington at cabinet level to talk to, once the Foreign Office found that he had been frozen out his evaluation of events in the United States, much of which remained sharply cogent, went unheeded in London. President Wilson's representative in the real world held court in New York and a personable, semi-detached proxy like Guy might be the key to the diplomatic door which had been shut in the embassy's face. 'I'll give you a letter to Colonel House,' he said to Guy.

'Just one more thing, Sir Cecil ...'

Springy got someone to open the safe and put $2,500 in an envelope.

Counsellor Lansing, whose friends had taken to calling him Duke, had firm advice. 'Must stay at the Biltmore, old man,' he drawled in his renovated diction. 'Only place in town.' Dead right, Guy realised when he saw the place. New York had many wonders but the newly opened Biltmore Hotel was top of the list. The twenty-five story tower built over Grand Central Station, the city's main railway artery, had cost $10 million, an enormous sum. Every suite included a 'Chicago' bathroom, as first seen at the World's Fair in 1893: tub, shower, toilet and hand basin all together in the one space. There were bedside telephones and an operator on duty around the clock. Despite the crowds attracted to the flamboyant public rooms it was a shrine to discretion as well as luxury; perfect for covert meetings. A private elevator went all the way down to the mainline platforms below ground level, where trains from the north east pulled in and an escalator led to the subway that linked most of Manhattan. With a little care anyone could come and go without being spotted. If New York was Guy's kind of town, the Biltmore was his kind of place. He moved into Suite 1405.

Even if Springy had been on speaking terms with the president it would have been little help to Anglo-American relations just then. Wilson was distracted by grief. His wife died on 6 August , two days after Britain had gone to war, and months would pass before anyone could be sure that matters of state had his full attention. More than ever he depended on Edward Mandell House, his 'second self'. House was the seventh son of a seventh son able, for those who believed such things, to cure ills and foretell the future. It was true of him politically, at least. A reporter wrote of his 'ball-bearing personality; he moves swiftly, but with never a squeak or a rasp'.

Although he spent most of his early life in Texas, where he was born—and where he acquired his honorary title—House had gone to school in Bath for a few months, formed an affection for England and made connections that proved useful when he inherited the fortune his father had made running guns in the Civil War and moved into international banking. After some seventh level political witchcraft in Texas he became a power broker in the national Democrat party that had been out of office since 1897, largely because Bryan's weird economic theories alienated big business. Impressed by Governor Wilson's performance in New Jersey, House decided before ever meeting him that he should have the 1913 nomination. Once he had met him—and steered him through the election campaign that put him into office—House found the key to providing the 28th President with guidance he would have rejected from anyone but the artful kingmaker. For all his powerful intellect, lofty principles and Presbyterian reserve, Wilson had a ham actor's hunger for praise that House exploited shamelessly. 'Goodbye dear friend', he wrote to him, on his way to Europe at Wilson's bidding

> may God sustain you in all your noble undertakings...you are the bravest, wisest leader, the gentlest and most gallant gentleman and the truest friend in all the world.

Even so, getting Wilson to listen to advice that was at variance to his ideals was hard going. Only months before Germany invaded Belgium, the pre-emptive opening move of the war, House. presented the president's views to Asquith, French president Raymond Poincaré and Kaiser Wilhelm. Shaken by what he found in Berlin he reported to Wilson that 'The situation is extraordinary'... militarism run stark mad... .There is some day to be an awful cataclysm'. But neither then nor later even House could not persuade Wilson that the warring Europeans were not equally guilty.

The American ambassadors to London and Berlin were Wilson's own appointments but soon he was refusing to accept anything either of them reported. He decided that Walter Hines Page in London had gone native and become hopelessly pro-British. James Gerard in Berlin lost his confidence for the opposite reason: his reports about intransigent German militarism were not what Wilson wanted to hear. House's talk of 'cataclysm' had been bad enough but the colonel could be forgiven anything. Thus, the extraordinary situation developed in which neither Britain nor the United States had any faith in the diplomats representing each nation to the other. With the president withdrawn in mourning and profound reflections on democracy, House was left to arrange the details of how the world should work, from a small apartment on East 53rd Street in Manhattan, where Guy called to present his letter of introduction.

House claimed to have a poor constitution and Guy believed it: he was short, frail and bald as a twelve-inch shell. He rarely left home except to take the Congressional Special down to call on the president or speak at a Democrat fundraiser. Never went Downtown, the source of his wealth and much of his influence: Downtown came to him. The ninth floor apartment in which he lived with his wife, Loulie, was the hub of a network vastly more effective than the State Department. A telephone in the apartment was connected directly to the White House switchboard. Friends and contacts all over the world, many from the great banking empires, others as improbable as the Kaiser's dentist, contributed to it by letters and cables or dropped in to be genially debriefed. They may have been disappointed by what they got in return. House believed in keeping his cards as close to his chest as any Texan poker player. As he was to write:

Most of the trouble in the world, I feel certain, is caused by conveying information and misinformation from one person to another and from one government to another. That which was information to start with, becomes misinformation before it reaches its goal, and an infinite amount of trouble and misunderstanding results.

To reduce the risk, House dealt directly with the men who really mattered. Sir Edward Grey, the British foreign secretary, had given him a private code in which the two could exchange cables without State or the Foreign Office knowing. Just as Springy had hoped, House became the fuse that restored the circuit although it was Guy rather than he who plugged into it.

House took a shine to Guy. He was far less knowledgeable about the British World beyond England than about Europe and he was pleased to have an affable guide. He took in everything Guy had to tell him about the

Pacific, East Asia, Australia. Their discussions, always ball-bearing smooth on one side, jovial and provocative on the other, soon showed Guy that while House, like Wilson, cherished the hope that America would be able to persuade the warring parties to agree a peace plan he did not, as the president did, believe each side of the European conflict was as bad as the other. Nor did House share Wilson's view that big business was essentially evil, especially as the war was making Americans richer by the day.

Guy became a frequent caller at East 53rd Street, making full use of the Biltmore's advantages to be sure the visits he made were unobserved. The apartment was only a few blocks away but, always in plain clothes, he would take the escalator to the subway, jump on the first train to come along, switch to another after a few stops, double back along the route and alight at random and hail a cab. The subway system was as baffling as celestial navigation; he often surfaced in parts of the city he would prefer not to visit.

He was soon completely at home, however, in the no-man's land of conspiracy that stretched from the House apartment down to Wall Street, the trenchworks of the money trade. He had a desk at the British Consulate, at 233 Whitehall, just off Wall, although he was soon spending most of his time at the Cunard Line office on Pier 54 at West 12th Street. Consular Service chaps were a different breed from the diplomats and to Guy's mind more congenial, less concerned with arcane politics they could influence than with the practicalities of life and livelihood: business and trade: births, deaths and marriages, passports and visas, Distressed British Subjects and shipping. From the consulate it was only a few steps away to the New York Stock Exchange, Standard Oil, his friends at J. P. Morgan and the enemy. The German attachés had also decided that New York was the place to be: Boy-Ed at 11 Broadway, Papen at into 60 Wall. A short stroll up Broadway was the German Red Cross Commission, a brazen front for propaganda and espionage run by *Kapitän* Ewald Hecker, like Papen a cavalry officer complete with sabre scars, but a genuine Prussian.

Just as handily, Voska moved into the Hudson Terminal, an architectural marvel on the very tip of Manhattan that like the Biltmore had several entrances, one to the electric trains that shuttled to and from New Jersey in a tunnel under the river. As cover during his visit to Prague, Voska negotiated the American rights to a system of electric advertising signs.

His office had a receptionist out front to deal with customers who want to put up a name in lights but the back rooms housed an ingenious set-up for steaming open dozens of pieces of mail at a time and a massive Photostat machine. This was the pivot of British operations, although the only Briton who knew about it was Guy.

The Austrian consulate was only a few blocks away. Most lunchtimes, Zeno the mailroom man arrived with a selection from the day's incoming post. While he and Voska ate their sandwiches a newspaper artist called Joe Mràzek went to work with the Photostat. Zeno ambled back to the consulate and distributed the originals. Every evening after work Villa Voska brought her father the letters Dr Albert had given her to be processed before she posted them. Voska dropped off Guy's copies on his way home to East 88th Street on the fringe of Manhattan's biggest German quarter.

One of the early tales of mischief that House found sourly amusing concerned the traffic in American passports to help reservists from the interned German ships get home. A New York lawyer, Hans von Wedell, who was also a reserve officer was giving street bums $20 to apply for passports which he collected from them on the post office steps. What tickled House was that every passport was signed by the Secretary of State. It was one of the duties Bryan performed daily for his adoring fans.

For the sketchy reports he had begun to make to Blinker Hall and the even thinner ones to Springy, Guy worked up another set of pseudonyms. He continued to call himself No.1. Grey became Phoebus and House, for no discernable reason, Beverly. Springy was Nimbus, the cloud that obscures a god. President Wilson was Aaron, after the grandiloquent leader of the Israelites, and Ambassador Bernstorff was dubbed The Barber—of Seville; an off-key rendition of the Telefunken station at Sayville. Bernstorff worried Guy. The Americans were too comfortable with him. House in particular was impressed by his readiness to press the American point of view to his masters in Berlin.

Guy had no intention of revealing anything about the shipping arrangements he was working out with the Cunard and other lines but he did his best to get House to understand that a secret war was underway on America's neutral doorstep. He reported on most of what he and Voska discovered about German intrigues, although only rarely how they came by the information. He could see that his reports, worked up into anecdotes and delivered in his jaunty, full-on Colonial style, were more effective than the full frontal advocacy that made Springy virtually *persona non grata*. He had no doubt that whatever he said was conveyed to the president; House and Wilson spoke every day.

House reminded Guy of the resentment Americans were beginning to feel over the Royal Navy's interference with ships carrying their mail and goods. In part it was due to missed opportunities of selling to Germany as well as the Allies. Neutral ships carrying inoffensive goods were being allowed through the blockade but only after long delays in a British port while they were searched. Even if the purchase price of confiscated cargoes was eventually refunded and mail to anywhere but Germany eventually delivered but it was not an ideal way to do business. A loaded slogan was being muttered around: 'Freedom of the Seas', the principle for which Britain and the young United States had gone to war in 1812.

Guy found it irksome that House seemed unconcerned that Britons could no longer take to the high seas with the same insouciance as Americans. By the end of 1914 the Germans were sinking a hundred British merchant ships a month. To begin with both German submarines and surface vessels played by the 'cruiser rules' added to the Hague Convention on warfare in 1907, a last optimistic attempt to limit the effect of war to combatants. Belligerent nations could sink each other's cargo ships provided that crew and passengers were spared. A U-boat would surface and order all on board the intercepted ship to take to the lifeboats. The vessel would then be destroyed by explosive charges or gunfire. This chivalrous ritual did not last long. A feeble British scout cruiser, HMS *Pathfinder*, became the first ship to be destroyed by a torpedo from a submerged submarine, shaking the world's navies to the waterline. Many officers had doubted it could be done. More warships soon went the same way as the Germans tried to batter holes in the British blockade and this sneaky new weapon was soon being used to cripple the supply line Guy had begun to organise.

In October there was a foretaste of the unpleasantness to come when U-16 torpedoed an old French channel ferry, *Admiral Ganteaume*, as she made for Dieppe crowded with two thousand Belgian refugees. In January 1915 *Kapitänleutnant* Otto Dröscher of U-20 sank three British steamers in one day from the depths. His last torpedo missed the hospital ship *Asturias* by the width of one of the big red crosses painted on her side. No

Americans were involved but it was clear that by repudiating the cruiser rules Germany was upping the ante. State sent a mild diplomatic Note to Berlin warning that Germany would be held responsible for any damage to American property and any loss of American lives. Within hours Bernstorff hustled around to assure Bryan that there was no need to worry. It was well understood that neither American ships nor passenger liners out of American ports could carry war goods. German periscopes would give special consideration to both.

House's diary, a key record of the period, was dictated to Fanny Denton, the secretary who had come with him from Texas. There was no safe in the apartment so each evening Fanny took the day's entries, together with other sensitive documents, down to Rothschild's bank hidden in her muff along with a pearl-handled six-shooter that, like a good Texan girl, she was quite ready to use.

El Dorado

Guy, sunburned, dressed like a beachcomber, clothes stinking with sweat, kept his hand on the small automatic pistol in his trouser pocket while listening to a large German tell him of the pleasure that shooting an Englishman would give him. The German was under the impression—at least Guy hoped he was—that he was talking to an American called Grant. What else? They were deep in the jungle of central Colombia, at rest after shooting a stretch of river rapids in a flat-bottomed stern-wheeler. Guy was not grateful to Blinker Hall for getting him into such a position. The gun, he thought, would not stop a decent-sized rabbit and he resolved to improve his personal protection.

At the beginning of December 1914, Guy and Hall were still sounding each other out as best they could at a distance. The war was not going well for the fighting part of the navy. The *Kronprinz Wilhelm*, which had slipped out of New York before anything could be done to stop her, was well into a new career as an armed raider in the Southern Atlantic, sinking British and French merchantmen with guns that—just as Guy had foreseen— were awaiting her somewhere. The formidable Asiatic Squadron of

German cruisers, in whose ships Guy had often been entertained while on the China Station, was heading for home via Cape Horn. Off the Pacific coast of South America it sank most of the British force sent to intercept it and continued on its way, coaled and victualled by the freighters that Boy-Ed had chartered in New York. There were no British warships left in those waters to hunt it down.

Despite the prospects the Voska network had opened up Guy still had hopes of getting back to sea. Every time the *London Gazette* arrived he saw men lower down the Navy List being given commands, even decorated. Career time was slipping away.

Hall, his web centred in Room 40 at the Admiralty, was more alert than landlubbing diplomats to the threat that German raiders posed to Britain's supply lines. In October, his codebreakers, came up with a lead. What did Guy know about Telefunken wireless stations around the Caribbean? Nothing, really. Then he was to go and find out.

Blinker may have meant the Caribbean assignment as some sort of a test but as far as Guy was concerned it was all in a day's work for a spymaster learning on the job. Conventional attaché duties had acquainted him with the many British mates and skippers in the freighter fleet of the United Fruit Company, an outfit with more influence around Central America and the Caribbean than the State Department. The ships were joked about as banana boats but most of them were fast and up-to-date with spacious passenger accommodation. He got his baggage on board one of them well in advance and on sailing day strolled over to India House in Hanover Square, another sumptuous private club to which Roosevelt had introduced him.

He was already used to being followed. The Teutonic Twins, as he had come to think of Boy-Ed and von Papen,, were plainly worried by the interest he was showing in the German liners—although they never did wake up to the Czech connection. He usually had no difficulty shaking off his shadow with a bit of fast footwork on the subway but sometimes he wanted his movements to be reported, especially when he visited police headquarters. Guy and Voska had puzzled over what they should do if—or rather when—they found German operatives up to something criminal. The Czechs were already breaking the law by tampering with mail and should Guy be caught in some warlike act his precious immunity could be endangered. If the Germans did something criminal all Guy could do was tell the local police. There was a Bureau of Investigation at the Justice Department but the only foreigners it had so far dealt with were prostitutes, the 'white slaves' of the nation's whorehouses. Later in the year, largely as a result of Guy's reports to House—and once to the president in person—the Secret Service would be authorised to investigate espionage by foreign diplomats. But for the moment, he had applied his breezy, open-handed ways to winning the friendship of Captain Thomas Tunney of the New York Police Department's Bomb Squad, a redoubtable, bowler-hatted stalker of anarchists, and he hoped that being seen to call on him would un-nerve the opposition.

Guy made a conspicuous entrance up the canopied front steps of India House and never came down them again. After lunch among the usual crowd of bankers and shipowners he slipped out of the delivery bay at the back of the building and took a cab to the Brooklyn piers. A week later he landed in Cartagena, Colombia. As the banana boat entered harbour he had an excellent view of a tall wireless mast sprouting from the jungle surrounding the town.

Guy had never been in this particular South American port before but it was a typical scene, full of cheerful black labourers from around the Caribbean and surly officials who spoke nothing but Spanish. The only Europeans seemed to be Germans belonging to an interned steamer. The British consul confirmed that Telefunken engineers were indeed installing a wireless station but Colombia was a neutral country. What could be done?

It was no secret in Britain that the Kaiser dreamed of turning Brazil into Germany's India, the jewel in his imperial crown. Guy had already begun to wonder why the United States seemed so indifferent to the prospect of a German Raj in South and Central America. While American traders and investors stuck to the port and capital cities; their German counterparts took to the great rivers that were the trade routes of Venezuela, Brazil and Uruguay, planting themselves in strategically located settlements, hacking plantations out of the jungle, building factories, monopolising crops, underwriting banks. There were more Germans in Mexico City than Milwaukee.

He tried a little misinformation. At Walters Hotel—'the only spot in the town where you could get a decent drink'—he tried to pass himself off as an American: George Grant. He made friends with a Trinidadian who ran the iceworks, a gossip supermarket since it made daily deliveries to every substantial household. Were people aware, Guy asked the iceman, of the British warships that were lying offshore? There was no such presence within a thousand miles, but Guy was soon invited to call on 'the slick little man who was the big noise of Cartagena'—the governor of the province, actually. What was this talk of British warships?

Guy hoisted his true colours. 'Three cruisers,' he assured the governor. 'All Monmouth class. They can easily stay beyond the horizon and drop six-inch shells on this very building.' Britain, he warned, would regard messages being sent to German ships from the transmitter that he knew was being installed as an act of war and Colombia would have to take the consequences. The stern glare of a British officer, the long shadow of the Admiralty at his back, did the trick. The Cartagena station stayed off the air—for the moment.

But were there other Telefunkens? Room 40 had heard there might be one in the San Andrés Archipelago, 150 miles offshore and another in— yes!—El Dorado, the real one, the Fort Knox of the ancient Inca nation, now all but engulfed by jungle. Guy set out on an epic trek inland: days on the bony backs of mules, fending off monkeys, mosquitos, crocodiles, snakes, hostile Indians. Also the hostile German who seemed to accept that Mr Grant was American but kept talking about the pleasure that shooting an Englishmen would give him.

There was a month of this before Guy gave up the hunt and went back to Cartagena to take ship for the island of Curaçao, Dutch territory. One of the wandering German supply ships had sailed from there with twice the amount of coal she would need for herself, obviously intending to replenish a raider. After delivering a verbal broadside to the authorities on the obligations of a neutral nation, he hitched a ride on a fishing boat to Colón, the American enclave at the Caribbean end of the newly opened Panama Canal. He tried to bluff his way ashore, unshaven, unkempt and unwilling to explain who he was. The Americans, exasperated, locked him up. He was rescued by the British Consul and together they watched a battered freighter come through the canal. She was flying the red ensign and had an unimpressive three-inch gun on her poop. Her holds were full of coal intended for the British warships that had been sunk by the Asiatic Squadron. The consul had no idea what to do with the ship or its cargo. 'Give her to me,' said Guy.

The rustbucket's skipper accepted the consul's instructions to follow his mysterious passenger's orders to make for San Andrés. They had no charts for the dangerous shoals of the archipelago and could get close inshore but even from ten miles out Guy could see a wireless mast. Satisfied, he agreed on a course for Jamaica. News awaiting them there was galling. Admiral von Spee, overconfident from his victory, had rounded the Horn into the Atlantic heading for home when he made a fatal detour to the Falkland Islands. All but one of the German ships had been sent to the bottom by a pair of British battlecruisers rushed out from Britain. The admiral in command was Sturdee, Guy's old skipper in *Porpoise*. Worse, both battlecruiser captains were well below Guy in the Navy List.

Back in New York it was a slight consolation to hear that his forcefulness had been well received in London. The San Andrés installation had been discouraged by a visit from—fortuitously— an Australian cruiser, HMAS *Melbourne*. Guy's name had been mentioned appreciatively in the House of Commons. He said nothing to anyone about threatening to declare war on Colombia.

His absence from the United States, however, meant he had missed the overture to the German sabotage offensive, a series of events in the farcical style that was to characterise most of Papen's efforts. The German embassy had been reminded by Berlin that Britain would soon be relying heavily on Canada not only for food but fighting men. Everything must be done to discourage this huge chunk of the British Empire from lending a hand to the old country. Papen began to study some maps, particularly those showing the Welland Canal, a 40km waterway that carried ships filled with grain from the Great Lakes ports into the St Lawrence River from which they steamed out into the Atlantic. Blowing up the Welland would be a splendid contribution to the war effort but he had little idea of how to go about it until the appearance of another preposterous figure who joined the attachés in their persistent efforts to shoot off their own shiny toecaps.

Most Germans in America, hyphenated or not, must have been decent and law-abiding, even if they were ready to see a few liberties taken in the cause of thwarting British interests. However, those who volunteered for subversive mischief, seem to have been either indoctrinated ninnies or homicidal maniacs. Captain Horst von der Goltz's real name was Wachendorf. He borrowed his *nom de guerre* from a Prussian field-marshal who spent a quarter of a century training the Turkish soldiers that were to prove so effective in the Gallipoli campaign. He had been a soldier of fortune—as mercenaries of the time liked to think of themselves—in Mexico, on different sides at different times in the three-cornered civil war that was rumbling on. He insisted that it was the call of duty to the Reich that brought him to New York rather than an itchy feeling between the shoulder blades but anyway he was just the kind of useful idiot Papen needed.

There were several locks in the Welland, all unguarded and vulnerable. Papen gave Goltz a fake American passport in the name of Bridgeman Taylor, $300 and three hundred pounds of '60 per cent dynamite'. The explosive was ordered from the ever-obliging Du Pont and delivered to the huge explosives depot at Black Tom Island, a speck of New Jersey across from the Statue of Liberty linked to the mainland by a railway bridge. Goltz hired a speedboat to collect the shipment and zoomed up the Hudson to the German Club on Central Park South. He and another five conspirators, three of them stranded seamen, portioned it out between them and they all shuffled off to Buffalo.

Goltz kept up the momentum befitting a man of action by renting an aeroplane to help him choose his targets. But within a fortnight he was back in New York, the dynamite dumped on the baffled aviator who had flown him on the reconnaissance mission, his accomplices abandoned in Buffalo, penniless. Goltz insisted that the operation had been compromised but would not say how. Papen was embarrassed—afraid, even—of the reaction from above. He had primed Berlin to expect a dramatic outcome. He insisted that Goltz go over to Germany and explain himself. Meanwhile, he would try to put together another attack on Canada.

For that, Papen talked a half-demented army reserve officer, Werner Horn, into trying to blow up the international railway bridge across the St Croix River, a section of the border. The idea was to cut off the rail traffic that also brought grain into the United States to be shipped on to Europe. Papen gave Horn a couple of thousand dollars to buy his own dynamite, some work clothes as a disguise and a train ticket to the town of Vanceboro, last stop on the American side. He also gave him two armbands in the red, black and yellow of the German flag that he was to put on before planting the charge in the middle of the bridge. The insignia would serve, Papen assured the poor sucker, as a symbolic uniform and thus ensure that if caught he would not be shot as a spy.

The blast occurred on 2 February 1915, the very day a banana boat brought Guy back to New York. It did not seriously damage the bridge but most of the windows in Vanceboro were blown out. Trusting in those armbands, Horn did little to hide his movements and was soon arrested. Why, investigators asked, had he risked attracting attention by travelling in a first class carriage dressed in workman's clothes? To say nothing of booking a second sleeping berth for his carpet bag full of explosives? Horn replied frostily that a German officer would never be found in second class, as Papen had obviously understood when he bought the ticket. Horn was sent to prison for eighteen months for breaking the windows and transporting explosives, the only charges American prosecutors could bring since the deed had actually been carried out on the Canadian part of the bridge. The Canadians later extradited him and sentenced him to ten years imprisonment. After the war he was declared insane and sent home to Germany.

Guy found that the Czechs had missed Goltz but knew all along what Papen was up to. Villa overheard gossip in Dr Albert's office about a 'Canadian operation' and they soon picked up Horn, following him when he went to collect the dynamite and do his shopping. But without Guy and his Bomb Squad link Voska feared that warning the police might compromise his people. Since the target seemed to be in Canada and not likely to kill anyone they let Horn do his stuff. Also, as Voska said, 'We thought such an exposure … was worth a little damaged property to the British.' Guy was inclined to agree. It might be more important to publicise German mischief than prevent it. If Americans saw German saboteurs at work more of them might come to sympathise with Britain.

The war was not winning the American audience over. The South resented its principal export, cotton, being classed as contraband and it was eventually taken off the list of prohibited exports, even though it was an important ingredient in much war material. Out on the West Coast newspapers were dominated by hysterical warnings of the Yellow Peril:

Japanese immigrants. Not helpful, since Japan was an ally of Britain. The Midwest seemed especially hostile not—as Guy at first assumed—because of its large German communities but because Britain was stopping those neutral ships with grain sold to Germany. and confiscating the cargo. The purchase price would eventually be refunded and the mail eventually be delivered but The ideal of Freedom of the Seas had become reinforced with robust greed. At least on the East Coast the travelling classes began to take the matter seriously when they found they could no longer make reservations on the boat train from Dieppe to Paris.

The long way home

1912. The other Gaunts were relieved, although not particularly surprised, when Minnie turned up in London at the beginning of October safe, well and with dog. Once she had decided on China as the next *Alone* project she developed a distinctly proprietorial attitude towards the Chinese founded to some degree on old William's role as Protector. It was at full throttle when she set out to collect commissions to pay her way. Werner Laurie wanted a new book, of course; more than one, if possible. *Every Man's Desire* was to be published at the beginning of January 1913 and with that the African lode ran out. The American magazine *Century* contracted for two China pieces at £30 each—which covered a first-class trip out on the Siberian Express—plus 12/6d per photograph published. *Harper's*, too, would welcome travel pieces.

As ever, Minnie exploited every likely contact, starting with Chinese Morrison. She swooped on him when he passed through London in 1910; they knew each other slightly from Ballarat; in fact they were virtually related via Lance Gaunt's marriage to Violet. She wrote him quite a bold note after that meeting: 'I dreamt about you so vividly...'. If she was being flirtatious the effort was wasted. Morrison returned to London in 1912 married to his secretary, Jennie Robin, a New Zealander. A series of political upheavals in China that he helped bring about, resulted in the president of the first Chinese republic, Sun Yat-sen, being replaced by the warlord *di tutti* warlords, Yuan Shih-k'ai. Morrison was the new government's adviser on foreign relations.

Britain's main interest was to see China kept intact, politically and geographically. The displaced Qing regime, dregs of the Manchu Dynasty, had been a useful partner in trade and diplomacy and China had to be retained as a market for the mass produced goods of Birmingham, Coventry and Sheffield. The Chinese had no serious territorial ambitions, unlike the Russians and Japanese but Britain stood to lose more than any other power with a foothold in China if the national territory was to be reduced by annexation.

Morrison's influence was more important than ever and he was in demand around Whitehall and the City. He was also drawn into the activities of Sir Edmund Backhouse, a *louche* young aristocrat he employed as an assistant. Morrison's language skills were limited and he relied heavily on Backhouse's mastery of Mandarin and Manchurian in his dealings with the Chinese bureaucracy. Now Sir Eddy, who had come over at the same time, was attracting attention in his own right by donating thousands of ancient scrolls he had somehow come by to the Bodleian Library in Oxford. He was even being offered the Chair of Chinese Literature at King's College, London. The admiring dons might not have known, as Morrison did, that Backhouse had perfected his linguistic achievements in the gay brothels of Peking, or that he counted among his conquests Queen Victoria's second-from-last prime minister, Lord Rosebery, as well as Oscar Wilde—and Lord Alfred Douglas. He was yet to air the claim that he owed much of his insight into Chinese affairs to having serviced the late Dowager Empress Cixi 'between 150 and 200 times', or to be exposed as a greedy trickster but Morrison was well aware that his little helper was a smouldering bundle of trouble that might explode at any moment.

Minnie persuaded Morrison to endorse her plans and give her a letter of recommendation. Slyly, he delayed delivering the letter until the day before his departure, leaving no time for discussion; and subsequently dodged the series of niggling questions with which she pursued him. Should she send her safari kit ahead by sea? How could she get money on the journey out? How much should she pay porters? What kind of transport should she use in China? How would she find an interpreter for the return trek she had in mind, following the Old Silk Road across China into Mongolia or Tibet?

Nonetheless, Minnie was confident that the Morrisons' invitation to stay with them in Peking held good and when her train left Charing Cross on 31 January 1913 her destination was the house in Wangfujing. She arrived on 22 February, the day the Dowager Empress died. That was Longyu, who Sir Eddy's old Cixi had compelled to adopt the last heir to the Manchu throne and thus become Empress Regent. A year earlier, when the boy, Puyi, was six, Longyu signed the abdication order that ended the line of Manchu succession. When Puyi grew up the Japanese enthroned him as the puppet ruler of Manchuria and he was subsequently introduced to wider fame by the film 'The Last Emperor'.

Minnie was worried that people did not seem to respond to the style of pidgin that had got her through Africa. She said so to one of her fellow passengers on the last leg of the rail journey, a smug young Englishman.

'Oh you'll be all right,' said he. 'The Chinese will like you because you're fat and ol ...'. And then he checked himself seeing, I suppose, the dawning wrath in my eyes. The Chinese admire fat people and they respect the old, but I had not been accustomed to looking upon myself as old yet, though I had certainly seen more years than he had, and as for fat, well, I had fondly hoped my friends looked upon it as a pleasing plumpness.

Minnie was a mere fifty-two. And, as she would have been saddened to discover if she had been able to peek at her host's diary, plumpness was not her only shortcoming in Morrison's eyes. On 25 February he noted:

Mrs Mary Gaunt makes a very poor impression – very fat, almost hunch-backed, imperfect manners and forever discussing herself, and her mind a blank about China.

The Morrisons may have been put out because Minnie turned up two weeks ahead of the letter in which she told them when to expect her and they came home to find her taking a bath. But even if the harsh diary description were true her mind was unlikely to remain blank about anything for long. She was soon out to discover everything she could about her new topic, much of which would not have arrested Morrison's refined gaze but was, she knew, what her readers wanted. But it was true that she was becoming both eccentric and egocentric. Before that family Christmas of 1912 Lucy's daughter Ellinor had found going around London with her something of a trial. Her diary said:

> I will refuse dinner parties with Aunt M in future. Going there she slipped and fell in the mud, frightening the life out of me, but she only giggled in her usual fashion and proceeded all over mud, hat on one side, etc. but as cheerful as ever.

The ornate funeral ceremonies for the empress were a bonanza for the magazine commissions. Minnie slipped into the Forbidden City, to which the deposed royal family had been confined, joined the throng of white-clad mourners and bowed to Longyu's portrait amid the sounds of gongs, bells and trumpets. A choir of Chinese girls from a mission school sang 'Auld Lang Syne' and another local favourite, 'Way Down Upon the Swanee River'. Vivid copy was cabled off to New York and London; pictures bundled into the mail. She was a more accomplished photographer than in her African days and she took hundreds of slides, most of them unexpected images packed with information.

After a couple of weeks with the Morrisons and a few more in the intriguingly cosmopolitan Hotel Wagons-Lits she found a cheap and peaceful place to work, a tumbledown little abandoned temple in the Western Hills, just beyond the city outskirts. From there she made excursions to the Great Wall and the spectacular tombs of the Ming emperors and empresses. Friends she had made in Peking provided her with the company of

> a small black and white k'ang dog, about six inches high, but his importance must by no means be measured by his size. I owe much gratitude to James Buchanan for he is a most cheerful and intelligent companion.

K'ang meant a charcoal-warmed bed; implicitly the place for a pekinese or some similar breed. Why the little mutt was given the name of America's only gay president and by whom Minnie never did say; the prime suspect has to be Sir Eddy.

The first book she produced was *A Woman in China*, about her discoveries from one day to another in endlessly exotic Peking. Open-mouthed, open-eyed and open-minded, she brought to life a turbulent stir-fry of gowned Manchus, feckless Russians, sinister Japanese and British with attitude; bazaars, nights at the Chinese opera, the counterpoint of privileged, sanitised life in the foreign legations and the squalor of the stinking streets. The quaint and shifty ways of the servants she hired also made good copy. Her chef's only idea of portable food was hard-boiled eggs, of which she was compelled to eat dozens on those outings.

She felt none of the empathy she had expected to with the Chinese. The people of the crowded northern capital seemed to have little in common with the hard-working southern rustics who went to Australia to wash for gold. Nor was she particularly sympathetic to Chinese women. By contrast with the stalwart, independent Africans—such as the ones that had lugged her around in her litter—she thought them artificialised and subservient. Binding women's feet in some warped ideal of sex appeal was still widespread despite the outspoken opposition of Western missionaries to baby girls being systematically crippled. She was made sharply aware that it still went on in her expeditions to villages beyond the city walls where in the relative quiet at morning and evening she would always hear children crying.

The little girls cried because the bandages on their feet were being drawn more tightly. Always it is a gnawing pain, and the only relief the little girl can get is by pressing the calf of her leg tightly against the edge of the k'ang. The pressure stops the flow of blood and numbs the feet as long as it is kept up, but it cannot be kept up long, and with the rush of blood comes the increase of pain—a pain that the tightening of the bandages deepens. If the missionaries do but one good work, they do it in prevailing on the women to unbind their feet, in preventing unlucky little girls from going through years of agony.

The campaign against that barbaric practice apart, she was no more impressed by the work of missionaries than she had been in Africa, even though once she began her homeward trek she had to depend heavily on their protection. Since she enjoyed both cigarettes and liquor, she was irritated that the mission workers preached against both; the Chinese had so few pleasures. 'Personally I should encourage smoking, because it is the one thing people who are as far apart as the poles might have in common.'

She thought trying to Christianise the Chinese was futile. What they needed was Western medicine and she was prepared to admire the work of medical missionaries, especially some who had received cruel treatment at the fists of the Boxers but returned to their work.

She sent *A Woman* off to Werner Laurie a year after her arrival and turned to her main project. She was set on becoming a Fellow of the Royal Geographical Society, an honour so far bestowed on only one woman, Isabella Bird, in recognition of adventures in Persia and Turkey. Her lone trek along the Old Silk Road—alone but for the usual entourage—would do the trick. She had a contract from Werner Laurie for the book about the journey to be called *Across Asia*, and a handy advance. The *Daily Chronicle* assured her it would take whatever copy she could send en route.

She tried out one transport option on a visit to the Summer Palace of the Mings about 450 kilometers from Peking, a four-day trip. The Peking Cart was a local version of the wagons that won the West, a buckboard pulled by a mule, a kind of canvas bonnet shading a plank seat.

> The Chinaman sits on the floor and does not seem to mind, but the ordinary Westerner, such as I am, packs his bedding and all the cushions he can raise around him, and then resigns himself to his fate. … as it tosses you from side to side, you yourself are one sore, bruised mass.

A chubby, stubby matron full of hard-boiled eggs being tossed around in an unsprung mule cart was not the image of the intrepid explorer she wished to offer the RGS. Since the cart experience had shown that wheels were not the answer to China's daunting roads, she decided on a mule train, a dozen animals in all, with handlers and other helpers.

Not only had Minnie's romantic notions about China and the Chinese faded, her stay had done little to solve the central problems of life.

> It has been a curious and lonely existence away in the hills, in the little temple embosomed in trees, among a people who speak not a word of my language; but it had its charm. I had my camp-bed set up on the little platform looking out over the place of tombs, with the great Peking plain beyond, and there, while the weather was warm, I had all my meals, and there, warm or cold, I always slept. When the evening shadows fell I was lonely, I was worse than lonely, all that I

had missed in life came crowding before my eyes, all the years seemed empty, wasted, all the future hopeless, and I went to bed and tried to sleep, if only to forget.

Introspection, however, was not a durable quality among the Gaunts. Experienced manipulator of outlets that Minnie was, she made sure everyone knew the risk she was running. If she was killed, she wrote to Werner, think of the publicity it would mean for *A Woman*. She wrote to Morrison of whom she had not seen a great deal in the year gone by. 'I have the money for that trip I consulted you about, and that you don't recommend.'

Since he had originally encouraged her, he felt obliged to provide her with introductions along the way. He knew how insecure the rule of his patron Yuan was in distant parts of the country and advised Minnie to move directly from one mission station to another. All she need do, he said rather wickedly, was tell the missionaries she was his mother 'and they will kill the fatted calf'. There was other advice. 'The Chinese are fiendishly cruel.' She should take a revolver 'and remember to keep the last cartridge for yourself'. Minnie had little confidence in her ability to handle a gun; she would be as likely to give herself the first bullet as the last. 'Then have something made up at the chemist,' he told her, 'and always keep it on your person.' She hired a tall, strong headman to lift her on and off her mount and over obstacles, and an interpreter who turned out to know various local dialects but very little English to tell her what was said in them. Her standard safari kit of beds, tables, chests, tent and bath was supplemented by a load of medical supplies she thought might be more useful on a journey of 1,700 km than a revolver or a suicide pill.

She set out from a Presbyterian mission north west of Peking that she had reached by train. The missionaries had not forgotten the atrocities the Boxers inflicted on their predecessors and the constant danger of bandits. There were worrying rumours that a brigand-king called *P'ai Lang*, the White Wolf, was ravaging territory through which she must pass.

Within two days she was back at the mission. Rocking along side-saddle had triggered an asthma attack. Her helpers fashioned a litter similar to the hammock of West African but slung fore and aft between a pair of mules. Reclining on cushions, and with Buchanan in her lap—looking to the Chinese much like emergency rations—Minnie lurched out along a tributary of the Yellow River. Everywhere they stopped there were reports that White Wolf was about to swoop. The missions were generally too far apart to be reached in a day's trek and the only other shelter for overnight stops, small walled cities, shut their gates well before dark. They pressed on but soon the sight of a headless body on the side of the road spooked her team badly. She persuaded them to take her as far as the banks of the big Yellow but had to accept that she could go no further. 'Well, I had failed!' she wrote. 'The horrid word kept ringing in my ears... I come of a family that does not like to fail.'

But failure like success is relative and, although Minnie needed a couple of months to reorganise, she took a different way home that was no less adventurous. She was happy to be leaving; China had served its purpose. 'Everything that I particularly dislike in life have I met travelling in China.' She meant dirt, noise, confusion, corruption, condescension. It did not seem to occur to her that this was the natural order in most of the exotic lands she had always longed to visit.

She set out from Tientsin by train, north across the top of Korea to Mukden and Harbin in Manchuria. No entourage, just Buchanan. She had not lost the knack of putting herself in the way of hospitality nor, with her direct and open approach, of making friends. The British Consul in Harbin had known Ernest when he was the Commissioner at Weihaiwei. In Vladivostok there were people who remembered Guy from his days patrolling the seal rookeries. 'I sometimes wonder,' she wrote, 'if I could get to such a remote corner of the earth that I should *not* meet someone who knew one of these ubiquitous brothers of mine.' She covered more than three thousand kilometres in Chinese and Japanese trains before reaching the vast Amur River along which she continued westwards in Russian river steamers, luxuriating in food she could identify: chicken and lamb, sturgeon and caviar, freshwater crayfish. It was early summer. The fertile plain through which she chugged could have been the pasture land around Warnambool except that all the men around were dressed in belted Cossack blouses and high boots—and the far bank was China. Her one complaint was that even on the balmiest nights all portholes were closed. Russians dreaded fresh air and draughts.

In Kharbarosvk, still in the Eastern reaches of Russia, she found that

Austria and Serbia were at war but did not grasp what it might mean. She had not realised Serbia was a country. It took a little while longer to discover that Russia had gone to Serbia's aid, Germany had joined Austria and Russia had declared war on them both. She had been wondering why everyone was suddenly so unpleasant to her: they thought she was German. Only when the ship reached Blagoveschensk, did she learn that Britain, too, was at war. Reborn as an *anglisky*, she waved her British passport under the nose of everyone who had been rude to her and was swept off to lunch in an open-air restaurant. She wanted the bandleader to play 'God Save the Queen'. He knew—as she apparently did not—that it was the tune of a German hymn. He would be torn to pieces, he told her. They settled for 'Rule Britannia'.

She reached St Petersburg in the first week of September, nearly two months after leaving China. The city's name was being changed to Petrograd to sound less German. Unable to cross Germany she had to go from one side of Finland to the other by train and the take a ship to Sweden. She was appalled to hear that Sweden had a strict ban on dogs. She bought some sulphonal, a sedative, and when they were about to land gave Buchanan a dose, dumped him in a large basket with clothes on top of him and, haughty with trepidation, wafted through customs. Once the knock-out drops wore off he was to all intents a Swedish dog. They could go on to Norway with no problems and from there, at last, to Newcastle-upon-Tyne. It was the end of September 1914. Down-channel, a U-boat had just sunk three British cruisers. The Germans had occupied Belgium. There was a British army in France. She had no idea where any of her brothers might be. The world was changing fast, even the World. But never mind that. First she must find somewhere to live. Then, she had a book to write.

1915. In January the president sent House back to Europe for another shot at persuading the Allies and the Central Powers to stop fighting. On his pre-war trip around the crowned heads House had paid his own way. This time it was on the White House for Loulie as well and Miss Denton with her trusty six-shooter. Wilson was making the odd partnership public and official. They sailed in the *Lusitania*, which could easily outrun a submarine. However, just to be on the safe side, as they neared British waters where the U-boats hunted, her master hauled down the Union flag and ran up the Stars and Stripes. The Admiralty had advised British merchantmen to disguise themselves by flying a neutral flag. It also reminded skippers that a submarine on the surface was vulnerable and that they should ram any that came near them. This aggressive response led the Germans to abandon the niceties and soon after the House party landed the *Admiralstab der Kaiserlichen Marine*, the German navy high command, declared the seas around Great Britain and Ireland a war zone in which any ship merely suspected of carrying war supplies was liable to be sunk without warning

House was to be away nearly five months and Guy missed him badly, especially when, on 25 March, the SS *Falaba*, an Elder Line steamer bound for West Africa, was sunk by U-28 just south of Land's End and the grim potential of the new German policy became evident. Among the 104 men and women who perished was Mr Leon C Thrasher of Hardwick, Massachusetts, a mining engineer. He was the first American victim of the cold-blooded submarine campaign. The U-boat captain, Baron Georg-Günther von Forstner, had been decent enough to order the passengers into lifeboats but when a British armed trawler hove into sight he loosed off a torpedo before most of them could get off the ship. That single American casualty at last focused the nation's attention on the war at sea. Newspapers around the United States described a massacre.

Wilson seemed stunned. He, too, missed House. Also, as the mourning clouds lifted, he had been distracted from affairs of state by negotiations with a stately widow, Mrs Edith Galt. A spectacular misprint in the *Washington Post* reported that he had spent an evening *entering*, rather than entertaining, her.

It was left to the Secretary of State to deliver a feeble and conciliatory response. Bryan did not want the nation provoked into a hasty reaction. America must roll with the punch. His diplomatic Note merely warned Germany that it must stop doing that kind of thing. Bryan was insistent that neutrality obliged the United States to treat all belligerents equally and in that spirit Britain also got a prim Note about the use of the American flag, even though it had been flown to protect Colonel House.

Duke Lansing, primed by his regular meetings with Guy, was furious with his boss; he argued that sinking the *Falaba* had been an act of war. But Bryan's even-handedness became sterner yet when the British, even with

House in London pressing the American case for Freedom of the Seas in person, declared a total embargo on shipments to Germany. Nothing would now be allowed through the blockade no matter where it came from or what ship was carrying it. This total refutation of the sacred Freedom could have caused mortal damage to Anglo-American relations but, encouraged by getting away with the *Falaba*, the Germans came to the rescue. On 2 April the American steamer *Greenbrier* was sunk by a German mine in the North Sea and on 10 April, the *Harpalyce*, a British ship which had just delivered American humanitarian supplies to Belgium, was torpedoed.

Despite the growing peril on the sea, Margaret decided that if her husband was stuck on the other side of the Atlantic she had better join him. She steamed across from a grim world of war to one of heady, rackety glamour in the SS *Minnehaha*, an elegant little one-class steamer that was a byword of unostentatious luxury among seasoned travellers. Like the larger liners she was thought to be safe because of her speed—and because most of the passengers would be American. On 16 April, the day Margaret came safely ashore in New York, Germany announced that British ships even *suspected* of carrying war supplies would be attacked without warning, implicitly even when there might be neutrals—meaning Americans—on board.

Powering the Press

The case against the United States coming to the help of the Allies in any way, let alone joining in the war, was put forcefully in every issue of *The Fatherland*, a weekly newspaper founded by George Viereck, a widely admired German-American poet who treasured a violet he had picked beside the grave of Oscar Wilde. He was proud to have composed the first love poem ever written in a Zeppelin, a claim never contested. Indeed, he turned some quite saucy lines for those times

> *Before me, in defiance bold,*
> *Now all your little being stands.*
> *Your breasts like two small birds I hold—*
> *I feel their heartbeats with my hands.*

His father, it was said, had been an illegitimate son of Kaiser Wilhelm I. 'My American heart was at war with my German heritage,' he explained when he later found himself on the wrong side.

The Fatherland, enthusiastically advertised in by German businesses and subsidised by Dr Albert, appeared several times a week and put the case for the Central Powers forcefully. The Allied cause was getting mixed treatment from the mainstream American press and Guy and his Bohemian Brigade had no equivalent in which to present their arguments. Voska's *Voice of the People* spoke only in Czech. How to get the maximum impact out of the incriminating material they began to dig up about German activities was a major worry.

Guy made friends with newspapermen in both Washington and New York but in an atmosphere tainted by resentment of high-handed British ways it was hard to gain their sympathy. Like their readers, other than those who defined themselves by a hyphen or were making a buck from it, they were yet to focus on the distant war. He came across the solution in the lobby of the British Embassy, a bulky figure in a huge linen jacket that flapped around him like a loose topsail, trying to bluster his way in to see Springy, 'My name's Rathom, I'm the editor of the *Providence Journal*. Also, I'm an Australian, and I guess it's about time I did a bit for the old country.'

Who John Revelstoke Rathom really was, whether any of that resounding moniker really belonged to him, and where he actually came from remains a mystery to this day despite the efforts of many industrious reporters including, years later, those from his own newspaper. Hardly anything he said about himself survived scrutiny, even the accounts he gave of how he came to know Guy. The version he offered Voska was that they had met during an escapade in Asia that Rathom was covering as a newsman. He claimed to have reported most of the major events of the previous twenty-five years including the Sudan campaign, the Spanish–American War and the Great Fire of Chicago. Since most of this would turn out to be nonsense it seems best to accept Guy's account of coming across him and his unexpected pleasure at meeting—as he believed—a fellow-countryman.

'Melbourne Grammar School,' said Guy

'Scotch College,' said Rathom.

Like all good conmen Rathom had done his homework. The encounter with Guy is unlikely to have been accidental. But Guy was impressed. He had been to Providence, Rhode Island, up the New England coast. The New York Yacht Club was an important presence in the state, organising races out of the millionaires' rookery of Newport. He knew the *Journal* was an influential newspaper. He was even more impressed when Rathom claimed to have worked at the *New York Times* and to be able to place stories in it.

Soon, a highly effective triple act was worked up. The Little People did the legwork— more importantly, the earwork. Voska delivered the raw material to Guy who distilled from it a report for Blinker Hall and notes for his conversations with Duke Lansing and Roosevelt. then passed it on to Rathom to be converted into sensational stories of German perfidy. The *NYT* and a few other helpful papers around the country would be invited to reprint the *Journal's* version. Then as now newspapers were often ready to use stories once they had acquired velocity—though not necessarily veracity—by being published elsewhere. The *NYT* had been aiming for even-handed coverage but Rathom's stories proved such a boost to circulation that it began to jump the gun and run the latest crop of anti-German items under the standing headline '*The Providence Journal* will say today....'. None of the stories was ever connected to the real source. Many were even true, although heftily embellished. Rathom never saw an angle that he could not make acute.

Nevertheless, news still travelled slowly, tapped out in Mr Morse's code along the Western Union wires. Most reports were distributed via Associated Press, a co-operative that would pick up an item from a member paper, process it into a standard format and distribute it to subscribers on ticker tape. In New Jersey that February the Roebling Chain Company in Trenton burned down and the Du Pont Powder mill at Haskell blew up. In March there was another explosion at Du Pont and one at a guncotton factory in Wallington. Eight men died in these incidents and on 1 April another five were killed in a blast at the Equitable plant in Alton, Illinois. But the AP was wary of overexciting its clients and rarely linked events or provided an overview. Few Americans realised that throughout 1915 and well into 1916 their country was beset by blasting and burning; still less that an underground river of hatred ran from the forests of Oregon to the cabbage fields of New Jersey, surging and spitting like a lava flow.

The German equivalent of Guy's threesome was headed by Bernstorff himself. Unlike Springy, who never wanted to hear about what Guy was up to, the ambassador took instructions not just from the German foreign office, the *Auswärtiges Amt*, but directly from *Abteilung* III, the intelligence bureau of the General Staff.

If Bernstorff was entertaining lady friends he put up at the Ritz-Carlton Hotel, 40th Street and Madison Avenue. If he had the countess in tow they usually stayed in a gothic mansion at 993 Fifth Avenue belonging to Edmée Reisinger, a popular German-American widow who was ready to put her money where her hyphen came from. She was the daughter of Frederick Pabst, a Milwaukee brewer who went back to Germany—Prussia, actually—to devote himself to the nationalist cause. His name lingered on in the Pabst Bar and Grill in Columbus Circle, another hangout of German conspirators. Edmée was At Home to every important German passing through New York and ready to reach out beyond them. Meeting Guy on the social round she coyly explained that she could hardly invite him to drinks with his country's enemy but hinted that they might trade information. He let her think that might be possible but there was no need. The governess who saw to Edmée's children's, Mila Jarushkova, gave Voska a regular summary of everything she overheard being discussed in the house.

Berlin was getting worried at the slow progress in preventing American-made war goods, particularly ammunition, from reaching the Allies. Boy-Ed and von Papen, on whom Bernstorff relied to manage the dirty work, took pride in the sabotage going on but laden freighters were arriving in France, Britain and even Russia every day. The Horn episode had not even stopped the trains from Canada. Boy-Ed explained to the *Admiralstab* that his efforts against British ships in American ports were being foiled by counter-measures directed by the British naval attaché. German admirals had been shaken by Guy's success in silencing the Colombia transmitters, which made it difficult to pass orders to German raiders down there. The main station at Nauen could not reach the Caribbean or South America directly so to relay signals onwards they were having to set up stations in Mexico City, Dutch Guiana, Peru and Brazil. The *Admiralstab* needed a Captain Gaunt of its own.

An obvious candidate was *Fregatten-kapitän* Franz Dagobert Johannes Rintelen von Kleist, a thirty-eight-year-old reserve officer in naval intelligence whose peacetime career had been with Deutsche Bank, the national treasure house. He had worked for the bank in New York and had many friends there who would remember his charming ways and excellent English. On the eve of war he pulled off a remarkable stunt that went a long way towards ensuring that Turkey would join in on the German side. Admiral Wilhelm Souchon in the battlecruiser *Goeben* took his ship and the light cruiser *Breslau* the length of the Mediterranean to Istanbul, shaking off British pursuers that were supposed to sink him the moment they legally could. The ships were presented to the Turkish navy, although the crews stayed on board, swapping their caps for the fez.

Germany promised to maintain the ships. Souchon told the *Admiralstab* he needed five million marks in gold immediately. The Deutsche Bank had closed by the time his cable reached Berlin but Rintelen rounded up two governors who had keys to the vault. He organised a special train, persuaded Romania and Bulgaria to clear the tracks for it and within twenty-four hours Souchon had the money. He then took his talents to Denmark where Russian agents were collecting a consignment of French machineguns. He fooled the Russians into loading the crates on to a ship that took them to Germany instead. Home again, he invited the American Legation in Berlin to use the Nauen wireless, thus allowing German experts to crack the State Department code. Rintelen certainly looked like an ideal trickster to go head to head with the wily Captain Gaunt but as things turned out he ended up being shaken down for $300,000 by a Wall Street shark, double-crossed by Boy-Ed and Papen, steered into a trap by Guy and spent several years in a federal penitentiary. Before that, however, he arranged to set fire to at least thirty-two valuable cargoes destined for Britain, a useful contribution to the German war.

Margaret Gaunt was not sure about the Biltmore, especially after she had been shown the ladies' passageway on each floor that let women move around without fear of molestation. New York men, it seemed, were hard gropers as well as hard drinkers. It was not at all like Staffordshire. Although she was glad to be away from England it was strange to be among people whose life was not dominated by the war that had become dismally real at home: daily lists of killed and wounded from Flanders, German warships bombarding the coast, Zeppelin airships dropping bombs near the royal residence at Sandringham. After eight grim months, people winced if they were reminded that it was all supposed to have been over in half that time.

If Gaunts Wood seemed far distant so, in some ways, did her husband. There were a couple of uniforms in the Biltmore closet for the times he needed to make an official impression or dazzle a Manhattan hostess and a dinner jacket for his evenings in the clubs; otherwise Guy Gaunt, of New York City, got himself up like a fashionable lawyer or a gangster. Snappy fedora until Memorial Day—the beginning of summer, he explained to her—then seersucker suit and straw boater until Labor Day in September. Long jackets were in style, all the better to hide the bulge of a .38 Browning automatic in his hip pocket when he went to cover the waterfront. He had indeed upgraded his defences after the South American experience. New York was a much more dangerous place than the Colombia jungle; there were any number of disgruntled Germans around who would be delighted to shoot an Englishman.

Margaret wondered if Washington might be less hectic than this flashing, bustling, clanging high-speed city. Guy had kept his apartment there and also had the one on the West Side that he rented for his first meeting with Voska. She thought she might prefer to live there rather than at the Biltmore, where even the ladies' corridor often seemed as busy as the sidewalk of East 42nd Street outside. She half expected to meet Rathom in it one day. He seemed to be everywhere else, coming down from Providence several times a week, slipping up from the depths of Grand Central like a huge spider from a crevice.

To begin with, Guy rarely met both of his fellow conspirators at the same time and then well away from the Biltmore. Voska had several apartments around the city: one on Sixth Avenue kept especially for meetings with Russians. A Russian Supply Committee stormed into town like a regiment of Cossacks and took over a floor in the Flatiron Building that soon reeked of vodka and herrings, anarchy and graft. They might have been allies but the British and French were wary of them; no one wanted to ask a Russian home.

Papen's diplomatic status had been in question ever since the Horn fiasco.

Now it was Boy-Ed's turn. A German naval reservist, Richard P Stegler, was caught using forged documents to apply for an American passport. The government had became more vigilant once Guy's discreet tips to House filtered down; a clerk had already been sent to prison for three years for selling passports at the inflationary rate of $200. Stegler claimed that Boy-Ed briefed him to go to Britain and spy on shipping movements. Boy-Ed denied everything but Stegler's wife Annette, a good-looking 22-year-old blonde from Atlanta, Georgia, wrote to President Wilson insisting that her husband was telling the truth. A couple of reporters from the *New Yorker Staats-Zeitung*, the city's largest German-language newspaper, tried to bully her into changing her story. At three o'clock in the morning she was lured to a hotel room by a woman and between phone calls to and from their office the reporters offered her money and threatened to smear her reputation. At one stage some of her clothing was removed but, Annette later explained in court, 'I still had my gloves on,' She hit one of her tormentors with a bottle. Indignant, he called a cop and demanded she be arrested. The cop arrested the reporters.

The *Staats* men told Magistrate Arthur Barlow they were merely trying to protect Boy-Ed from false accusations. One, Albert Sander, said: 'No German is safe with such a person as Mrs Stegler free to talk.' Victor Ridder, son of the proprietor of the *Staats*, testified that there might have been a little 'misdirected zeal on the part of two able and loyal members of the staff' but he saw no need for disciplinary action. Mr Barlow disagreed. If there had been more corroborative evidence, he said, it would have given him 'unbounded joy' to send the Ridders' heavies to prison.

This sinister operetta enthralled the regular press. Stegler was given sixty days in jail. Boy-Ed's status spared him a court appearance but any cover he enjoyed was blown away. Not until three years later did it emerge that just before the Stegler incident Bernhard Dernburg, chief of the German Information Service, had made the *Staats* a $30,000 'loan'.

A series of explosions at sea that Rathom was enthusiastically hyping up got Guy particularly worried. Between January and March, three British ships leaving American ports lost most of their cargoes of cotton to mysterious fires caused by time-bombs. Unexploded devices were found in the holds of other vessels arriving in France and Voska was yet to discover who had put them there. Papen, who seemed ready to hand out sticks of dynamite to any bloodthirsty compatriot, was the obvious suspect but he seemed preoccupied with another barmy plot to choke off Canadian support for Britain: an epic, almost Wagnerian, plan to raise a secret German army on American soil.

Papen believed that thousands of former German soldiers now living in the United States would sign up for a massive raid across the border in order to give Canadians such a fright that they would insist on keeping their army at home. These shock troops, armed with 50,000 surplus U S Army rifles, antiquated Krag-Jorgensons he had tracked down in a federal depository, were to be ferried across Lake Ontario by an armada of motor boats. Expressions of interest were coming in from along the fault line of hatred when it was quietly arranged, via the Little People, Guy and Duke for the president to hear that Papen had submitted a tender for the Krags. Assuming they were to be exported to Germany, Wilson vetoed the sale.

Fregatten-kapitän Rintelen landed in New York on 3 April 1915, the day after Margaret. He strode ashore from the thoroughly neutral SS *Kristianiafjord* out of Sweden with a passport that showed him to be M. Emile Gaché and Swiss. It had been issued to an Emily Gasche but forgers in Berlin altered the name to Emile and added the chic accent. In addition he carried a Kaiserpass, a sort of imperial *laisser-passer* that gave him authority over anyone else in the German pecking order in America, not just *Kapitän-zur-See* Boy-Ed, who was two ranks his senior, but Ambassador Bernstorff as well. It did not, however, give him the diplomatic immunity the others enjoyed.

The operational and reputational disasters Papen and Boy-Ed had caused made it all the more important that Rintelen got quickly to work in America and explains why he was provided with such extraordinary powers. But although Rintelen was to do a notable amount of damage to the Allied cause he was as much of a fool as the others, if only to judge by the memoir he produced well after the war. Entitled *The Dark Invader*, it is a marvellous document, written in a style beyond parody and packed with claims beyond belief.

Rintelen, and for that matter the *Admiralstab*, had been taken in by an American named Malvin—more likely Melvin—Rice, although both names were probably invented, who had shown up in Berlin claiming to be a director of Du Pont and ready to sell Germany as much in the way of explosives as she might want. Getting the goods back home would be subject to the usual difficulties with the British blockade. Unlike the Allies, Germany was not short of munitions nor even at that stage of the war, food. But Rintelen and his minders saw a chance of choking off the flow of ammunition and explosives to the enemy. With the help of Mr Rice they would simply order everything that Du Pont and other war suppliers had on offer and store it away, leaving nothing for the Allies to purchase. A start-up fund of $500,000 was sent to Deutsche Bank in New York. 'I'll buy up whatever I can', Rintelen promised as he set out to board the *Kristianiafjord*. 'And what I can't, I'll blow up.'

At the dinner parties Guy attended in uniform, or the snug, smug black-tie gatherings at the Yacht Club and other exclusive watering holes to which a widening circle of influential friends introduced him, he pushed the British cause with breezy charm. He brought up a Rolls Royce Silver Ghost tourer from the embassy that made Packards and Cadillacs look drab. 'Must have a Rolls, old man,' he told Willert of *The Times*. 'Got to show the flag.' The masters of the 1915 universe and the mistresses of their drawing rooms knew nothing of the less visible company he kept but word soon got around that there was more to Guy than glamour. At the Cunard office they had no doubt of it. Under the frequently averted eye of Dudley Field Malone, the Collector of Customs, he built up a flourishing export scam.

Mr Malone was the principal federal officer stationed at the Port Authority and, the joke went, chief of the 'neutrality squad'. He had to enforce the shipping restrictions. To begin with he did, even accusing the British of bending the rules by sending out tugs with stores for the cruisers stationed offshore in case one of the German liners should break out. The federal attorney's office began an investigation in which Guy swore that the warships were entirely victualled from the huge base at Halifax. The only items sent out from New York had been 'bottled beer, mineral water, cards, chess, books, newspapers and, occasionally, 'flowers for the officers' wardrooms'. Nothing was done and Malone was soon less obstructive. He may have been reminded that the list of appointments in which he had been transferred from a dull job in the Treasury was drawn up by Colonel House.

In the case of a dodgy shipment, Guy and his helpers would draw up a provisional cargo manifest, nothing controversial mentioned, for Malone to sign off. Once the ship in question had sailed, a revised manifest would be submitted listing what had actually been put in the holds. If Malone felt he had to raise a token objection, Guy would hang his head, grin disarmingly, and offer to buy the martinis.

Guy used dozens of ships, Cunarders and others, for the questionable cargoes he put together but whenever possible he chose the *Lusitania*, the largest and fastest liner still making regular crossings. Even before she had been completed the Admiralty had taken an interest in her. It paid the Cunard £75,000 a year for having made it easy to convert her into an auxiliary cruiser with a few design tricks: an ammunition magazine, protective plating along the waterline, deck gun mounts. The guns had actually been fitted when war broke out but taken off again and the Cunard told to put her back on the Atlantic run. She had a civilian captain and crew but her orders came from the Admiralty. Homeward bound, the Cunard was informed, her vast cargo space was to be placed entirely at the disposal of the naval authority in New York, Captain Gaunt.

1915. Margaret did not enjoy the restless time-spinning she had to put in until Guy returned from some mysterious errand or an evening at one of his masculine strongholds like the Yacht Club. He had agreed they should stay in the West Side apartment whenever they could, mainly because he worried from time to time that one of Papen's crazies might be heading for the Biltmore with a bomb. The tree-lined neighbourhood was more pleasant than midtown but there was little she could do to while away the crisp spring days. She called on the big Fifth Avenue stores, Lord and Taylor, Bergdorf Goodman, to keep up their interest in Wardle fabrics. She might have done more but back in Leek the looms were idle, the dye-vats empty: men gone to the war, women into munitions factories. She longed to move to Washington where she could be a proper diplomatic hostess. Guy was about to hear another application from her on the matter when the war came vividly home to the United States. On 7 May, the *Lusitania*, seven days out of New York, was torpedoed by a U-boat as she approached the west coast of Ireland. Of the 1198 passengers who died

128 were American. It was the *Titanic* all over again.

No one could say they had not been warned. Ten days before the *Lusitania* was due to leave New York this advertisement appeared in fifty daily newspapers across the United States—and in *The Fatherland*.

NOTICE!

Travellers intending to embark on the Atlantic voyage are reminded that a state of war exists between Germany and her allies and Great Britain and her allies; that the zone of war includes the waters adjacent to the British Isles; that, in accordance with formal notice given by the Imperial German Government, vessels flying the flag of Great Britain, or any of her allies, are liable to destruction in those waters and that travellers sailing in the war zone on the ships of Great Britain or her allies do so at their own risk.

IMPERIAL GERMAN EMBASSY
Washington, D.C. 22 April 1915

The warnings were placed by the poet Viereck. The sharp spike in tension caused by Mr Thresher's death and the damage to American ships had German-Americans worried. At a meeting of the German-American Committee at the Red Cross Commission three weeks earlier many of those present were, like Viereck, torn between a German heart and an American head. If the United States was to enter the war, which was beginning to seem a less distant possibility than it had been a few months earlier, even native-born and naturalised Germans would become the enemy. Their friends, too, as they assumed most speakers of German to be. American headline writers were already lumping Germans and Austro-Hungarians together as 'Teutons' a hostile label.

'Sooner or later,' Viereck predicted, 'some big passenger boat with Americans on board will be sunk by a submarine. Then there will be hell to pay.' At least that is what he later claimed to have said as the justification for urging that Americans be given clear warning of the danger they could face on the high seas. Something should be done, he told the meeting, before the next important transatlantic departure—which happened to be the *Lusitania*.

Viereck assumed the advertisements would appear in the name of the committee but Papen told him to attribute it to the embassy. Many of the papers to which it was wired it, together with Western Union money orders from Dr Albert to pay for the space, declined to publish it. Viereck, knowing where to find a sympathetic ear in the government went down to Washington to see Secretary Bryan.

The moment seemed timely. On 28 April an American oil tanker, SS *Cushing*, had been bombed by a German plane as she neared the French coast. But what really convinced Bryan to endorse the *Lusitania* warning were cargo manifests of her earlier departures that Viereck produced, showing that she regularly carried munitions. These were public documents, routinely published in the shipping pages, but they came as a revelation to the secretary of state. The Remington Arms Company, as keen as any to profit from the vast market created by the war, had found a way to ship rifle and machine-gun cartridges under rules meant to apply to birdshot and hunting ammunition sent around to California. The only requirement was that the crates be labelled 'Non-explosive in bulk'. Guy had taken full advantage of this dodge and the Germans were livid. At that very moment, Viereck told Bryan, millions of rounds of military ammunition were waiting at Pier 54 to be loaded on board the *Lusitania*. They didn't know the half of it. The holds were being jammed full of questionable gear.

Guy never accounted for the preparations he made for the *Lusitania*'s last voyage. In his piecemeal autobiography he seemed hurt by the suggestion that he could have been in any way responsible for the huge explosion that sank her so quickly. Preposterously, he claimed that he knew she would not be carrying anything dangerous because the passengers on that trip included Lord Rhonda, a Welsh coal magnate prominent among the British munitions carpetbaggers who had begun crossing the Atlantic in shoals.

This insouciance does not sit well with an account given a few months later by one of Voska's sources in the Austro-Hungarian embassy, Dr Karl Ritter von Rettegh, a chemist who claimed to have spoken to Guy in Washington a few days before the *Lusitania* 's departure. In a sworn statement that Lansing sealed in his files, Ritter said Guy had been particularly interested in the possible effect of seawater on the chemical pyroxylin, a component of the gun cotton the British were now buying in large quantities. Contact with salt water, Ritter told him, would cause an explosion. Whether that was true or not, in the following days Guy filed a report to the Admiralty about another subject Ritter said they discussed, U-boat fuel, and Du Pont billed J P Morgan for six hundred tons of pyroxylin delivered to Pier 54.

Under the sporting ammunition dodge, the *Lusitania* sailed with 4,200 cases of Remington-made .303 cartridges, the British rifle and machine-gun standard—a thousand rounds to a box—as well as explosives by the ton. Other items in her hold were less likely to have been covered by the 'non-explosive in bulk' rule: 1,250 cases of three-inch shrapnel shells and eighteen cases of fuses. Lethal as these sound, both fuses and shells held only small charges, too weak to cause a major explosion. That was also true of other items that nevertheless ought not have been there. Bales of 'furs' put on board by the helpful Alfred Fraser were probably Guy's guncotton; containers labelled butter and cheese the pyroxyline.

Not until 1982 were divers able to assess the wreck and not until 2012 did the Foreign Office disclose that at the time it had warned they could face 'danger to life and limb'. Documents released under the Thirty Year Rule made it plain that the government had always known there was much on board that a liner should not have been carrying. Noel Marshall, head of the North America department wrote:

Successive British governments have always maintained that there was no munitions on board the *Lusitania* (and that the Germans were therefore in the wrong to claim to the contrary as an excuse for sinking the ship). The facts are that there is a large amount of ammunition in the wreck, some of which is highly dangerous.

He worried that others in Whitehall were still not telling everything they knew.

The Foreign Office and the Ministry of Defence agreed to stick to the line that there had been no munitions aboard and that it had 'always been public knowledge that the *Lusitania*'s cargo included some 5,000 cases of small arms ammunition'.

Marshall was left 'with the uneasy feeling that this subject may yet—literally—blow up on us'.

It did not, though. The pioneering divers came to no harm; nor have any of those who followed them. No exploration has found anything to suggest an explosion in the holds. All evidence indicates that the torpedo hit caused a shattering boiler explosion which opened up the sideplates and took old *Lucy* to the bottom in just eighteen startling minutes.

Bryan's approval persuaded the reluctant newspapers to run the German warning but it did not appear in most of them until the eve of the *Lusitania* 's departure. Passengers going on board the next morning were filmed, photographed and peppered with questions by reporters waving front pages that had turned the advertisements into news. Telegrams arrived for some of the first class passengers advising them not to sail. The Western Union operator handed the messages to the New York manager of Cunard, Charles Sumner, who decided not to deliver them. One was addressed to Guy's friend, the railroad magnate Alfred Vanderbilt who was setting out on the impeccably neutral mission of replenishing the bloodstock in his stables and acquiring some new foxhounds. The message he never got to read was:

> Have it on definite authority that the Lusitania is to be torpedoed. You had better cancel passage immediately.

Like the others, that telegram had been sent by Rathom's office boy from the Western Union counter next door to the *Journal*. Vanderbilt died like a gentleman, giving his lifebelt to a lady even though he could not swim. His widow offered $1,000 for his body when the going rate among Irish fishermen for a recovered corpse was $2 but there was never a taker.

The nation was, of course, shocked and appalled. 'Dastardly is the word on millions of American lips,' roared *The Sun*. The *Tribune* delivered specific instructions to Secretary Bryan. 'The Department of State must go to the Imperial German government in Berlin and demand that the Germans shall no longer make war like savages drunk with blood.'

Only days before, Bernstorff had assured Bryan yet again that despite the escalating threats to enemy vessels Germany would sink passenger liners only if they tried to escape or resist being boarded or searched. He took advantage of his audience to ask that the president persuade the British to ease the blockade and allow neutral ships to get to German ports. Wilson might even have been willing to try but on the day the *Lusitania* sailed another American tanker, the SS *Gulflight*, was torpedoed without warning off the Scilly Isles. She made port but two crewmen drowned and the captain died of a heart attack.

Germany pre-empted American protests with the accusation that the *Lusitania* had been armed and was therefore a ship of war and a legitimate target. The British had no one to blame but themselves, went the defensive explanation. Sad though it might be that so many of Americans had died

> The Imperial Government must point out that on her last trip the Lusitania, as on earlier occasions, had Canadian troops and munitions on board, including no less than 5,400 [*sic*] cases of ammunition, destined for the destruction of brave German soldiers. The German government believes that it acts justifiably when it seeks to protect the lives of its soldiers by destroying ammunition destined for the enemy.

The Germans were confident they could get away with it. Kaiser Wilhelm's imperious view was that Wilson was in thrall to the foolishness of democratic government. The German-American vote that helped the Democrats win in 1912 was a guarantee that the United States would keep out of the war. The solid majority Wilson enjoyed had already been alienated by the Vera Cruz fiasco and would need to be won back before the 1916 election. America could protest as much as it wished but democracy meant that its Congress must decide on whether America went to war. An American president did not lead, he followed.

Bernstorff told Bryan he had affidavits from upright German-American citizens attesting that they had seen that the *Lusitania* was armed with heavy guns. Gustav Stahl of Hoboken claimed to have touched one.

> They were covered with leather but the barrel was distinctly to be seen. I unfastened the buckles to ascertain the calibre... .

When this was reported, Americans began to ask if the British might have brought the disaster on themselves; more importantly to the innocent neutrals on board. Collector Malone assured a siege mob of reporters that the *Lusitania* had been inspected before departure. 'No guns were found, mounted or unmounted. No merchant ship would be allowed to arm in this port and leave the harbour.' That might have been true but it seemed beside the point. While the non-explosive munitions may have been on board legally other items in the holds breached federal law. But the Germans had known nothing about the really questionable items of cargo. They merely tacked an assumption on to their accusations about guns on board and the derisory claim about Canadian soldiers. Certainly the true culprit, *Kapitän-Leutnant* Walter Schweiger of U-20, had no information that could justify his actions. He had form for sinking ships without warning and could not resist the opportunity. The devastating effect of his single torpedo surprised him but he did not know what ship he had fired at, only that it was a large passenger liner. He did not go home to a hero's welcome. Germany had not wanted to antagonise the United States further and even by Germany's own undertaking the *Lucy* as a passenger vessel, should not have been sunk without warning.

Although the Stahl affidavits got plenty of headlines in America, it soon became clear that the main German defence simply would not play. The Secret Service and the NYPD got straight on the case and Stahl confessed that he had been paid $2000 for his 'testimony' by Paul Koenig, the Hamburg-Amerika security chief who was Boy-Ed's main man on the docks. The claim about Canadian soldiers rested on military papers found on the first body recovered, that of Robert Matthews, an Englishman who had indeed held a commission in a Canadian militia unit. However, he was not on his way to Britain to fight for king and country: he was running away with a lady named Annie, for whom he had deserted his wife in distant Saskatchewan.

Even with the nation shocked and outraged, survivors' stories splashed across American newspapers and played out with melodramatic captions in movie houses, the British feared that Wilson would not be ready to make a decisive response to Germany. He seemed preoccupied with the shambles of his Mexican intervention. Venustiano Carranza, whom he had endorsed as Huerta's replacement, was struggling to get the country under control. If his makeshift regime could not establish order, Wilson warned, the United States might step in to show it how. Once again it was left to Bryant to remonstrate with Germany.

A few days after the sinking Guy went to Washington for one of his regular meetings with Lansing. He was anxious to discover what advice the president might have received from House, who was still in London. House would have taken the loss of the *Lusitania* personally: he had expected to come home in her. At the Shoreham Hotel, Guy found that Lansing had invited the Secretary for War, Lindley Garrison, and Wilson's private secretary, Joseph Tumulty, to join them at lunch. In the absence of House these three top-table Democrats were Wilson's regular sources of information and advice. They were in a mood to celebrate, having just that morning persuaded the president to go beyond the meandering and anodyne objections Bryan had made in the Note he drafted and give Berlin a warning to in his own words. Unusually, Wilson listened. He went to his new Hammond 12—he had worn out the first machine—and drafted a second Note scorning German attempts to justify the sinking. He was not repudiating the views he shared with Bryan. The founders of the nation had been right in wanting to keep it free of involvement with grasping and decadent European empires. But he was beginning to see that the day would come when America's modern navy might have to be sent further afield than Mexico and the army turn its hand to something more than ethnic cleansing out in Indian country. The Note was Wilson in a new mood of defiance: eloquent, righteous, uncompromising. Americans, he told Kaiser Wilhelm, had an inalienable right to go wherever they wanted on the high seas in whatever vessel they chose and in safety.

Whatever be the other facts regarding the Lusitania, the principal fact is that a great steamer, primarily and chiefly a conveyance for passengers, and carrying more than a thousand souls who had no part or lot in the conduct of the war, was torpedoed and sunk without so much as a challenge or a warning, and that men, women, and children were sent to their death in circumstances unparalleled in modern warfare.

Any more actions affecting American citizens, Wilson wrote, would be regarded as 'deliberately unfriendly'. In diplomatic terms that represented an ultimatum. The Kaiser thought he had never received a greater insult.

Realising he had fallen among hawkish plotters who were ready to keep up pressure on the president even if it led to war, Guy slipped into his most guileful mode. He confided that as the *Lusitania* was passing down Long Island Sound three German stowaways had been discovered. The captain stopped the ship and signalled the Cunard office. Guy ordered that the men be taken on to Britain locked in the brig, where presumably they drowned. They had been caught, Guy told his enthralled companions, with 'a device'. He left the implication hanging, deciding not to explain that the device was nothing but a camera that had been sent ashore together with its photographic plates, none of which had been exposed.

With his audience's attention ensured, he adroitly let slip that cables deciphered in London had shown that Germany intended to scorn American protests and continue the unrestricted U-boat campaign. They would understand that he could not reveal his sources but he had it on unimpeachable authority that if America entered the war the German embassy had plans to unleash armed insurrection in the streets of New York and Chicago.

The first of these mischievous confidences was sly surmise, the second pure inflammatory invention but they worked all too well. Garrison, who was the most senior member of cabinet, took Guy's stories straight to the president and within hours Wilson issued an executive order widening the powers of the Secret Service, effectively the only national investigative agency. He instructed its head, William Flynn, to monitor the activities of the German ambassador and all his associates—an unprecedented departure from diplomatic practice—and specifically authorised him to tap their telephone wires. Gratifying as it was to know he had prodded the president into action, this was not really what Guy wanted. The more trouble unruly Teutons caused in America the more it helped his cause.

Although they must have realised time was running out on them the sheer cluelessness and ineptitude of the German trio and their leg men beggars belief. The bid to establish that the *Lusitania* carried guns had been spectacularly counter-productive. Stahl, whose account did much to destroy Bernstorff's credibility, was convicted of perjury and given eighteen months in prison, recorded in stacked headlines. Papen's arrogance bordered on *folie de grandeur*. It is not surprising that a few years hence he would conspire with Adolf Hitler to undermine the Weimar Republic, Germany's postwar democratic government, and become a founding member of the Nazi Party. He insisted that his office suite on the 25th floor of 60 Wall was extra-territorial, an outpost of the German embassy, and that activities there were immune from American intervention. Even if that had been so it would not have insulated Papen from suspicion, justified or not, that he with the help of Albert was bankrolling the amateur saboteurs who began to pop up like U-boats all around the United States.

In the case of Erich Muenter, the star turn among these enthusiasts up to then, he did not. Muenter, a deranged professor of German at Cornell University, was entirely self-supporting and self-motivated. He had dropped out of sight a few years earlier after killing his wife with arsenic but began writing to newspapers demanding an end to American support for Britain. He complained that payment for war goods was being laundered by J P Morgan & Co., which was hardly news. His first practical contribution to the war effort was to come up to New York from New Orleans, where he had been skulking, and smuggle a bomb on board the *Minnehaha* as she prepared for her return to Britain after delivering Margaret. The ship had already sailed with it nestling in her fore hold. The timer Muenter devised, which depended on acid eating through cork at a calculated rate, worked as scheduled. The bomb exploded on 10 June but the cargo of cordite for artillery shells that Guy had arranged to put on board was in the after hold. The ship made port before the burning cargo could sink her.

On 5 July 1915, the day Colonel House got back from Europe, Muenter turned up in Washington to make a protest in person. Unchallenged in those peaceful days he wandered into the Capitol building after hours, carrying a large package that he set down behind the telephone exchange in the anteroom of the Senate chamber. Later in the evening the powerful explosion it produced blew out the door of Vice President Thomas Marshall's office, brought down all the chandeliers and ruined much of the decor.

With the satisfying blast still ringing in his ears, Muenter hopped on board the Congressional Limited and the following morning showed up at Jack Morgan's mansion in Glen Cove, Long Island where, as it happened, Springy was being entertained. He and Morgan had been discussing the loans Britain was negotiating to pay for the war, which seemed to be growing zeros by the day. Muenter had planned to take Morgan's wife and two children hostage until Jack promised to stop helping the Allies. But when he shouldered his way into the house with a revolver in each hand, both Jack and Mrs Morgan went for him. Muenter got off two shots before the butler crowned him with the fire tongs and sat on him until the police arrived. Springy was deeply impressed by this display of American defiance. 'I see that the thing to do is to close at once with the assassin,' he reflected afterwards, 'and not let him put his hands out.' Morgan was hit twice below the navel, but not seriously. Muenter had aimed low, perhaps to put invisible writing out of the question.

Now the Secret Service was officially in the game, Big Bill Flynn felt able to call in a few favours. Guy was asked for all the information he had on the German plotters. The *Lusitania* advertisements had marked Viereck out as a more dangerous influence than he really was and he became a prime target. Big Bill set Agent William Houghton to follow him on a visit to the Hamburg-Amerika offices. Houghton was joined by Agent Frank Burke and when Viereck and another man emerged the feds stayed on their tail over to the El station on Rector Street. The agents did not know who the second man was but from one of the profiles Guy provided—six-foot tall, heavy build, blond hair, stubble moustache, sabre cuts on the right cheek—he looked like Villa Voska's boss, Heinrich Albert.

Former boss, actually. After six months in the commercial attaché 's office Villa had been outed by *The Fatherland* as a daughter of the enemy. Viereck had no idea of the scope of Voska's subversive activities but the Bohemian Alliance was stirring up anti-German feeling in public and he wanted to hurt it however he could. Albert was on the return half of his daily commute. Every morning he took the Sixth Avenue El from 50th Street, the stop nearest the Ritz-Carlton Hotel at 40th Street and Madison Avenue, where he lived, to Rector and went home the same way each evening. He always carried a large briefcase. At the 33rd Street stop heading uptown Viereck shook Albert's hand and got off. Agent Houghton followed him. Burke stayed on board in the seat behind Albert, who had wedged the satchel between himself and the side of the carriage. As the train clattered on Albert dozed, not waking at 50th Street until a warning clang signalled that the train was about to move off. He sprang up and jumped out of the rear door of the car. A woman passenger who saw he had left the briefcase behind called out but Agent Burke scooped it up like a football and shot out the door at the front. Albert came back on board, saw fingers pointing and ran downstairs to the street where he spotted Burke with the trophy under his arm. Burke swung on to a moving streetcar. He was being harassed by a nutcase, he told the conductor, pointing to Albert racing along behind them, waving and yelling. The conductor called to the motorman to skip the next stop.

Albert went immediately to the German Club to tell Boy-Ed and Papen about his loss. While the conspirators huddled together, sabre scars glinting in the occasional flare of match to cigar, their conversation was pieced together by *malí lidé* waiters, giving Guy and Voska much to chortle about even before they knew the full story. Oblivious to the surveillance enveloping them, the Germans decided the snatch must been the work of a common street thief. On 27 July the New York *Evening Telegram* carried an advertisement.

> Lost on Saturday. On 3:30 Harlem Elevated Train, at 50th St. Station, Brown Leather Bag, Containing Documents. Deliver to G.H. Hoffman, 5 E. 47th St. $20 Reward.

The contents of the briefcase staggered all who beheld them, especially Treasury Secretary William McAdoo, who was responsible for the Secret Service. Papers and chequebooks documented a nationwide campaign of espionage, sabotage, and propaganda. Activities under way or in the planning included organising strikes in armaments factories, secretly taking over newspaper companies and financing propaganda films. Apart from a project to buy out the Wright Brothers in order to acquire their aircraft patents there was little that Guy's shadowy triumvirate did not already know something about but here was hard evidence that would change many American minds about the Teutons' true intentions. McAdoo remembered thinking, 'I'm morally convinced that the Allies were doing the same thing but we had no documentary proof.' Worth every martini Guy had bought him. The documents were photographed and returned to the briefcase which was delivered to the address in the advertisement. A secret serviceman posing as a police officer explained that it had been recovered from ... a common street thief.

When McAdoo, who was one of the cabinet hawks—despite being the president's son-in-law—showed him the Albert papers, Guy presumed to advise on what might be done with them. He had made a friend of Frank Irving Cobb, the chief editorial writer on the New York *World*. In the early months of the war Cobb had filed stories from the German side for the *Saturday Evening Post*, powerful, even-handed pieces that won him a unique tribute. A composer, Guy Earl Holmes, was inspired to write 'The

War Correspondent's March' and dedicate it to him. No score, alas, seems to have survived. The *World* splashed the choicest finds in the Albert papers over several pages, irrefutable evidence of what the Germans had been up to. Cobb saw that Guy, too, received due recognition. The Wyandanch Club in Suffolk County, Long Island, where they went to ride and shoot ducks, made an addition to the breakfast menu: 'Fried Ham Captain Gaunt', heavy on Worcestershire sauce and cream.

Wilson was still digesting the gloomy reports House delivered when he returned—in the American liner *St Paul*, escorted by a pair of Royal Navy destroyers. Crowned heads had been happy to receive him—he went to Germany via Holland—but the Kaiser showed no interest in the hint Ryan had squeezed into the first *Lusitania* Note of a peace settlement brokered by America. Ambassador Gerard assured him that

> It is the German hope to keep the *Lusitania* matter 'jollied along' until the American people get excited about baseball or a new scandal and forget. Meanwhile, the hate of America grows daily.

Although it had been no more than tactical guesswork, Guy's prediction that the Germans, heartened by the *realpolitik* of Wilson's situation, would tough it out proved correct. The war was going well for them. They were holding the French and the British on the Western Front and the Russians on the Eastern Front; Turkey, their strategic ally in the Middle East, was paying for *Goeben* and *Breslau* by spiking the Allied attempt on the Dardanelles at Gallipoli.

House had been more warmly received in London than Berlin but left in no doubt that Britain intended to see Germany completely defeated. Asquith and Grey listened courteously when he spoke of the deep resentment about British interference with American ships and cargoes but gave no sign that anything was likely to change. Nor did he find a visit to Buckingham Palace for a chat with Guy's old shipmate Herring any more helpful. At least, after the haul from Albert's briefcase, the president was ready to admit that at least some of what House had passed on to him from Guy must be true. The country, he grumbled, was 'honeycombed with German intrigue and infested with German spies'.

Young Roosevelt, who loved a conspiracy as much as he loved a cocktail, took to carrying a revolver when he went to meet Guy at the Biltmore, letting his jacket swing open to offer a glimpse of it. Guy was trying to get him to do something about the Telefunken transmitter at Sayville. He argued that the station was relaying messages to German raiders, an abuse of its neutral site. His real interest was that since only brief messages could be passed on the Dutch or Swedish cables which Room 40 was reading anyway, Sayville was the link by which German activists reported to Berlin and received their instructions. But he plotted their chats around the interests of the navy, reminding Roosevelt that while the first generation of U-boats were small and their range limited, bigger ones would soon be built. Germany would want bases around the Caribbean—America's Mediterranean—from which to attack ships going to or from the Panama Canal. Such operations could be directed by the Telefunken chain.

Roosevelt was interested but even more intrigued by how Guy got to know these things. The conversations tended to veer towards espionage and counter-espionage, swirling like a slow-moving typhoon around unmentionable British activities at its centre. Guy would not even hint at his ever more fertile sources but he brought up the question of why the United States had so few. Why, despite the latitude the president had decreed, were the Bureau of Investigation and the Secret Service, so limited in what they could do?

The question interested Roosevelt. He was in charge of the Office of Naval Intelligence, an outfit meant to gather low-key intelligence on foreign navies but mainly used to watch out for devilry on the lower deck: socialists, saboteurs and skivvy-lifters. It was still working on the sinking of the *Maine*. Guy suggested that the United States should create a dedicated organisation that would be able to operate anywhere in the world. Roosevelt did what he could while Assistant Secretary to expand the ONI and in World War Two, when he was president, he used it as the foundation of the Office of Strategic Services which later morphed into the Central Intelligence Agency. There was more to those martini moments than gin, vermouth and an olive.

The main difficulty in persuading Roosevelt to act on Sayville was lack of evidence. The coded wireless messages were ephemeral, existing only for the brief time it took for the operators at Nauen to note them down. Without time to translate them and work on the ciphers who could say what they contained? As so often before, Voska came up with the answer. An early radio ham with links to the *malí lidé*, Charles Apgar, devised a way of recording the transmissions on Thomas Edison's wax cylinders, something the Germans had not thought possible until Big Bill Flynn played the result back to them. In early July the transmitter was taken over by the United States Navy. The Germans could continue sending messages, Roosevelt told them, but only in English and they would be tapped out by navy operators. Rathom boasted to his readers that the illicit German transmissions had been detected by the *Journal's* very own wireless station.

Bryan had resigned as Secretary of State rather than let Wilson's *Lusitania* Note go out over his name. It was an honourable gesture and Wilson would have kept him as the chief pacifist in cabinet had not Bryan's self-righteousness tripped him up. In a private chat he assured the Austrian ambassador that America would not be going war no matter what Germany did. Dumba could not wait to report this misplaced confidence to Vienna nor Vienna to pass it on to Berlin; the stern warning Wilson had handed out was undermined.

Apart from his bewilderment at finding that Wilson still nursed a faint hope that the antagonists could be brought to see reason, House was appalled to find the severe and reserved president once again dominated by personal emotion. Marriage to Mrs Galt was in the summer air. It was only ten months since the first Mrs Wilson died and House dreaded the effect an early conclusion to his mourning might have on voters in a year's time. More immediately, he was concerned that the romance was demanding too much of Wilson's attention at a critical moment.

Lansing became secretary of state and Guy went to work on him with only slight variations of the hints and warnings about the Panama Canal that he had tried on Roosevelt. As it happened, the Caribbean was at the top of the pile on Duke's desk. The island of Hispaniola, one half of it the Spanish-speaking Dominican Republic, the other French-speaking Haiti, was shaping up as a fresh challenge to Wilson's determination to teach such places to elect good men to govern them. In Haiti, a mob murdered the president, Vilbrun Guillaume Sam, and dragged his body through the streets. Wilson ordered three thousand United States Marines to take the country over until its people were made to see what was best for them. Just before Bryan quit he received a delegation of New York bankers worried about loans they had made to Haiti. 'Think of it,' the former secretary had said wonderingly. 'Niggers speaking French!'

Guy could not see how to turn events in Haiti to his purpose but there were other possibilities. Denmark, a small country so far untouched by the European war, owned some strategic specks of territory in the Virgin Islands. Nearby Puerto Rico, which Spain had ceded to the United States along with the Philippines, was now the nation's most important regional base. How would the navy feel, he asked, about finding itself next door to a U-boat nest? America had tried a couple of times to buy the islands but the deals fell through because it might have meant giving citizenship to niggers speaking Danish. But if they were to start speaking German? Lansing dusted off the files.

Backstage meddling led to farce as often as drama. House told Guy that Aaron—as Number One and Beverley sometimes remembered they should refer to the president—was impressed by the information being passed on to him and would like to meet its source. Guy was thrilled. 'No doubt a trifle curious concerning the people who were turning the country into a diplomatic battlefield,' he said. Man-to-man, he might be able to put the British case to the president in a manner less resistible than Springy had ever been able to do. The meeting would have to be secret. It would not do for it to be known that Wilson was willing to receive the British naval attaché while his superior, the ambassador, was being kept at arm's length.

Guy, in plain clothes, of course, was to go the White House at ten o'clock in the evening. For fear that German informers—or worse, reporters—might spot him, he must not use the main entrance on Pennsylvania Avenue. He should present himself at a side entrance to the garden and go to the back door. The Secret Service man at the gate nodded him past but word of his visit had obviously not been passed along. The black butler who answered the door refused to believe the president was expecting him. Even that he was a British diplomat. 'No, suh,' Guy recorded being firmly told. 'Youse can't see the president. Ah know nuthin about you.'

House was hugely amused by the embarrassing setback and another appointment was made. The audience took place in a 'plainly furnished, parlour-like room'. Aaron was not known for setting people at ease and it was apparent that he expected Guy to do most of the talking. Close up, Wilson was a disconcerting presence. His head was disproportionately large and he seemed to have more than the usual number of teeth. He greeted Guy by saying, 'House thinks a great deal of you, your sources of information and opinions.'

He asked me to sit down on an old-fashioned sofa, while seating himself on the head of it. From his great height and this position of advantage—just about as satisfactory as sitting in a low arm-chair while your vis-a-vis is walking about a room—he looked down on me with a quizzical expression, doubtless saying to himself: 'Here's another of them trying to swing me around.'

That was true enough, but deciding that the president must have heard enough about Teutonic perfidy, Guy decided on an oblique approach. He argued that joining in the war would help weld together the many different strands in the United States population that did not seem to be all that united: the various hyphenates as well as the different races. Wilson confined his response to 'nodding comprehendingly' from time to time but Guy was pleased to hear from House that he had 'put his points well'. He probably put them as well as anyone could have hoped to at that stage. 'Explain the naval and military situation to him you could not; apparently it mattered not one iota to him which side was winning.'

1915. August 19. Forty passengers and crew drown when the British passenger liner RMS *Arabic* was torpedoed. Two were American. Wilson accepted the possibility that the German U-boat commander believed the ship had been trying to ram his vessel. Nevertheless, he descended from his nirvana of non-commitment and thumped out another Note, which Berlin finally took as meaning that the United States might, after all, be provoked into declaring war. The Germans came up with the Arabic Pledge, a promise that merchant vessels would be given thirty minutes warning of being sunk; time for those on board to take to the boats.

Invader in the Dark

Using the name Frederick Hansen, Rintelen set up a couple of phoney businesses at 57 William Street, the Bridgeport Projectile Company and the Transatlantic Trust Company. Both were used to buy large amounts of explosives from Du Pont and other suppliers which did indeed mean there were occasionally shortages of stock when British buyers came along. In another persona he opened an office at 55 Liberty Street just around the corner, where he invited representatives from the waterfront unions to consider his propositions for delaying or refusing to load cargoes for the Allies. If they were fined or fired he would pay them double whatever it cost them. Less a Dark Invader than a dim one. Rintelen did not know that the president of the main waterfront union, the American Federation of Labor, Sam Gompers, born in the East End of London, was one of Guy's key waterfront contacts. Nor that David Lamar, the financial consultant he had trusted to manage his half-million dollars, was known to rewrite men in every Manhattan newsroom as The Wolf of Wall Street (snappy labels are rarely new).

He also got in touch with Victoriano Huerta who, finally dislodged from the presidency of Mexico, had been allowed into the United States, the better to be kept under surveillance. Huerta would surely be interested in being helped back to power? In exchange he might be persuaded to start a fresh war with the United States. It did not seem to occur to Rintelen that Big Bill's boys would be keeping tabs on Huerta. They duly logged this Senõr Frederick Hansen, whom they did not know, and a friend he had made whom they did: Andrew Meloy, a crooked gun dealer. But if Rintelen was no great judge of character where foreigners were concerned he knew exactly who to blame when, only four months after arriving in the United States, he ended up in London, sitting across from a Royal Navy captain who winked at him all the time.

...one incapable man, one self-complacent dilettante, one petty spirit, one pitiful intriguer, with no nobler drive than jealousy, was able to bring it all to nought with his sheer genius for evil. Papen!

Nevertheless, before he was spectacularly double-crossed by Papen, Rintelen got one thing explosively right. He recognised the potential of a brutally simple gadget being touted around by another homicidal improviser, Dr Walter Scheele. Scheele had the distinction of being Germany's only pre-war intelligence agent in the United States. He was a proper spy, a graduate science student recruited as a lieutenant in the reserves. He even had an appropriate pedigree: his grandfather had discovered chlorine, which the Germans would soon use as a battlefield poison; his father died while experimenting with hydrogen cyanide, known to a later German generation as the Zyklon B the extermination camp gas. No wonder the army gave him a scholarship to study chemistry in America and $1500 a month to report on militarily useful developments.

Scheele coasted along in America for twenty-one years before he justified the army's investment by developing a 'cigar bomb', an improved model of the device that Muenter had put on board the *Minnehaha*. A lead cylinder the thickness of a decent havana was divided internally by a copper disc. One chamber was filled with sulphuric acid the other with picric acid and the ends sealed. The acids ate through the copper at a rate determined by its thickness and the mingling liquids produced an impressive explosion. Rintelen thought he could use as many of these useful items as Scheele could produce. By-passing Boy-Ed, who had nominal authority over the ships tied up in Hoboken, he set up an assembly line in the *Freiderich der Grosse*'s engine room. Bridgeport Projectile provided the lead piping, Scheele the acids, and the ship's engineers the workmanship. Bombs were produced in batches of fifty, timed to ignite in fifteen days. Altogether, thirty-six ships had their cargoes destroyed at sea, although none sank and, miraculously, no one was killed.

The success of the Scheele bombs and the other plots Rintelen was nursing along showed Boy-Ed and, in particular, Papen how it should be done. The attachés did not enjoy the lesson and Papen set out to restore the balance by blowing the Invader's cover. A letter arrived at the Deutsche Bank addressed to *Herr Kapitän-leutnant Rintelen*. No one recognised the name until the clerk in charge of Frederick Hansen's affairs, who knew who his client really was, spotted it. He passed it to Rintelen who was shocked to see his true identity used, to say nothing of giving him a lesser rank.

Was the letter a trap? I decided to open it nevertheless, and saw it was from the Military Attaché of the Embassy. I was furious at his thoughtlessness and stupidity in addressing me in such a fashion. Or was it done deliberately?

Was the Kaiser German?

A Little Person at the bank also saw the letter but could not say to whom it had eventually have been given. Nevertheless, Voska reported this indication that a hitherto unheard of German naval officer was drifting around. Might he be the source of the annoying firebombs? Notes were soon being compared on both sides of the Atlantic. A *Kapitän-leutnant* Franz von Rintelen appeared in the German navy list but Room 40 could see no reason for him to be in New York. There was nothing to connect him to the known German conspirators there or—most frustratingly—show what he might look like.

Guy did not believe he and Rintelen ever actually laid eyes on each other. It certainly seems unlikely from Rintelen's account of a conversation he claimed they had once had and his description of Guy as 'tall, broad-shouldered, with a clever face expressive of great energy'. Guy, built to the stocky Gaunt specifications, was greatly amused when he read that years later. 'My best friend could not call me tall, nor markedly broad-shouldered', he wrote. 'As for my face, well ....'

There is, nevertheless, much in Rintelen's highly imaginative memoirs to suggest that he modelled himself on Guy. He seems to have missed being able to wear his uniform, especially when he read society page accounts of the popular British naval attaché Captain Gaunt being entertained around town in a glitter of gold braid. He wrote of having convinced a pair of ladies with whom he conducted a fleeting flirtation that he was, in fact, a Royal Navy officer and a friend of Guy. He claimed that, like Guy, he frequented the New York Yacht Club, indeed that he had been breakfasting there on 6 July 1915 when Boy-Ed phoned and summoned him to a nearby street corner where he handed him a typed slip.

To the Naval Attaché at the Embassy. Captain Rintelen is to be informed unobtrusively that he is under instructions to return to Germany.

The message, received by the roundabout cable link, had actually been sent to the German embassy by Room 40. The Swedish circuit had long since been tapped into and the standard *Admiralstab* code cracked. Hall decided, almost as a joke, to try to shake the Dark Invader out of the shadows. It shook him right enough.

I wondered whether I had fallen a victim to intrigues, such as were usually concerned only with the 'big guns'. Or was I being recalled to Berlin in order to report how matters stood in America?

Although he was aware of the attachés' hostility towards him it does not seem to have crossed Rintelen's mind that the summons might have been related to Papen's simulated blunder with the letter to the bank; even that it might have been fabricated by Boy-Ed.

I could not understand why this telegram had been sent to me, and only knew that if I obeyed it immediately, I should leave things in frightful confusion. Our strikes had begun to boom again, and we were still placing bombs on the transports. All would now come to an end.

However, he was confident that M. Gaché would be able to bluff his way through the British blockade.

The word 'fear' did not and does not exist in my vocabulary; so danger or no danger, the journey had to be made, for I was a German officer and had to obey orders. I fetched out my Swiss passport and managed to obtain a letter of recommendation to Count Ignatieff, the Russian Military Attaché in Paris ... a celebrated connoisseur of claret, and I soon had documents printed to provide evidence that I was a Swiss citizen travelling to France from the United States to purchase wines.

Since Guy had no idea what Rintelen looked like he could not tell whether Blinker's improbable ploy had succeeded. Voska narrowed the search down to a group of Germans who had arranged a rendezvous at the Manhattan Hotel with Huerta and his cronies, the most open approach they had so far made to one of the players in the amorphous Mexican revolution.

The meeting with Huerta gave Guy and Voska the chance to field test the latest advance in eavesdropping, an ingenious new device patented as the Detectograph. A microphone only slightly smaller than a soup plate was mounted behind a drape and its cable led through a hole bored in the window frame to a receiver in the adjoining room. An Edison device recorded what it picked up but since the cylinders were only good for twenty minutes an operator had also to use headphones and take notes. The Detectograph established that the Germans were offering Huerta the huge stock of explosives Rintelen had bought up in return for Mexican help. Huerta seemed more interested in cash. Ritalen had none left, alas. What had not been paid over to Du Pont had been gobbled up by the Wolf of Wall Street.

The Secret Service gave Guy a mugshot of Meloy the gun dealer and a vague description of one Frederick Hansen with whom he had been seen. Voska, waiting outside the hotel, picked out Meloy as he left with the German delegation, one of whom might or might not be Hansen, who might or might not be Rintelen. He and Guy were still trying to puzzle out which might be who when Rintelen, with his usual off-kilter judgement, decided to take Meloy back to Germany with him on the Dutch liner SS *Noordam*. Once he found that Hansen had been transformed into Gaché, Guy was sure he must be Rintelen. When the *Noordam* steamed up the English Channel on 13 August, bound for neutral *Tribune*, a British cruiser directed her into the Thames Estuary. Special Branch detectives took the two suspects up to London. Rintelen might have got away with his Gaché impersonation if Meloy had not been carrying documents about guns for Mexico awaiting him in Germany. Blinker Hall had no doubt that his improbable plot had landed the right man and, fearful of being shot as a spy, Rintelen confessed.

Guy and Voska, though, felt no need to slacken the pace of their own efforts. They turned their attention to nailing the Teuton attachés with such efficiency that they also did for Count Dumba. Until he passed on Bryan's unfortunate slip, the Austrian ambassador had passed for a mere amiable bumbler. He caused a mild upheaval early in the war by suggesting that Austrians who had come to America to avoid conscription might be forgiven if they returned home and joined the army. It had to be pointed out to him that to recruit American citizens— as many such immigrants now were—for a foreign army was against the law. But the Bryan affair enhanced his standing at home and he was keen to tell Vienna about the fresh effort he planned on behalf of the emperor: a campaign to discourage Austro-Hungarian nationals past or present from taking jobs in factories that supplied the Allies. There were

> thousands of working men in the big steel industries, natives of Bohemia, Moravia, Carniola, Galicia, Dalmatia, Croatia, Slavonia, and other peoples of the races from Austria-Hungary, who are uneducated

and who do not understand that they are engaged in a work against their own country.

Unless, of course, the working men were working for Voska.

Austrian communication problems were even worse than Germany's and Dumba was delighted when a full-blown American eccentric sympathetic to the Central Powers offered to carry mail for both embassies on a trip he was about to make to Europe. This was James Archibald, who had popped up in Mexico and other small wars as a correspondent for various fringe publications. His by-line was J P J Archibald, which led colleagues to call him 'Alphabet' Archibald. For several months he had been presenting himself to lecture audiences across the Midwest as 'Captain', the honorary status bestowed on war correspondents by the Austrian army, to which he had briefly been accredited in 1914.

Zeno, Voska's priceless presence in the mailroom, duly reported the plan and a little person in the German embassy told of documents were being microfilmed, a level of technology beyond the Austrians. Archibald booked a cabin on another of those handy Dutch liners, the *Rotterdam*, for 21 August. As the date neared he had several meetings with Teuton diplomats at the Ritz-Carlton, where the waiters picked up puzzling jokes about 'caning' and 'the hidden sword'. Guy worked out that the German microfilm was to be concealed in a swordstick.

Second only to Zeno as an asset in the Austrian consulate were two young women stenographers. One had helped steer an earlier shipment of documents into British hands. The consul-general, Alexander von Nuber, caught her in the act of marking the packing case to help British searchers pick it out among the cargo. Quickly she converted the doodle into a heart, explaining shyly that she had been daydreaming. Nuber, a gallant Viennese, took her red crayon and completed the outline of entwined hearts pierced by Cupid's arrow. The British naval officer who boarded the ship in Falmouth had no difficulty finding the right box. Now the stenographer typing up the list of documents being sent with Captain Alphabet slipped in an extra carbon copy.

Sealed and wrapped in stout waterproof canvas, the precious bundle was handed by Nuber himself to the doorman, a loyal employee of many years named Jacob Schnal who was more loyal still to his native Bohemia. Voska had counted on Schnal being chosen to deliver the parcel and given him specific instructions. He was to stay on board the *Rotterdam*, mingling with the farewell crowd until All Visitors Ashore was called, to be certain that neither Archibald nor the package left the ship. Thus, Schnal was able to observe an official from the German consulate arrive and depart minus the cane he had been carrying when he came on board.

Once the *Rotterdam* had cleared harbour Voska reported to Guy and handed over evidence of the parcel's origin: offcuts from the wrapping and a length of the cord used to tie it up. 'He didn't pause to express his joy,' Voska recalled. His mind, as usual, began to work in flashes. He reached for the secret schedule of ships about to sail which he always kept on his desk … .' Guy picked out a faster ship that would reach Britain before the *Rotterdam* and bundled a courier on board her with the material. A ciphered explanation went off to Hall; Guy and Voska headed for some martinis.

The message Guy received from Hall a week or so later was sobering. The *Rotterdam* had been held up at Falmouth for the last two days. Armstrong had been detained. Ship and man had been thoroughly searched. Nothing. American and Dutch authorities were lodging protests about the British action. What do you advise? asked Hall.

Shooting himself, might have been the most appropriate answer, Guy thought. Two neutral but friendly governments gravely offended at a stroke. An international incident in the making. His credibility was at stake; perhaps Hall's as well. That of the hitherto invaluable 'Voska' most of all. Voska never forgot his summons to the Biltmore.

Mrs Gaunt … was at her husband's side. Their faces were as calm and expressionless as marble statues. That is how the British always look in a crisis. It is one of their strengths. Beside them I must have appeared like a wretch waiting for the hangman. 'Have a cigarette?' asked Mrs Gaunt calmly.

Voska was inconsolable. He could see that the entire edifice of the Alliance about to come crashing down. He had given everything he owned to the Bohemian cause, bankrolling most of the activities of the Alliance. He had sold his quarry and was on the point of mortgaging his house. Guy had never been able to help. His own extracurricular, extremely undiplomatic, activities were not just low-budget but no-budget. The suite at the Biltmore, the tabs at the clubs, backhanders to postmen, chauffeurs and other informants all came out of his own pocket—and sometimes Margaret's purse. Only occasional handouts from Springy's slush fund kept the Rolls on the road and let him to take trains to debrief his contacts in Chicago, San Francisco and other Teutonic flashpoints.

The two men re-examined every link in the chain of events. The Austrian package and the German cane had been double-Czeched on board the *Rotterdam*. The guard at the foot of the first class gangway had been another of Voska's men. He refused to believe that any of the Little People involved had failed him. Voska stood by his story. Guy stood by his Voska. He cabled the advice Hall wanted: look harder.

Hall stood by Guy. Another few days of suspense went by in which Guy and Voska felt like men sharing a cell on Death Row. The American press flung itself hungrily on to the case of a United States citizen detained while going about his legitimate business, the worst kind of high-handed British behaviour. The Dutch were just as indignant at a gross breach of neutrality, legality, sovereignty. The *Rotterdam*'s captain repeatedly refused to allow the naval searchers access to the safe in the purser's cabin. Exasperated, Hall abandoned all restraint and threatened to have its door blown off. The captain delivered a final formal protest, produced the key and there was the Austrian parcel.

Hall sent a courier back to Guy with copies of some of the documents it contained. From Guy's point of view the greatest treasure was a letter from Papen to his wife telling her how pleased he was at the way the war was going.

... how splendid on the Eastern Front. I always say to these idiotic Yankees that they should shut their mouths and better still be full of admiration for all that heroism.

Those idiotic Yankees were about to be thoroughly enraged. A surge of furious public opinion would push the government in the direction Britain wanted. But the Foreign Office got cold feet. The papers had been obtained by disturbingly unorthodox means that had offended two neutral nations. The United States citizen, Mr Archibald, had committed no crime. It was all very ... undiplomatic. Guy decided that the story must be broken somehow but safely distanced from Voska and himself. He turned to his friend Cobb. The story, backed by facsimiles of the documents, appeared under the byline of The *World*'s London correspondent Joseph Grigg: the most powerful scoop of the war.

Within weeks Dumba and the countess, Guy's erstwhile glamorous dinner companion, were on their way home. But not until October did Wilson acknowledge that under the shield of diplomatic immunity the German attachés had doled out nearly $30 million to saboteurs and propagandists on American soil and declared Papen and Boy-Ed *non persona grata*. He explained to Congress:

> A little while ago such a thing would have seemed incredible. Because it was incredible, we made no preparation for it. We would have been almost ashamed to prepare for it as if we were suspicious of ourselves and our comrades and neighbours.

> They have formed plots to destroy property, they have entered into conspiracies against the neutrality of the Government, they have sought to pry into every confidential transaction of the Government in order to serve interests alien to our own.

There was, of course, no mention that this was precisely what Guy had been trying to get him to appreciate for months but it was now obvious to all that any secret British operations against the Teutons were entirely justified.

November 1915. In spite of the Arabic Pledge, an Italian ship SS *Anacona* was torpedoed in the Mediterranean. Of two hundred passengers who drowned, nine were American. The submarine surfaced and broke out the Austrian flag, a deceit as well as a grim courtesy since Germany, unlike Austria, is not yet at war with Italy.

The expulsions of the German attachés spurred Rathom into manic action. Guy let him have a carefully regulated dripfeed of facts, including some about the Dark Invader, to which the *Journal* applied the sensational treatment its readers had come to expect. The disclosures were strung out for weeks, the big whammy delivered on 8 December in a stack of *New York Times* headlines which left little need to read on.

On the Western Front
Guy went to see for himself and returned convinced that unless the United States joined
the Allies the war might be lost

(National Library of Scotland)

Father William
A Victorian patriarch whose children
would never do as he wanted

(State Library of Victoria)

Lady Writer
Mary Gaunt as rarely seen.
Particularly by herself

(Yvonne Gaunt)

Gaunt's Brigade

Guy shows his Redtops how to do it

(Powerhouse Museum NSW)

Tulia the Samoan Girl

Guy's personal treasure

(University of Canterbury, NZ)

Thomas Tonkin
alias John Ridgewell Essex. The very
model of a modern-day adventurer

Alone
Except for those who took up the white woman's burden

(Yvonne Gaunt)

Minnie on Wheels
Who took the picture?

(Yvonne Gaunt)

HMS *Centurion*
Ready for her sea trials

(Maritime Quest)

Sinking the Lusitania
German commemorative postcard with Admiral von Tirpitz sharing the glory

(Maritime Quest)

Edward Mandell House
President Wilson's 'second self'

Woodrow Wilson and First Lady Esmée
Wedding postcard

(Corbis)

Victor Voska
As US Army captain in Prague 1919

John Revelstone Rathom
Never saw an angle he couldn't
make sharper

Sir William Wiseman Bt
A man with a Cause

Margery (Lady) Cruise
Tulia the Samoan Girl under a different sky

(Bassano/National Portrait Gallery, London)

Four Winds
Bought for a song

Maude Allen
The Case of the Clitoris

Millions Man
Guy Gaunt at David Jones lunch, Sydney 1931

(National Library of Australia)

Guy the Spy
Sailing from New York as
Commodore First Class

UNCOVER GERMAN PLOT TO EMBROIL U.S. WITH MEXICO

VON RINTELEN CAME HERE, BACKED BY MILLIONS, FOR THAT PURPOSE, GOVERNMENT LEARNS.

NEW REVOLUTION WOULD DIVERT FROM ALLIES THE FLOW OF MUNITIONS

Rathom was fascinated by the mysterious cane and the microfilm it was thought to contain. In the *Journal's* fanciful accounts the stick became the Holy Grail of dark secrets; he envisioned it elegant and capped with gold, being passed from hand to hand in the European shadows. Guy assumed that Archibald, unable to be sure of a hiding place, dropped it overboard.

Happily, the data in Rathom's stories were more convincing. In listing forty incidents of sabotage that cost at least twenty lives the irreproachable *Journal of Commerce* credited the *Journal* as its main source. Insurance claims running into hundreds of millions of dollars helped wise up America to the crippling cost of allowing the Teutonic terrorists to operate unchecked for so long.

Papen was the first to ship out, granted safe conduct through British and French ports. When his ship reached Falmouth, the British authorities airily declared that the immunity granted him applied to his person, not his personal effects. His suitcases contained a mass of documents even richer in revelations than the Captain Alphabet package or Albert's briefcase: receipts, cheque stubs and lists recording exactly how the German funds had been spent on the plots and conspiracies Wilson had finally acknowledged. Bernstorff, whose part in the conspiracies was still not clear to the Americans, made a sanctimonious gesture, telling Secretary Lansing that if events had tainted him in the eyes of the American people he, too, was ready to ask for his passports. There was no chance of Bernstorff's offer being accepted. Persisting against all evidence and advice in the belief that he could yet stop the war, the president had begun to use The Barber as a conduit for the continuing proposals he was making to the German government. To Lansing's alarm, he decreed that Bernstorff be allowed to convey his proposals to Berlin using the State Department cable circuit to American embassies in Europe via Copenhagen—and London. The

British were not supposed to know about this arrangement but, as with virtually every other cable link around the globe, Room 40s ear was so close to the State wire that it was called the Main Line. With his straight diplomatic face in place Lansing wrote to Bernstorff: 'You are in no way included in this episode … .'

Gumshoes

Guy was crouched in the forward hold of a freighter tied up at the West Side piers, a Secret Service agent named Murphy beside him in the dark. Two more agents were in the after hold. All were armed, Guy with his elegant Browning. Murphy had a revolver but if their expectations were fulfilled his weapon of choice would be an eighteen inch-long sap, a hefty leather salami shape filled with lead. 'Never known anyone it wouldn't put to sleep,' he said, showing it to Guy in the back room of the waterside bar where the party had assembled.

The ship was due to leave for Liverpool in the morning Guy had chosen it at random in the hope of catching someone in the act of planting the nasty little incendiary devices that were the Invader's legacy. Rintelen himself was locked up in a British detention centre for enemy officers and Scheele had fled to Cuba but cargoes were still catching fire. Guy and Voska were driven to distraction trying to find out where the exploding cigars were being made and who was smuggling them on board ships.

Got up as rough-looking sailors, the party had rowed a dinghy around to the seaward side of the ship and climbed on board out of sight of the gangway watch. They sat for hours in the stifling blackness but in vain. They did this a score of times with the only result much loss of sleep and ratshit on their trousers Rintelen, they would find out much later, had enlisted Captain Fred Hinsch, North German Lloyd's gang boss in Baltimore, to carry on planting the bombs. Hinsch went about the work with enthusiasm until a more important assignment came along and he subcontracted it to local talent: Edward Felton, chief of the African-American Waterside Workers. Even if Guy and Voska had known where to turn, no paleface mole could have infiltrated those ranks.

Felton also introduced an early biological weapon. Allied forces depended on regular shipments of horses, less for cavalry—the Maxim gun and winter mud had sidelined mounted soldiery—than transport. Mules, too, for hauling artillery pieces and ammunition. Auctioned off to British buyers in Missouri and Kansas City, animals by the thousand were railroaded to Newport News, Virginia and loaded on board special transports.

German agents first tried sprinkling fine pieces of wire into the animals' fodder, which did for a lot of them. Then an German-American doctor, Anton Dilger, returned from a visit to the old country with a supply of anthrax and the equine disease glanders. He had a day job at Johns Hopkins Hospital but for his extermination programme he set up a laboratory at his house in Chevy Chase, Maryland, After the war Ed Felton told a public enquiry how he and a band of helpers simply roamed around the enclosures in which the animals were mustered, jabbing needles into as many as they could. Dead and dying animals in their hundreds were dumped at sea.

Hard pressed as he was towards the end of 1915, Guy had not been pleased, to get word from London that two representatives of the SSB would shortly arrive in New York. He was to give them whatever assistance they required. He had all but forgotten about his few days with C and so far as he knew the organisation had never shown any interest in the United States. Remembering the amateurism and departmental rivalry, he foresaw trouble.

The SSB had never gelled in the way it was supposed to. Keith Jeffery, the author of *MI6: the history of the secret intelligence service 1909-1949* had access to the SSB archives of the period. He devoted several pages of his magisterial analysis to relations between the tripartite factions without being able to say who was really in charge during the first two years of the war. The Foreign Office paid the bills but found the whole thing rather distasteful. It had been agreed that Kell's putative MI5 would confine itself to domestic activities and C would control all agents abroad, including those representing the army and navy, but the services did not give up on their own covert operations. Apart from providing Guy with an interface, Hall concentrated his efforts on code-breaking with spectacular results that he ensured were seen as entirely due to the navy.

The War Office continued with its own shifting array of military intelligence units: MO6, MI1c, GM. America had not really been on C's map at the outbreak of war. When the SSB was conceived there had been little thought of operations on friendly territory, except to the extent that the European neutrals were useful places from which to monitor the activities of hostile players, but Guy's achievements, regularly laid on the table by Blinker, showed what could be accomplished in New York and Washington. A bizarre drama of June 1915 showed C that it might be time to grab a piece of the action over there.

Because of the huge Indian Army the War Office nursed a fixation with the subcontinent. Revolt had been rumbling along since the turn of the century. The Raj feared a second Mutiny could cut off the supply of trained and capable Indian soldiers being exported in the service of their imperial masters; indeed there had been a savage though short rebellion in Singapore in which Lance Gaunt's part was more than a walk-on. The most active faction was the marvellously named Silk Letter Movement, a Muslim conspiracy that looked to Turkey for leadership. The Caliph Mehmet V issued a *fatwa* asking the faithful to fight the British. Conspirators went to Berlin to sell the German government on the idea of fostering a revolt and papers seized from Alphabet Archibald showed that Papen had been ordered to find a way to ship guns and bomb-making material to India. Indian immigrants in the United States formed an organisation to support the insurgents back home but unfortunately for the Hindu revolutionaries on the ground, the janitor of the building they chose as a headquarters, 364 West 120th Street, had been born in the same province as Voska.

Although Guy was reluctant to consider it anything more than a sideshow he could not ignore waterfront whispers that $200,000 worth of rifles and explosives had been loaded on board a decrepit schooner in San Diego, the *Annie Larsen*. Commanded by a German officer, *Kapitän-leutnant* Paul, the *Annie* was to rendezvous with an old oil tanker, the SS *Maverick*, at Socorro Island, a barren volcanic speck six hundred miles off the Mexican coast. The transhipped cargo was to be taken to Burma then smuggled into India. Guy found the *Maverick* in a San Francisco dry dock and going nowhere but he missed the *Annie*. British consulates in the various American seaports were expected to provide information about ship and cargo movements but not all did the job properly. In some, the staff were local employees, some vice consuls, even consuls not even

British. Guy worried about loyalty as much as competence and in several instances used his clout with the consul-general in New York to have a few suspicious cases transferred or sacked. Grumbles from London soon faded but he was to find that the Foreign Office had a long memory for meddlers.

Perhaps because the conspirators knew the *Maverick* was being watched she did not leave San Francisco until nearly a month after the *Annie* had sailed. By that time, Skipper Paul had discovered there was no water on Socorro nor anything else to ease a long wait. With the crew on the point of mutiny *Annie* struggled back and tried to hide out in a logging port in Washington state. All on board were soon arrested and several versions of the events made headlines. The German Embassy claimed there was nothing illicit about her cargo and demanded it be handed over. But the local harbourmaster auctioned off the rifles to settle port fees.

Eighteen months later, when the United States had entered the war, those involved in the fiasco were put on trial together with half the staff of the German consulate in San Francisco, 105 defendants in all. Proceedings were enlivened when the leader of the conspiracy, Ram Chandra Bharadwaj, was shot dead in the courtroom by another of the accused who believed he had turned informer. The assassin, Ram Singh, was blown away, smoking gun in hand, by a United States marshal.

Partly to accommodate the army's obsession with Hindu dissidents, C flirted ineffectually with a couple of freelance cloaks and a few *poseurs* who claimed to know their way around the darker corners of the United States, including the shaman to the fashionable and credulous, Aleister Crowley, aka The Great Beast 666 and, by his own measure, The Wickedest Man in the World. But someone who might be capable of planting the SSB flag firmly in America came along, seemingly by chance: William Wiseman, the son of an old shipmate. He had lived Mexico and Canada before the war, as well as the United States and was now an army captain waiting to be declared fit for active service after having been gassed in France. In his unsecretive way, C mentioned the difficulty he was having in finding the right sort of help and Wiseman asked if he could have the job.

Sagely, Guy did not come up with an unhelpful response when C announced he was sending over a pair of SSB spooks. He left the objections to his most formidable American collaborators: Edward Stettinius, whose views carried the weight of J P Morgan & Co., and Frederick Whitridge, a distinguished attorney whom he consulted whenever he feared he might be testing the limits of diplomatic immunity. Both men wrote to Springy offering the opinion that it would be most unwise of the British government to introduce officially sanctioned clandestine agents into the United States. The very mention of a secret intelligence service evoked images of conspirators or spies for hire, even—as Stettinius spluttered—'amateur gumshoe merchants'.

But the gumshoes were already on the water, arriving at the consulate on 28 October 1915. They told immigration officers they were 'merchants' with business at Touche & Niven, a firm of accountants at 30 Broad Street. They were a strange pair. The older, C had been persuaded by the army, would know what to do about troublesome Indians because of his service on the North West Frontier. His true identity has been shuffled out of the annals but he called himself Sydney Mansfield. The other, short, plump and aged thirty, introduced himself as Smith. C, who had been both Smith and Mansfield, decided that these two bold pioneers of the service could not be expected to infiltrate unknown territory under their own names. Take mine, he offered. Take two. It was obvious to Guy that the names the men used were assumed but it does not seem to have struck him that they came from C's attempts to improve on his own.

The consular staff were as disconcerted as Guy by the appearance of the SSB twosome. They received regular reminders from the Foreign Office that their precious diplomatic status must not be imperilled by inappropriate activities or associations. Guy's furtive coming and going was bad enough but strangers representing an organisation that was not supposed to exist were a bit much. Grumbling messages went back and forth across the Atlantic and between Hall and C in London and after a few weeks Mansfield was recalled. Smith, who soon reintroduced himself as Wiseman, hung around for nearly two months, much of the time spent with bankers he knew, particularly those at J P Morgan's main rival, Kuhn & Loeb & Co. To go by correspondence between Guy and Wiseman years later, Wiseman had been dismayed to find how little he could expect to accomplish in America since most of the things C expected him to do had already been done—by Guy, on behalf of the Department of Naval Intelligence. One of Guy's letters reminded him of an extraordinary scene in which just before he left for London, Wiseman had burst into tears in the Biltmore suite, sobbing that he had been, in effect, set up in some way by the contra-rotating forces within the SSB. Guy never saw Mansfield again but before long he was to see all too much of Wiseman whom he had gravely underestimated.

1916. The United States and the Allies had revised their attitudes. The French now thought it was America's democratic duty to enter the war and Britain was beginning to want the same thing, if not for the same reason. House could see that while that decision might have to be made eventually America would be the only participant motivated by an ideal. 'What the Allies want is to dip their hands into our treasure chest.'

> While the war has become a war of democracy against autocracy, not one of the democracies entered it to fight for democracy, but merely because of the necessity of self preservation. If we go in, it will be because we believe in democracy and do not desire our institutions and the character of our civilisation changed ... unless the United States is willing to sacrifice hundreds of thousands of lives and billions of treasure, we are not to be on good terms with the Allies ....

Picking up on the new British mood Guy began to apply pressure, even warning House that America's reluctance to join the fight was causing grave displeasure in Australia.

Playing Der Tag

1916. Guy's yearning for a seagoing command became acute. *Der Tag* fell on 31 May 1916, when the German battlefleet at last came out into the North Sea and ran into Vice Admiral David Beatty's battlecruiser force patrolling off the Jutland peninsula. The main British dreadnought fleet, commanded by Admiral John Jellicoe, stormed out of its anchorage in Scapa Flow to join in. It was to be the mighty clash for which both sides had built their mighty ships, trained the crews and inspired a generation of officers: a modern Trafalgar.

Following Jellicoe's wake in the afternoon haze, Rear Admiral Ernest Gaunt peered out at the three dreadnoughts of the First Battle Squadron following his flagship HMS *Colossus* in line astern. A captain's eye should be ahead, the saying went, an admiral's aft. Looking ahead was the job of his flag captain, the future First Sea Lord Dudley Pound. Looking sideways, had visibility been better, Ernest could have seen *Centurion*, Guy's lost prize, steaming parallel in the Second Battle Squadron. When she had been ready to return to sea, the Admiralty, in its unfathomable way, had given command of her to Captain the Honourable Horace Hood, prosecutor at the court-martial.

Moved by the occasion, Ernest had an Nelsonian message semaphored to his squadron: 'Remember tradition of Glorious First of June and avenge Belgium.' Officers in the ships astern might remember that Admiral Howe's clash with the French in 1794 had not been all that glorious; most would have forgotten that this war had begun over the German invasion of Belgium. An historian thought the signal 'somewhat incongruous', but Ernest's blood was up.

The two British fleets comprised twenty-eight battleships and nine battlecruisers, the German sixteen and five. Including cruisers and destroyers, 250 warships were hurled into a frustrating free-for-all between early dusk and the following dawn. *Colossus* sank a German destroyer then turned to face a trio of enemy battlecruisers only just visible in the gunsights. The forward twelve-inch turrets landed several hits on *Derfflinger*, which had just helped sink two of Beatty's ships, and in return achieved a bizarre distinction: she was the only one of Jellicoe's battleships to be hit by enemy fire, her casualties half-a-dozen wounded. The British lost 6,784 men and three of their prestigious battlecruisers; the Germans suffered only 3,039 casualties, the loss of one battlecruiser and an old battleship. They kept quiet about several more that had been crippled beyond repair. Captain Pound wrote a stark description of steaming through a twilight seascape littered with crippled and sinking ships. Ernest submitted a report of his squadron's part that included a sharp reference to the battlecruiser fleet commanded by the ineffable Beatty having blocked the line of fire between his ship and the enemy; bold criticism of a superior. The Admiralty botched its account of the battle, letting the Germans get away with framing the shambles as a victory.. But the German fleet never came out again; there was never another *Tag*.

1916. The year got off to an ominous start. On January 16 the enigmatic Wiseman returned. Some kind of understanding had been reached in London, but Hall assured Guy that he remained Number One and that there was no reason why the interloper, who had no official or diplomatic standing, should get in his way. In token of that, Wiseman accepted the codename of Number Two. There was also a Number Three. Once again Wiseman arrived with company, Norman Thwaites, an army major who spoke excellent German. He had been recommended by an intriguing figure at the Mexican embassy in London, Manuel Del Campo, who had known Wiseman in Mexico and Thwaites from the pre-war West End social round.

Guy had to accept the situation, even if it meant that the line of command in New York would be as blurred as it was in Whitehall. In fact, he hoped to shift some of his workload on to the others, particularly Thwaites who knew New York and the newspaper scene well: he had given up a youthful career as an actor to become a reporter, then private secretary to Joseph Pulitzer, owner of the New York *World*. After Pulitzer died he stayed on at The *World* but when war began went home to enlist. Back in New York, the midtown flat he shared with P G Wodehouse awaited.

To begin with, Guy may have been a little jealous of the newcomers, both of whom had seen action. The damage a German machine-gun bullet had done to Thwaites's jaw was more conspicuous than a Prussian sabre cut, making it hard for him to go about unrecognised but Guy found it useful to have a deputy ready to service the shadier contacts he had nurtured. Since the expulsion of Papen and Boy-Ed his diplomatic status was more at risk than ever from German attempts to expose his questionable activities.

Thwaites soon made himself useful. A telephone call told Guy that he might find out where those cigar bombs were coming from if he sent someone over to Hoboken who spoke German and was ready to part with $2,000. The answers to questions with which he kept the conversation going suggested that, unusually, the man on the other end of the line might know what he was talking about.

The New Jersey waterfront had become a dangerous place. The German shipping lines had cut the wages of their stranded crews to a third. The men still ate and slept in the ships but most of the time there were hundreds of them loitering around the piers, frustrated and hostile. 'Better take a gun,' warned Guy.

Suitably tooled up, Thwaites kept a cautious rendezvous with a young German-American, Adolf Witte. He paid him $50 on account and fixed a second meeting back in Manhattan. Guy arranged for a German-speaking plainclothes cop to hide behind a curtain in the Prince George Hotel and take notes as Thwaites led Witte through his story again and gave him the rest of the money. Arrested, Witte was soon ready to give evidence against Scheele and some engineers of the *Freiderich der Grosse*. The police drew up warrants and Guy got his $2000 back—less the $50 Thwaites had paid out.

Because the *Friederich* was effectively neutral territory neither the police nor the federal agencies would raid her. Even so, no more bombs came out of the engine room. 'But for Guy Gaunt's prompt action in hearing that voice on the telephone,' wrote Thwaites. 'Dr Scheele and his colleagues would have continued their destruction of ships for months, and Scheele himself might never have been caught.' Scheele was not actually nailed until Cuba expelled him towards the end of the war. Rather than send him to prison, the Americans treated him much as they did Nazi rocket scientists after World War Two. They gave him his own laboratory near Baltimore where he spent many productive years developing chemical weapons on behalf of the United States.

The going was not always so heavy. Thwaites went for the weekend at the Long Island house of a glamorous couple he knew from his West End days, the millionaire racehorse fancier Oscar Lewisohn and his actress wife Edna May, the original *Belle of New York*. The couple were just back from a party in the Adirondack Mountains, a fashionable refuge from Manhattan's humidity, that had included Bernstorff. The countess was taking a trip back to Germany and the Barber risked a public appearance with a couple of the girl friends. There he was in the Kodak pictures Oscar Lewisohn showed Thwaites, posing on a springboard in his bathing costume, a similarly underclad young lady on each arm. Deft as a cardsharp, Thwaites slid one of the little prints into a handy book. 'I should like to read this,' he said to Oscar, holding it up. 'Take it to bed with you,' said his gracious host.

Thwaites took it instead to his chauffeur, who drove back to Manhattan and delivered the picture to Guy. It was copied and returned to Thwaites by breakfast-time. A day or two later the Russian ambassador, Boris Bakhmetieff, held a reception to mark a rare victory on the Eastern Front. On the mantelpiece of the embassy salon for *le tout* Washington to see stood a framed enlargement of Bernstorff and his poolside friends. Even by the stickiest standards of the day the picture was hardly scandalous but it struck a sour note among Germans who were taking the war seriously; more so a few weeks later when it made a full page in *Tatler*, the London picture paper edited by Guy's old friend Clement Shorter. The caption read: 'Even during the stress of war a representative of the Central Powers in America finds time for a little relaxation.' The German-American Alliance issued a marvellously pompous claim that the picture had been faked: heads superimposed on the incriminating bodies. The Russians awarded Guy the order of St Anne. Thwaites's taste for such light-hearted but effective capers and his readiness to come back from the badlands and slip into white tie and tails for a night on the town made him Guy's kind of guy. It also helped that he unfailingly referred to Guy as 'my boss'. But Guy had been well disposed towards him anyway from the moment he discovered that Thwaites played a tough game of polo and that his regiment was the Fourth Dragoon Guards, in which Cecil Gaunt was once more saddled up.

Back in the saddle

Cecil retired from the army a few months before the war, a major with an imposing array of campaign medals and clasps. He and Helen moved to a wisteria-draped bungalow in Bangalore, a domed and minareted city unrecognisable in the Silicon Valley simulacrum it is today. The house was close to the cantonment, the club and above all the racetrack and polo field. The couple had no children; the horse in every shape and purpose was their main interest in life. But when the trumpets began to sound Cecil knew where he belonged. The Fourth, its India service long past, was already in France but there was a need for experienced officers closer by.

Only four months after the abysmal defeat at Gallipoli, the British went at the Turks again in another ill-conceived campaign. Ottoman

Mesopotamia, now Iraq, shared a border with Persia, part of today's Iran. The Anglo-Persian oilfields, only tapped in 1912, were essential to fuel British warships, vehicles and aircraft. The Turks had to be kept away from Abadan, the Persian Gulf port where the pipe-line fed into tankers.

The Indian government sent a small force to take Basra, which would have been an adequate base from which to protect the wells. But the War Office wanted a 'spectacular' to wash away the bitter taste of Gallipoli. A plan was laid out to capture the Mesopotamian capital, Baghdad. The 6th Indian (Poona) Division, about 10,000 Indian and British troops led by Major General Charles Townshend, landed at Basra in November 1915. Cecil was with them, commanding, in the absence of his dragoons, an infantry battalion, the 1st Seaforth Highlanders. He was given the vital job of setting up and managing a depot from which the division's advance up the Tigris would be supported.

The river spread into vast marshlands on either side: not enough water for a navy but too much for an army. Nevertheless a navy of sorts assembled, a few river gunboats, a flotilla of *tarada*, flimsy canoes used by the Marsh Arabs of the region, and the airboat *Ariel*. Pushed by a giant fan, this was the prototype of the craft in which tourists now skim the swamps of Florida. Cecil had no idea where such a futuristic item came from but it was one of the few useful pieces of kit the penny-pinching Raj provided. He was dismayed at the shortage of everything a fighting advance would need, from food to medical supplies. General Townsend had been assured he would be able to capture everything he needed in Baghdad. On you go, old chap.

A squelchy trek upriver culminated in the capture of Kut-al-Amara, a dusty collection of huts around a dilapidated liquorice factory. Townsend wanted to regroup and replenish with whatever Cecil was able to send up from Basra in *tarada* armoured with metal plates against sniping from the wetland reeds. But his bullish superiors in Delhi insisted he press on. About twenty miles short of Baghdad, at Ctesiphon, the ancient capital of Persia, a fresh Turkish army awaited. In command was Field Marshal Baron von Goltz, the genius whose name had been pilfered by Papen's Welland Canal bumbler.

Many of the Turks were veterans of Gallipoli and welcomed the chance to settle unfinished business. They were defeated but it was a pyrrhic victory; the Indian division suffered so many casualties it could not go on. Townsend retreated to Kut with 1,600 prisoners and more than 4,500 wounded. Goltz rallied his forces and surrounded them. About 13,500 soldiers and sepoys were trapped at Kut, together with a local population of six thousand Arabs. They held out through four months of winter. Only the incessant freezing rain that spread the wetlands even wider saved them from being over-run. As it was they suffered shelling, sniping and bombing from Turkish aircraft. The Raj had no air power at all so Cecil was delighted when a ship arrived in Basra bringing a handful of Australian flyers with half-a-dozen ancient Farman Shorthorns in crates. The flimsy biplanes had a top speed of about 50mph but they made warfare history: the first airdrops.

It was Mafeking all over again but with none of the Baden-Powell spirit of cheerfully sitting things out. The besieged soldiers were starving. Vegetarian Hindus would not eat the horses and mules, bullocks and camels that kept the British alive, if barely. There are stocks of wheat but no way of turning it into flour for *chuppatis* One of the Shorthorns staggers into the air with a 70-lb millstone and dropped it on a huge parachute, narrowly missing the liquorice factory.

In desperation the Raj negotiated the recall of two seasoned Indian divisions from the Western Front and an all-British division blooded at Gallipoli. The best Indian regiments were Muslim and it had been feared they might not be enthusiastic about attacking co-religionists; even take Caliph Mehmet up on his *fatwa*, but the situation was desperate. A relief column assembled in Basra and Cecil saw it on the way upriver. The Turks commanded both banks and every mile was defended.

It occurred to Townsend that he might be able to buy his way out. He told the War Office so and Thomas Edward Lawrence (of Arabia) was sent to offer the Turks a couple of million pounds in gold. The Turks politely declined. They had a whole other army in reserve on the Gallipoli peninsula; they must win in the end.

The surrender of Kut on 29 April 1916 was a shattering blow to British prestige, the worst defeat since the Battle of Yorktown in the American War of Independence; worst until the fall of Singapore a quarter of a century later. In Basra, Cecil held the fort—literally—while yet another force could be raised to avenge the disgrace and capture Baghdad.

That took nearly a year, during which Ernest Gaunt's performance at Jutland won him the prestigious appointment of commander-in-chief East Indies Station, the naval realm stretching from the Gulf to Bombay. On his way out he brought his flagship, the ancient four-funnelled cruiser HMS *Euryalus*, in to Basra, where Cecil had been recommended for a DSO, the award Guy so longed for. Guy grumbled that he could not even adorn his chest with the 1914–15 Star, a medal bestowed on practically everyone in the navy who had been to sea since the beginning of the war.

In League

The surreptitious correspondence that Colonel House and Sir Edward Grey kept up in their exclusive code produced a Big Idea. Foreign Secretary Grey might merely have been trying to dampen down Wilson's grumbling from the sidelines, but he hit on something that offered a focus for Wilson's chronic idealism. In response to the persistent American canvassing,

London had always insisted that an objective that made it essential to continue the war was 'the elimination of militarism and navalism'. Grey put it to House that in order to sanctify this intention a grandly dispassionate American president might be persuaded to allow one of his ideals to acquire capital initials and propose the formation of 'a League of Nations binding themselves to side against any power which broke a treaty'. Only the United States, said Grey, had the power and influence to put such an idea across. House grabbed at the idea. 'This is the part I think you are destined to play in this world tragedy' he wrote to Wilson. 'And it is the noblest part that has ever come to a son of man.' House could see clearly what Wilson was not yet ready to concede. That to exert the required leverage once the war was over the United States needed to be among the victors. He applied a gentle push towards the battlefield, assuring Wilson that the country would follow him along such a path 'no matter what the cost might be'.

Wilson was obviously taken by Grey's notion because in January 1916, days after he and Edith Galt had been married, he made a firmly neutral speech offering to organise a peace conference that would allow the enemies to shake hands and return to their respective corners with honour and security. He packed House off to Europe yet again to put across the message to Germany that the United States might well be ready to intervene on the side of the Allies if only to be able to shape a peace settlement that would include all the well-known Wilsonian aims of arms limitation, binding arbitration and, crucially, Freedom of the Seas.

Until then, few Americans had heard of House but this mission put an end to that.' Although he holds no office and never has held any', said an editorial in the Atlantic City *Review*

> he far outweighs Cabinet officers and bureau heads in Washington affairs. He may not be the power behind the Presidential chair but he is he power alongside of it. He is a figure without parallel in our political history... he has been called the 'assistant President'—a new name for a new and puzzling figure.

House estimated that at least fifty reporters and photographers were on the pier to watch him and Loulie board the *Rotterdam*, together with a battery of 'moving-picture machines'. Some at least were there because, as they had been delighted to discover, another first-class passenger was the disgraced German naval attaché. Throughout the voyage, House managed to keep well clear of Boy-Ed but a German newspaper used darkroom trickery to create a picture that seemed to show them chatting. Guy had arranged for the Houses to be taken ashore as soon as the ship arrived in Falmouth. The rest of the passengers were kept on board for twenty-four hours while all baggage was searched and Boy-Ed locked in his cabin until the ship sailed for Holland. House had given Wilson yet another code in which to send back reports about the arguments he was pressing against continuing British interference with American trade. The presidential newly-weds sat together in bed deciphering them.

24 March 1916. The French cross-channel ferry *Sussex* was torpedoed. Several American civilians were injured although there were none among the fifty drowned. This was a clear breach of the Arabic Pledge of seven months earlier—that merchant ships would be given half an hour for passengers and crew to launch boats. Lansing argued for an immediate break in diplomatic relations, the final step short of a declaration of war. Bernstorff rushed to see not the secretary of state but the 'assistant President'. He assured House he was doing everything possible to get his superiors at the *Auswärtiges Amt* to grovel. And he was. Neither he nor the countess wanted to see an end to their sumptuous plenipotentiary life. Nor did he want to be parted from the substantial fortune that he and Dr Albert had made by investing in the American industries that were supplying the Allies. In addition, The Barber was none too sure of the welcome he could expect in Berlin because of the bathing suit pictures.

The *Auswärtiges Amt*, however, dug in its spurred heels and blustered. Mistaking a ferry for a troopship was a simple error that any U-boat skipper could make. The ship had not been sunk, merely had its bows blown off. No Americans had been killed. What were they doing on the ship anyway? The best offer Bernstorff was allowed to convey was a promise that Germany would abide by the promises already made—on the usual condition: the United States must insist that Britain lift the blockade. Wilson told Congress that his latest warning to Germany was final.

Bernstorff's position had never been in danger. Wilson had begun to believe that the cryptic exchanges he was having via the Main Line with the men who gave Bernstorff his instructions were having an effect; that his standing offer to negotiate an honorable end to the fighting—a 'peace without victory'—was being seriously entertained. Another sorry milestone was set up, the *Sussex* Pledge. Passenger ships would not be attacked unless they disobeyed orders to stop. Merchant ships would not be sunk unless they were known to be carrying munitions. Even if a search found contraband, the safety of passengers and crew would be assured before the ship was destroyed.

Throughout the tense aftermath of the latest sinking House repeatedly sought Guy's views on likely British reactions. They were sternly realistic. Let the Germans do their worst and see where it led. Asking Britain to lift the blockade was a ludicrous idea. If the government could not be persuaded to do it in the name of Freedom of the Seas it was not going to do it to please the Germans. Guy knew nothing about Wilson's backdoor link to Berlin but from the point of view of his operations he did not want a diplomatic break just yet. With the attachés gone The Barber was the best source of secrets he and the Little People had. House thought that both Guy and The Barber had been extremely helpful.

I told Gaunt he reminded me of Bernstorff, inasmuch as he had courage and good temper and viewed matters like a sportsman. I wish Gaunt was British Ambassador and that Bernstorff was Minister for Foreign Affairs in Berlin. It is my intention to suggest to the British Government that they handsomely recognize Gaunt's services...

Wilson had a reason to play it cool even more important than the election drive getting under way: a spectacular display of disrespect on the part of Pancho Villa, the psychopathic Mexican warlord. After being outmanoeuvred by Carranza, who unilaterally declared himself president of Mexico, Villa began marauding around the north of the country at the head of a murderous rabble, charging across the border into New Mexico to rob banks, steal weapons and molest American womenfolk. The usual exchange of protests and excuses took place with Carranza's makeshift government but after a series of particularly outrageous incursions Wilson decided on the strategy adopted generations later by George Bush and Barack Obama of going for the guy at the top. Every Hearst newspaper across the country came out with the headline 'Pershing ordered: Get Villa Alive or Dead'. Given command of a Punitive Expedition, Major General John 'Black Jack' Pershing had difficulty scraping together five thousand men. Two-thirds of the army and most of the Marine Corps were in the Philippines, Panama, Hawaii, Haiti, Costa Rica. The United States was simply not ready for a major land war. The ultimatum to Germany was as hollow as the German pledges. Army and Navy were finally being allowed to get on with some serious preparations but for months to come Wilson would be hostage to any trigger-happy German U-boat captain. Another cold-blooded sinking that took Americans to the bottom would force his embarrassingly empty hand.

Working wounded

What the enigmatic William Wiseman was doing in America remained a mystery to everyone in the consulate and even the embassy, where he went to pay guarded respects to Springy. If C had wanted him to use his Mexican connections to influence Huerta in Britain's interests he was out of luck. The day he arrived in New York the old jackal, caught trying to escape from the United States, died in an army prison, poisoned, it was said, by his own cook.

Wiseman had come down from Cambridge University without a degree but with a Blue in boxing—bantamweight. For nearly a year he had been sparring lightly with Guy, dancing around out of reach, waiting for an opening. He was a little plump now but still fast on his feet if he had to be. In the interest of a peaceful accommodation, Wiseman agreed to deal with the stream of British seekers after American military treasure that surged through the consulate daily. He found himself an office and put a sign on the door:

Transport Department
Ministry of Munitions

Thwaites told Guy he understood that he and Wiseman had been chosen simply because only wounded or gassed officers could be spared for intelligence work. The Germans had introduced gas earlier in the year—against the Canadians that Papen had been so keen to keep at home. Rudimentary masks were soon in use, hoods with round eyepieces that made soldiers look like Caspar the Friendly Ghost, but Wiseman, four months in France, got a whiff just the same.

His medical record showed 'Relapsing conjunctivitis ... slight and not permanent'. He was to avoid dust and wear tinted glasses. After a couple of months a medical board would decide if he was fit to be sent back to the front. That was when—apparently—his course converged with C's. The medical service made several attempts to reach him but he had dropped out of sight. His record was amended: 'With MO6 [sic] since 15 September, 1915, Room 217, War Office'. By the time he got to New York he no longer wore glasses.

Guy seemed not to have been told much of this. As he would write to Wiseman later: 'I didn't know you had been gassed. Blinker had quite a different view.' How different?

It remains difficult to get Wiseman's debut as a spook into focus. Many of the business contacts he had made during his time in Mexico were now in New York, safe and usually richer. Kuhn & Loeb stayed top of his list, however. No matter that the partners were beginning to attract attention by its dealings with the revolutionary Bolshevik movement, which was a good deal better organised than the official Russian delegation. As bankers the partners could hardly agree with the Marxist doctrine personified in Vladimir Lenin and Leon Trotsky but they were Russian Jews whose families had suffered in various Czarist pogroms. They regarded anything that might end the repressive rule of the Romanoff dynasty as a deserving cause.

C might have thought Wiseman was working exclusively for the SSB but he never really parted company with the War Office. M06, where the medical service lost track of him, was an army intelligence department. Some things he reported to one set of spooks, some to the other. Some he kept to himself. He was polite and deferential, well-spoken and respectful to elders and superiors. Very good at getting people to confide in him. He also had a talent for intercepting credit that was rightfully due to others.

Guy took the Transport Department sign at face value and handed over the scheduling of cargoes. His concern was to keep the shipments of war materials safe. Despite the best efforts of Voska's moles and regular tip-offs to the NYPD, the Secret Service and the Bureau of Investigation, explosives plants around the country were still being blown up. Von Papen had left a to-do list with a junior secretary, Herr Wolf von Igel, who moved into 60 Wall. But Americans had at last begun to take Teutonic sabotage seriously, although Irish dissidents, Hindus and anarchists all came in for a share of the blame. A federal district attorney, Joseph Baker, raided the Igel's nest with three Bureau of Investigation agents— all of whom, interestingly, had Bohemian names. Pushing aside a 'giant German guard', they collected thirty kilos of paper, although not without resistance. 'I must say Mr von Igel is quite a scrapper', Baker told the *New York Times*, 'Every time we seized a new document or opened a drawer he was on us like a wild man.'

Taking the papers, Igel blustered, would be an act of war against Germany. It may have been another small step in that direction, if not in the way he meant. There was no breach of diplomatic protocol: the embassy had never got around to registering von Igel for immunity. The seized documents identified the men involved in the Welland Canal fiasco and prosecutions followed.

Beyond trying to keep Irish-American longshoremen away from

cargoes meant for Britain, Guy managed to stay clear of the simmering bitterness that characterised that particular tribe of hyphenates, at least until the Roger Casement affair stirred them up. Casement, a former British diplomat who sympathised with the movement for Irish home rule, had been in New York when war broke out, raising funds for the Irish Volunteers. One of the early strokes of mischief Bernstorff had come up with had been sending him to Germany to try to induce the Irishmen among British prisoners of war to form an Irish Brigade and fight on the German side. Few were interested but Casement persuaded the Germans to provide weapons for an insurrection in Dublin planned for Easter and take him over to Ireland to participate. Room 40 decrypted all the wireless and cable traffic involved. The ship carrying the arms was intercepted and scuttled by her German crew. A U-boat put Casement ashore near Dublin where he was captured, taken to London, tried for treason and sentenced to be hanged.

Many Americans, not only those of Irish background, believed Casement had been framed. Congress passed a motion calling for clemency. In response the British government discreetly circulated the 'Black Diaries', a record of Casement's homosexual exuberances in Africa years earlier. Sympathisers assumed they were forged, or at least doctored, although years later they were proved genuine. Forgeries or not, Guy made sure copies of the hair-raising journals reached the most vocal American critics of British justice and Rathom turned in one of his finest hatchet jobs. It might not have been the most admirable exercise in black propaganda the old firm ever pulled off but support for Casement—and the problem for Britain that he represented—fizzled out.

Black Tom

On 29 July 1916. Margaret and Guy retired early in the suite at the Biltmore. It had been another trying month. Germany's domination of the underwater world entered a new dimension. Larger U-boats, easily able to cross the Atlantic, were being launched and the first of them docked in Baltimore earlier that month to a barrage of admiring headlines, a clamorous welcome from the German community and some confusion. The 2,000-ton *Deutschland*, the first U-boat seen in America, belonged not to the German Navy but to North German Lloyd. It was to manage her arrival that Hinsch gave up his job as Rintelen's successor in the exploding cigar business. *Deutschland* was unarmed and, according to her master, Paul König, a merchant ship like any other.

She was also, apart from having no torpedo tubes, a U-boat like any other and Allied naval circles took a poor view of her being treated otherwise. Guy and the French naval attaché put up the somewhat feeble argument that she could not be regarded as a merchant vessel because the ability to submerge meant she could not be stopped and searched for contraband. They suggested to Lansing that if she did not leave within the 48-hour limit allowed belligerent warships she should be interned. The US Coastguard and port officials looked the puzzling vessel over and certified that she carried no weapons or means of causing destruction. Lansing decided there was nothing in maritime law to prevent a ship from carrying her cargo under water.

The greater part of the cargo *Deutschland* carried was a consignment of dyes produced by the sophisticated German chemical industry that was greatly welcomed by the New York rag trade. It sold for more than it had cost to build her. There were also precious stones and gold bullion, surety for loans from American banks. Glumly—and correctly—Guy assumed that *Kapitän* König also handed over new naval and diplomatic codes that would set Room 40's work back for a while.

The rapturous welcome made *Deutschland* a propaganda treasure chest. Her crew became celebrities and not just among German-Americans. A Broadway producer begged König to star in his vaudeville show. The writers of an Irving Berlin musical, *The Century Girl*, cobbled together a scene set in a submarine and squeezed it into the opening night performance. König was the guest of honour, The Barber alongside him. Guy piled on all his gold braid and Margaret her best jewels to sit in the row behind the drably dressed civilian skipper: the Royal Navy, ever vigilant. The dark allure of *Deutschland*'s visit faded with her departure, however. Running down Chesapeake Bay, the cargo bulges along each side stuffed full of rubber and other industrial treasures Germany needed, she rammed the tug escorting her, capsizing it and drowning the five crew. Guy might have been able to take a vicious pleasure in the incident had not Fred Hinsch, on board the tug to wave *Auf Wiedersehen*, been the only survivor.

A sister cargo sub, *Bremen*, also set out for the United States. The *Admiralstab* had her tracked by the fully-armed U-53, in order to show Americans what the real thing looked like. *Kapitän-leutnant* Hans Rose startled the navy base at New London, Connecticut, by slipping into the anchorage and going ashore to enquire for news of *Bremen*. When he was told she had been sunk by a British submarine, he took the news bravely and invited the American officers on board U-53 for a drink. After Assistant Secretary Roosevelt telephoned the base, Rose got the feeling he was not welcome to hang around. Off the Nantucket lighthouse, just outside the territorial limit, Rose put on a day-long spectacular. The farewell escort, a flotilla of American destroyers, watched helplessly as U-53 lay on the surface and picked off three British ships in a row, then a Dutch freighter and a Norwegian. All the merchantmen were abandoned without loss of life and the destroyers ferried the crews ashore. It was a bad day for Anglo-American relations but neutral meant neutral and the Americans could not intervene. Guy was outraged. 'I have never seen him quite so perturbed,' wrote House. 'The sinking... was a little too much for even his staunch nerves.'

Deutschland made one more Atlantic crossing but the cargo-carrying submarine was not an idea whose time had come. When the United States joined the war she was fitted with torpedo tubes and enjoyed a respectable career sinking enemy freighters. After the war she was bought by the legendary British trickster Horatio Bottomley who moored her by Tower Bridge and charged a shilling to look her over.

The Gaunts were sound asleep when a shattering explosion shook the New Jersey shore and Manhattan. It was eight minutes past two on a Sunday morning. All around the financial centre on the downtown tip of the island shards of window glass crashed down like giant icicles. In Trinity Church off Wall Street gravestones were blown out of the ground. A *tsunami* of thunder and vibration rolled up the midtown avenues, parting on the great prow of the Flatiron Building, surging around Grand Central, shaking the Biltmore from the railway tracks beneath it to the flagpole on its roof. Across the Hudson, the Lehigh Valley Railroad terminal on Black Tom Island, last stop for massive shipments of explosives to Europe, as well as the pickup point for German saboteurs, had disappeared. A dozen huge barges and eighty freight cars, packed with high explosive destined for Russia, that were waiting to be ferried to freighters out in the harbour disintegrated.

On Ellis Island, half a mile away, immigrants spending their first night in America in the cheerless Great Hall shrieked in panic. Closer still to the blast, the Statue of Liberty's skirts were peppered with shrapnel. She has never been the same; repairs went on for years. Astonishingly, while hundreds of people were injured in various ways, mainly by flying debris, the only fatal casualties were three barge hands and a baby blasted out of his crib in New Jersey. Nothing like this had ever happened in the United States; nothing would again until the Twin Towers were brought down eighty-five years later.

Guy, rolling out of bed, thought there must have been an earthquake. No one was answering the telephone but before he had got into his clothes Voska arrived. Only the day before they had been worrying about Black Tom. Some of the watchmen who worked shifts there were, naturally enough, on Voska's payroll. They reported a worrying discovery. Crates that should have contained artillery shells and other ammunition for Russia were filled with scrap metal and bits of old T-model Ford parts. The obvious culprits for the explosion were Germans out to prevent the munitions reaching the Eastern Front. But it was always possible that the original contents had simply been pilfered and sold. If the scam had been on the point of being exposed whoever stuffed the cases with junk might have blown up the lot to destroy the evidence of a massive swindle.
Guy's response to the discovery had puzzled Voska.

Gaunt had one of the sharpest, quickest minds I have ever encountered. With him decision was usually a matter of a split second. This time he hesitated. 'It's awkward,' he said. 'We might mix things up frightfully by stepping in.'

Guy had realised that there could be a tricky diplomatic dimension. He told Voska:

The rotter who's behind this must be one of the high Russian officials. We're supposed to be friendly with all of them. Some of them are important to other things we're doing. So far as the British are concerned, it's best to keep clear out of it until we know exactly who's responsible.

The official Russian intelligence chief in New York was a Professor Sergei Syromiatnikov whom Guy had met in an official capacity and found his doleful personality as difficult to come to terms with as his name. 'Why don't you put the case to him?' Guy suggested to Voska.

Voska met Syromiatnikov in a hotel room on the morning of 29 July, less than twenty-four hours before the explosion, and told him about the junk-filled crates.

Neither by word, expression, nor gesture did he [Syromiatnikov] betray any surprise. I had an intuition that my story was not news to him, and that he was wondering hopelessly what he could do. He asked only one question: 'How did you learn all this?'

The Russian could hardly have expected Voska to tell him. But he seemed grateful for the information and asked that the matter not be mentioned to anyone else. 'It might interfere with my work.'

That afternoon Voska called at the Biltmore. Over their teacups Guy mused, 'I wonder if we haven't made a mistake in telling the Russians.'

The Russians never came under public suspicion, although the usual Irish-Indian-anarchist suspects passed briefly through the frame. Most of America had no real doubt about who was responsible. Black Tom was a turning point. German-American influence began to fade. Even its visibility. Many a Schmidt became a Smith; many a Braun a Brown.

After the war the Lehigh and United States government demanded $50 million compensation from Germany for damage done by the blast and Papen, by then a prominent Nazi, persuaded Hitler to pay part of it for the sake of good relations. But a joint German-American commission rejected the claim. No doubt the terminal had been 'a shining mark for the activities of agents of destruction'. But, the commission concluded: 'We are quite a long way from being convinced that the fire was caused by any German agent.' Guy too.

November 1916. With House laying out the election strategy, Wilson won thirty of the forty-eight states and just under 50 per cent of the popular vote. The boldest banners in the campaign read: He Kept Us Out of the War. There was a Democrat majority in the House of Representatives and the Senate. The hasty marriage to Esmée had not, after all, told against them and the confirmed First Lady set out to punish House for having counselled against it. Also, she hated the portrait of her that he had commissioned as a wedding present.

The war itself seemed frozen in winter mode, all quiet on both European fronts, the great navies once more holed up in harbour. Guy could take stock. He had stopped pressing the case for American entry into the war because it had come to seem to the Royal Navy that the present state of benevolent neutrality was a better idea for the moment. If Germany were to turn the full power of her underwater capacity against the Atlantic traffic the damage would likely outweigh any advantage. Wait and see, he now advised House. For the moment, Voska's people had The Barber and his remaining henchmen ring-fenced. Thwaites was well plugged in to the law enforcement connections they had set up. Wiseman's Transport Department seemed to be keeping the cargoes moving. He had accomplished much in America but he felt isolated—insulated even— from significant events. He resented missing the action the fleet had seen; also, the promotion imperative had become as powerful as the urge of a migrating bird.

For the leap from captain to admiral he needed up-to-date sea time in command of a serious ship of war. Arthur Balfour, who had been First Lord when Guy's achievements began to be recognised at the Admiralty, had passed down a vague assurance that Guy's long dry stretch need not be a barrier to advancement and indeed Blinker Hall, who had spent the entire war in Room 40, had just been made a rear-admiral. But Balfour had moved on to replace Grey as Foreign Secretary and Guy knew how easily the Admiralty could switch between approval and indifference. Then there was his marriage. Margaret, fed up and missing Gaunts Wood, had gone home in mid-August. He welcomed a suggestion from Blinker that it was time the two of them met face to face. Lloyd George had replaced Asquith as prime minister and Hall wanted to show his star performer off to the new government. He would have to go along with that while reminding everyone he dared that his appointment had run well over the customary two years. He arranged six weeks leave and under the protective cover of Grant—George Grant—booked a passage for early December. Bad move.

Although neither brother mentioned it in his memoirs, Lance was still in London in the weeks before the war, when Guy was learning how to be an attaché. He and Violet left for Singapore on 30 July 1914, taking the ferry to Calais then a train to Marseille to join the P&O liner *Malaya*. France was mobilising: railway stations packed with *poilus*, bands playing. It was all very exciting but he had to get home. Allen & Gledhill, the firm of solicitors where he was now senior partner, were impatient for his return.

Even in ordinary times, life in the Settlements was rarely dull. The practice took him up and down the Malay Peninsula, even across to Borneo where the Sultan of Sulu paid his fee with a couple of diamonds the size of kidney beans. Another sultan, Ibrahim Iskandar Al-Masyhur Abu Bakar, the ruler of Johore, the mainland Malay state across the narrow strait from Singapore, invited him to shooting parties, snipe and pigeons mainly, but sometimes pigs. He tried for a tiger once but missed.

In Singapore brother Clive and his fiancée Evelyn Morrison—Violet's sister—would be waiting to meet them. Rangoon, where as Chief Crown Prosecutor Clive worked the opposite side of the law from Lance, was only two nights away by steamer and the couples frequently exchanged visits. A friend of the family who visited both couples, Nancy Adams, thought that if Lance's life was Somerset Maugham, Clive's was Joseph Conrad. In his early days he had to be taken to the distant parts of his circuit in a dug-out canoe paddled by head-hunters. Burma was the hind end of the Raj, only tenuously connected to Delhi. Like many hind ends it was more appealing than the frontal aspect, an enchanting land of mountains and teak forests, great rivers that rose in far-off Tibet, treasures of gold, amber, jade and rubies; even petroleum. It was quite a different place from the sub-continent with its teeming millions: a small population, most of them easy going, cheroot-smoking Buddhists. It had been in the embrace of the Raj for less than a century; its administrators were less deeply rooted and stratified than their counterparts in India, youngish men enjoying a life-style their incomes could never buy elsewhere. In the courts many junior counsel and magistrates were Burmese but there was no nonsense about racial equality. This was the British Empire, not the British World.

Lance and Violet were just settling in for their voyage when, four days into August, Britain's declaration of war imminent, one of those Forrest Gump moments unfolded. Two warships broke out of the morning mist astern of *Malaya*. Morse signals could be heard chirping from the liner's wireless cabin and officers with binoculars soon identified the *Goeben* and *Breslau* on the way—had anyone known it—to their new owners in Constantinople. Lance watched German rangefinders swivel towards them. Would the pursuers open fire? Capture the *Malaya* with all on board? Nerves straining, the passengers watched the Germans slip past, As in that far-off Samoa experience, Lance was gripped by longing Those menacing ships belonged to the world that Ernest and Guy so confidently bestrode and of which he was a mere onlooker. He held a captain's commission in the Singapore Volunteer Artillery, but at thirty-nine he was too old for active service and a pillar of the community could not uproot himself on impulse and roll off seeking adventure. Even a Gaunt.

Evelyn was indeed waiting at Singapore but with news that Lance found disconcerting. They had probably passed Clive somewhere in the Indian Ocean. Two years Lance's senior, even less eligible for military service, he had jumped on board a homebound ship determined to join the colours, another older brother doing what Lance really wanted to.

News of the far-off war reached Singapore in frustratingly short takes: cable bulletins in the *Straits Times*, casualty lists. The garrison, a battalion of the Yorkshire Light Infantry, was shipped to France and replaced by a mainly Muslim unit of the Indian Army, the 5th Bengali Light Infantry. Not all the fighting was far off. In November there was high drama offshore: The Australian cruiser *Sydney* sank the German marauder *Emden* in a stirring duel, the first British victory at sea. Three hundred and fifty survivors were brought to Singapore and either hospitalised or imprisoned. The German presence helped inspire a plot by the usual troublesome imam, in this case one Nur Alum Shah, whose war news presumably wafted over from India on a silk hankie.

Sepoys of the 5th Bengali became persuaded that troopships were coming to take them to Europe or the Middle East where they would be made to fight their brothers in faith. In fact, they were to be sent to garrison Hong Kong. Nur Alum's plan was that at midnight on 15 February, Chinese New Year, a big holiday for the multiracial island, the Bengalis would set the *Emden* prisoners free. They would then take over the gasworks that provided the town lighting—only the Raffles had electricity—and Fort Canning on Government Hill, the highest point of the island.

Sensing trouble, the army command sent trucks to the barracks to collect all ammunition there. The sepoys reacted by shooting several of their British officers. A stray bullet also accounted for Nur Alum Shah and the plot fell apart. The Bengalis fragmented into aimless gangs, roaming the town, shooting at random.

There was uneasy muttering in the European enclaves about the Mutiny of 1857 that had also been sparked off by disgruntled sepoys. These events were nowhere near as momentous but forty-seven people had been murdered, most of them innocent civilians, and the machinery of retribution creaked into motion. A decrepit corvette, HMS *Cadmus*, was in harbour on its way home with Rear-Admiral Thomas Jerram after his stint in command of the China Station. It put bluejackets and marines ashore with their trusty Maxims and sent out a general SOS. By the following day a motley armada of French, Japanese and Russian warships began to arrive and send off landing parties. In running shootouts the mutineers were pressed back into the jungle that in those days separated the island's various settlements.

Jerram knew his fellow admiral, Ernest Gaunt, and certainly knew of Guy. The younger Gaunt would surely be made of the right stuff, too. Lance was called away from the stately three-storey office in Raffles Place which was daily besieged by clients chest-deep in the fortunes of war: tin, rubber and coconut oil, an important ingredient of margarine. Appointed Intelligence Officer, he was to find out immediately where the fugitive Bengalis were hiding. Lance knew that many of them would have headed for Johor to seek sanctuary with his friend Sultan Ibrahim, the local religious authority. He and five other Volunteer Artillerymen piled into a pair of jalopies and set out along the rough unlit road to the far side of the island.

The multinational reinforcements were more of a threat than the mutineers. In the four hours it took the Volunteers to reach the north shore they were challenged eleven times by trigger-happy soldiers and sailors of eight different nationalities, none of whom had much idea of where they were or why. With kitchen Malay and scrappy French the British insisted they were not German. As it turned out, only a couple of dozen *Emden* prisoners decided to walk. The rest preferred to stay in jail.

The splendid causeway that now joins Singapore to the mainland was yet to be built. They commandeered a launch. Even though it was only just after dawn the Sultan is the spirit of hospitality and reassurance. Indeed, he said, about sixty bedraggled Bengalis had arrived at his palace door begging his protection. They would not give up their rifles and ammunition so he sent them off to sleep in the prison attached to his palace compound, ostentatiously leaving the doors open. When the scoundrels came out to wash before morning prayers he would order the doors locked, cutting them off from their weapons, and bar the gates of the compound. The police could come and collect the naughty fellows whenever they wished.

Back in Singapore the hunt for fugitives went on. The stories Lance wrote out in longhand years later of picking his way through the cellars and attics of mosques and *godowns*, revolver in hand and heart in mouth, may have been a little stretched but they read convincingly as close-quarter stuff more dangerous than anything Guy or Cecil got up to. The fugitives had little to lose; they were bound to be executed. Some would have been ready to take an infidel with them. Nevertheless, the pages seem stamped with the shadow of Samoa: Lance drawing on Guy's experiences in order to enhance his own.

Two hundred insurgents were put on trial and forty-eight who participated in the first day of the mutiny sentenced to death. The rest were shipped off to serve long sentences in solitary confinement at the notorious Cellular Jail in the Andaman Islands, a masterpiece of Victorian penal architecture transplanted to the tropics. Lance confined his description of the chilling events to the first two to be executed before an audience of about fifteen thousand Singaporeans.

The shooting party consisted of 10 and they took up their position in the centre of the wall end of a square the other three sides of which were made up of troops; the mutineers were then escorted out from the jail walls; the Proclamation setting out the reasons of the execution and the authority was then read out first in English then in Malay, Chinese and Tamil and as the last sentence was read the Commandant passed the order to the officer in command of the firing party to carry out the sentence; one could not help admiring the splendid way those two faced it all; they declined to have their eyes bandaged and the only movement noticeable was an attempt shortly after they had taken their places to face towards the West so that they would be facing Mecca; at the first command they both lifted their voices and called to Allah but there was no cringing or struggling; they met their death with stout hearts; I was anxious to know the opinion of a Company of Sikhs who witnessed it all and approached them for that purpose; there was no doubt what they thought Yes Sahib it is good they should all be shot.

This whiff of action had a transformative effect on Lance. The Gaunt compulsion to get to where things were happening—an inversion of the Gump effect—proved irresistible. In December 1915, having turned forty, he went back to Britain and joined the Royal Horse Artillery. This was an undeniable one-up on Clive, who had been rejected as unfit and returned to Burma, buckling up with the Rangoon Port Defence Volunteers.

Assuming that his days with the Rupertswood Battery and the Volunteer Artillery would be seen as a qualification, Lance expected a commission but none was on offer and he hated being a mere trooper. He was far too grand as well as too old to be mucking out stables on freezing mornings alongside lumpen teenage recruits. Once again, 'a certain Admiral', as he archly referred to Ernest, mustered some of that old-fashioned interest. In May 1916 Lance was commissioned a lieutenant (Temporary) in the Royal Naval Volunteer Reserve, At least that is what he seemed to think. His service record shows it was actually the Royal Naval Reserve. The only real difference between the two was the shape of the rings on a cuff, but it seems strange he should not have known which he belonged to.

The navy took note of his artillery experience and after two-months of gunnery school sent him to the battleship *St Vincent* with the Grand Fleet at Scapa Flow. Jutland had come and gone and the huge armada was waiting impotently, in the vile weather of the remote anchorage, for the Germans to show themselves again. The wait went on until the end of the war but the ships and the thirty thousand men in them were never idle: drills and maintenance in harbour, provocative sorties to the protective German minefields, regular firing exercises.

Lance was put in charge of a pair of twelve-inch guns. Closed up at action stations for long hours in a great steel turret he and the gun crews depended on voice pipes and telephones to tell them what was happening, even whether it was raining outside. When the guns opened up at a practice target the turret filled with cordite fumes. Heads rang concussively; earplugs and cotton wool were considered effeminate. Nevertheless, he felt close to the real war: hope of sighting the German fleet flared afresh every time his squadron steamed out into the North Sea. He enjoyed the on-board camaraderie: concert parties, dances with midshipmen partners, the 'lady' shuffling gracelessly astern. Even the pleasures of shoreside Scapa grew on him: the sodden peat golf course, pigeon shoots along the cliff tops.

While Lance had been swinging around a buoy in Scapa, Guy spent the better part of two months in Britain. He went to visit Minnie, who had moved out to New Eltham, Kent, where she was waiting impatiently to be allowed to travel again. She had found a house called, quaintly, 'Mary Haven'. Lucy's son Pat was there, convalescing after being shot in the head at Gallipoli. At the beginning of the war T Werner Laurie had brought out a collection of Minnie's stories that was selling well. Some were tales of the sea for which Guy had been technical advisor. Others had been inspired by her adventures. She was at work on the crucial China book but wondered if it would ever appear. Publishing had become haphazard, ink and paper in short supply like everything else, money included. She had been turned down for a job writing propaganda handouts and brooded that the blimpish old colonel who interviewed her simply could not imagine that a woman might be capable of doing the work. She took up reading manuscripts for her earlier publisher, Edward Arnold, at fifteen shillings a time. A girl had to do what a girl had to do.

Absence makes the heart grow fonder ... to which the traditional sailor's response was, 'fonder of some other blighter'. Guy had barely passed the Nantucket Light on his way over when he was badly missed by both House and Springy. In the Cabinet reshuffle that followed Lloyd George taking over from Asquith, Grey had been replaced as foreign secretary by Balfour and House's private link had gone dead. The Foreign Office, deprived of guidance from above, turned to Springy to find out from House if he had received any hint from Germany of the terms on which it might be ready to end hostilities.

Springy was wary of what House might make of a direct enquiry from him; he wanted an informal tip-off, the kind of thing he had come to rely on from Guy. With no one else in New York he could depend on he telephoned the new chap who was working with Guy. Wiseman. Would he mind calling on the colonel to see if he could find out something discreetly? He would send up a letter of introduction. Wiseman was delighted to oblige; House, too, was ready to help. The pair got on from the start. Among their interests in common: an insider grasp of big banking. Wiseman had had expected to read for the Bar after Cambridge but had to get out in the world to make the family some fast money. He found how to do so, if only with modest success, in Mexico, where British entrepreneurs and engineers were renovating the decrepit infrastructure the better to exploit the country's resources: building railways and ports, setting up banks and factories, often in competition with German counterparts. At the outbreak of war he was back in Britain, married with two children, as chairman of a fund that managed the family investments: the Hendens Trust.

Guy arrived back in America on 27 January 1917 in the White Star liner RMS *Adriatic* as tweedy George Grant. Reporters on the shipping beat recognised him instantly and made sure to get his *nom-de-guerre* in their stories. He regretted not being in uniform and able to show off the decorations he had acquired. The DSO he yearned for could only be won under enemy fire and if any of that came his way in America he would have to keep quiet about it but the Admiralty had invited him to become a CMG. He thought he had better not turn it down as he had the Foreign Office offer after Samoa. Also, someone pointed out to him that the rusty old collier he took around the Caribbean looking for Telefunken masts had carried a four-inch gun on her poop. Thus he had the sea time in a ship of war required to qualify for the 1914–15 Star. He had the ribbons of the two awards stitched to his jacket for a visit to the Western Front. In France the Allied commander, Field Marshal Douglas Haig, took him through a pile of re-drawn maps of the Somme to demonstrate that the new alignment of trenches had been worth sixty thousand casualties, then handed him over to John Buchan, the pace-setting thriller writer who was, in effect, the General Staff's publicity man.

As when Guy he had gone over in 1916 Blinker had sent him to brief Lloyd George about America's reluctance to fall into step. It had been an impressive enough performance for him to be invited to continue the following day, after which he was invited to repeat some of his points for several Foreign Office honchos—who might not have been flattered to be receiving guidance from a mere sailor, and one with murky connections, it was rumoured.

Guy assured the shipping reporters everything he had seen and heard in Europe convinced him the fighting would be over in months. He did not say that he feared an Allied victory was far from certain. He had seen for himself that the British armies in France were suffering a cruel winter and everyone at the Admiralty knew that the U-boat offensive was sending British ships to the bottom faster than they could be replaced. A few months of such attrition and there would be no food, ammunition, raw goods, even reinforcements with which to continue the war.

As with many a deceived and demoted suitor, Guy was slow to grasp what was going on. He could not help noticing that the Transport Department had expanded, a certain Signor Del Campo whom Numbers Two and Three treated as an old friend installed had been installed, but the discovery that Wiseman was handing out business cards as Walter Wisdom, director of W. Wisdom Films Inc. put matters in perspective. Posing as a moviemaker was as dodgy a device then as it is today. If Wiseman could do no better than that he was not much of a threat to Guy's turf. He should have taken C's man more seriously. House had.

Wiseman consolidated his deft courtship of House by insinuating that, alone among the government's British contacts, he was untainted by association with the Republicans, particularly Teddy Roosevelt, who while not a candidate had rallied much opposition to Wilson in his first election campaign. He made much of being a member of the Conservative and Unionist party, to which Balfour belonged. After their first meeting, House was infatuated. He wrote to Wilson praising his caller as

> the most sensible Englishman that has been connected with the embassy here since the war began. He has intelligence enough to go with friends of the Administration rather than its enemies.

Since those friends had to include Guy that was a cheap shot Springy may never have seen any reason to give up his old Republican friends but although Guy had enjoyed some boisterous meetings with old Roosevelt, an unalloyed warmonger, he soon saw the danger of being tainted by association and kept at a safe distance.

House was worried about the erosion of his own standing. As Wiseman had stepped in front of Guy, the new Mrs Wilson interposed herself between the president and his vital supporter. House was no longer welcome to turn up at the White House whenever he cared to come down from New York. He and Wilson continued to exchange notes and letters daily but the tone of them had been retuned. The customary earlier salutation 'Dear dear friend', was now plain 'Dear House'.

It was not merely that Wiseman was personable, deferential and, it seemed to House, exceedingly well informed about what was going on in London. He was *Sir* William George Eden Wiseman Bt. The title he dropped so disarmingly denoted not some grubby political knighthood but a hereditary baronetcy running back to the court of Henry VIII. For anglophiles like House and Lansing, this was the very essence of what they expected from Old England. Their faith in republican government might run deeper than religion but they dearly loved a lordling.

Sir William had something else going for him: he was a bold and strategic liar. He told House that he rather than Springy—and certainly rather than Guy—was now the British government's chosen conduit to the United States. He told C that he had established a direct link with President Wilson. Neither claim was true at the time but on both sides of the Atlantic wishing soon made it so.

After their first few meetings House wrote to Wilson that Wiseman had told him

in the gravest confidence a thing which I had already suspected and that is that he is in direct communication with the Foreign Office and that the Ambassador and other members of the Embassy are not aware of it ... I judge he reflects the views of his government.

This was outright deception on Wiseman's part and wishful thinking on that of House. The British government in the sense of the Foreign Office and the War Cabinet, the five-man *junta* with which Lloyd George now made the critical decisions, had never heard of Wiseman. His reports to C were circulated in the form of anonymous secret memos but no matter how exasperated everyone might be with Springy he and the equally unappreciated American envoy, Walter Page, remained the only recognised conduits between the two countries.

Despite what he had told the president, it soon became evident to House that irrespective of his claims the new *protégé* was not really getting through to a level of the British government that mattered. But to re-establish a direct link with Britain and win back Wilson's dependence on him House was ready help. First he had to sell the unorthodox arrangement to Wilson and there was an unnerving moment when House showed the president a message Wiseman had sent in which he implicitly criticised a speech Wilson had made to the senate in which he spoke of his enduring hope of bringing the European enemies together in that victory-free peace of his dreams. In Wiseman's view, the president's insistence that the European enemies must stop fighting and settle their differences by arbitration was not a useful approach. Wiseman's opinion—one already firmly held in London and Paris—was that before those differences could be discussed the Allies must prevail. Faced with Wilson's cold raised eyebrow, House rushed to assure him that this was not really Wiseman's view. 'He had been saturated with the unfriendly attitude of Spring Rice and for the moment it warped his vision.' Springy's attitude was anything but 'unfriendly'; it simply did not cater to Wilson's unswerving views.

Wiseman was wise enough to give Springy carefully crafted accounts of his developing relationship with House. In an explanation he provided for an edition of the House diaries in 1925 he said:

Sir Cecil replied without hesitation that anything should be done in any way that would help the Cause; and that his own position in the matter was not to be considered.

That does not seem to be the way others remember things, although it is interesting for its use of 'the Cause', a term that Wiseman later applied to a piece of extraordinary private enterprise.

Grateful that Guy was being understudied, Springy, seems merely to have asked Wiseman to inform him if a political dimension developed out of the contacts with House. One did, of course—the only one, really, but Springy bit his stiff upper lip when Wiseman showed him his first contribution to Anglo-American relations, a lengthy memorandum for the Imperial War Conference in London that March, summarising American attitudes towards the impending war. Most of it was no more than Springy himself—and Guy—had been advising for months, particularly the counsel that if America did join in the war it would not mean that Washington agreed with the Allies on everything, especially what would happen once peace came. The difference now was that House had shown Wiseman's draft to Wilson, who thought it a 'just statement'.

Weighing up the mutual dependence between Wiseman and House, the historian of American diplomacy, Wilton Fowler, identified a late-onset filial relationship to explain their matching needs. Wiseman had been only eight when his father died and House, the seventh son, had no son of his own. 'In many ways Wiseman was a young House with an Oxbridge accent.' Wiseman, the wise quasi-progeny, provided House with 'flattery, devotion and a protégé's admiration'.

1917. Germany stuck to the *Sussex* Pledge for several months. Wilson never tried to convince Britain to scale down the blockade and Berlin lost patience. Whale Guy was in mid-Atlantic a message on the Main Line told Bernstorff that on 1 February, Germany would begin unrestricted submarine warfare. German hawks were counting on the likelihood that the United States would soon be distracted from the European war by the fruitless campaign in Mexico. The Punitive Expedition had failed to nab Villa and Carranza was swaying and swirling like a matador to evade Wilson's attempts to bring him into line. He poised the sword of righteousness between Washington's shoulders. The sovereign Mexican government of which he was head, said Carranza, would talk no more while American invaders were in its territory. In an unusually decisive response to Carrranza's intransigence, Wilson pulled Pershing's force back across the border. But the Mexicans were not at all grateful. State told House that Carranza seemed more ready than Huerta had been to listen to sales talk from the Germans, responding with hints of what might be on offer: sites for munitions factories, Telefunken stations. U-boat bases? Guy found this ominous when Lansing leaked it to him. There were more Germans in Mexico City than Milwaukee. If they became seriously active down there the Admiralty could lose the Tampico oilfields in the Gulf, more important to the Royal Navy than the wells of Persia or Burma.

On the last day of January Berlin sent a Note to be delivered to State informing the United States that ships approaching the British Isles that *appeared* to be carrying war goods might be sunk without warning. American ships would be given specific routes to follow in European waters but they would be searched. This ran contrary to everything Bernstorff had counselled. Such a restriction on the sacred Freedom was virtually a declaration of war in itself, he told the *Auswärtiges Amt*.

... the president will view this as a slap in the face and war with the United States is unavoidable. The war party here will gain the upper hand and...there will be no end of the war in sight, since the power resources of the United States are very great ...

Although House began a regular exchange of information with Wiseman he was not ready to give up Guy; he timetabled his rendezvous with each of them as carefully as The Barber managed his girlfriends. Guy, of course, could be as flexible with facts as Wiseman, at least when it came to pursuing the goal which, had he only known it, had already been won. He had yet to hear Tumulty describe Wilson's private response to the German submarine ultimatum.

... first, blank amazement; then incredulity that even Germany could be guilty of such perfidy; then gravity and sternness, a sudden grayness of colour, a compression of the lips and the familiar locking of the jaw which always characterized him in moments of supreme resolution. Handing the paper back to me, he said in quiet tones: 'This means war. The break that we have tried so hard to prevent now seems inevitable.'

The wavering compass needle of Allied policy settled on the course it needed America to follow. Faced with unrestricted U-boat attacks and now short of manpower for the offensives needed to overcome Germany, Britain and France wanted the United States to come out fighting. House could see what Wilson did not wish to: Bernstorff was no more influential with the German government than the British and American ambassadors were with theirs. The Germans, he wrote to Wilson on 10 January, were

slippery customers ... with the English, one knows where one is. They may be stubborn and they may be stupid, but they are reliable.

That week, Guy was 'my most interesting visitor'. House summarised the situation as he understood it from Bernstorff, clearly intending for Guy to pass it on.

The Kaiser, the Chancellor [Theodore von Bethmann-Hollweg] and Germany generally desire peace. [Generals] Von Hindenberg and Ludendorff, who control Germany, believe that peace can be secured quicker by the sword than through negotiations. The Chancellor and the Kaiser therefore will not be able to offer such terms as the Allies can accept.

To belittle whatever sources House was using, Guy began to needle him. His masters in London knew about everything going on in Berlin. On his last visit he had seen Room 40 intercepts that showed the Germans believed they could do whatever they liked with no fear that America would enter the war or even break off relations. He had even, he assured House, seen a letter from Bernstorff to the *Auswärtiges Amt* boasting that he had the colonel 'in his pocket'. House never got to see this taunting message for himself but it gave him something to brood about when he boarded the Congressional Special on the last day of January for the most critical conference he had ever had with the president. On 2 February, New York blanketed in freezing snow, Guy took to his bed in Suite 1405. The phone rang at 3.00am.

'Do you know who's speaking?'

'Of course. Beverly.'

'What do you want most in the world?'

It could not be a declaration of war. That would be for Congress to make. But it had to be the next best thing. The talking was over, House assured him. The announcement would be made that afternoon. Guy used his most secret code for a cable Blinker was to decipher personally.

```
The Barber gets his papers at 2.p.m. today stop
I'll probably get soused.
```

Wilson summoned a joint session of Congress. His explanation of why he was at last severing diplomatic relations was entirely based on the maritime issue. Germany had broken all undertakings to allow American ships free passage. The latest declaration put American lives at risk as never before. Even then, though, he stopped short of the brink.

Notwithstanding this unexpected action of the German Government, this sudden and deplorable renunciation of its assurances ... I refuse to believe that it is the intention of the German authorities to do in fact what they have warned us they will feel at liberty to do ... . Only actual overt acts on their part can make me believe it even now.

He did not have long to wait. Within hours the SS *Housatonic*, with a cargo of grain out of Galveston, Texas, was torpedoed off the Scillies. It was done politely and in accordance with the rules by *Kapitän-leutnant* Rose, the cheeky predator of U-53 who six months earlier had popped in and out of New London then picked off five ships before supper.

The Telegram

On the same day that Wilson stood before both Houses of Congress and listed the offences Germany had committed against the nation, Blinker Hall was presented with the first draft of the document that represents the greatest single espionage feat of all time. The Zimmermann Telegram was not the sole—not even the main—reason America finally declared war on Germany; that had become a matter of when rather than whether. But it provided the final spurt of acceleration. Guy's personal contribution to this monumental piece of mischief is—like much else about Telegram—far from clear, even today.

Arthur Zimmermann was the new German foreign secretary. The Telegram was one he sent to Bernstorff on the Main Line to be passed on to the minister in charge of the German Legation in Mexico City, Heinrich von Eckardt. Assuming that the American government would soon open hostilities against the German Empire, the message said, Mexico was to be invited to enter an alliance—that might also include Japan—to launch an invasion of the United States from south of the border. Once the dust of war settled, Germany would ensure that Mexican territories the United States had annexed in the previous century—Texas, New Mexico, Arizona—would be restored.

Although Room 40 was routinely reading the all the Main Line traffic, the Zimmermann Telegram ran to a thousand four and five-letter groups in a code designated 00075 that—as Guy had feared would happen—had been delivered by the submarine *Deutschland*. Blinker's team did not know where to begin.

The message had already raised eyebrows at State when it arrived there on 19 January. Lansing had never been happy about the Germans using the link and a cable of such length was unprecedented. He consulted House, who reminded him that the backstairs exchanges with Berlin were being made at the express wish of the president. The Telegram was sent over to Bernstorff. It did not occur to anyone at State that it was meant to be passed on to somewhere else. It had not occurred to anyone at the *Auswärtiges Amt* that the German legation in Mexico City did not have the key to 00075. Embassy clerks had to convert the Telegram into an older code, 13040, and send it to Mexico by good old Western Union.

By the time Room 40 had begun to grasp the significance of what they were working on, Bernstorff was on his way home. Warned that he might be in for a cool reception he asked State to let him go to Cuba, where pro-German insurgents were on the point of seizing power. Lansing was not inclined to do him any favours. On 15 February, The Barber, his countess and some two hundred diplomatic staff including the paymaster Albert, were bundled on board the Danish liner *Fredrick VIII*. She pulled out of Hoboken to a defiant wail of sirens from the laid-up German ships whose crews had been ordered to get them ready to move. When war was declared they were to use what coal they had to power a Valkyrie ride out to sea. If the Americans tried to prevent them they must scuttle and block the harbour entrance. Alas for *Götterdämerung* on the Hudson, the engines, idle for months, needed so much attention that the plan had to be changed to wrecking the machinery so the vessels would be useless as prizes.

By early February, Room 40 knew what the Zimmermann message was offering the Mexicans. If, as now seemed likely, the United States declared war on Germany, the proposals would only be of incidental interest. But if Wilson kept putting off the critical moment the Telegram could be vital. The challenge was to find a way of putting it into play without letting the Americans know that the British had been reading their mail. The solution lay with the Western Union version that had been sent directly from the embassy coderoom.

Blinker to Guy, 5 February 1917:

Essential to try and get copies of all telegrams from German Embassy Washington to German Minister Mexico since Jan 18th. If procurable wire in original to me.

The recently replaced chargé d'affaires at the British Legation in Mexico City, Thomas Hohler, had been able to buy copies of a few German messages from local telegraph office clerks. As Hohler told the story years later, the methods involved a currency forger, an honest printer, a mistaken arrest, an understanding with the police and a grateful relative of the forger who happened to work in the telegraph office. It was a plot worthy of Italian opera and just improbable enough to be true. Guy, briefed Hohler's replacement, Edward Thurstan, to try it again. Perhaps it was also true that Guy had no idea of the content of the telegram he was soon able to pass on to Blinker. His surprise may even have been genuine when, eventually, House tipped him off about the sensational content of the deciphered text before it was shown to the president.

Nearly four weeks passed between the arrival of the original Telegram in Room 40 and word of it reaching Washington. As soon as he had an inkling of its significance Blinker went to the Foreign Secretary. Balfour knew and trusted both Hall and Guy. He left Hall to work out an effective way of getting Zimmermann's proposal into American hands without any British fingerprints on it while he convinced the War Cabinet that this was the development that would nudge Wilson into taking the plunge.

Hall took the risk of confiding in Ambassador Page, whom Wilson still mistrusted as a war advocate. Page agreed to help fudge the Telegram's origin. He cabled Washington that the British were handing over the information gathered in Mexico 'in order that our government make be able without delay to make such disposition as may be necessary in view of the threatened invasion of our territory'.

But Lansing was worried about wily British ways. He had the original German message to Mexico retrieved from Western Union and sent to Page. Blinker invited Page to nominate an American citizen to decode the message for himself. Page sent his deputy, Eddie Bell, to take the Western Union form to Room 40 where he was given the cypher key and a German-English dictionary. It took Bell several hours to be satisfied but finally he said, 'That's torn it!' He meant Wilson's last hope for peace.

As soon as he heard what was going on at the American end Guy let Blinker know, adding a request for something he and Rathom could exploit.

Gaunt to Hall, 24 February:

Aaron has got hold of a cable to Barber directing him in the event of a break at once to conclude an alliance with Mexico. This information will most likely become public property by Wednesday morning. Can you send me any information which would make information fuller and more decisive.

Wilson's first reaction when Lansing showed him the Telegram was that it must be a fake—presumably a British one. Lansing pointed out that the message passed on to Mexico by Western Union must have been received on the Main Line at the time Bernstorff's efforts to fend off the submarine offensive and, supposedly, get his government to see reason were at their most intensive. 'Good Lord!' said Wilson. It seemed never to have occurred to him that the cable link he had offered the Germans might be used for mischief. 'Good Lord!' he said, again and again.

Hall to Gaunt, 27 February:

Germany guarantees assistance to Mexico if they will reconquer Texas, New Mexico and Arizona. Also proposes alliance with Mexico to make war together. Do not use this till Aaron announces it, premature exposure fatal. *Alone* I did it.

Blinker was using *Alone* in the Minnie Gaunt sense. *Alone* except for the tireless cryptologists who squeezed meaning out of the German ciphers. *Alone* but for the couriers and pilferers who got the material to where it was needed and a few more helpers on both sides of the Atlantic who ensured that the Telegram was eventually accepted as authentic. Guy fell into more than one of those categories, even if he might not always have been aware of the role he was playing.

On the evening of 28 February Guy reported to Hall, again on the basis of a tip-off from House, that Lansing was about to hand a version of the text to Associated Press. Hall obviously wondered if the exuberance of his earlier message had been misplaced. On 1 March he cabled:

Imperative that knowledge of this affair should never be traced to British source.

That was too late for anyone capable of associating cause and effect. On the day the *Washington Star* filled its front page with the Zimmermann revelations an article inside headlined

SYSTEM OF SPYING IN THE BIG CITIES
'Intelligence officers' of foreign nations are busy

The writer likened what was going on to a sporting contest but concluded

> The British intelligence system is believed to be the finest thing of its kind ever put into operation in the world. It is known to be in charge of Captain Guy Gaunt. R. N., the youngest captain in the British navy, an Australian, who is as much at home in the country houses of Long Island as he is in Washington. Captain Gaunt is described by those who know him as the ideal of the romantic type of modern intelligence officer, a man of indomitable energy, to whom could possibly be applied the old fashioned detective phrase, 'He never sleeps'.

With what cover he had enjoyed now completely peeled away it would have been too risky for Guy to go back into the shadows. The slick suits stayed in the Biltmore closet; the Browning was passed to Thwaites. The Admiralty created a new role for him: Naval Liaison Officer to the United States. He became Commodore Gaunt, three of his captain's rings welded into a single gold band as broad as a Veuve Clicquot label, the fourth left to represent the first rung of the admiralship ladder. In the Royal Navy commodore was more an appointment than a rank; if he did not move up to rear admiral he would revert to captain when he left his post. But the title had a particular resonance for Americans; their greatest naval heroes—John Paul Jones, Matthew Perry, George Dewey—all won their fame as commodores.

Rathom, manic with excitement, came down and they mapped out an onslaught of ingenious disinformation to suggest how the key to the Telegram might have been obtained. The captain of *Deutschland* had been mugged on Broadway. The code book had been captured in Brussels by renegade soldiers who sold it to State for a fortune. Countess Bernstorff had been blackmailed by a lover. It gave them an amusing few hours but Guy saw that he might have trouble keeping Rathom's imagination within acceptable boundaries.

Even with headlines blazing around the country—'Prussian Invasion

Plot' was a favourite— even with four American ships torpedoed in the ensuing days, Wilson clung to the hope that war might still be averted. But the Telegram did everything the British wanted and more. Arcane arguments over freedom of the seas might never have aroused the vast landbound masses. Away from the eastern seaboard indignation over torpedoed ships was short-lived. Even the *Lusitania* outrage faded as months passed. But German-Mexican armies pouring over the border to snatch back Texas was a threat that everyone with their feet on United States territory could understand. Popular indignation bounded ahead of presidential indecision.

Wilson's continuing hesitation to go beyond cutting diplomatic ties revitalised the German-American press which fiercely denounced the Telegram as a forgery. They and the politically aggressive Irish organisations insisted it must be a plant by British agents. Nor were all of Guy's influential friends and contacts convinced. On 2 March he was invited to dinner by the Round Table, a powerful but circumspect group of lawyers, industrialists, bankers and political heavyweights to whom the *Washington Star* article would have come as no surprise. Many of them would have been aware that a report from army intelligence agents in Europe, filed a few weeks earlier, said that it was 'generally understood' that

> the principal contre-espionage work in America has been directly [sic] by the British Naval Attaché, and, we believe, to a certain extent through the medium of some of the representatives of J. P. Morgan and Company.

Anticipating a warm reception from these distinguished co-belligerents to be, Guy went in full glittering fig, *aiguillettes* and all, since he was still the attaché, the white enamel Maltese asterisk of the CMG on its ribbon around his neck. Eighteen of the thirty Round Table members turned up. Nearly all of them were pro-British; most had already decided that America could not stay out of the war much longer, but they did not like being taken for suckers. Not one was ready to accept the Telegram as genuine; it had to be a trick and the most likely trickster was Guy. 'After dinner they all drew their chairs up around the fire and went for me,' he told Blinker.

The attack was led by Joseph Choate, a former ambassador to Britain, and Elihu Root, who had been Theodore Roosevelt's secretary of state. Choate declared outright that the Telegram must be a forgery. Root demanded to know what part Guy had played in producing it. On the spot and afraid of dropping even a hint of British intrigues, Guy returned fire, asking his inquisitors why they did not question their president and secretary of state rather than an innocent bystander like himself ;but it was an unpleasant experience which suggested how differently things might have turned out had not the following day Zimmermann himself admitted that the Telegram was the real thing.

Zimmermann assumed the German codes had been cracked by the Americans. If the United States decided to prove the Telegram by releasing more messages the full range of German duplicity would be revealed. Happily for Guy the Zimmermann admission came just after Viereck 'and all the rest of the inkslingers got their yarn into the papers pointing out how obviously it was a British fake'. For Guy this devastating embarrassment for the German propagandists was a neat demonstration of the nasty German term *schadenfreude*. For Viereck, it was an enduring reminder of the English proverb about revenge being a dish best eaten cold. He was not finished with Guy.

In the course of their acrimonious falling out years later, Wiseman claimed that Guy had 'forgotten which service he belonged to'. That was rather more true of himself. Most of what Guy did in 1914 and 1915 was what the SSB ought to have been doing. Most of what Wiseman did ought to have been done by the diplomatic service. Any doubt about the extent to which the SSB depended on the naval intelligence operation personified in Guy would seem to be settled by the grovelling letter C wrote to Blinker in 1917 to congratulate him on his knighthood. The salutation was 'My Dear Chief' and C, still a captain, referred to himself as 'one of your "lieutenants"'.

For all the time he spent running clandestine operations Guy had never neglected his serious naval work. Now there was more of it than ever. He barely noticed that it was a springtime of conspiracies. Some were still directed at the enemy; others bubbled up among the co-belligerents. Perhaps because he had been shut out of the Zimmermann caper—Blinker did not mention the Telegram to C until the navy's ownership of the project

217

was secure—Wiseman intensified his courtship of House to the point that the British government was induced, in effect, to openly disown its own ambassador. The Americans merely went back to ignoring theirs. A timely warning from Voska meant that the Port Authority got armed guards on board the interned German ships in time to limit the sabotage. Most of the liners were to be converted into transports for the American army that would—surely?—soon be heading for France. Actually, the less glamorous freighters were needed more badly as so many British ships were being sunk. In early 1917 Britain wanted material more than manpower; the empire was still good for gunfodder.

The Admiralty, still fearful that another encounter like Jutland could lose the war in an afternoon, had begun to drop heavy hints about the dozen American dreadnoughts that had survived all Congressional efforts to torpedo Teddy Roosevelt's dream of making the United States a sea power to equal Britain. With a few of those added to the Grand Fleet the Germans would be irremediably outgunned. It also had a greedy eye on the smaller, nippier cruisers to take on U-boats. This was not necessarily what the president wanted to hear from the British Naval Liason Officer when Guy had a chance to discreetly raise the matter. Wilson had no greater understanding of the details of sea warfare than of the battlefield but he knew that Britain had 5,360 warships and the United States 223. Why could the British not use that powerful fleet of theirs to escort merchantmen? His admirals, however, understood. All navies conformed to the big-ship doctrine: an immutable numbers game. As long as the Royal Navy could deploy more dreadnoughts than the Imperial Navy the Germans would not dare to confront them. Detaching even a few heavy ships for other tasks would be an unacceptable risk. What the Americans found strange was that the British did not do more to provoke an encounter, lure the Germans out.

Ambassador Page persuaded Navy to send someone across to discuss how the two fleets might work together: Rear Admiral William Sims, a technocrat who, it was said, taught the navy how to shoot. If he wanted to do the same for the Royal Navy there was plenty of scope. In every engagement so far German gunnery had been superior. Sims admired the Royal Navy which was not the case with all his fellow officers, some of whom still nourished the spirit of 1812. 'Don't let the British pull the wool over your eyes', the chief of naval operations, Rear Admiral William Benson, warned him. 'It is none of our business pulling their chestnuts out of the fire. We would as soon fight the British as the Germans.'

Sims felt he should make the crossing on an American ship but flying the flag was all that the one he chose had going for her. Earlier in the century the SS *New York* of the American Line had been a marvel of elegance; now she was so worn-out that her owners had done away with first class: the choice was second class or steerage. Once Guy had put Sims on board on 6 April he cabled Blinker that second-class passenger Mr S W Davidson was really the admiral they were expecting and Mr D J Richardson, with whom Sims was compelled to share a cabin, was his assistant, Commander John Babcock.

Great secrecy has been maintained here. Request landing facilities and all courtesy shown. I am anxious he send back a glowing report of his reception as he represents the pro-English party in the US Navy Department and it will strengthen them.

On board the *New York* the American officers did their best to pass for civilians. The ship's captain, who did know who they were, locked a tin despatch box containing their documents in his safe. They brought no uniforms with them but a cabin steward reported that initials embroidered on the men's pyjamas did not match their names. A crewman who had served under Sims recognised him. Both men were sworn to silence. But when, in mid-Atlantic, a wireless message reported that the president had at last gone before Congress and asked for a declaration of war the need for secrecy evaporated.

Guy was embarrassed when the landing facilities and courtesies were not what he had hoped for. Entering the Mersey, the *New York* struck a mine. Welcome to the war. Damage was slight but passengers were ordered into the boats. An excursion steamer returning from the Isle of Man changed course to pick them up. On board it, Sims realised he had left the tin box packed with details on the navy's wartime dispositions in the lifeboat. He yelled for it to be retrieved but it was the day after the Easter Bank Holiday and, as Sims's biographer Elton Morison explained, 'no one in the steamer was quite sober'.

... a sailor told Sims to 'stow his bloody lip' or be put back in the lifeboat. Lip was stowed and the despatch box was returned later by a thoughtful passenger.

Lance's chilly idyll at Scapa came to an end in May 1917 when, as a scratchy iron nib noted in his record, the Admiralty sent him 'to assist Commodore Gaunt at Washington USA'. This was an extraordinary development. It may have been brought about by the benign hand of Ernest or Guy himself might have applied some interest while he was in London at the beginning of the year. If so, he came to regret it. Minnie would surely have been in touch with Lance but Guy's account of this time makes no reference to him. Neither does Lance mention Guy in his. He records his appointment as Assistant Naval Liaison Officer without bothering to mention that the Liason Officer he was meant to assist was his more famous brother. A recollection that did not fade was that for the duration of the posting he was made a lieutenant-commander. This was a new rank to replace senior lieutenant. It was still marked by two-and-a half rings, but in the chronically stratified confines of the navy its real value was that the holder would be addressed as 'commander'.

Guy certainly needed some help. The Navy department and various shipbuilders demanded most of his time. The Admiralty is impatient to know how many American cruisers and destroyers are being readied to hunt submarines and how soon they would get to sea. The German open season on shipping was catastrophic. In the first three months of the campaign U-boats sank 470 ocean-going merchant ships: one in four freighters leaving British harbours would not return. Unsettling questions were being raised about whether American troops could be lost before they reached France. In earlier years the Allies had not been worried about America's unreadiness to fight. Then what they needed had been guns and ammunition; now it was gunfodder.

Rathom rampant

The United States in the war at last, forests of flags and the blare of Sousa bands everywhere was too much for Rathom. He flipped out of control. Until then Guy had kept him in hand like a steeplechaser prone to bolting, constantly emphasising that nothing the *Journal* published must be traceable to him or Voska, checking to see that its heavily embroidered stories were only a few strides ahead of the facts. Rathom accepted the strictures Guy imposed while America was neutral but now he wanted the world to know what he had achieved. Understandable, really. There could be no doubting the effect of the two year-long catalogue of German crimes and misdemeanours recorded in hundreds of *Journal* news items that had been spread far beyond by the *New York Times* and other client papers. In the 1930s, well before crossfire broke out over who had done most to ruin Germany's image, the first American historian to assess the events, Horace Peterson, wrote

> It is useless to criticise Great Britain for the propaganda—for spreading falsehoods and exaggerated interpretations of their own and their enemies' actions ... the United States would have done the same.

He named the man most responsible: Guy Gaunt. That propaganda, together with the determined counter espionage campaign that exposed Dr Albert, the malevolent Teutonic Twins, the Dark Invader, Alphabet Armstrong and the clumsy German efforts to exploit the *Lusitania* events was almost entirely the work of No 1's threesome. Even with the main objective achieved, two of them preferred the lid to stay firmly in place on their mischief; Guy because of sensitivity over his diplomatic status, Voska because the Little People were still working towards the destruction of the Austro-Hungarian Empire from within. But there was no holding Rathom. The best the others could hope for was that no one would believe the wild claims he now began to spout. But of course they did.

Before radio and television, the best opportunities for a personal appearance were offered by the flourishing public lecture circuit or banquet audiences. Rathom went both ways. In June he made his debut before a congenial after-dinner crowd at the Empire Club in Toronto, opening with a rousing account of the dangers he had faced from dastardly German agents. 'In spite of the fact that the *Journal* was guarded night and day the front of our entire building was blown out'. It was true there had been an unexplained 'fire and explosion' on the third floor of the Providence office back in March 1916 that caused a mere $3,000 damage. At the time the paper disposed of it in five paragraphs. Rathom inflated the event into a German attempt on his life. He then hit full stride with an enthralling description of the *Journal* as a hub of the Allied war effort, plucking coded messages from Sayville out of the ether with its own wireless receivers, marshalling an army of secret agents, infiltrating Teuton embassies and consulates, foiling sabotage plots. Respecting Guy's stricture on mentioning him or Voska freed him of any need to share the glory. *Journal* revelations, he boasted, had been entirely responsible for the expulsion of Ambassador Dumba and the German attachés. Even the Zimmermann Telegram. He worked up a particularly entertaining version of the hearts-on-the-box episode in the Austrian consulate. Instead of Herr von Nuber, of whom no one had heard, he put the crayon in the hand of a far better target for ridicule, the villainous Papen: 'a man with a weakness... for beauty and talent in feminine form'. But of the many fantasies with which he enthralled his listeners the most compelling was a version of the Albert briefcase saga. As though the true story was not gripping enough, Rathom pitched it to his listeners like a scenario for the one-reeler melodramas the early movie studios were beginning to make.

Albert was followed into a shop by one of 'our' operatives who watched him order an elegant briefcase and sketch out the monogram to be inscribed on the lockplate. Having memorised the design, the 'tail' buys an identical satchel and has it replicated by another engraver. On the El another Rathom agent creates a disturbance. While Albert's attention is distracted the briefcases are switched. Not until days later does Albert open his to find it stuffed with old newspapers.

Someone somewhere had already become curious about the immoderate entry Rathom submitted for the 1912 edition of *Who's Who*. An investigator examined each detail and provided a devastating deconstruction that left virtually nothing standing, except his title as editor and general manager of the *Journal*.

Guy never seemed to doubt Rathom's claim to be Australian and to have gone to Scotch College and Harrow. But no John Revelstoke Rathom ever attended those schools. If Rathom had, as he told *Who's Who*, been born in Melbourne on 4 July 1868 the event went unrecorded there or anywhere else in Australia. Nor had the *Argus* sent anyone of that name to report the campaign in the Sudan (when, by his own account, Rathom would have been eighteen). Thus, the vivid description he often delivered of watching General Gordon's head roll down the stairs at Khartoum after the dervishes had lopped it off was open to question. Neither had two epic explorations in which he claimed to have participated, one to New Guinea and the other to Alaska, ever taken place.

The first demolition job on Rathom was an anonymous report drawn up in 1914 by, to judge by the inclusion of sworn statements from most of the sources, an attorney; although perhaps a superior kind of gumshoe. It is among the private papers of Adolph Ochs in the New York Public Library. Ochs was the owner of the *New York Times* when it regularly reprinted the rabid *Journal* stories that helped lift the daily sale from 230,000 in 1914 to 368,500 by the end of the war. The report was, presumably, available to him all the time his paper was dealing with Rathom and afterwards when both of them were directors of the Associated Press, an organisation devoted to accuracy and objectivity. It is a marvellous guide to how to succeed in journalism as liar, thief and imposter. And when it was written Rathom was only halfway through his project of self-renewal.

The first confirmed sighting of Rathom was in Victoria, British Colombia, in 1881 when—by his reckoning—he would have been twenty-one. He told people he had come from Australia but no Rathom was to be found in landing registers. 'Having an engaging personality, abundant energy and a brilliant pen,' the anonymous investigator reported, 'Rathom found employment on *The Colonist* where he left a lasting impression. 'About as unscrupulous and unreliable as anyone I ever met,' said *The Colonist*'s owner, remembering a libel suit he had been left to settle. Rathom developed a risky sideline in putting together exposés of gambling dens and bordellos and demanding money for keeping them out of print. 'He was a smooth article,' one of his targets recalled. 'And while he did not act like a regular grafter he got the money just the same.'

Life on a weekly newspaper left time for a second job as part-time secretary to the mayor of Victoria on whose bank account Rathom regularly forged cheques. Hustled out of town, he repeated this pattern of swindling and shady journalism on papers in Oregon and Washington state for three years. In his own account of this time, Rathom confirmed the main recollection retained by his badly misused first wife, Mary De Veulle, that he had a 'very fertile imagination'. He said he had spent those years in the Chinese navy.

One *Who's Who* entry was true in part. He did work for the *San Francisco Examiner* and became, briefly, its star reporter, despite borrowing money all around the newsroom and never paying it back. The paper did, as he claimed, send him to Cuba to cover the war with Spain that followed the sinking of the USS *Maine*. But, rather than being badly wounded, as he related, he went down with fever as soon as he arrived and never filed a story. According to managing editor George Fitch he 'rendered very little service but spent much money for which he did not account and claimed most of it had burned up in a fire'. Even so he was kept on.. 'In view of his marked ability and his offer to make restitution we overlooked it,' Young explained. 'But he never did repay the money.' The *Examiner* did not, however, send Rathom to cover the Boer War, as he said it had done and thus a deep friendship with Lord Kitchener to which he would often refer remained unverified.

What the *Examiner* could not overlook was finding that it had to carry stories about its chief reporter's scandalous love life. Rathom's mistress, Florence Mildred Campbell, tried to consolidate her position by posting herself a box of poisoned chocolates made to look as though it had been sent by Mrs Rathom. The plot was too amateurish for the police to take seriously but it was reported in other San Francisco papers and the *Examiner* had to follow. Rathom left town in a hurry—with Florence.

From then on it was, surprisingly, all uphill. In Chicago, he got a job on the *Record-Herald* where, according to the biography he put on file at the Rhode Island Historical Society, he was 'in charge of the Iroquois Theatre disaster for his newspaper'. The 'lead' of that story, consisting of several thousand words written under pressure in three hours, is one of the classics of American newspaper history.

There could be a kernel of truth in that boast, although the feat does not seem to have made an impression on American newspaper historians. Rathom's job was on the copy desk, writing headlines and marking up typefaces. But the theatre fire was the city's biggest story for years; more than six hundred people died. Piecing together copy from the army of reporters and barely literate legmen out on the street would call for real journalistic skills and if Rathom had pulled it off he could expect a reward.

Certainly, something got him promoted to the more glamorous

job of feature writer. Better paid, too, although he and Florence made regular moonlight flits to avoid paying the rent, working their way along the converted brownstones on one side of Superior Street where the investigator found a string of disgruntled landlords. At the final lodgings they sold the furniture to buy railroad tickets to Rhode Island, where they arrived with not much more than Rathom's colourful CV and a sheaf of equally fake clippings.

The owners of the *Journal* had always been ready to take a chance. They tried broadcasting before there was wireless. A busker with a megaphone stood at a second floor window and shouted out sports items from the AP wire, stopping short of the results. With a crowd assembled in the street, newsboys moved in with papers inky from the press carrying final scores. Soon Rathom was managing editor and the paper was on the way to becoming the most profitable in the country after the *New York Times*. He and Florence got married before his divorce from Mary, but no one would imagine they were bigamists. Outwardly they were as respectable a couple as any in New England. She went regularly to church; Rathom became a Boy Scout commissioner.

For the 175th anniversary of its founding, the *Journal* gave its reporters the assignment of unearthing the real Rathom. An article headlined 'Fiction Writer', concluded that the illustrious editor had been 'a shameless show-boater, and a liar with a fantastic imagination'. An Australian genealogical researcher provided 'circumstantial but strong' evidence that Rathom was the son of Judah Moss Solomon of East Melbourne and his wife Adele. Even if that had been so, why, when and how he left Australia could not be explained.

Rathom eventually ran into trouble when the popular magazine *World's Work*—owned by Ambassador Page and edited by his son Arthur—commissioned a series of articles about his exploits. 'More thrilling than fiction,' the standfirst to the opening instalment read, 'it is the modestly told story of a brave editor and resourceful reporters who beat the Germans at their own game.'

The Secret Service, sensitive about its belated debut into counter-espionage, resented being written out of the script. Until then the federal agencies and various police forces that, once aroused, had done plenty to thwart the Teutons were merely irritated by what they heard of Rathom's bragging. Speeches were ephemeral, reported only in local newspapers and usually ignored by the AP. This was different. Articles in a national magazine would become an early draft of history with their contribution ignored. The Bureau of Investigation offered Arthur Page the true story of Rathom's wartime activities—or as much as it knew about them—and after the opening instalment, which was an entirely fabricated account of a bomb planted at the *Journal* by the German military attaché that 'almost achieved its purpose'—the series was cancelled. Rathom vainglorious episodes were replaced by copy produced by *World's Work* staffers and introduced with a note on quality control.

By courtesy of the Bureau of Investigation of the Department of Justice the facts and documents of this narrative have been verified.

If House had not been off in Paris with the president, sorting out the postwar world, he could have ensured that matters stopped there. But the Attorney General, Thomas Watt Gregory, whose ruthless Sedition Act had stifled any lingering opposition to the war, threatened to haul Rathom before a federal grand jury. To avoid being examined under oath Rathom agreed to write a letter admitting that many of his anecdotes were exaggerated or invented.

> ... sources of information have given us valuable knowledge of a great many matters ... we have felt compelled to cover them up by intentionally suggesting sources which did not actually exist.

Even that ignominious confession need not have surfaced. Rathom persuaded Gregory not to make it public if he promised to shut up and behave himself. That was never going to happen. In 1920 the *Journal* stirred up indignation over a homosexual scandal in Newport involving young sailors. Rathom wrote an editorial accusing Franklin Roosevelt, who was still effectively running the navy, of neglecting the men's welfare. Roosevelt had been one of the trio's best friends and had fond memories of their mischievous machinations. But that was war and this was politics. Rathom's embarrassing admission to the Attorney General was leaked, to the delight of headline writers everywhere except at the *Journal*. Said *The Nation*:

> The vaunted exploits of his editors and reporters he has now admitted were myths, and what little information he did have as the basis for his

sensations was supplied by British secret agents whose tool he was, and who used him for their own purposes.

Well, yes. And vice versa. In Rathom's life fantasy prevailed over fact and other men's headlines left him unscathed. He remained the *Journal's* editor until he died in 1923 and an effusive obituary in *Time* magazine ticked off all his fictional career milestones without questioning a single one.

Balfour decided to see for himself how America planned to go to war. It was a testing experience but he pulled it off, impressing powerbrokers and public meetings around the United States with respect for the American viewpoint and gratitude for what Britain was about to receive in the way of reinforcements. The visit also gave House the opportunity to ensure a role for his protégé in the haphazard transatlantic alliance being pulled together. As Wiseman explained:

> Colonel House arranged that Balfour should cable in a special British Government code direct to me in New York, and that I should make it my chief duty to attend to these cables and bring them immediately to Colonel House, who could telephone them over a private wire to the State Department or to President Wilson. In this way Balfour, speaking for the British Government, could get an answer from President Wilson, if necessary, within a few hours. This would have been utterly impossible had the communications gone through ordinary channels.

Thus, House, whom Wiseman had deceived into believing that he was linked to the highest level of the British government, stepped in to validate the equally dubious claim Wiseman made to his superiors of having a vital connection with the United States. In this way House got the British cabinet back on line. Balfour saw for himself that Springy had been bounced out of the game and that Wilson scorned anything that came through Page. He may have thought it was time the Foreign Office got something for the money it was paying out for the SSB but it was most likely a matter of what America wanted America got.

House was relieved, as his diary for 23 May said, that the visit had given young Sir William a splendid 'Boost'.

> They found out how much I think of him and how much I trust both his integrity and ability, and they reciprocated by following my lead. I

am looking forward to Wiseman's future career in English politics. I should like to see him go far.

Alas, the *protégé* was already shaping his future towards private profit rather than public life, although the time Wiseman spent at Kuhn, Loeb was useful in more ways than one. The firm's senior partner, Jacob Schiff, was especially anxious to see the war end: his two brothers were bankers in Germany and he feared for their future. He loathed the Czarist regime for its treatment of Jews; he had largely raised the money that allowed Japan to go to war against Russia in 1908. While Guy's operation had to scrape along on handouts from Springy's petty cash, Schiff gave Wiseman $75,000 to subsidise anti-German propaganda for which, by then, there was little need.

House, though, did not abandon one attachment simply because he had acquired another. He remembered the gratitude he felt for Guy and told Balfour he wanted

to express my high regard and appreciation of Captain Gaunt. I doubt whether you can realize the great service he has rendered our two countries. His outlook is so broad and he is so self-contained and fair-minded that I have been able to go to him at all times to discuss, very much as I would with you, the problems that have arisen.

Guy was not particularly disturbed to discover how firmly Wiseman was digging himself into the political relationship between Britain and America. The success of his own work in exposing German influence in America had been recognised, if discreetly. He had done as much as he could to ensure that Britain got all the help possible from American industry and, when the time came, to bring the United States into the war. He was prepared to leave Wiseman to the business of making himself indispensable to the main players as though he was the only second in a sparring match, rushing from corner to corner to urge one man on or cool the other down. There were other contenders for his attention. One was brother Lance, now on his way over to the United States; another was Leon Trotsky.

The overthrow of Czar Nicholas II in the February Revolution of 1917 meant little to Guy until he was told that on 27 March an important Russian revolutionary had sailed from New York in the SS *Kristianiafjord*.

Wiseman's Department of Transport, which had taken over surveillance of outgoing passenger lists, knew that Mr and Mrs Trotsky and five comrades had embarked but Guy thought he had better make sure that letting them go was the right thing. He supposed that Trotsky was a scheming Bolshevik like the rest of the unruly gang in the Flatiron whom he mistrusted more than ever since Black Tom, and better kept under surveillance than left to roam the world causing mischief.

Trotsky was not a Bolshevik at that time but the distinction was lost on Guy. He had found his way to New York after being released from prison in Spain, living in Queens and working as an electrician at the Fox film studios in Fort Lee, New Jersey. Guy signalled Halifax to intercept the ship and lift the party off. Ensuing moves gave the first indication that he and Wiseman might not always be steering by the same star.

Wiseman used the Schiff donation to hire some extra help. One new outworker was Casimir Pilenas, a freelance snitch whose previous employees included the Czarist secret police and Scotland Yard. Another was a journeyman spy currently known as Sidney Reilly who was roosting among the Flatiron Russians. Once the Bolsheviks had picked up momentum Reilly was sent to Russia as an agent for the SSB. He and a former consular service officer, Bruce Lockhart, also recruited by C, shared many adventures, some of which are better documented than others they subsequently described.

According to Pilenas, Trotsky and friends were taking a large amount of gold to Russia that had been provided by Jacob Schiff to help keep Czarist factions from regaining power. The naval party that boarded the *Kristianiafjord* found no gold among the Trotskyites, not even much money, but Guy asked for the Russians to be held in Canada until he got some instructions from Blinker. A month later a man dressed like a country squire turned up in Halifax with credentials effective enough to arrange their release. Provided with fresh documentation and travel expenses they were sent on their way, Trotsky to the epochal partnership with his significant other, Vladimir Ilyich Lenin.

The mysterious stranger was Major Claude Marjoribanks Dansey. He was controlled not by C or Blinker Hall but by Vernon Kell, who had managed to keep a murky stretch of no-man's-land between the SSB and his War Office operation. The new relationship with America stirred up bareknuckled competition among the London intelligence industry for a new franchise to operate there. Dansey, who had made a brief appearance in the United States with the Balfour mission, was Kell's nominee to replace Wiseman. Then a well-turned out forty-seven, Dansey had retired from the army after a colourful career, re-enlisting when war broke out. Between times he had been secretary of the Sleepy Hollow Country Club on Long Island, which Kell considered suitable grounding for a spymaster since he would have made the acquaintance of many influential Americans.

It seemed at the time that Dansey had been ordered to intervene in the Trotsky affair to embarrass Wiseman and therefore the SSB. But according to his account, released from the Foreign Office archives in 2001, he acted to free the Russian party on his own initiative in order to spare London the embarrassment of a protest from the new Russian government. And, perhaps, to score a point over the SSB. Either way, the chain reaction was to ripple through the century. Had Trotsky not got back to Russia he would never have teamed up with Lenin; there might never have been a Bolshevik revolution, a Soviet Union, a Comintern, an Uncle Joe Stalin, Communist China or the Cold War. Even if decades of turmoil and slaughter could be traced to Dansey's intervention it did not prevent him from going on to become deputy director of MI6 for most of World War Two. The confusion Guy felt over this episode endures. Today's internet is clogged with suggestions from many a foam-flecked keyboard that a pile of Schiff gold was awaiting Trotsky somewhere along the way. More soundly, the question remains of why Wiseman had been indifferent to his departure from the United States.

By the middle of 1917 relations between Springy, Wiseman, the Foreign Office, the SSB and Blinker's DNI had become so entangled that Wiseman and Thwaites went over to London to unravel them. Thwaites had originally understood he was to take his orders from 'a department of the navy' in the person of Guy but recently some had been coming from other directions. The usual Whitehall medley of nods, winks and slight adjustments of the old school tie ensued. The SSB was under attack from the army which wanted all intelligence matters brought under its control. The Directorate of Military Operations had already captured Kell's internal security service, the incipient MI5, and designated it MO5 (g). The generals preferred to keep civilians under control, including unruly men in suits with whimsical notions about foreign politics or hearts-and-minds. What they wanted from spies was hard information about troop movements, supplies and ammunition. Around C the only uniforms were worn by the lady driver of the somewhat unpatriotic Mercedes tourer he had acquired and the chef seconded to the SSB canteen from the Savoy Hotel.

Under pressure from the War Office, C took on a new hand—Colonel Dansey. And a new perspective. Balfour had received strong hints from both House and Lansing that while earlier activities on the part of certain British representatives had been understandable, now the two countries were marching in step one spying on the other seemed to be...not quite cricket. Rather than raise the level of intelligence gathering in the United States, Britain ought not be running a spy shop there at all. Thwaites was sent back to New York as the British Provost Marshal, a strange appointment in a place where there was no British jurisdiction and only a handful of British servicemen.

While Balfour was still in America he asked Cabinet to find a replacement for Springy, someone who could shake out the tangle of Allied purchasing commissions, loan negotiators and other supplicants surging around Washington, duplicating each other's work and confusing the Americans. He was appalled to be told that after a token attempt to choose a new ambassador his fellow ministers had decided to leave Springy in post and send an emissary of a totally different kind at the head of a British War Mission, a national figure who would personify British energy and resolve. This was Lord Northcliffe, the Rupert Murdoch of his day: owner not only of *The Times* but, at the other end of the spectrum of influence, the popular and populist *Daily Mail*, a paper written—as Balfour sneered—by office boys for office boys but selling a million copies a day.

Springy, shut out but not shut up, was withering when he heard. Northcliffe, he informed the Foreign Office, would be seen as a 'rigorous hustler and loud-voiced propagandist; one who will tell them with utmost emphasis not merely what the Allies would like to see done but what America ought to do'. Wiseman by contrast was delighted. The key Northcliffe man in the United States, Willert of *The Times* was now one of his SSB helpers and when Northcliffe arrived in New York only Willert was there to greet him. Taking the absence of the ambassador as a diplomatic snub, Northcliffe at first threatened to stay on the ship and go back home.

Then he changed his mind and went to a hotel where he could use several telephones at once. His first call was to Guy, who bustled around in uniform to present Springy's apologies. He had not gone up, nor sent anyone from the embassy, because he assumed the arrival was a secret. That would have been a less transparent excuse if the usual horde of shipping reporters had not been waiting and been given an expansive explanation from its master of what the Mission intended to do. Willert, thought Guy was a 'thick-skinned bouncing fellow'—useful attributes, actually, when dealing with a fully accredited bully like Northcliffe. He remembered him emerging from the meeting looking 'disconcertingly amused'. Thin-skinned Willert was not to know that Guy and Northcliffe were well-disposed towards each other from a meeting in France a couple of months earlier when they were visiting the front at the same time. Northcliffe also wanted to talk to Wiseman. Willert tracked him down at Kuhn, Loeb.

The British deputations and delegations Northcliffe was supposed to be disentangling and the American government departments he needed to deal with were all in Washington but because of Springy's attitude he refused to go there except for an audience with the president. Wiseman and Willert arranged meetings in New York with all the influential Americans they could find and with whom, according to Willert, Northcliffe was

voluble and superficially frank, Napoleonic, domineering, downright in question but genial ... The more important people were entertained at heavy lunches washed down by a sweet white wine.

The rest of the Mission, most of them from the *Daily Mail*, were still on the way over so Wiseman loaned Northcliffe his own secretary from the Department of Transport. He arranged for Northcliffe to use the Foreign Office code and was thus able to read all his messages. After talking to Wilson, Northcliffe wrote a report for Lloyd George. Before it was sent Wiseman showed it to House. 'Northcliffe does not realise,' said a House diary entry, 'how he is being moved on the chessboard and how carefully he is being watched to keep him from making mistakes.' All unaware, Northcliffe was soon describing Wiseman as 'one of our most valuable people here'. Historian Wilton Fowler, a less impressionable American, saw Wiseman's role as 'a sort of chaperone' on behalf of the wily colonel.

The two were soon closer than ever, geographically. Wiseman took a second-floor apartment in the building on East 53rd Street. He told the Foreign Office:

> I am thus able to see him several times a day and we are working together even more closely than previously. As you know he has a private telephone to the State Department and the White House, so I could not be in closer touch if I were in Washington.

The closeness was startlingly evident when House led a reciprocal mission to London and Paris towards the end of 1917. He asked Balfour to accredit Sir William to the American delegation, which was to make the crossing in a cruiser, 'I had planned for him to come with me on the warship,' House explained, ' but we think it would be better for him to travel by American liner to avoid any possibility of jealousy among the other Allies.' Wiseman warned the Foreign Office that the Americans were accustomed to 'steam heating'. They could not be expected to face the British winter with the same stoicism as their hosts. It was not a well-timed arrival. New place names had been added to the atlas of tragedy: Caporetto, where the invasion of Austria that Italy had been persuaded to embark on by the promise of a postwar chunk of territory had collapsed; Brest-Litovsk, in Belarus, where the Bolsheviks who had taken over in Russia were bartering for an armistice with Germany, their delegation led by Leon Trotsky.

The Americans must have been kept warm and well fed, for House was gushing in his thanks for the arrangements Wiseman had made, adding at the end of the visit: 'I hated to leave you last night in Paris. I have come to feel that your place is by my side.' I shall miss you, too, when I return to the United States and shall look forward to your coming back.'

Wiseman was staying on in London for a few weeks. There had been such a radical reorganisation of intelligence interests in London that the SSB was all but lost in the shuffle. In the structure that was to evolve into MI6 the alphanumerical mix was enriched by Roman numerals. C's original operation was restructured into Sections I to VI. IV Military, and V Political, were run by Dansey from whom Cumming would, at least in theory, take orders. But C remained in control of established SSB agents and, more importantly, the Foreign Office cashflow. Section III— 'Naval'— of C's domain stood little chance of getting Blinker Hall to take any notice of it. He was now a rear admiral, outranking everyone in sight. Room 40 steamed serenely ahead, tossing the other spooks about in its wake.

Slow starters

Lance was characteristically evasive about his brief time in New York and Washington and his account of it ends, mystifyingly, in mid-sentence. Some of his anecdotes read like a rear-vision view of Guy's experiences. In one he describes being invited to a patriotic event in Manhattan while Guy was out of town and being greeted as Captain Gaunt. Americans were prone to exaggerate the rank of a man in uniform, he explained, but he does not seem to have corrected his host. Once again he seems, in memory, to be occupying his older brother's space, and once again Guy is never mentioned, at least not by name. '... my hours were long and arduous hours since the S.N.O. had been called to England and I was left in charge'. Presumably the Senior Naval Officer was Guy, who went back across the Atlantic again in late 1917 to warn his superiors of misgivings sloshing around the Department of the Navy over the prospect of having to steam in tandem with a British fleet that despite its size and power seemed disinclined to close with the enemy.

Months after Wilson's fateful April day before Congress, Lloyd George and his cabinet felt much the same as that about the entire American war effort. As winter approached there was little sign of the horde of fresh and battle-ready New World warriors the Allies had come to count on. All over America the blare of Souza mingled with dozens of jingoistic jingles. George M. Cohan's hit *Over There!* was top tune, belted out from every vaudeville stage, scratched out on every phonograph. 'The Yanks are coming'... it promised. 'The Yanks are coming ... .' But when?

The situation on the Western Front had become desperate. First the French then the British failed in a major offensive; their armies were on the point of disintegration. Among the French, whose casualties were the most numerous and futile mutiny was widespread. Many British units were also reluctant to fight on. On the other side of Europe the Austrians had driven the invaders back almost to Venice and half the Italian army dissolved. The

Allies no longer needed steel, nitro-glycerine and wheat. They need men.

The difficulty was that the United States did not really have an army, at least as the concept now applied in Europe. Some states had a National Guard militia but the National Army consisted of a mere two hundred thousand riders and riflemen, good enough for killing Indians and chasing Mexicans but utterly unprepared for the kind of war that had developed Over There. It had no artillery worthy of the description, no trench mortars, no hand grenades, no proper marching boots. The lack of equipment did not worry Allied generals. They had plenty now, partly thanks to American manufacturers. Their plan was simply to feed America's inexperienced troops into their depleted armies as reinforcements. They could be fitted out in British or French uniforms, and given the few weeks rudimentary training raw recruits now received before being hustled into the killing fields. The French planned to put half the strapping, corn-fed Americans into labour battalions to repair bridges and dig trenches while the rest were learning to follow orders in a new language.

These airy assumptions appalled the Americans. Wilson insisted that the United States was not becoming a formal ally of Britain and France, merely fighting on the same side. The order appointing his favourite soldier, 'Black Jack', now a full general, told him that 'the forces of the United States are a separate and distinct component of the combined forces, the identity of which must be preserved'. Also, Wilson made clear in increasingly testy exchanges with Lloyd George whom he had come to dislike, that he would not allow Americans to support the colonial policies of the Allies or any territorial aspirations they might have. That included helping the Anglo-French campaigns in Mesopotamia and Palestine by opening hostilities with Turkey. The European imperialists need not think that spilling across the North American continent, decimating the native population, annexing huge territories belonging to Mexico, conning Panama out of the Canal Zone, hanging on to the Philippines, Cuba and other useful assets picked up from Spain had made the United States a colonial power; it was merely fulfilling its civilising mission. His own was to continue to press his plans for peace although the only leader now listening was the pocket-sized Pope Benedict XV who, having solemnly declared the Vatican neutral, had begun to push a peace plan of his own.

Pershing meant to slip over to Europe to size up his task as discreetly as Admiral Sims had gone across but even though they were dressed as civilians the staff of two hundred that boarded the SS *Baltic* with him on 25 May did not fool New York's eagle-eyed shipping reporters. Besides, the battery on Governor's Island opened up with the four-star send-off that was his due: a seventeen-gun salute that thundered around Lower Manhattan like an echo of Black Tom. Once he had heard what his French and British counterparts had to tell him and visited the sulking and demoralised front, he cabled the War Department his minimum requirement: a million men.

Guy, no longer spy nor counterspy, had begun to think of what might come next. He had hinted as often and as forcefully as he dared that he was ready to go back to sea but when he returned from London this time he knew there was little hope of it until the two navies had become comfortable with each other, a process of which he was an essential part. He had been right to plug Sims as a friend to Britain, although Sims himself had to work hard on the Admiralty, Cabinet, even the king before the true extent of the nation's plight was revealed to him. When he had scrambled ashore at Liverpool clutching his tin box there was only enough grain in Britain to feed the country for three weeks and most essential war material was in perilously short supply. He was all the more appalled when so many people he spoke to seemed resigned to losing the war. It was impossible to fend off the wolfish U-boats. The Royal Navy had those mighty battleships and battlecruisers that were the ultimate deterrent against Germany but before there was a chance to use that mighty weapon, Sims feared, control of the seas would slip away. Within two weeks of his arrival in London he told the Navy Department what must be done: send every available destroyer and light cruiser to patrol the crucial Atlantic run. Build more of them. Build more freighters, too; transports to bring the troops over there.

American admirals were delighted by the prospect of their star performers getting a piece of the action, especially the chance of showing the Limeys how to shoot straight. There were also a few things to smooth out. Flag and wireless codes were different. Exchanging signals with the British would be bad enough but what about the French? Many at Navy also resented the idea of having to follow tactical plans they had no part in making. And there was a major obstacle to getting those prestigious new battlewagons over there. The newer battleships of both navies burned oil but Britain had trouble finding enough fuel for her own.

The Department expected Sims to keep clear water between their ships and anyone else's but he had persuaded it that the American anti-submarine force of cruisers and destroyers should be based at Queenstown in Ireland, the British terminus of the Atlantic run, where their movements were directed by a Royal Navy captain. American ships under British command? Had Sims gone native?

In fact he had gone bows-on with the Admiralty to push the idea that merchant ships should cross the ocean in convoys. The British had always resisted this simple notion but younger officers saw merit in the idea. When David Beatty, who had succeeded Jellicoe of Jutland as commander-in-chief, gave his support to Sims convoys of forty or fifty freighters were soon organised and it worked just fine. The chances of a freighter being attacked shrank dramatically and the Atlantic lifeline was preserved. Cargo reaching British and French ports increased by thousands of tons The American patrols sank only one U-boat and of the four vessels lost one was rammed by a British transport. The destroyer *Jacob Jones* was the first to go, torpedoed by U-53: at the periscope *Kapitän-leutnant* Hans Rose, who had made that impertinent visit to Rhode Island. Rose sank eighty-one ships altogether. *Jacob Jones* was the only warship.

Guy's absences did not leave Lance alone and friendless. Margaret had returned after nine months at Gaunts Wood. Lance would come up from Washington to share her re-entry rounds: cocktails, gossip and whispered secrets, some of them about Guy's extramural activities which were now openly talked about, especially the latest coup he was credited with pulling off. A few weeks earlier a posse of Secret Service agents called on the widow Reisinger at 993 Fifth, where Bernstorff and Albert, Papen and Boy-Ed had so often been entertained. On the roof of the five-storey mansion they found just what Bill Flynn had briefed them to expect: a wireless installation, its antenna neatly strung beneath the concealing eaves. If conditions were good, it could bring in Nauen.

Himmel! exclaimed Edmée. Whoever could have put that there? The explanation she came up with was the butler who, it seemed, was no longer turning up with the teacups. His name was Alexander Kagan, soon found to have been an officer from one of the Hoboken ships and a naval reservist. Because Mila the Czech governess was quartered with the

Reisinger children two floors below, the wireless had probably been in use for some time before she reported it to Voska and word was passed along. Although America was being swept by the kind of spy phobia that had gripped Britain three years earlier Edmée got away with it. How was she supposed to know what went on up there in the servants' quarters? She threw herself and her fortune into patriotic causes and with the return of peace reconnected to the social whirl by marrying an American war hero.

It is frustrating to have so little real idea of what went on between the brothers when they were supposedly working in harness—and with Margaret—in this odd period together; whether Guy felt that Lance had been foisted on him; if he kept him sidelined rather than share the glory he could now bask in as a visible personification of the gallant ally that America had embraced. But by the time each brother got around to writing his memoirs their relationship had been irretrievably—and publicly—blighted. Whether Lance performed adequately as an assistant or whether Guy simply did not want him underfoot, his time in America came to an end within days of Guy's return. By November the United States Navy had four coal-burning battlewagons ready to join the Grand Fleet, older vessels but as formidable as anything in the Royal Navy. A liaison officer was required to help understand strange Limey ways. Lance was bundled on board the flagship USS *New York*, back to Scapa Flow and the futile wait for *Der Tag*.

The Cause

Wiseman gathered up all the SSB files from the Transport Department and took them home to 53rd Street. He proposed to C that he stay in business covertly, running a secret service inside the Secret Service:

> a small organisation which will be directed and controlled by myself, principally for the purpose of obtaining IRISH and MEXICAN affairs.

This would be done in the name of 'The Cause', a term he told Charles Seymour that Springy had used to justify accepting his covert link through

House connection. Then 'the cause' was winning America over to the Allied point of view. Now, it seems, The Cause was a private venture of Wiseman. In his pitch to C, Wiseman emphasised that his reports would no longer be copied to the military attaché in Washington and thus would not reach Vernon Kell at MI5. In addition to the ubiquitous Del Campo and Willert, he enlisted the assistant military attaché at the embassy, Lieutenant-Colonel Arthur Murray, who had been Grey's parliamentary private secretary before the war and was still a member of parliament. After a few months of grooming Murray was persuaded to leave the army and go into the Foreign Office as the London connection of the Cause. 'The circle is now complete,' Wiseman wrote.

Who or what Wiseman was actually working for, apart from his own interests, remains open to question. He later insisted to Willert: '... I represented not M.I.5 (*sic*) but what is discreetly called "a department of the Foreign Office"'. That is pure dissimulation. Neither MI5 or MI6 was in existence at that time; the part of the SSB operation that C supposedly controlled, Section IV, remained MI1(c) to the army. C might have assumed that Wiseman belonged to him but at the Paris peace conference after the war he appeared kitted out as a lieutenant-colonel, the red tabs of the General Staff on his lapels.

The Transport Department's work fell back on Guy and what help the consulate could provide. The entire United States war project all but disintegrated at the end of 1917 when the national rail network, an uncoordinated tangle of tracks, jammed solid, unable to cope with the combination of demand and foul winter weather. Coal and oil could not get to eastern ports and the Atlantic traffic faltered. One hundred and fifty ships lay in the New York bays unable to sail for lack of fuel. Time was short. The Bolsheviks, of whom Leon Trotsky was now one, were pulling the bearskin out from under the remaining Allies by a separate peace with Germany. Soon dozens of seasoned German divisions might be free to move from the Eastern Front to the Western. The Americans needed to get there first. Jolted into action, Wilson ignored the squeals of the railway barons and effectively nationalised their operations, lines, locomotives and rolling stock.

1918. The extent to which servants of the Crown were at the mercy of

Whitehall's capriciousness became sharply apparent in March. Despite Balfour's earlier decision to leave Spring Rice in post to act as a lightning conductor for American discontent while he used the House–Wiseman link for real deals, poor old Springy was ejected from his post by a cable less that a dozen words long. Guy shared the general shock at such callousness. He had become fond of Spring Rice, understood his foibles and admired both his crystalline vision of American politics and his loyal friendship to those, like Teddy Roosevelt who had been his early guides.

It was fashionable in England to attack him—by people who knew nothing of the conditions pertaining in America. They seemed to imagine the country was theirs for the asking.

The effect of Graves' Disease was worsening and Springy decided to break his journey home in Ottawa: his wife's cousin, the Duke of Devonshire, was governor-general of Canada. That was as far as he got; he died in the official residence, Rideau Hall, and was buried in the national cemetery in Toronto. Before leaving Washington he tried to make peace with people to whom he had been a particular trial. He sent William Jennings Bryan a poem written during an earlier posting in Sweden, *I Vow to Thee My Country*. Bryan, a sentimental Christian, circulated it and eventually Gustav Holst set it to a theme from his *Planets Suite*. It was soon Britain's top tune to be buried to, chosen by Margaret Thatcher for her funeral and sung at Princess Diana's memorial service, whether she had wanted it or not.

Springy's successor, the Earl of Reading, born Rufus Isaacs, was one of the stranger diplomatic appointments ever made since while acting as an Envoy Extraordinary to the United States he continued to preside as Lord Chief Justice of England and Wales. When he began to worry that he was neglecting one job for the other, the Foreign Office seriously proposed that he could be shuttled between them by a battlecruiser.

Guy had known him since he had come over in 1915 at the head of an Anglo-French mission that with the help of Jack Morgan pulled together a $500 million loan to pay for Britain's earliest war splurge. The two had much in common. At the age of sixteen Isaacs had been a young tearaway disinclined to settle into the family's wholesale fruit business in the City of London. In the hope that discipline would help, his father sent him to sea as ship's boy in the *Blair Athole*, a three-masted barque bound for Melbourne. He got back a year later after trying to jump ship in Rio de Janeiro. At nineteen he borrowed his father's identity to join the Stock Exchange where a member had to be twenty-one. Within two years he had been 'hammered'—unable to pay for shares he had bid for—and tried to flee to the Continent. Two of his brothers manhandled him off the boat train and drew up a debt management plan. The law seemed an obvious career choice.

Rufus became a brilliant barrister, counting among his clients Guy's old shipmate Herring, who while Prince of Wales had been embarrassed by allegations of a secret marriage that suggested he was a bigamist. So adroitly was the matter disposed of that when the royal client became King George V the first of his subjects on whom he bestowed a knighthood was Isaacs QC. Even so, advancement was not smooth. In 1912, together with Lloyd George, then Chancellor of the Exchequer, and two other ministers, Rufus was accused of using insider information to make a killing in Marconi shares. His brother Gerald was managing director of the company in England. He had cleared his debts by then but the Stock Exchange matter resurfaced. Nevertheless, he survived to represent the Board of Trade at the *Titanic* enquiry, which gave him a broad view of misfortune at sea that Guy could appreciate. They also shared an interest in Roger Casement. Guy's hard sell on the Black Diaries had done much, in America at least, to justify the death sentence that Chief Justice Reading passed on their author.

Consoling as their chats were, Guy knew they would soon end. His own relief had been announced in February and he expected orders for home any day. He was to be replaced by Rear Admiral the Honourable Victor Stanley, an officer of no particular distinction but plenty of interest. The battleship he commanded at Jutland had not got off a shot but his brother was the secretary of state for war, Lord Derby. Guy made sure that newspaper coverage reflected both the hopes he held for the future and his past achievements. The *New York Times* headlined:

SEA COMMAND FOR GAUNT

The story explained that he had been in post longer than the usual two-year stint 'because of the importance of the special duties he was performing'.

Commodore Gaunt has maintained headquarters in New York for some time, and his activities have brought him into contact not only with officials in every department of the government but with men prominent in the business life of the nation.

While Margaret was still around, the farewells to those priceless contacts were fairly sedate. In Washington, Reading turned out an array of the eminent and powerful to pay their formal respects. But after she had boarded the *Adriatic* for Liverpool in mid-March things became raucous. The India House Club took over the main dining room at Delmonico's. There was an elegantly printed menu of one word: Everything. Waiters carried in a salver on which Guy's uniform caps and his fedora-about-town drenched in brandy were blazing like a Christmas pudding. He was given a humidor inscribed with the signatures of all present and a silver martini shaker. The Secret Service and the Bomb Squad towed him around their more dubious haunts. But New York and Guy had not seen the last of each other.

Mystery voyage

June 1918. Guy and Colonel House looked out on the Hudson River from the admiral's walk of HMS *Leviathan*. The light was fading but downriver they could make out markers of the risky, rackety years in which Guy had done as much as the wily old fixer to bring their countries together in arms. They could see as far as the Statue of Liberty and the gap in the lights of the Jersey shore where Black Tom had been. Arc lights glared over the German–Amerika piers where he had wrecked the elegant speedboat and, later, watched The Barber push off for home. Some of the troublesome liners were being loaded with soldiers and horses for France. They could get there soon enough. A massive new German offensive was pushing the front line further than ever into France. The Germans were out to gain as much ground as possible before American troops got Over There.

House had not expected to see Guy again so soon but Admiralty bureaucrats could display benevolence as well as malign wit. The Sea Lords may have seen the chance to give him a last brass-buttoned voyage. Or he might have been given a final mission too sensitive to discuss even twenty years afterwards.

Guy's is unhelpful in many respects, even puzzling. In the chapter of *The Yield of the Years* dealing with this twilight period of the war, an entire section seems to have been lifted out with no regard to what went before or came after. Similar frustrating flaws occur throughout the autobiography: developments in events not mentioned earlier, references to characters not previously introduced. The simple explanation may be failing memory, especially since he had few records to consult; some omissions and obscurities may be the fault of his ghostwriter, Sidney Feldstead. It is possible that when Guy saw the draft Felstead produced he decided that some stories ought not be published after all, and dropped them, leaving holes that neither of them got around to patching up. It is also possible that Felstead deliberately skated around delicate areas. A few years later he would sometimes mention his close acquaintance with Captain Kell.

Guy was to have taken passage back to Britain from Halifax. Awaiting him there was *Leviathan*, flagship of the West Indies squadron, an armoured cruiser launched at the turn of the century that, because she went through fuel like a bushfire, had spent most of the war in Bermuda harbour. He was to bring her back home leading a convoy of transports and troopships.

A ship! A ship at last. A flagship! The very idea added punch to the cocktail of regrets and fulfilment with which he toasted his departure. *Commodore* Gaunt was a flag officer, entitled to fly a swallow-tailed pennant, the red cross of St George on a white background, at the mainmast. It got better. When he got to Halifax—by means undisclosed—where the convoy was assembling, Guy says he was ordered to take *Leviathan* on a round trip back to New York to 'show the flag'. The daughter of a J P Morgan partner came across him buying up silk stockings in Lord and Taylor. 'What are you doing here?' she asked. 'I thought you'd sailed.' 'Hush, hush', Guy replied. 'These are war times.'

The Admiralty files have nothing to say about this mysterious detour, simply confirming that Guy had been given *Leviathan* 'for voyage home only', but whatever the reason it was a peerless opportunity for flaunting. He tied up in the Hudson at midtown, Pier 81, and invited his cronies to bid him farewell once again, this time in his true habitat. The old cruiser may have been past her best but with a good scrub-down and a few dabs of paint the flag captain, Francis Austin, got her ready to party: marine band arrayed around the after nine-inch gun, stewards in white jackets serving champagne—which Guy had to pay for. Beneath the quarterdeck an admiral's quarters spanned the beam, opening on to the airy walkway over the stern to which Guy led Colonel House for their parting conversation.

They must have discussed the real reason *Leviathan* had come to New York. To collect an important passenger? Pick up something too valuable to be trusted to a merchant ship: sensitive documents, bullion or currency? Guy does not say. He was ready, though, to recall telling House that he had been brooding over his prospects. He had little idea of what might await him immediately but however and whenever the war ended the navy would be halved. Even assuming he made admiral he could not expect a lengthy career. He had vague notions of getting something moderately prestigious—president of the Jockey Club, governorship of a small colony—but such sinecures needed a private income to subsidise them. 'I haven't saved a cent,' he told House. 'Rather the reverse.' The meant the contribution Margaret made to his lifestyle. House, who was used to dealing with men whose price was as clear as the tags at Lord and Taylor, might have thought this a heavy hint, although Guy seemed to take his reply as a joke. 'I don't know anyone who could make money in a short time better than you,' House said. 'You know more about us than anyone. If you start in I'll have to find a hundred thousand dollars somewhere to keep your mouth shut.'

If there was an ulterior purpose to the *Leviathan* voyage it remains a mystery. Finally setting out for Britain, Guy seems to have alarmed the Admiralty by taking the convoy far north of the usual course. Blinker Hall signalled him directly to warn of signs that he was being stalked by a pair of U-boats and he kept radio silence until, within sight of Ireland, a message 'from the Government' demanded to know where he had got to: 'Cannot impress upon you too much the importance of your mission.' Whatever the mission might have been.

There were conversations with Lord Reading similar to that with House on *Leviathan*'s sternwalk and when Reading returned to London a few months later, having been appointed to the War Cabinet, he came up with an idea. But first he gave Guy the good news of the day: a knighthood was in the works. This is a point at which Guy's autobiographical ramblings move wishfully off course. 'You are about the first man since the days of Nelson,' he has Reading say: 'To come up through the hawse-pipe and work aft to command a squadron in time of war.' What could he have been thinking? The metaphorical crawl up the hawse-pipe described a man from the lower deck working his way up to a commission. Guy had gone into the merchant service as an apprentice officer and he joined the navy as an officer. The only formation he had ever commanded was the *Leviathan* convoy.

More accurately, Reading pointed out that Guy would be the only captain—as he soon would be once more—to be knighted during the war. A rueful irrelevance to Guy's way of thinking. Admirals received knighthoods almost routinely—although Ernest was never to get one—so if there had been a choice between rank and title he knew which he would have preferred. Admirals could look forward to regular promotion even in retirement, each notional extra ring a raise in pension. But that was Admiralty business, well outside Reading's remit. The plan he had for Guy was to find him a berth in a place where, as an elder of the Liberal Party, he did have some influence. 'You would do well in the House of Commons.'

PART THREE

Prospects of Peace

1918. That glittering world of doubletalk and double dealing that the brothers briefly shared in New York would have made their older sister's typing fingers twitch. While all the Gaunt men found adventurous roles for themselves poor Minnie was stuck with the dreary realities of life on the home front, cut off from the exotic stimulation she needed for new projects. *The Ends of the Earth* had been published after all and she embarked on a novel inspired by her experiences in China, *A Wind from the Wilderness*. The heroine, Rosalie Grahame, was a doctor who took a less stern view of drinking and smoking than the missionaries with whom she worked. Identification with the author is not difficult. Dr Rosalie finds herself in danger from a bandit known as the White Wolf, has an ill-fated romance with a chap called Miller and owns a little dog called McTavish who 'loves me as no-one in the world ...' Minnie's faithful James Buchanan lay buried in the Mary Haven garden.

In the dreary backwater of New Eltham people no longer bothered to complain about shortages that meant even fewer comforts than Minnie had enjoyed in Africa. There was sometimes farm produce to supplement the food ration but cigarettes and whisky had all but disappeared. She was often lonely, as hungry for family news as for decent food. Like much else destined for Britain mail often ended up at the bottom of the sea. Even so, some of her reports to the *Argus* reached Melbourne, close-ups of the civilian war and what she thought it meant. A piece that appeared in November 1916, when the country was still coming to terms with more Australians having been killed on the Somme than at Gallipoli, described the nightly spectacle of searchlights seeking out Zeppelins dropping bombs on London sixteen miles away. She saw a marauder hit by anti-aircraft fire.

The view was magnificent. The burning Zeppelin, like a flaming world, came down sweeping through the night sky. We could see each other's faces in its glare, and it was as if all the millions of London had joined in one rousing cheer. That homes are wrecked and women and children are killed and maimed can be of no military value to the Germans. But to the English I think it is of immense military value. In country and seaside towns, in villages such as the one I dwell in, even on the outskirts of London, with soldiers marching every day, the people would have realised nothing of the horrors of war had not the Germans seen fit to bring it home to them. For every woman and child killed, for every poor home wrecked, a thousand, nay. ten thousand citizens, who ordinarily would be perfectly content to leave the issues of war and peace in the hands of their Government, have been turned into active partisans who will endure hardships, submit to taxation, give the last penny of their hard-won gains, give their best beloved, their stalwart sons, and say only with deep drawn breaths that the victims of the Zeppelin raids must be avenged—the Allies must win this war.

And win they did, after a fashion. In June 1918, a year, a month, a week and a day after the United States entered the war, the American Expeditionary Force at last went into action. Only some 100,000 were battle-ready, or almost. Their artillery, machineguns, hand-grenades, even the steel helmets they wore were French or British. America, land of the automotive assembly line and the cradle of aviation, never managed to put a tank on to the battlefield or a warplane in the sky. Nor could the Expeditionary Force have got there except for the commandeered German liners and a fleet of British troopships. The unblooded infantry went willingly into battle but in the earliest encounters the only units that really knew how to do it were the marines, seasoned by those skirmishes in the Caribbean and trained, as Guy was always ready to point out, by the navy.

Wilson warned Lloyd George that the American people would not accept a prolongation of the sullen, static trench warfare of the previous three years. The people of France, Britain—and Germany—felt much the same but in the long months of waiting for the Americans to arrive the war moved out of the trenches. The German spring offensive ran out of momentum and by the time Guy delivered the *Leviathan* convoy to

Greenock in June, the Allied armies, so exhausted by the years of attrition when Pershing first saw them, had been revitalised and the Germans proportionately demoralised. The effect was less due to those hundred thousand or so doughboys in the front line than Pershing's million—and more—that the draft had, by then, delivered to France where they were being trained up. The Germans gave way. But it was a fighting retreat, falling back on the Hindenberg Line, a maze of defensive fortresses two miles deep. There would have been plenty left for the Americans to do if the Germans had not asked for an armistice. On 12 November, the day after an agreement was signed, Lloyd George called Britain's first election in nearly eight years.

The four months of war that remained after Guy arrived back in Britain were spent in Room 40 alongside Blinker and his intellectual rabble of decoders and black propagandists: 'half the members of the Garrick Club ... actors, barristers poets, and what not'. The atmosphere carried a lingering whiff of the scandalous events into which the Admiralty had been drawn earlier in the year. Among the what-nots in the intelligence thickets that had sprung up across Whitehall was an American who joined the British army in 1915, Harold Sherwood Spencer, a captain of artillery with a thin moustache and a fixed stare. No one seemed to know how or when he found his way into the secretive community but he was soon shown the way out, discharged from the army as well. He was an unstable fantasist and thus perfect material for his next employer, Noel Pemberton-Billing, independent Member of Parliament, visionary aircraft designer and all-round nutcase.

Billing founded the Vigilante Society and supported the National Party, a breakaway group from the Conservatives. His magazine *The Imperialist* argued that Britain faced many dangers: Jewish capitalism, the hedonism of the governing classes, the antics of 'flappers' but, above all, homosexuals. A network of depraved German *agents provocateurs* was 'exterminating the manhood of Britain' by converting upright young British men into 'urners'—men from Uranus. The pun is fortuitous; that is what they were called in German.

Agents were specially enlisted in the navy, particularly in the engine rooms … Incestuous (*sic*) bars were established in Portsmouth and Chatham. In these meeting places the stamina of British sailors was undermined. More dangerous still, German agents, under the guise of indecent liaison, could obtain information as to the disposition of the fleet.

Spencer offered Billing a scoop for *The Imperialist* that he could not turn down. He said he had a Black Book—compiled by the king of Albania, as it happened—listing the names of 47,000 prominent British men and women whose fear that their sexual proclivities might be revealed put them in the power of the German subversives. Lesbians worried Billing even more than urners and he seized the chance to work the Black Book into an article that also accused an American actress playing in Oscar Wilde's *Salome* on the West End stage, of leading a 'Cult of the Clitoris'. Few people at the time had even heard of this item but Billing was convinced that in lesbians it was notably enlarged and somehow responsible for their inclinations. The danger was obvious.

Wives of men in supreme positions were entangled. In Lesbian ecstasy, the most sacred secrets of State were betrayed. The sexual peculiarities of members of the peerage were used as a leverage to open fruitful fields for espionage.

The peerage kept quiet but the actress, Maud Allan, a sumptuous redhead, sued for libel and the trial produced the most sensational evidence about arcane sexual behaviour ever offered in a British court. The Black Book itself was not, however, produced. Spencer claimed that for safe keeping he had given it to the head of naval intelligence, Rear Admiral Hall. He could, however, remember some of the names it contained and with Billings's encouragement he blurted them out from the witness stand. Margot Asquith, wife of the former prime minister, was one. Another was that of the judge conducting the trial.

Spencer managed to avoid revealing in court that the reason for his discharge from the army was 'delusional insanity' (or that he had then been given a job as an aircraft inspector) but it was apparent to all but the most wild-eyed of Billing's followers that he was several stages removed from reality. Blinker denied ever hearing of either Spencer or his book, although he was not given the opportunity to say so on oath. He was summoned as a witness but the proceedings became so chaotic that the exasperated judge wound them up without his testimony. There was a comparable level of diversion outside the courtroom. A local chapter of the Church of Christ Scientist concluded that Billing must be the Messiah they were expecting. In case he was sent to prison—a possible consequence of criminal libel—they wanted a tangible object of adoration left behind. A female volunteer was offered up for him to impregnate. Billing obliged but declined to take an interest in the resulting offspring.

Billing conducted his own defence and despite the farcical witnesses and his own outrageous antics Ms Allan lost her case. Like everyone able to read a newspaper, Guy was enthralled by this legal circus and its sideshows but his course did not converge with Billings's until they became neighbours at The Albany, the secretive bachelors' warren in Piccadilly.

Guy had little to do in Room 40 but he was in demand elsewhere. Northcliffe had convened, rather late in the day, a Committee for Propaganda in Enemy Countries, whose objective was to convince citizens of the Central Powers that their rulers had lost the war. Guy went to its meetings as the DNI delegate, sitting with Wickham Steed and John Buchan to discuss the effectiveness of airdropping leaflets into Poland and Bulgaria. Since the SIS had no visible existence it could not be represented but Guy was shadowed by his counterpart from Military Intelligence, a brigadier general. Between sessions he ambled over to Buckingham Palace where Herring tapped him on the shoulder with a dainty sword blade and he arose Sir Guy.

He was on call as a minder for influential Australians, one of whom was the Honorable Hugh D. McIntosh, a thick-necked bruiser. He was Honorable because he had inveigled his way into the New South Wales Legislative Assembly but not in most other ways. 'Huge Deal' was the prototype multimedia magnate. Evoking the bulky shade of Rathom, he alternately claimed to have spent his boyhood peddling hot pies in the streets of Adelaide or fossicking for silver in Broken Hill. Whatever his beginnings, Huge was the most spectacular of Australia's free-wheeling entrepreneurs and by far its noisiest. The noise, amplified by several newspapers he owned, was directed at the British government's failure to treat Australian soldiers with the respect they deserved for winning the Old Country's battles for it. London was awash with unruly British World troops and the government, short of ships to take them home, was beginning to talk of corralling them in the parks like brumbies.

McIntosh could not be ignored: he was an influential member of the Empire Press Union, an early non-governmental organisation formed to manage cable communications across the far-flung World. Huge conferences every few years pollinated editorial attitudes across the red-mapped parts of the globe with views shaped in the corridors and clubs of Home. He was also president of the Australian branch of the British Empire League, another imperial logrolling fraternity. The Colonial Office co-opted the chairman of the EPU, Baron Burnham—whose father had been Mr Edward Levy-Lawson before he bought the *Daily Telegraph*—to get Hughie to turn down the volume. Guy got the job of guiding his troublesome *compadre* into a sort of political honeytrap.

Neither Guy nor McIntosh knew what awaited them but when Burnham showed them into the library at Hall Barn there was Lloyd George himself. Burnham made the introduction. Did the prime minister know Sir Guy? Of course he did. This was the occasion on which—according to Guy—the words were uttered that, understandably, lingered in his memory: 'It's hardly likely,' Lloyd George said—or Guy says he said—'that I should forget the man who brought America into the war.'

'Very kind of the P.M.,' wrote Guy. 'If perhaps slightly too flattering.' Only *slightly* too flattering.

Whether it was the antipodean affinity or the benevolent mugging he got from the political big beasts in their stately lair, McIntosh went back to town persuaded that his perspective on the war from 12,000 miles distant was skewed. The truculent Anzacs eventually got home but McIntosh moved to Britain living—and eventually going broke—in some style. In the 1930s he opened the Black and White Milk Bar in Fleet Street, a first-aid post for the newspaper world's early starters and late finishers. A chain of Black and Whites around Britain was planned but trying to launch it was a huge deal too many.

In the final three months of fighting in France, Americans at last in the front line, it became clear, even to the Germans, that some sort of ending had to be arranged. Wilson, distracted by trying to keep the pope from elbowing his way into a peace conference, let House put together the delegation that was to sell his Fourteen Points, the formula that would reshape the world. Some of the people who gathered at Curzon House were recruited for the British delegation staff, among them the ghost of Guy's future, Sidney Felstead, a captain in the army with intriguing tales of his own to tell. He had been a field intelligence officer in Belgium, where the Germans carried out an atrocity comparable to sinking the *Lusitania*: the execution of Edith Cavell, a British nurse who helped wounded British soldiers evade captivity. In the chaos that followed the German surrender he strode in to their headquarters in Brussels and gathered up all the files about the event. They would make a riveting book. So might the adventures of Captain Gaunt that were hinted at in their comradely chats.

Rear Admiral Gaunt, actually. On 26 October Herring had signed an Order-in-Council, a kind of waiver that allowed government departments to evade their own rules, and Guy's sea time shortfall was forgotten. This was not a new career chapter, though. The navy was being shrunk to peacetime size; there would be more admirals than ships. On the day the promotion was gazetted he resigned from the service. The Naval Committee of Congress sent over a token of its appreciation for 'all the energy, tact and good common sense' he had shown in his dealings with it. Enclosed was a gold cigarette case engraved with his name, spelt 'Guant'. He was not at all offended. It became his favourite keepsake, more prized even than the blue and gold Navy Distinguished Service Medal that followed with a citation for 'exceptionally meritorious and distinguished service in a position of great responsibility to the Government of the United States'.

Sidney Felstead might not have been the best choice of ghostwriter to help with *The Yield of the Years* but he was probably the only one Guy knew— apart, of course, from Minnie. He was an Australian but of a different ilk from the Gaunts. He was born in Balmain, then a tough harbourside suburb of Sydney, today a gentrified residential sector. He had come to Britain at the age of twenty-one in the wake of a minor encounter with the law: obtaining a gladstone bag and a pair of binoculars by false pretences. Arrest and prosecution may have decided him on the career he was soon pursuing, crime reporter for the *Morning Post*.

Many ghosts, though, encounter the hazard he faced when he set out to shape Guy's memoirs. The putative author does not want to let him include the very material a reader might find most interesting. Their collaboration began with Guy letting Felstead use some of his experiences as material for short stories. A collection published in 1930 as *Strange Company* supposedly related episodes in Felstead's career as a crime reporter. A couple of them had been constructed by dismantling accounts that only Guy could have given—a device, perhaps, to camouflage events the government might prefer to keep quiet about—and reshaping them around Felstead. The stories were set in wartime New York where 'Captain Gaunt' was 'head of the Secret Service'. There were adaptations of Papen's plan to attack Canada, the exposure of Rintelen, the raid on 50 Wall Street, all centred on Felstead, the intrepid reporter. These scrambled versions seem closer to the truth than anything Guy was willing to relate under his own name when *The Yield* was published nearly twenty years later. One incident that Felstead related in the melodramatic first person was just the kind of caper Guy and his loyal sidekick Thwaites got up to in their waterfront days.

> Just as I was about to leave my office, there had come a telephone call from one of the British Secret Service agents in New York to say that I might, if I liked, make one of a party that night to solve one of the most sinister mysteries of the war. 'And mind you come heeled,' said my friend warningly. 'There'll probably be some shooting.'

There followed Felstead's account of hiding with the agent's team in the hold of a freighter to catch a German saboteur in the act. Guy certainly did such things; Felstead could not possibly have been there. Indeed he could not have been a reporter in New York, unless it was an entirely different Sidney Theodore Felstead with the same date of birth and the same address in Finchley Road, London, who joined the Royal Gloucestershire Regiment in 1914 and ended his war appropriating the Edith Cavell dossier in Brussels.

All change

London in the years immediately after the war seemed to Guy much like New York in 1914. The mood was euphoric for those with a little money and style. There were plenty of smart shiny cars. Black jazz was in the air, or at least on a lot of gramophones, and the West End jiggled to the rhythm of the cocktail shaker. Hemlines were up, necklines down; the women who wore them often on the arms of—in Stanley Baldwin's arresting description of his fellow members of the first post-war parliament—hard-faced men who had done well out of the war.

Guy's account of his political apprenticeship is entertainingly slippery. He insists he responded to Reading's suggestion by protesting he had neither the education nor the brains to be in parliament, a transparent dissimulation for someone who had spent four years in the company of master politicians. He does not mention that his first attempt to win a seat in the Commons failed and—in much the same way as Minnie transposed experiences from one period to another—he moves events and references around, fudging the early defeat. In all he was elected three times out of the four that he stood.

Wartime governments had been shuffled together from members elected to the House of Commons in 1912 and peers in the readily manipulated House of Lords. The 1918 election was meant to lay down the foundation of a new Britain. Many candidates pushed their war records as a prime qualification with campaign literature full of pictures of themselves in uniform. Guy's posters and handbills were more impressive than most, decorations, knight's badge and sash, *aiguillettes*—although on the right shoulder rather than the left, since as an offhand mark of personal favour Herring had made him a royal aide-de-camp.

In preparation, the traditional parties—Liberal, Conservative, Unionist—divided, reformed and divided again, rival Liberal wings choosing either Lloyd George or Asquith to lead them. The maturing Labour Party looked nearly as powerful of any and certain to attract significant support. Voters were more numerous. Before the war only male property owners had been eligible but the Representation of the People Act passed earlier in the year gave the vote to servicemen aged nineteen, all other men at twenty-one and women at thirty—as long as they lived in the right kind of house or were university graduates.

The count was delayed for weeks while votes from soldiers and sailors scattered abroad were collected and the outcome was a confusing clash of factions in which Lloyd George clung to office despite a Unionist-

Conservative coalition that outweighed his National Liberals. Guy had been selected as a Lloyd George Liberal in the Gaunt home ground of Leek where the family name was thought to carry some weight. He was beaten hands down by a Labour candidate representing the silk workers on whom the early Gaunt fortunes had depended.

Minnie gave up the house in New Eltham and stayed at Gaunts Wood while she put together a new escapade. The paper supply had improved, publishing was picking up and her second China book, *A Broken Journey*, brought her back to public attention. Her asthmatic lungs needed sunshine. England was a deeply unhealthy place, racked by the influenza epidemic which was to kill more people than had died in the war. The endlessly helpful Horsfalls offered her introductions in Jamaica, where they owned a sugar plantation or two.

Other Gaunts were also in re-deployment mode. Ernest came back from India to take over as Commander-in-Chief Western Approaches. Cecil returned from Baghdad with his Highlanders. He had not been coerced into wearing the kilt; he stayed a cavalryman to the end, spurs and shako in dress uniform. Lance showed up at the Admiralty, applying for his temporary rank of lieutenant-commander RNR to be made permanent. It had been a disappointing time for the United States Battle Squadron. After the embarrassment of discovering from exercises in the churning North Sea that their gunnery was not so hot after all, the American did their full share of lumbering, gale-lashed patrols aimed at luring the enemy out but never laid their sights on a German until the rusting remnants of the High Seas Fleet steamed over to the Clyde to be interned. The day after that Admiral Rodman took them all home. The Admiralty turned down Lance's application 'with regret' and he went back to Singapore still a lieutenant.

His passage home crossed that of his mother, heading for Home. Now that travel was possible again, Elizabeth Gaunt was showing a touch of the family wanderlust. She wanted to visit relatives who had gone to farm in Rhodesia but did the rounds of her offspring in Britain first. None of them had seen her for years and they were shocked to find that by dinner time their mother was something of a liability. Elizabeth, the spirited matriarch of the goldfields, the confident horsewoman of their childhood, had become a genteel drunk. The image spins and sharpens of William driving the cart into Ballarat after the fire, Elizabeth with the Chinese vase in one hand and in the other the decanter of whisky. The sons insisted she take a 'lady's companion' with her to Africa, briefed to keep her away the bottle. None of them could have known much about alcoholic resolve.

For all the smarts Guy had shown in dealing with villains on behalf of Crown and country he was painfully naive when he went into business with 'an enterprising speculator in land', Sir Ernest Fawkes. They did all right for a while, parcelling off the surplus acreage of large estates to accommodate the post-war housing boom. They wanted to try something similar in America and put up £50,000 for a piece of Louisiana. Only when Guy went to inspect it did they discover that a crooked landowner and his friendly valuer had sold them a useless Mississippi flood plain.

The experience convinced Guy he was not meant to be a businessman and after a few months of desultory shooting and fishing around Gaunts Wood there seemed nothing for it but to give politics another try and—in the Minnie manner—pretend it was his first. The Louisiana Purchase was bad judgement; a Gaunt could count on good luck when it was needed. A fellow admiral already on board let down a ladder: Blinker Hall was now a Conservative MP for Liverpool.

The 1922 election caused a far greater upheaval than that of 1918. The Conservative Party broke out of coalition with the National Liberals and fielded its own candidates. Guy switched parties like a polo player swapping ponies and Blinker helped get Guy adopted as the Conservative candidate for Buckrose in Yorkshire, a place he had never been near. No matter, he was accepted by the local party despite showing up for his interview wearing a shirt with a soft collar rather than the stiff winged version and twice being heard to say 'damn'. Out came the posters, gold braid and decorations still acceptable currency. His Labour opponent, a local blacksmith and a Methodist lay preacher, countered with his own dressy picture placards. He made a splendid straight man for Guy when a crowd at the hustings launched into a noisy semiotic deconstruction of rival images. He had seen hundreds of horses shod, Guy joked, but he had never seen a man doing it while dressed in a white shirt and high white collar. The pious smithy took his posters down and Guy squeaked in by a couple of hundred votes. His mother was not there to show her pride.

Elizabeth came back from Africa, her minder worn out and defeated. Christmas at Gaunts Wood confirmed that the problem was serious. She was sent to a home for inebriates in Folkestone, where on 3 February 1922 she turned eighty-seven and three days later died.

Political turbulence meant a fresh election in 1923 and another in 1924. Guy was an asset to his new party. Being elected in the eponymous year made him a founder member of the 1922 Committee, an influential group of backbenchers devoted to keeping their leaders on the Right track. Strong nerves and speedy firing rate with amiable demotic comebacks made him a natural campaigner. As well as defending his own seat he was on call as a troubleshooter for struggling Conservative candidates. He made his maiden speech in the House in the debate over a proposal by the dedicated anti-booze campaigner Viscountess Astor. Her immediate goal was to get the drinking age raised from fourteen to eighteen but she was out to achieve the total prohibition of alcohol that had been inflicted on the United States at the beginning of 1920. She confronted him before they went into the chamber, accusing him of being out to wreck her Bill. Throughout his speech she turned to glower at him and interjected: unsporting treatment for a first-timer. A dipsomaniac mother was not enough to convince Guy and nor could this assertive puritan. His argument meandered a bit but he had been in America recently and seen the trouble criminalising alcohol could bring.

> At the age of seventeen I worked in San Francisco, very scantily clad and certainly short of boots, and I carried kerosene tins for very small remuneration under a hot American sun. I was a slight figure, not at all strong and muscular. It was all I could do to get water enough to keep me going ... therefore, I used to go into a dive and buy beer.

Violet Astor was a useful enemy. Conservatives were poorly received in working class areas; often run out of meeting halls, their cars trashed. At a meeting in South London Guy and a candidate he was supporting were greeted by demonstrators croaking out the Internationale. A group of husky brewers' draymen demanded to know which of the two gents was the admiral. Guy's inclination was to point to his companion but it turned out that anyone who took on Lady Astor was all right with these beer-soaked heavies. What could they do to help? 'Just spread yourself around the hall', Guy begged as red flags were broken out all around. 'But don't do anything unless I throw the water bottle.' Hecklers were readily silenced by a beefy hand on the shoulder, the bottle stayed on the table and when the nervous Conservatives were escorted back to their car its windows were intact.

In 1923 a huge Labour vote meant a hung parliament. A desperate Conservative offensive was mounted to regain the lost ground. Guy was less than delighted to find another Gaunt in the front line. His fraternal shadow Lance had retired from Allen and Gledhill and brought his Singapore fortune to the Home Counties where he resumed his curious mimicry. Since he was ready to finance his own campaign, the Conservative Party was ready to take him on as a candidate, although only for a sacrificial constituency in Hull. On the stump he would sometimes cup a hand around one ear, explaining he suffered slight deafness from the guns of Scapa Flow.

November 1924 saw Conservative dominance re-established. Guy increased his majority by three thousand votes, one of the better results. Lance's Liberal opponent had been the Honorable Joseph Kenworthy who as a straight-ring lieutenant commander and the heir to a barony outclassed him on two counts. He had also been the navy's heavyweight boxing champion. Lance took his knockout manfully, Guy joyfully in all likelihood, although this was another episode unreported in the autobiography.

Politics was engrossing as a way of life but not really a living. An MP's salary was £400 a year; an admiral's pension £600. It took ten times that to keep Gaunts Wood going, which Margaret must have provided. The Louisiana Purchase debacle meant that he needed more than ever to make some serious money. Then the government opened up the Kenya colony to settlers and ex-servicemen were offered staggering stretches of fertile uplands on which to grow tea or coffee, shoot lions and exploit the locals. Guy made a solo trip out to take a look at this late flowering of the World, an adventure in itself: ferry across the Channel, train to Marseille, steamer down the Suez Canal and around to Mombasa, train up to Nairobi. He spent three months there, some of it driving around remote parts of the country in a borrowed car, an echo of Minnie's adventures. He was no more alone than she had been: a native bearer in the back and beside him in the front seat, someone else who was also feeling the way to a new kind of life.

He came back with happy memories but no inclination to grow coffee in East Africa. Something would turn up. He was only fifty-four, highly-respected, with contacts all around the world; he was even warmed by royal favour. And more than ever in demand by his party.

Cruising

House of Commons activity was frenzied, most business done at night and into the early morning hours. Guy took a 'set' of rooms in The Albany— he used the definite article which some, snobbily, preferred to drop. He shuttled between London and his constituency as well as responding to distress calls from hard-pressed fellow Conservatives. There was little time for Gaunts Wood. Margaret became a Westminster widow and turned her attention to getting her mother's vast needlework picture history restored and displayed at Reading.

There was plenty for the new parliament to get its teeth into, the issues disconcertingly familiar in 21st Century Britain: housing, pensions, youth unemployment, education, gender equality, Russia. Then Guy had a motoring accident. The car he was driving overturned and caught fire. He was trapped under the wreckage by one arm. Gaunt luck saw there were people around to haul him out. A new fracture was added to the steeplechasing damage and he showed up around the Commons wearing an impressive sling. But a few months later he stopped appearing there or anywhere else around London. Around Britain. Just disappeared.

Her name was Margery Cruise. Lady Cruise, wife of Sir Richard Cruise the eminent ophthalmologist—Surgeon-Oculist Extraordinary to King George V and Queen Mary. There are photographs of her in the National Portrait Gallery taken in December 1922 by the royal photographer Bassano on those wonderful glass negatives. She is a beauty in the new style: hair in a bob pushed under a cloche hat, silk shift with scooped out neckline and cap sleeves, long rope of pearls, precision lipstick. *Brideshead* yet to be visited. She looks straight into the lens, frank and knowing. Tulia the Samoan Girl under a different sky. She was thirty-five when the pictures were taken, married for nine years. One daughter.

Her maiden name had been Woolcombe-Boyce; the family home was in Gloucestershire where she made her mark for sporting womanhood as a junior golfing champion. She and Guy had met much earlier in her debutante years; how, where and with what consequences none can tell. Well brought-up girls were cautious about dalliance; reputations were precious, contraception messy and undependable. A married woman could be more adventurous. Margery had been in Kenya visiting friends when Guy was out there. Another Happy Valley, north of Nairobi, was a metaphor for sexual exuberance rather than racing. Are you married, the joke went, or do you live in Kenya?

Not a hint of the destructive romance that ensued is to be found in Guy's recollections. But with a little hindsight it seems the more likely cause of an attack of angst and self-doubt about which he was characteristically vague.

> Financial difficulties and continual worries broke my health down so badly that I became a victim of insomnia. I tried aspirin and used to take it practically by the pound, but with no effect. Night after night I tramped the streets vainly seeking sleep, until I knew every rut in Piccadilly from The Albany out to Sloane Square and back again.

Not the slightest clue there to the slow-burning fuse and eventual detonation that would blast Margery out of her glittering social orbit and Guy out of the Commons, out of Gaunts Wood and both of them so far out of royal favour that there was no hope of return. In Guy's version of why he left London, the Conservative chief whip, Stanley Jackson, a famous Test cricketer with a moustache as broad as a set of bails, suggested a long holiday to restore his spirits. 'I applied for the Chiltern Hundreds and dropped out of public life.'

Not quite. He applied for the Stewardship of the Manor of Northstead, a notional post that—like the Stewardship of the Chiltern Hundreds—is used to get around a rule that prevents MPs from resigning during the life of a parliament. Each Stewardship is 'an office of profit under the Crown', something a sitting MP is forbidden to hold. Awarded the fictional job, a member automatically forfeits his or her seat. But Guy did not make his application until 14 April 1926. He had come back from Kenya early in 1924 and what happened in the two years between could hardly have been improved on by his idol Robert Louis Stevenson.

'Roaming across the world in search of distraction,' Guy—or Felstead—wrote:

> I found myself standing on the wharf of Lake Union, Seattle, USA. I watched a beautiful, four-masted schooner of some thousand tons arrive in ballast from Tasmania. Their day was done; steam had defeated them.

He seems to have been pointed towards this remote spot in the Pacific North West by his fellow denizen of The Albany. Pemberton-Billing might not have been everyone's choice of neighbour but he was entertaining company so long as no one mentioned Germans, urners, lesbians, Jews, any of his former girlfriends or Christian Scientists.

Billing built only two aircraft that flew. One was a four-winged wonder called the Nighthawk that had been meant to attack Zeppelins with a small cannon but could not climb high enough to reach them. The other was a seaplane. The company he founded, Supermarine, went on to develop elegant floatplanes that became stars of modern aviation, evolving into the emblematic Spitfire. He sold the company but remained convinced that hulls and floats were aerodynamically superior to the wheeled undercarriage of landplanes and as soon as he finished marketing another invention, an early long-playing gramophone disc, the World Record, he would be back at the drawing board.

The Boeing company shared his view of seaplanes and built them beside Lake Union, the location of the movies *Sleepless in Seattle* and *An Officer and a Gentleman*. Nearby there were great forests of sitka spruce from which to make airframes nearly as strong as aluminium, just as light and far cheaper. Billing was out in Sydney demonstrating the World Record when Guy showed up in a P&O liner and set about chartering a small steamer to cruise around the Pacific. Just the man to size up the spruce market for him and how best to get the timber to Southampton.

No one was going to come looking for Guy, at least for a while. The Conservatives had a secure majority in the Commons; no need to fret about no-shows. Unless a crucial vote came along a member's time was his own. Nor did constituents expect to see much of their representatives unless there an election was in the offing. It is a measure of how little anyone really expected of a back-bencher that the better part of a year went by before people began to wonder what had happened to the Member for Buckrose.

The last interested party to have seen him kept quiet. Margery's husband had been with Guy at some weekend sporting event about the time he was last sighted around Westminster. Like Guy, Sir Richard Cruise was a steeplechaser. Like his wife, he was an enthusiastic golfer, a sporting attitude he carried over into the delicate work of cataract removal and glaucoma in which he specialised. In the operating theatre, he would advise junior doctors to adopt a confident stance; address the eye 'as one would a golf ball'.

The two men had a delicate discussion. Out of guilt or some warped notion of chivalry Guy decided to inform Sir Richard that he had become, in the words of the Cruise v Cruise divorce petition a couple of years later, 'overfond' of Margery. He had therefore decided that the honourable course was for him to leave the country. Only Guy knows why he needed to blurt out such an operatic declaration rather than simply get on his way. Cruise would have realised soon enough that something was up. When he got home from his weekend there was no Margery, just a note: *Dear Richard ... .*

Someone must have asked Margaret what had happened to her husband but it is unlikely she could or would have been helpful. She may have been the source of an explanation passed around that he was recuperating from a riding fall. Other Gaunts had their own preoccupations. Cecil was by then a widower, his life centred on polo. In 1925 Ernest hauled down his flag and retired to Monaco: a grand apartment with a view of the Grand Prix circuit and within easy reach for Minnie who had decided that the French Riviera was a more suitable setting for an eminent lady author than the West Indies.

Eighteen months in Jamaica had worked wonders with Minnie's asthma but the first book that resulted did not fulfil her hopes. *Where the Twain Meet* was a straightforward popular history of Jamaica from the time of slavery and pirates to the resultant mess of miscegenation and social turmoil. It was a story little known in Britain or America and it deserved to do better. She had been introduced to the hallowed firm of John Murray, which had published Jane Austen and Lord Byron. Its archives in the National Library of Scotland record the book's production in detail: printing costs, author's contract, reader's report and stiffly polite correspondence between Minnie and the Murrays, father and son. The publisher's reader concluded that 'If it were half its present length it would be twice as good a book.' Minnie cut the manuscript from 140,000 words to 90,000.

Reviews were respectful. 'Mrs Gaunt writes with a rare sympathy for all she sees and learns,' said the *Morning Post*. 'Her point of view is impartial and she sees through her historical knowledge the progress of events marching to a happier future.' Sales, alas, were derisory. The print run was 1,250 copies. Fewer than a thousand were sold in the first year of publication,1922, and by 1926 only a sorry single copy left the warehouse. It had been wrong of her, Minnie said, not to have called it simply *JAMAICA*. She was still on the island at that time and saw rich Americans hunting for books about the place 'but they don't even know mine is about Jamaica'. A rival writer, Richard Hughes, changed the title of his story of underage sex and mayhem from *An Innocent Voyage* to *A High Wind in Jamaica* and it became a global bestseller. Entirely due to the title in Minnie's sour view. 'Local colour is wrong; some of the book is disgusting and the rest uninteresting. Yet it's making its fortunate author piles of money.' If Murray were to follow up with a cheap edition, she said, please call it *JAMAICA: Where the Twain Meet*.

Before *Twain* was in print, the energetic Mr Brown also sold the Murrays *As the Whirlwind Passeth*, a historical novel Minnie had begun in Warrnambool a quarter of a century earlier and finished while she was in Jamaica. Published in 1923 it did far better, running to four editions. By then she was back in Europe, drafting a fresh chapter of her own life. She had gathered valuable impressions to help model another of her independent heroines. Charlotte Maxwell Hall, a white Jamaican, was 'young, extremely good looking, if she will allow me to say so, charming, and, above all, she is strenuous and vivid with energy—indomitable'. Not yet thirty, Charlotte had a job as the government meteorologist, managed a cattle station inherited from her English father and ran a medical clinic for farm workers—a life, Minnie frankly confessed, that she would love to have had for herself. Charlotte is readily recognisable in Fabia Vrooman, the heroine of *The Forbidden Town*, published in 1926; a West African reprise that exuded the fascination inter-racial sexual tension held for Minnie. She would have been the least likely of the Gaunts to raise an eyebrow at Guy's roaming; boys would be boys and a cheerful sex life was fine with her as long as those involved were the same colour.

Rolling home

That first glimpse of the schooner *Eric* laid down a completely fresh course for Guy to steer. The ship had been built in 1898 at Port Blakely on the other side of Puget Sound. The Burns-Philp company sent her tramping around the Pacific, her hold full of dressed logs, more on deck, stacked as high as the main boom. Worn out, she was on the point of being turned over to the sawmills herself. But beneath the peeling paint and battered planks Guy could see the lines of a thoroughbred. He might be homeless, jobless, fairly broke and at the mercy of a reckless passion but there was something in his power that none of the eminent men he knew could match. He could go down to the sea in a tall ship, master under God—or at least under the wide blue heavens—bestride the deck like a buccaneer, beautiful female prize at his side, and sail wherever in the world he wished. 'I bought her for a song ...', wrote Guy. Or Feldman.

Whatever the song, it soon swelled into a mighty chorus. Eight years earlier the schooner had changed hands for $67,000. Even if Guy got her for a fraction of that, installing a pair of diesel auxiliary engines, refrigeration plant, repairing the work-worn hull, sails and rigging, to say nothing of converting her from cargo hulk to gentleman's yacht cost many thousands more. By the time he had finished the huge cargo space below looked much like a set in the Albany, although more luxurious: three guest cabins and a master's suite, each with its own bathroom. Only the suite, though, had its ample bed slung in gimbals to keep it level when the ship heeled. One end of the main saloon was screened off by a grille as an aviary for exotic birds, at the other bookshelves framed a wood-burning fireplace and carved mantelpiece. There were racks for the India House humidor and martini shaker, only a couple of the mementoes on display: the panelled bulkheads were hung with paintings and sketches, photographs of Guy in his several lives.

At least a crew could be had on the cheap. While the ship was being worked on Guy took passage on a freighter across to Hong Kong and came back with two dozen Chinese: engineers, deckhands, cook and stewards. He put them in bell-bottom rig: blue for seaman, white for stewards. A motor car was swung on board by the main boom, and he and Margery spent months on a shakedown cruise around the pine-fringed waterways of Vancouver Island and Puget Sound.

Eventually, whispers began to circulate in London. Guy's opaque past encouraged gossip. There had been another motoring accident, far more serious. He had lost his memory. Taken on a new identity to protect him from … something. Members of the Opposition began to ask mischievous questions in parliament. Was the Honourable Speaker aware that the good people of Buckrose seemed to be no longer represented in this House? The first sighting report drifted in from Hong Kong when some travellers remembered Guy arriving there nine months earlier. According to the Sydney *Evening News* of 25 May 1925 he had been heard saying that he meant to cruise the Pacific islands, preferably those 'on which there were no white men'. The story was illustrated with a picture of him in a homburg hat. On 17 February 1926 the Reuter news agency filed a story datelined Victoria, BC. It was brief but the newspapers that picked it up obviously saw there would be more to come and treated it playfully.

FOUND
Missing Admiral

Rear Admiral Sir Guy Gaunt, whose movements for some time were not within the knowledge of his friends but who is understood to have left London a year ago on a health trip, has arrived here. He is having the schooner Four Winds fitted out for a cruise of the world.

When Guy changed the ship's name he gave his address as Gaunts Wood and with splendid cheek registered her in Cowes on the Isle of Wight, home port to the Royal Yacht Squadron of which Herring was patron. He had been over impressed when he had first seen her. Rather than a thousand tons she was closer to six hundred, but plenty of ship nonetheless. At 174 feet, not counting an impressive bowsprit, she was nearly as long as the grim old *Britisher* in which he had first gone to sea, although shaped to different needs. Those broad-beamed square-riggers were only happy with the wind aft or over the shoulder. A schooner's sails were set fore-and-aft, meant to press her slender hull upwind.

With Guy at the wheel, the big schooner went down the West Coast like a toboggan, off to give Margery a carefree retrospective of Guy's former lives. The steady onshore Pacific breeze on her beam powered them along but the rollers that came with it made for a rough ride, bursting spray, lee deck awash, life on board at a sharp angle except in the gimballed bed. Soon there was another report from San Francisco where the splendid yacht's arrival under full sail could hardly have been more different than Guy's first visit in those youthful Barbary Coast days. South again they closed on a big passenger ship of Glasgow registry drifting along just outside territorial waters before they realised that a swarm of baleful looking speedboats were running past them with crates of illicit liquor. Prohibition brought more hazards than the moral dangers that worried Lady Astor; ruthless rum-runners and the United States Coastguard, one as trigger-happy as the other. Danger crackled on the breeze; the blood-black schooners of the Kuril Island seal poachers came to mind. Guy hauled away for the island of Socorro, four hundred miles offshore. Toting a Winchester, as he had for the big brown bears of Kamchatka, he went ashore, this time to shoot a few unresisting wild sheep for the cook. Then on to Baja California, where barnacled whales surged alongside like friendly submarines and great sea birds flew low air cover. In Acapulco, where he had taken HMS *Challenger* on her 1911 tour of the Pacific, he introduced himself to the Mexican *commandante* who insisted that he inspect the garrison guard. In the fortress a grey squirrel on a chain reminded him of the pet bear of old HMS *Swift*. He named it Mexican Joe and took it on board *Four Winds* where it would spook the crew by hurtling around the rigging. They tacked far out again to Cocos, the silent enigmatic island that inspired *Jurassic Park*, the only humans for hundreds of miles around.

Sir Richard soon put together everything he needed for his divorce petition: a letter from Margery saying she was not coming home, another that she had written to a friend explaining where she was and with whom; the testimony of a gumshoe that she and Guy had shared a room at the Oak

Bay Hotel in Vancouver as well as their close quarters afloat. All concerned were fortunate that restrictions had just been imposed on the reporting of divorce cases: newspapers had to limit themselves to a bare outline of the evidence. Even so the papers did their best, decorating the brief accounts with references to the 'Will o'the Wisp Admiral'. 'Breezy' was used a lot.

Four Winds swanned between the Pacific and the Caribbean through the Panama Canal. At the time of the *Challenger* tour it had yet to open for business but Guy had looked over the mighty workings and sent a report to the Admiralty. Now he was intrigued to discover that the governor of the Canal Zone, the American enclave enclosing the waterway, knew exactly what he had written at the time: the buildings being put up in the Zone were too big, 'simply a bit of American advertising'. Did he still think that? their host teased. Of course not, Guy had to say. But how on earth did the governor know what he had written back then? Silly question for someone who had spent years dipping into other governments' documents.

On the other side of the continent they tied up in Colon, where Guy had commandeered the old collier to hunt for Telefunken stations. After that the ports of call were those of today's cruise liners: the Virgin Islands, Jamaica, Cuba then on to Miami. Not that all was plain sailing. Leaving Havana, Guy recalled

> standing by the man at the wheel, piloting the ship out when the jiggermast above us was struck by lightning. A shower of wood and the after rigging a mass of flame was the only thing that happened except for a minute or two the steering compass played the fool.

The busier East coast waters were more dangerous than the West. Guy feared that seaborne gangsters running booze from Cuba might try to hijack *Four Winds* for their outlaw fleets. He kept loaded shotguns on deck to repel boarders. It was a relief to drop anchor in Boston where Margaret's lawyers had sent the Gaunt v Gaunt divorce papers. Her address was given as Villa Trianon, Rue Principe, Monaco. Good old Ernest had come to her rescue.

It was time to go home—or where home had been—although getting there was no fun.

> I can strongly advise anybody who is his own captain not to tackle the North Atlantic, with the winter months coming on, in a big schooner

under canvas with a Chinese crew. With the glass falling, I had to shorten down very early, as I found the men much too small and light to handle the big sails.

The Cuban lightning left its mark. When a gale struck it became frighteningly evident that the wire rigging of the jigger, the aftermost of the four masts, had deteriorated and they had to work hard to save it. But on they went to

Bermuda, the Azores, Gibraltar, and, at last, thank goodness, Marseilles, where I was lucky enough to sell my craft, thus ending my sea career as I started, i.e. under sail.

And who was the buyer Guy had been so lucky to find? Lloyd's Register records the sale to Noel Pemberton-Billing c/o The Albany, Piccadilly, London W1. Cowes was just across the water from Southampton and the Supermarine hangars. This goes some way to explaining where the money came from. Billing may have been, in effect, the real owner ever since Guy took the ship over, paying for the lavish conversion on the understanding that she would eventually be delivered to him. It is a more appealing possibility than the thought that Guy raided his wife's fortune for a project to impress his mistress.

As for the mistress herself, there is no knowing whether she made it as far as Marseilles or jumped ship before the Atlantic crossing. But the affair was over, Margery left with the sour aftertaste of a reckless romance and the prospect of firmly closed drawing room doors back home. Women of the gilded circles from which she had bolted took their cue from Queen Mary, who would sooner have offered her gloved hand to Guy's Chinese cook than to a divorced woman. Even the innocent party might be royally shunned, although expediency may have spared Sir Richard. He remarried, had a couple of children and retained his royal appointment, continuing to write prescriptions for the stern old dear's *lorgnettes* long after widowhood made her the Queen Mother.

The newspaper reports took care to include Guy's age, titillating when the woman involved was some twenty years younger. His own divorce was concluded just in time for Christmas 1927, the year he became the fictional Steward of Northstead, the year that Charles Lindbergh flew the Atlantic, that the Chinese took time out from a civil war to discover the Great Panda and when everyone everywhere was whistling *Ain't She Sweet*. There was a regretful tone to the *New York Times* report, recalling 'an intelligence officer of unusual talent and pleasing personality'. He was fifty-eight, love life expired, homeless, and if not penniless uncomfortably short of money. That helpful wheeze of promotion in retirement made him a vice admiral and in another year he would reach top rank but the pension would not keep a chap in much style in modern Britain. Besides, he too had lost friends. At the United Service Club, 'The Senior', where the entry level was commander or colonel, fellow members were happy to stand him drinks but would never think of asking him to meet their wives or daughters. Even their mistresses.

Comfort Zone

Where was a chap to go for a decent climate, affordable living and trustworthy servants? He had an enduring fondness for Australia but, the servant problem apart, it was too far away. He wanted to be able to get to London or Paris in reasonable time. That also eliminated the West Indies and—even without its unhappy associations—Kenya. It did not take long to settle on Tangier, a sunny place for shady people before Somerset Maugham said that about Monte Carlo, a whitewashed enclave about the size of the Isle of Wight in the north of Morocco that in 1924 emerged from a squabble between colonising France and Spain as an International Zone.

Farcical as it seemed in many ways, the Zone was one of the more successful achievements of the League of Nations that Sir Edward Grey had encouraged President Wilson to create. At Versailles, implacable imperialists and new land-grabbers among the peacemakers had torn apart Wilson's fantasy of a new world order powered by self-determination and democratic principles. The fifty-eight nation League that was cobbled together did incorporate his sanctified Fourteen Points, but not all of them pointed in quite the direction Wilson had hoped. Much of the detail at the Peace Conference was delegated to House and Lansing but House saw little of his old friend. Wilson was in poor shape, an intimation of the stroke that a few months later would poleaxe him. House and Lansing often had to report to Edith, who would come back with the president's instructions and responses. Or what they had to accept were the president's; they came to suspect that sometimes she simply guessed what Wilson wanted to say. There was also help to be had from Sir William Wiseman, who had been appointed the British delegation's Advisor on American Affairs. His continuing closeness to House meant that the American delegation, whose interests were often at variance with Britain's, received just as much of his attention.

Sir William Wiseman as a Lieutenant-Colonel

Whether Wilson was well advised or not, the political hard men on the Allied side, George Clemenceau of France, Lloyd George and Winston Churchill, Secretary for War since the war ended, danced rings around him, although the lot of them failed to make the world a better place for long.

Back in the United States, Edith hid her husband's true condition from Congress and the nation for months. Wilson failed to persuade Congress to take the United States into the League, virtually ensuring that his main hope for it, the prevention of war, would not be realised. The League did, however, settle some border disputes. It decreed that the Tangier territory would be administered by a council representing eight European countries with the United States allowed a watching brief. Italy was specifically excluded, which Signor Benito Mussolini, the new prime minister, took personally.

Across Europe, power was shifting into the hands of men whose embittered followers proclaimed themselves by the colour of their shirts. António de Oliveira Salazar's *Estado Novo* set the style with a fetching shade of blue: the only fashion statement ever to come out of Portugal. In Spain the Falangists preferred their blue a little darker. Mussolini chose black for his *Fascisti*, Hitler brown for the Nazi party. In Russia, of course, they wore red.

The clang of new weaponry being forged was barely audible in Tangier. Within the boundary insulating the Zone from the Spanish territory surrounding it the original population of Arabs and Jews retained their traditional ways and means. Europeans introduce their own. French and English, Germans and Spaniards set up banks, post offices, courts and police. Many of the foreigners were drawn there by the opportunities for all kinds of mischief, financial, political and sexual, but as long as they did not do it in the street and frighten the donkeys they could behave pretty much as they liked.

The British, of course, imported snobbery, the twin pillars of which were the El Minzah Hotel, property of the Scottish but sun-loving Marquess of Bute, and St Andrew's Anglican cathedral. They fenced off a cemetery for themselves and another for their pets, built tennis courts, a golf course and organised a hunt. There were scores of retired officers like Guy whose pensions, converted at a ridiculously favourable exchange rate, bought a lifestyle they could never find anywhere else: those servants that Guy found essential and sun-filled houses; in his case, two that he converted into one.

A garden which rambles down the cliffs sprang up in time with a faithful native to help me rear the flowers and vegetables that flourish so well in this hard bright atmosphere. From the front windows I look straight down precipitous cliffs descending to the sea, stretching across the Straits of Gibraltar.

Below in the bustling Grand Souk he shopped for whatever else he needed, fascinated as much by the sellers as by what they sold.

All the women wear white, most of them showing only their wonderful eyes, not entirely due to nature, for the European sister cannot teach the women of the harem much when it comes to make-up.

The spread of civil aviation meant that Paris could be reached in a day from the Spanish airport fifty miles away, with only five or six fuelling stops en route. A British or Dutch liner on the Far East run called in every week; on a homebound P&O it took only two days to Southampton. In addition, there was a virtual hop-on, hop-off steamer route around the Mediterranean. A brisk run over to Nice let Guy visit Ernest and Minnie.

Minnie was still turning out a book every couple of years but it had become evident that writing would not provide for all her needs. Although neither brother had much money to spare they agreed to make her an allowance. She installed herself in the brazenly picturesque village of Sainte Agnès, 4,000 feet above Monaco; the dry air did wonders for her asthma. The French were building an enormous fortress there in case Mussolini's bombastic Fascists tried to reclaim territory that had been Italian a century earlier when people there decided they would be better off French. She was reminded of the ruined forts that lured her to Africa, crumbling monuments to attacks that never came.

Many of the British émigrés in Tangier were old India hands and the easily reachable Moroccan hinterland was ideal for the horsey sports to which much of their careers had been devoted. Guy collected a pack of hounds and was elected Master of the Hunt, whose quarry was scrawny desert foxes and jackals. There was a polo ground, too, but what he liked best was pig-sticking. He could remember when the young Gaunts had been so taken with the idea of this stirring encounter between man and beast that he and Cecil got into trouble for attacking a Ballarat farmer's prize sows with sharpened broomsticks. This was the real thing, though; there were wild boars in the desert, small but vicious, capable of crippling a horse or rider. Beaters would drive hogs out of the scrub, banging petrol cans and shouting, to the great amusement of anyone who understood, 'Get on, you Christian pig! Run, you dirty Jew!'

Whatever his talent for poetry or propaganda, Guy's old adversary George Viereck had a fine gift for making trouble. America's entry to the war meant the end of *The Fatherland* so with typical modesty he changed the title to *Viereck's Weekly*. Intimidated by Attorney- General Gregory's brutal Espionage and Sedition Acts, he kept the content anodyne and himself out of sight. With peace, however, he emerged as partisan as ever, launching *The American Monthly*. In 1919 he wrote in an editorial that the Versailles treaty meant that 'every German in the world would be dreaming of the war that is to come for the redemption of the land taken from the Germans'. In 1923 he was one of the first reporters to interview Adolf Hitler: 'This man, if he lives, will make history.' He got that right.

Then he put his own spin on those shadowy battles of Manhattan, first in a *Saturday Evening Post* article on 29 June 1929. The piece was bylined 'One of the War Propagandists' but Viereck was obviously its author. The account was repeated in a book published the following year that did carry his name, *Spreading Germs of Hate*. Somehow he or the publishers persuaded Colonel House to provide a foreword, which they must have regretted since House made it clear that he believed almost nothing of what Viereck had written—an opinion shared by most reviewers.

In Viereck's version the head of the British 'secret service' in New York was not, as most believed, 'the picturesque Guy Gaunt' but Sir William Wiseman. This might have been an arguable assertion but it was made particularly wounding by the malicious little anecdote in which it was embedded. Guy and Wiseman, Viereck's story went, had been together at a luncheon given by one of New York's 'upper Four Hundred'. Their hostess, whom Wiseman had not previously met, told him 'confidentially' that she would introduce him to 'the head of your secret service ... Captain Gaunt'. Whether she actually did was a detail Viereck ignored in the interest of inflicting maximum embarrassment on the 'energetic but not always discreet' attaché.

Poor Guy Gaunt squirmed in his seat but his tongue was tied. From the first cocktail to the last cigarette, the amiable hostess poured into the ears of Sir William Wiseman the marvelous exploits of Captain Guy Gaunt in his capacity as the head of the secret service.

Publicly, Guy shrugged off the slight, insisted that nothing of the kind had ever happened—although given the rivalries prevailing at the time it easily could have. On an Australian visit he made a year after Viereck's book came out he rattled off anecdotes about those New York days. He told members of the Millions Club lunching at David Jones department store in Sydney of intercepting letters from an American girl to her German lover in which she wrote that she had seen 'that beast Gaunt holding his head in his hands and saying 'The Germans have beaten me again.' He was just as disarming about his abandoned political career. 'I have no brains,' he told the enthralled audience. 'But I possess a certain amount of low cunning and pride myself on the gift of repartee.' He also possessed a heart swollen with pride in his feats of that heady time and Viereck's sly affront lodged in it like one of Dr Scheele's little cigars, the acids eating their way towards an explosion.

The clifftop house was ready when Guy got back to Tangier but he did not live there alone for long. In the three hundred pages of his autobiography there is only a single mention of 'my wife'—not Margaret but her successor, Sybil Joseph, a widow of independent whims. They married in December 1932. No photograph of Sybil as she was at that time survived the upheavals that were to come but she is remembered by a son-in-law as striking and spirited. She claimed to have galloped along the Tangier beaches at dawn as barebacked as her mount, which seems improbable. She may well have wanted to, though. Her early life brings to mind an edgy version of John Betjeman's limber Joan Hunter Dunne, 'Furnished and burnished by Aldershot sun'.

Sybil Victoria Grant-White was burnished—as much as anyone could be—by the sun of Heene, on the Sussex coast, where her father was a bank manager. She was twenty when the war ended, twenty-five in 1922 when she married William Octavius Joseph, a widower of sixty. It could not have been the match she and her family hoped for but a generation of husband material had been written off in the casualty lists and a girl had to take what she could get. He was an engineer working in Egypt for the Suez Canal Company and they went to live in Cairo. For better or worse, it was not a lengthy marriage nor were there any children. Within a few years, Mr Joseph died and Sybil moved to Tangier. When she married Guy she was thirty-four, he sixty-three.

Guy did not give Felstead much to work with about the Tangier period. Since *The Yield* was published in 1940—with the author described on the title page as 'Naval Attaché and Chief of the British Intelligence Service in the United States 1914-1918'— the causes of the disastrous feud with the Foreign Office in which Guy subsequently became embroiled have to be pieced together from the archives and correspondence and legal statements of several years later, jumbled and bile-tinged on Guy's part; aloof and disdainful on the diplomatic side. Felstead signed off well before the Second World War began, leaving Guy and 'my wife' in the idyllic house on the cliff he had named Four Winds.

PART FOUR

The war between the wars

1936. It was too good to last. No matter how hard the sybarites and scoundrels of Tangier tried to remain indifferent to what was going on outside their haven of privilege they could not ignore the loud noises from Spain after 1931, when a left-wing government dethroned King Alfonso XIII and proclaimed a republic. New elections in 1933 moved the government to the right, heartening Spaniards who wanted the monarchy restored—the army especially. The Republic survived but did not trust the generals. *Le Journal de Tanger* and the *Gibraltar Chronicle* kept Tangerines up to date on the career of the youngest of them, Francisco Franco, a well known monarchist. In 1934 the government assigned him to bring colonial soldiers over from Morocco to break up a miners' strike in the province of Asturia. The brutal operation in which some 2,500 were killed won the admiration of Rightists but when the 1936 elections improved the Republican grip on the country he was shipped off to command the garrison of the Canary Islands.

It might be thought that, in the spirit of the 1922 Committee, Guy would be inclined to favour a strong-armed monarchist like Franco. But he was never more than a middle-of-the-road Conservative with no taste for authoritarian politics. Unlike some of his British friends, most notably Pemberton-Billing, he had never been attracted by the homegrown Blackshirts, the British Union of Fascists. Not that his affable manner made him wholly egalitarian. All the Gaunts were officer material, confident in the standing that the World entitled them to, a presumption of superiority that shaded off into genial racism. Guy did not hesitate to refer to 'the nigger' or 'the Jew', never seeming to consider that he might be speaking of some of his best friends: Jack Morgan, Edward Stettinius, Lord Reading. Nonetheless, he got along fine with Moroccans, particularly the well-off and worldly who often entertained him and 'my wife'. Got on better, in

275

fact, with the Arabs, Berbers and Jews of Tangier than with many of the local Europeans as it gradually came to seem that the war in Spain was merely the warm-up for a larger confrontation.

Four Winds looked down into the crowded harbour where the coming and going of rival warships measured out the last days of peace. Italians were the most frequent visitors. Resentful of the obstacle that older navies posed to her claim to sole ownership of the Mediterranean, Italy was building a modern fleet. Its sleek new ships frequently sidled in to sniff at the tails of French super-destroyers and disdainful British cruisers from Gibraltar across the Strait. The Rock was only a couple of hours away by ferry. Ernest's flag captain at Jutland, now Vice Admiral Dudley Pound and commander-in-chief of the Mediterranean Fleet, had his headquarters there where Guy was always welcome.

Tangier was rarely short of an entertaining scandal. One began unreeling in 1933 when a new British envoy, Frederick Gye, arrived. The importance of the appointment, which meant a seat on the Committee of Control, was recognised in the job title of Envoy Extraordinary, Minister Plenipotentiary and Consul-General. Gye had an unusual pedigree for a diplomat. His mother was a celebrated diva, Dame Emma Albani, his father the director of the Royal Opera House. He was unmarried and his constant companion was a sleek young Arab servant. The relationship was so blatant that whenever the pair showed up at receptions, strait-laced Spanish *duennas* would sweep out of the room. For as long as he could Guy shrugged off the complaints brought to him in his Residents Association role, but eventually sent some of the stronger ones off to the Cabinet Secretary in London whom he knew, Maurice Hankey. Hankey was a famously tactful puller of strings and, according to Guy, he replied: 'After investigation action has been taken.' Certainly, Gye soon flounced offstage.

It is not surprising that the Foreign Office was irritated by Guy's interference. There were still people there who remembered the trouble and inconvenience he had caused in the past, especially over insisting that those suspect consuls in America be replaced. And all that backstairs stuff with Colonel House. And the Zimmermann Telegram affair in which the diplomats had been completely by-passed. Now here he was again, sticking his naval nose into diplomatic matters, a pompous has-been blowing off steam. Admiral Blimp.

As events in Europe unfolded intrigue flourished and Guy was soon drawn in. He did not have to advertise: people knew he had some kind of shadowy background in the service of the State. Whether he wished it or not he was soon at the centre of a new network of Little People—most of them, unfortunately, less able and dependable than the Voska network. Most of the information they brought in was just malicious gossip about the multinational bureaucrats of the Zone. What he really wanted to know was what the present generation of British spooks was up to. Something fairly disastrous, as it turned out.

In the summer of 1936 the Spanish army high command decided to unseat the Republican government. The conspiring generals were not confident that enough army units around the country would follow their orders for a *coup d'etat* to succeed. They needed the support of the Army of Africa stationed in Morocco, more than 100,000 turbaned colonial soldiers and Spain's elite Foreign Legion. The only man who could be sure of the loyalty of those fierce troops if they were ordered to rebel against the Republic was their erstwhile commander, General Franco. And to lead them to the mainland but he would have to be brought over from his virtual exile in the Canaries without arousing suspicion.

Who decided that Britain should lend a stealthy helping hand to destroy the legitimate government of a neighbour is still open to question. There had been several Cs since Cunningham. The outfit that Wiseman said was 'discreetly called a department of the Foreign Office' had split into a domestic MI5 and an offshore MI6, aka the SIS. Nevertheless, when the owner of the rabidly right-wing Madrid newspaper *ABC*, Juan Ignacio Luca de Tena, decided to give history a helping hand his London correspondent Luis Bolin knew where to turn. The editor of the right-wing and Roman Catholic *English Review*, Douglas Jerrold, referred him to a like-minded journalist, Hugh Pollard.

Pollard had been on the *Daily Express* before the war; he was now 'Sporting Editor' of *Country Life*. He had written twenty books, some about fishing, others about firearms, with which he claimed to be an expert. He had a parallel career as an army reservist, joining up well before the Great War and becoming an intelligence officer. During the civil war in Ireland he was a major attached to MI7b, one of the baffling War Office covens that had not been absorbed by the SIS.

The report of an official interview with Pollard among documents released by the National Archives in 2010 profiles an archetypal personality of the intelligence *milieu*. As well as his military background Pollard had an engineering degree from London University, knew French, German and Spanish, could shoot, ride, swim, drive, ski, sketch and read a map. Under the heading of Political Views, the report noted that he was vice chairman of his local Unionist Association and 'Extreme Right'. Other documents suggested he could be dangerous company. He had a tendency to discharge firearms in his working quarters.

Bright and early on 11 June, Pollard and another former army officer, Cecil Bebb, arrived at Croydon airport to board a plane chartered from Olley Airways. To reinforce the impression that they were well-heeled pleasure seekers off on an adventure they were accompanied by a pair of sporty-looking young blondes. In reality the women were Pollard's daughter Diana and her friend Dorothy Watson.

Bebb was a pilot and would fly the De Havilland Dragon Rapide, a smart-looking twin-engined biplane with a glassed-in cabin that seated eight. Unusually for a pleasure outing, Pollard had arranged for a short-wave wireless set to be fitted and hired an operator, George Bryers. Rapides were used on most short-haul routes around Britain but they had a range of five hundred miles. The adventurous foursome's destination, Las Palmas in the Canary Islands, was at least fifteen flying hours away; they would need to make refuelling stops in France, Portugal and Morocco. The people at Olley warned that maintenance skills might be in short supply in such places so they decided to take along a flight engineer, Walter Petre, known around the field as Pete.

All did not go smoothly. The long hops were tedious; people got on each others' nerves. During the stopovers Bryers drank too much and became objectionable. Before taking off from Casablanca for the last leg out to the islands Pollard dumped him. Pollard and Bebb then dressed up for their arrival. Only when Pete the mechanic saw them in military uniform did he realise this was no holiday.

Even then, there were days of waiting before Franco decided he was ready to go with them but eventually the tubby little general and a couple of his aides squeezed into the Rapide and were flown off to Tetuán, the army headquarters in Morocco. The girls were left to find their own way home.

Franco was now the fulcrum of the rebellion but there was still a major obstacle to dislodging the government. The Spanish navy remained loyal to the Republic and declined to bring the Army of Africa across to Spain. Franco knew the man to call. Adolf Hitler, just getting into his jack-booted stride, sent a fleet of Junker transports to airlift the first contingents. Mussolini did not want to be left out and Italy was soon sending whatever aircraft and elite Blackshirt volunteers could be spared from the invasion of Ethiopia.

Just as with Dansey's wild Trotsky move in 1917 the course of world events had been determined by a more or less whimsical piece of British spookery. Since Franco was the only man the Africans were ready to follow across to Spain, had he not been delivered to Tetuán there would have been no coup. The disastrous civil war might never have ensued, Germany and Italy would not have discovered that Britain and France—and the League of Nations—ran scared of them. The wider conflict that followed might have been delayed or averted altogether. Franco's victory gave the established dictators a chance to show their muscle and World War Two became inevitable.

Pollard may not have been on the SIS payroll when Bolin approached him but he was certainly with it in spirit and it with him. A few months later, with Franco's Nationalist army besieging Madrid and Russia pledging help to the Republic, the Whitehall spooks were having trouble keeping up with events. They briefed Pollard to go back to Spain and ask Franco what was going on. But he seems to have priced himself out of the job. In addition to a diplomatic passport and top of the range fees and expenses, he wanted the service to pay for a deer-hunting trip so that he could write about it for *Country Life*. Nevertheless, he kept in touch with the official spooks and they kept an eye on him. An opinion recorded in 1941 was that while Pollard seemed able to do certain jobs well 'he was definitely unreliable where money and drink was concerned'. By then he was the MI6 station chief in Madrid.

Most members of the League of Nations signed a 'non-intervention' agreement to prevent military aid to either side from being landed in

Spain and some sent warships to blockade the coast. British and French captains often turned a blind eye to freighters making for ports still held by the Republican government but Hitler's new navy, the *Kriegsmarine*, was blatant in its support of Franco. Passenger steamers ferrying the main Army of Africa across were protected by the eleven-inch guns of the pocket battleships *Deutschland* and *Admiral Scheer*. Both vessels would put in to Tangier where even the most deracinated emigrés now found it hard not to take sides. In addition to the internecine factions divided by shirt colour, the British objected to thuggish Italian sailors smearing Fascist graffiti on their post office, the French to the crew of the *Deutschland* singing *Deutschland über Alles* in the streets.

The new Envoy Extraordinary was Edward Keeling, promoted from the embassy in Rio de Janeiro where he had been Counsellor. He arrived alone, wife to follow, and Guy was one of the first to whom he turned for a briefing about what was happening. To begin with, the Gaunts got on well with him, exchanging dinner invitations and comparing notes. Sybil helped buy furniture for the Residence, some of it made to her own designs. Tangier had become a *louche* tourist destination and the Gaunts built several cottages near Four Winds that, rented to visitors lured by the beaches or shadier pleasures that were as easily available, made for a nice little earner.

They and Keeling were soon in agreement about the ways of the Tangerine bureaucracy, particularly the ineptitude of the British judge at the international court, Michael Rafferty— who was actually Irish. Guy merely thought Rafferty had a bias against British and French litigants. Keeling was harsher. He was 'an amiable, weak, gentlemanly nonentity who commands little respect'. Besides, he was 'incredibly stupid'. He thought Mrs Rafferty an even less admirable human being, 'half Greek and half Dutch, with many of the less attractive qualities of the former race—a great mischief maker and a writer of anonymous letters'. Such reckless candour set the tone of all Keeling's reports. They were often laced with contemptuous references to the Spanish Republicans and anyone who seemed in sympathy with them which, he must have assumed, was the kind of thing the Foreign Office wanted from him.

Relations with the Gaunts cooled, in Guy's recollection, after Mrs Keeling arrived. She was an Argentine and the widow of an Italian by whom she had two sons. Both were in the Italian army; one serving in Spain. Since by that time the presence of Blackshirt brigades fighting in support of Franco was a matter of international concern this created a certain awkwardness, in Guy's mind. So did Mrs Keeling's makeover of the consulate, which she redecorated 'to look like an Italian villa'. In 1937, the coronation of Edward VII imminent, the British community was disappointed to find that no celebration had been planned. Guy borrowed a few hoists of flags from a French destroyer—and Christmas decorations from the German Legation—to see that the Consulate did not go unbedecked.

These were trivial, if troubling, matters for the British community but when the Marquess of Bute's business agent and his lawyer informed Guy that Keeling had greeted some Italians in the bar of the El Minzah with a Fascist salute he could not let it pass. He did not confront Keeling (who had already reported to London that the Bute family were of 'rabid Left' views and that the lawyer was head of the local Communist party). Rather, he asked the agent, a Mr Grisswood, to swear to what he had seen and sent the affidavit off to Hankey.

Everyday affairs of the Zone were in the hands of the Administrator, M. Joseph Le Fur and his assistant Charles Vernon Dicken, French and English respectively. According to Guy, these two were so concerned by the aggressive behaviour of Italian residents and their visiting compatriots that they asked him to use his influence in London to get something done to calm the atmosphere. Early in 1938 he went to Britain: Cecil had been killed by a fall from the saddle. The DNI of the time, Rear Admiral James Troup, heard what he had to say and something was done. When Guy got back, HMS *Barham*, 30,000 tons and eight fifteen-inch guns, lay in Tangier harbour, a heavy hint that the Mediterranean Fleet stood ready to discourage Italians and Germans from misbehaving.

That year, Germany absorbed Austria and—with the virtual consent of Britain and France—Czechoslovakia. The Zone began to wonder if once the Spanish battlefields had been cleaned up, Franco might grab Tangier. Hitler and Mussolini would support him in the interests of keeping an eye on, or even capturing, Gibraltar. In September the ominous preliminaries to World War Two began to unreel, beginning with the meeting between Prime Minister Neville Chamberlain and Hitler that concluded with

Chamberlain's fatuous declaration that 'peace in our time' was now assured. Peace had been bought—for a while—by giving Germany back the Sudeten territories annexed by the Versailles planners to create the Czechoslovakia Voska had dreamed of.

After a second Munich meeting, optimism dissolved. In Tangier nerves were set jangling anew. Neighbours might any day find themselves on opposite sides. Some German residents hung out swastika flags. One of the U-boats Germany had surreptitiously deployed around Spain, *U-33*, made an impudent appearance in the harbour and, against the orders of the Council, topped up with fuel. The French, Italian and Spanish consulates sandbagged their windows and locked the doors. But when, on 22 October, Guy called at the British Legation for advice he found the building wide open, the only official on duty a recently arrived member of the Levant Consular Corps, a sort of auxiliary service. This time he complained directly to the Undersecretary for Foreign Affairs, Sir George Mounsey, who until earlier in the year had been head of the Western Department, responsible for Spain and Tangier. Where had Minister Keeling been when his countrymen needed him? 'Cannot something be done?' wrote Guy. 'AND AT ONCE.'

Mounsey had recently heard Guy's name in another context. In Washington, President Roosevelt asked the British ambassador, Sir Ronald Lindsay, to stay behind for a chat after a White House reception. He reminisced warmly about Sir Guy Gaunt and the Anglo-American intelligence co-operation during the First World War, hinting heavily at his own involvement. The ambassador realised he was being told that it might be time to organise a new trade-off of secret information. Neither the Foreign Office or the SIS took the hint so Roosevelt got the ONI to set up a secret link with the Admiralty. Another crafty by-pass and one the diplomats did not welcome.

As far as anyone could tell nothing was done about Guy's concerns and on 10 November 1938 James Maxton MP told the House of Commons he had received grave complaints about the government's representative in Tangier from 'a man in whose honesty I can place complete reliance, and in whose ability to weigh up a situation of that kind I can place confidence'.

It had been astute of Guy to choose Maxton as a mouthpiece. He was leader of the Independent Labour Party, a Leftward breakaway from the main organisation that was by then well established in Parliament, and an unswerving foe of Nazis and Fascists. He was delighted at the chance to shape up to the Under Secretary of State for Foreign Affairs, the Honorable R A Butler, who was to go on to hold several great offices of state but who at that time was seen as an appeaser of the Continental dictators.

Maxton outlined the case against Keeling, quoting from the letters in which Guy had briefed him. When Keeling arrived in Tangier

> he gave a large party to various Fascist leaders, Spanish, Italian, Portuguese ... . We Britishers here are more or less on a powder magazine, and this man is the match. We believe here that the Italians were planning a coup, and that British people could not approach the Minister on the matter because he would go straight to the Italians.

The House was told about Mrs Keeling's Italian connection, her Blackshirt sons, the alleged Fascist greetings and salutes. Most seriously, at a time when British residents were looking for guidance from their envoy he had been in Spain, visiting the Blackshirt boy. And this, said Maxton, scornfully, was His Majesty's Minister representing the nation's policy of non-intervention.

It took a few weeks for 'somebody called Butler'—as Guy told it—to come up with a refutation. It could be seen, the Under Secretary told the Commons, that the allegations had been made by 'a certain British resident in Tangier, who has for a considerable time past been conducting a campaign against His Majesty's Representatives ...'.

Butler quoted from—but did not publish in full—letters he said were from 'the majority of the senior members of the British community holding property in Tangier', from the British Chamber of Commerce and the local British newspaper all disassociating themselves from the accusations. As to the Italian connection, it was true, said someone named Butler

> that Mr. Keeling is married to a lady who, though not of Italian birth herself, was formerly married to an Italian subject and that one—not two—of his stepsons is serving in Spain. But it by no means follows that because Mr. Keeling has these family ties with Italy he allows them to affect his judgment.

The consul-general had not deserted his post during 'the recent international crisis', Butler insisted. The Foreign Office was aware that he was escorting his wife to San Sebastián 'where he stayed in a hotel and met his step-son, who had been ill. When he heard that the talks in Germany had broken down he returned to Tangier'. On his return Mr. Keeling reported that

> he had found everything quiet, though there had been some alarm among certain of the foreign communities. The British colony, however, apart from their natural apprehensions about the international situation, did not seem to have been unduly alarmed.

The tone of aloof dismissal that comes off the pages of Hansard suggests strongly that Guy was on to something which the British Government, and especially the Foreign Service found embarrassing. John Rathom could not have done a better job of blowing up a story to bursting point. Guy could not have done a better job of making an intractable enemy of the Foreign Office. And he had not finished yet.

Keeling's personal response was to inform the Foreign Office that agitation against him had been stirred up by Masonic lodges 'controlled from Barcelona and Moscow' as well as by the French who, even more than the Spanish, wanted to add Tangier to their North African territory. It was evident, said the British envoy, that his French counterpart, 'an incredibly slimy individual', was 'much more in it than I suspected at first and they ably played Gaunt's crazy personal feud for their own political ends'. Not exactly a cool, diplomatic response but in the FO files 'Gaunt' and 'crazy' were linked.

The first sanction was petty. The Mediterranean flagship, HMS *Warspite*, came in and held an Open Day for the British community. No invitation for Guy. Assuming that an innocent error had left the patriarch of the Residents Association off the list, he sent Sir Dudley a note. Embarrassed, the admiral explained he had instructions that neither Guy nor Mrs Gaunt were to be invited to any official occasion.

People did not need to be British to be unhappy with what was going on in Tangier. A plan to build wireless transmitter towers on the coast of Spanish Morocco was put up by a company that was, ostensibly, Dutch. Some of the communities feared that one European nation or another would use them to broadcast propaganda and thus make them a target.

Guy was reminded of the danger posed by the Telefunken network around the Americas but the project seemed to have Keeling's support. The Portuguese doyen of the Control Committee, Antonio Alfredo Barjona de Freitas, compiled a dossier of misgivings and asked Guy to go to London again—'at my own expense'—and show it to someone influential. He was reluctant to make the trip not only because he thought it likely he would be shrugged off. In the year of the Munich crisis, Sybil, then thirty-nine, had a baby, Penelope. Guy was a father for the first time—as far as anyone knew— at sixty-nine. Whatever they were doing right, they did it again. Less that two years later there was another daughter, Shirley.

On the first day of June 1939, Guy went to London yet again. Proofs of *The Yield* were ready although whether there would be paper to print the book was questionable. War was all but certain, essentials already in short supply. The Germans were poised to attack Poland which Britain and France were treaty-bound to defend. Air raid shelters were being dug in Green Park; in Pall Mall there were sandbags at the entrance of the Senior. London was not a comfortable place in other ways. A reputation for being a notorious adulterer carried a certain cachet in Tangier but he was still *persona non grata* in London drawing rooms. Even at the Admiralty he was given plenty of sea room: reports of his undiplomatic behaviour had got around.

Thinking it would be futile to approach the Foreign Office, Guy went to see Hankey once again. He had wasted his fare, Hankey told him a couple of days later. Whatever the Frietas dossier showed, it was not enough to unseat Keeling. 'They won't kick him out on this.' Nevertheless, work on the towers stopped and soon afterwards Keeling was posted to Venezuela. He got as far as Madrid en route when the Foreign Office recalled him and told him he was being retired.

Guy left London on 1 September, the day German troops crossed into Poland, arriving home on 3 September, the day Britain followed France in declaring war. To general relief, Franco, now Spain's undisputed dictator, let it be known that that Spain would be a 'non-belligerent'. With luck, Tangier would be able to sit out a brief war with minimal inconvenience. Once again, Guy would be a spectator on neutral ground.

The next Envoy Extraordinary was Alvary Douglas Frederick Trench-Gascoigne, more commonly known as Joe. To begin with he took to Guy, while letting him know why he was out of favour at the Foreign Office. 'You seem to have got under their skin in the last war when you kicked out some of their consuls.' No news there, but Guy was pleased to be told he was regarded as 'turbulent', presumably because of the Keeling affair. Personal relations with Joe Gascoigne were anything but turbulent. Whatever Guy's foibles and prejudices he was an important personage in the community, though not the only one. A shadowy figure, popular at the Legation if nowhere else, was Frederick William Ellis, the British delegate on the committee that ran the port. He was the 'local small businessman', in Guy's description, to whom Keeling had turned to rally support after Maxton's assertions in parliament. Ellis claimed to have been a lieutenant colonel in the Royal Army Medical Corps during the earlier war. He practiced as an optician in Gibraltar before opening a shop in Tangier and some of his compatriots had difficulty in reconciling that exalted service rank with the modest civilian occupation.

Guy never bothered to hide his mistrust of Ellis, particularly after he emerged as an energetic advocate of the wireless masts. When Gascoigne asked why nobody seemed to have a good word to say about the chap, Guy replied affably that it might be because the chap was dishonest, untrustworthy and an incipient bankrupt. Whether any of that was correct there was a question of identity the Foreign Office might not have been aware of—or that it might have helped arrange. Army records that would not have been publicly accessible then, show half a dozen William Frederick Ellises. Only one was a lieutenant-colonel in the RAMC and he died in 1939 when the Ellis in Tangier was being given the run of the Legation.

Minnie's War

Minnie was once again a serious worry. She had not stayed long at Sainte Agnés. The steep steps and walkways in the village proved difficult and the incessant drilling and blasting annoyed her. The fortifications being built were now spoken of as the Southern Maginot Line, a counterpart to the longer and larger version in the north-east, facing Germany. After sending off the manuscripts of *The Surrender* and *Where the Twain Meet* she returned to sea level and settled in Bordighera, a few kilometres across the frontier in Italy, a flower-bedecked resort often painted by Claude Monet and greatly favoured by the wintering English. She took a large apartment in a stuccoed pile called the Villa Camilla, installed a housekeeper, Anselma, together with child and handyman husband, and set up her typewriter on the shaded terrace. Her niece Yvonne was enrolled in a convent school nearby; Minnie would take the little girl with her to the International Library where they would read the English newspapers and chat to fellow expatriates, most of whom agreed that life in Italy had improved considerably under Signor Mussolini. The war in Abyssinia might not be going well but that part of Africa would benefit from European influence. And if *Il Duce* was outspoken from time to time about England and France, well that was just politics, wasn't it? In 1936 Lucy, the sister Minnie always generously described as the prettier, died in Melbourne. Ellinor Archer, her daughter, came over to visit, then went across to see Guy before going on to London.

For a while Minnie found inspiration scarce. Money, too. The allowance from Guy and Ernest paid her rent but not much more. She tapped out a pot-boiler for a series published by A C Black called *Peeps at Great Men*. Her personal peep was at George Washington, 'the man who made the American Revolution'. She targeted *The Times* with letters on Employment for Women, Emigration in the Empire and Nursing as a Profession. Then she chanced upon another intrepid explorer who, just like Tonkin/Essex, could provide the exotic colouring she needed for fresh novels. Colonel Harald Swayne had mapped the frontier between British Somaliland and Abyssinia and hunted desert game around Aden. She raided his reminiscences for *Saul's Daughter* and *The Lawless Frontier*, both of which were dedicated to him. 'But for the public's dislike of two names on a title-page,' Minnie wrote in a letter

> yours should have been alongside mine as part author. If I wrote the story and thought out the characters, the local colour is certainly yours.

Perhaps sharing a title page did for the Ridgewell/Essex collaboration. There were two more works of fiction to come, each dedicated to one of the benevolent brothers, *Joan of The Pilchard* to Guy; *Worlds Away* to Ernest.

The Pilchard was a West Country inn and William Bligh of *Bounty* figured in the plot; Guy, as usual, provided seafaring advice. Ernest needed cheering up. He and his beautiful but doomed wife had moved back to Britain, all but wiped out financially by chasing cures for her chronic asthma; their daughter Yvonne estimated that they had consulted at least five hundred doctors in a dozen countries. The Irish brewery money had dried up; the grand Monaco apartment had to go. They set up again in a small flat in South Kensington where Geraldine died.

After Britain and France declared war on Germany, Mussolini began to make noises about re-taking some French territory and ordered several divisions to the frontier. The expats of Bordighera began to wonder if Italy was the best place to be. Minnie decided to move to Menton, just inside France. She locked up Villa Camilla and sent Anselma home to Reggio Emilia further inland. But after several weeks in a grim little *pension* it looked as though Italy was going to remain on the sidelines. Guy got a letter from her in June 1940 saying she was back in Bordighera: the last he heard.

Nearly eight months of uneasy optimism followed until the German *Blitzkrieg* overwhelmed the French army. Everyone British was advised to get out of France and Italy while they could. Minnie made it as far as Nice once again with a single suitcase and her typewriter; everything else she owned had been abandoned, every file, every photograph, every letter and manuscript, as cruel a wrench for her as the loss of a child.

Mussolini, taken by surprise at the French collapse and fearful of missing out on the spoils, declared war on the Allies after all. After a few days of the most inept campaign in modern warfare, the Italians had failed to retrieve more than a few kilometres of their lost terrain but after the surrender Hitler let them occupy the southern French coastline as far as Marseille. Minnie did not surrender. A woman who had trekked through West Africa and been ready to face up to the White Wolf was not going to let a rabble of scruffy *soldati* stand in her way. In the operatic disorder of the Italian invasion she somehow managed to return to Bordighera to see what she could retrieve. Villa Camilla had been commandeered by Blackshirts. Ludicrously, the post office was still accepting mail for Australia. A letter to Ellinor dated 22 September, 1940 arrived in Melbourne via Switzerland only a few weeks later.

The house is in chaos ... all my linen, silver, in fact most little things have departed ... young soldiers in the house might be trusted to ruin everything.

Minnie's asthma had not been treated since she first fled the villa and an attack immobilised her. The letter ended, 'I can hardly walk at all now'. She got back to France as inexplicably as she had got to Bordighera but for long weeks no one knew what had happened to her.

Ellinor demanded that the External Affairs department in Canberra track down her aunt, the 'well known novelist'. She undertook to pay for the necessary cables and the neutral United States got its consul in Nice on the case. Minnie was found to be one of some forty foreigners holed up in hotels and pensions around Vence, a town in the hills where 'the French are friendly'. With the help of the British estate agent John Taylor, whose name lives on over a chain of offices around the Riviera, accounts were set up that allowed Guy to send out £5 a week via the American embassy in London. The collaborationist government in Vichy agreed that stranded foreigners could receive 'harmless' letters via Thomas Cook and messages of twenty-five words on 'family or business matters' through the Red Cross. Minnie could pay for her lodging at the *Pension Rosarie* but there was no medicine to buy and not much food. Any local produce left by the Italian occupiers went to feed the Germans in the north. She wrote to Clive, now retired in Melbourne.

We are not starving but we are always hungry. ... Everyone is very thin. I never knew I had so many bones in my body.

She described revolting meals of stewed lettuce, flavourless couscous and dry bread. There were vegetables grown in the garden, so

I believe we are better off than anyone else in this town which used to be so wealthy ... It is the lack of all fats that is so trying.

Minnie stranded behind enemy lines, Cecil dead, Ernest sick and broke, Guy about to feel the full weight of Foreign Office revenge: the luck of the Gaunts was on the wane.

Spanish jackboots

1940. Britain was now at war alone. *Alone* in the Minnie manner—since it had the support of the World and the rest of the Empire: huge resources and far more manpower than the homeland could produce. Even so, it seemed to many, including Guy's old chum Roosevelt, that London must soon be forced to make a humiliating peace. But while most of Europe lay in the deep freeze of German occupation and a struggle to keep the Suez Canal open surged to and fro at the other end of the Mediterranean, Tangier became one of the weirder sideshows of the war, an insulated polyglot hub of espionage and intrigue: Manhattan 1914 with muezzins and jackboots of Spanish leather. On the day the Germans marched into Paris a Spanish army sauntered into the International Zone from Morocco and took over. Merely a temporary measure, Franco assured the world, until events elsewhere settled down. The frontier of the Zone were clearly marked and guarded but residents were able to stay in touch with the outside world, even visit it. The various post and cable offices stayed open; mail arrived and departed on neutral ships or the air service from Tetuán to Spain and Lisbon.

All key posts of the Zone were given to Falangists. Nevertheless, Joe Gascoigne felt able to report that the new administrator Manuel Amigra y Escadon, hitherto manager of the Spanish hospital, was 'not anti-British'. In fact, he 'makes an excellent impression'. The new chief of the gendarmerie, Pedro Aurioles-Aurioles, might be 'a fanatical Falangist' but the head of the port police Edmundo Carleton—whom Guy found a useful contact—was actually a British subject by virtue of being 'the illegitimate son of His Majesty's consular agent at Alcazar'.

People had to choose their friends more carefully than ever, sometimes change them. In addition to those whose countries were occupied and the pro- or anti-coloured shirt factions of the occupiers, the French community was divided. Most accepted the Vichy government but some were attracted by the Free French movement set up in London by the refusenik Colonel Charles de Gaulle. The only disunity among the British community was caused by Guy and his outspoken views about Ellis, who had been installed in an annexe to the Legation and seemed to have taken on the roles of general advisor, press spokesman and commercial mentor. Since Ellis was still running various businesses, Guy—spurred he insisted by other residents—complained that this meant a 'small local tradesman' was being given access to business cables and thus had an unfair advantage over competitors. His intensifying criticism of Ellis annoyed Gascoigne to the point where, said Guy

> we both got a little heated but at the end of the interview, he came across and shook hands saying 'Let's call it quits, old boy, don't let you and I quarrel.'

The French colonies in north and west Africa stuck with Vichy but dissenters wanting to join the opposition begin to trickle through Spanish Morocco to Tangier. Worried that the Spaniards might intern the bolters, Guy and Sybil built a bolthole for them inside one of the cottages. Their first guest was the French grandson of an English aristocrat whom they collected in Tetuán. They organised a regular escape route, bribing fishing boats to drop fugitives on the Spanish coast just ten miles away from where a Republican network would pass them on to Gibraltar.

Between a glass of mint tea in the Grand Socca and a cocktail in the Minzah bar Guy could stroll up to the great fortress of the Kasbah and watch Italian dive-bombers trying to put one down the funnel of a ship in the Gibraltar dockyard. They rarely did real damage but it seemed only a matter of time before the Axis, with or without Spain's help, would capture the Rock, choking off Britain's supply line through the Mediterranean. There were greater threats than the *Regia Aeronautica*. Memory of the devastation caused by U-boats a generation earlier made Guy particularly sensitive to the presence of a couple of Italian submarines that limped into Tangier in November 1940, *Michele Bianchi* and *Brin*. The Germans had set up a base at Bordeaux from which to launch a new generation of Atlantic raiders and these two were on their way there to join in raids on Atlantic traffic when they were attacked by destroyers from Gibraltar, *Brin* on the surface, *Bianchi* submerged. Damaged, both took refuge in neutral Tangier.

For four weeks the subs lay in the harbour, British destroyers waiting offshore. The Italian crews become familiar figures around the waterfront; the skippers, *Capitani di Fregata* Luigi Longanesi-Cattani of *Brin*, and

Adalberto Giovannini of *Bianchi*, regulars at the El Minzah bar. Guy kept a discreet distance, relying on his amateur spies or *Jefé* Carleton to keep him informed but no one was aware that engineers had been smuggled in from Italy to get the boats back in working order. Even so, Guy was appalled when the British patrol was discontinued and protested to Gibraltar. That his complaint was put politely would not have made it more welcome. The last thing the Gibraltar command needed was a feisty old admiral shouting advice and complaints from his clifftop across the Strait.

On the night of 12 December the crews of both Italian submarines swarmed into Tangier on a raucous pub crawl. While the sailors partied in dens and dives, the two captains dined out just as conspicuously in the more salubrious part of town. It looked as though the Italians had settled in for the rest of the war. As the night wore on and shutters were pulled down the carousing submariners vanished. So did the submarines. Guy was livid but saying he told them so made his fraying relationship with the navy even worse.

1941. Guy decided on yet another visit to London. It seems surprising that more than a year into the war such a trip might be possible but German-occupied Europe was quiet; the Battle of Britain had discouraged an invasion and the real fighting was much further north and east. Hitler had been foolish enough to invade Russia which tied up most of his assets; the rest were over in Libya, stiffening the Italian desert campaign against the British. Tangier—and Spain and Portugal—took every advantage of their spectator status.

The couple of little airlines that linked Tetuán with Lisbon were still flying. From there, a traveller who could somehow manage a booking could go on to Southampton in a British Overseas Airways Corporation flying boat, a mighty Boeing 314 Clipper built in Seattle. Ships bound for Britain still dropped into Tangier, if only to time a night passage through the Strait that would make them less tempting U-boat target.

A sea passage was only slightly easier to arrange than a flight and exactly where it might end would only be decided once the ship had reached home waters. When a sailing was due, the Zone administration gave each consulate a quota of berths to distribute among deserving nationals. Guy applied for a passage to see his Harley Street doctor. His collection of knitted-up bones was giving trouble and there was no one suitable in Tangier to consult. He also wanted—another indication of how oddly normal life in the Zone remained—to arrange a mortgage on Four Winds. There are no more sea-sex-dope tourists to rent the cottages and the Gaunts missed the £1,000 or so a year they had brought in.

Guy did not record the name of the vessel he boarded but on 13 July, after nearly two weeks at sea it dropped him off in Glasgow. He was expected. A stock character in raincoat and moustache handed him a letter from the Second Lord of the Admiralty marked 'Very confidential and private'. It asked him to 'say nothing to the press about the terrible affair in Tangier'. Which terrible affair? The escape of the Italian subs? Ellis? Mystified, Guy replied: 'No intention of saying anything to anybody.' After three weeks in London he went to the Foreign Office to collect the exit permit he needed to go back to Tangier. He was told he could not have one. In fact he could not go anywhere. The passport he left to be endorsed would not be returned.

This was devastating. Everyone and everything belonging to him was back in the Zone. What about his wife and children? If Lady Gaunt was able to make her way to Britain, came the bland response, she would be allowed to enter. He cables Sybil asking her to get Gascoigne to intercede. She replies that she found their old friend Joe 'hostile'. If he had known Guy was going to Britain, Gascoigne told her, he would have warned them that he would not be allowed to return. But Gascoigne *had* known. He had helped arrange Guy's passage. It had been paid for with a cheque made out to the Legation. What was going on? Sybil had no choice but to lock up Four Winds and everything in it. She buried the family silver in the garden, abandoned the car at Tetuán airport, and got on a plane with the children and a small suitcase each, all they were allowed.

Whatever the Gaunts might have suspected, it was not spelt out until the release of Foreign Office documents thirty years later.

The fact of the matter is that Admiral Gaunt had been making himself a thorough nuisance to the Consul General in Tangier and was undermining the prestige of the Consul General in the Zone and interfering with the proper performance of its duties. ... his further presence in Tangier during the war would have been contrary to the national interest.

The archives let Gascoigne off the hook to some extent. As he wrote to a chum in the Foreign Office, the action had been taken

entirely independently of me by the Foreign Office, although it was of course due to the great trouble which I had with Gaunt in 1940 and 1941.

Great trouble? Guy certainly made a nuisance of himself with Gascoigne's predecessors but should the Foreign Office not have been concerned that a British envoy was consorting with the next enemy but one? That German U-boats were boldly refuelled in Tangier? Or Italian submarines allowed to go on their way to sink British ships? As rascally Germans had found in his waterfront days, Guy had a master gunner's compulsion to single out a target and concentrate his fire: Keeling had been caught in the crosshairs, Ellis, too, although there may have been a touch of envy that led Guy to zero in on him. Ellis was obviously a welcome participant at some level in the kind of action Guy still had a taste for. It ought to have been evident that he was either an agent of some kind or that the Legation, if not the Foreign Office, found him a useful idiot.

Guy's true offence seemed to have been drawing attention to failings that ought to have been remedied. There were, beyond doubt, plenty of conscientious and competent men in the diplomatic service but there were too many, especially in the upper tiers, who viewed the world as though it was their country estate. Guy was seventy-three, an admiral (rtd.) of the Royal Navy—a *British* admiral—a knight of the realm, a former member of parliament, the legendary hero of Gaunt's Brigade. Even if Lloyd George did exaggerate, he had changed the course of the Great War, at the least: more directly than the Zimmermann Telegram. He had even defied Lady Astor! Forcing him into exile, wrenched from home, livelihood, even perhaps family, was nothing but shabby and vindictive bureaucratic revenge.

When it became clear he was not going to get anywhere with the Foreign Office, Guy turned to the High Commission for Australia, somewhere he thought the Gaunt name might merit support and waded into a swamp of complications that made his plight even worse. Stanley Bruce, the High Commissioner, was an effective diplomat. He had been prime minister of Australia in the 1920s and later chaired the League of Nations. At the outset of the war he was on the best of terms with Churchill, who replaced Chamberlain, and his foreign secretary, Anthony Eden, but after Japan came into the war and it seemed Britain might be ready to cut Australia loose he made them uncomfortable. The Foreign Office was not about to do Bruce any favours either.

Somewhere amid a flurry of meetings and correspondence Guy got the idea that the Australians thought the immediate answer to his plight was for the British government to buy up his property in Tangier. After months of fruitless wrangling this seemed the only course; at least it would provide some capital. He set a price of £12,000 on Four Winds and the cottages and submitted his proposal to the section of the Foreign Office that— he believed—Bruce had specified and years of claim, denial and counter-claim got under way. No one in the Foreign Office would ever admit to suggesting such a solution. Nor would Bruce or anyone at Australia House. The archival record of what happened is confused and incomplete but Guy was in no doubt of what was going on: 'To put it shortly, half-a-dozen foreign office clerks have started out to ruin me and succeeded.'

Guy had not lived in London since the 1920s when the afterglow of the Cruise scandal and his undefined but widely wondered about American activities ensured that people knew who he was. Now he was just another elderly ration-book holder looking for somewhere to live, which ended up being a scrappily furnished suburban villa in Hillcrest Gardens, Esher, Surrey, as far away in spirit as could be imagined from Four Winds, let alone the Biltmore Hotel. It was an ill-omened place. As the family was were settling in, a stark note forwarded to the Senior from the Foreign Office informed them that Minnie had died on 19 January, 1942.

Ellinor scraped together some details. Her aunt had been taken to Sunny Bank, the British hospital in Cannes, suffering from asthma and general disability but little more could be discovered until after the war when foreigners stranded in France were able to tell their stories. The Germans were not supposed to be active in the unoccupied part of the country but the flow of family mail and money to Minnie attracted attention. Gestapo agents made repeated visits to her bedside. They knew that Guy and Ernest were her brothers but even if she had any information about them the questioners had no more chance of getting a word out of Minnie than she did from her last treasured possession. Her final letter to Ellinor apologised for the cramped handwriting.

> I cannot use my typewriter simply for lack of half a teaspoon of oil to make it work.

The generation of achievers that old William and Elizabeth had produced was on the way out. Only two brothers left and they were not speaking to each other.

The historians

1945. As soon as the war in Europe ended, Guy came out fighting. The family had moved from Esher to Chertsey, another town in Surrey; now he made a strategic decision to settle in Woking, where the member of parliament produced by the 1945 election was Arthur Marsden, a retired captain RN who had a destroyer sunk under him at Jutland. Between them—and with the help of an energetic firm of solicitors, Cohen & Cohen of Finsbury Circus—they would bring the Foreign Office to account. There was cause for optimism, too, in an entirely different matter. The origins and conduct of the two wars were now attracting massed scholarly attention in the United States, although one of the strands historians had pursued in the 1930s was the effectiveness of British propaganda in changing America's national stance towards Germany.

In 1939 Horace Peterson, an American academic, published *Propaganda for War*, which argued that the most important reason America had eventually gone to war in 1917 was that British influence had swayed the national mind against Germany.

> People under the influence of the propaganda came to look upon the struggle of 1914–18 as a simple conflict between the forces of good and evil ... In the minds of American leaders there was developed a blind hatred of everything German.

Professor Peterson did not feel things should have been that way.

> The propaganda blinded men completely to the actual forces at work... economics, nationalism, power politics and the rise and decline of

nations.

But he had to admit that it worked. Two-and-a-half years of plugging away at public opinion was what had ultimately brought about America's entry.

It is useless to criticise Great Britain for the propaganda—for spreading falsehoods and exaggerated interpretations of their own and their enemy's actions. Locked in a life and death struggle it was only natural that she should have vilified her enemy and have done everything in her power to gain help. The United States would do the same thing.

Peterson's was the clear 1930s American view, uncluttered by the squabbles and territorial disputes that were to develop, of which British operatives had been doing what in the critical early years of the Great War,

The person in charge in the United States was Captain Guy Gaunt, the Naval Attaché at Washington. His chief assistants were Sir William Wiseman, Sir Geoffrey Butler and Colonel Norman Thwaites.

Blinker Hall's success in deciphering messages to and from Berlin identified the most important German agents in the United States. This, said Peterson, had led to Papen and the others being constantly shadowed until it became impossible for them to do anything 'without the knowledge of the American Secret Service and Captain Gaunt'.

Wealthy universities, Yale, Harvard and Princeton in particular, began scouting for original source material but classifying and de-classifying official documents would take years. Impatient researchers set out to track down individual players who might have treasures squirreled away: correspondence, diaries, photographs. Guy was excited to receive an enquiry from Yale asking if he had anything to offer. Sir William Wiseman, he was told, had sent it a large collection of documents and a promise of more to come; a matching contribution from Admiral Gaunt would be greatly welcomed. Alas, Guy had nothing. *The Yield* was produced largely from memory. His few papers had been abandoned at Four Winds. An unpleasant feeling developed that he could easily lose the only means of buoyancy that had kept him from going under during the last miserable years, his reputation. Even when history was being written by the victors the vanquished could score points by getting their version in first. If the spiteful Viereck take on events found its way into those Wiseman files, an ephemeral flick of spite could become enshrined in the historic narrative.

But first, Guy needed to get the Foreign Office to honour the undertaking that, rightly or wrongly—and probably wrongly—he believed it had made. He was told he could now return to Tangier but that was not what he and Sybil wanted. Pillaged and dilapidated, the house they had been forced to give up was no longer their home. They wanted the deal on which, as Guy saw it, the Foreign Office had reneged: the £12,000 compensation he remained convinced he had been offered. His efforts stalled right away because the 1945 election resulted in a Labour government and Anthony Eden was swept out of the foreign secretary's chair. Captain Marsden, a Conservative, had to go back to the beginning with Ernest Bevin, a Labour stalwart with little time for minor concerns of the officer class.

The Foreign Office view was summarised by the deputy under secretary of state, Oliver Harvey. His memo is an artful construct of distortion, elision and evasion. Guy's assertions, said Harvey, was

> just part of a campaign which this rather pathetic old naval officer carries on without respite to try and secure some retribution or compensation for what he regards as ill-treatment at the hands of H M Government.

Most people would indeed regard what had happened to Guy as ill-treatment but Harvey explained that when he had wanted to return to Tangier in 1941 exit permits 'were only granted to persons travelling on journeys in the national interest'. Giving him one would have amounted to 'preferential treatment'. Then, blandly contradicting himself, Harvey goes on to say

> he was refused an exit permit because his return to Tangier would have been a serious embarrassment to Gascoigne...

'I need hardly say', said Harvey—saying it—that the Foreign Office had never offered to relieve the rather pathetic old naval officer of his property. The briefing paper he prepared to steer Bevin away from talking to Guy offered an explanation for Guy's persistence that became perpetuated in the Foreign Office.

The root of the trouble is that Admiral Gaunt's mind has become deranged as the result of a motor accident which he had some years ago.

Some *twenty* years ago. Since then Guy had, until he saw things happening in Tangier that he could not keep quiet about, been well, happy and accomplished. There was no evidence whatever that an old car crash had affected him mentally. To the straightforward question of whether his dogged determination to get equitable treatment from the Foreign Office had developed into an *idée fixe*—monomania to the psychiatrists whom Guy would never have consulted—the straightforward answer is yes. It may even have indicated the onset of dementia, a condition barely recognised in 1948, let alone respected. But it was almost certainly aggravated by the disdainful revenge inflicted on him, perhaps enhanced by that Viereck smear, an echo from the Manhattan past, piercing as a downbeat snatch of jazz.

Determined not to allow his achievements to be overwritten, Guy trained his big guns around and, in 1949, at the nadir of his hopes of getting satisfaction from the Foreign Office, fired off a series off explosive letters to Wiseman. They are badly typed, scrawled over and not always coherent. In one he asks to be forgiven for the typing: 'my Sec has given her appendix away'. Thomas Troy, the CIA historian who set out years later to unpick the conflicting claims about who had been in charge of what in New York and when, suggested the messy pages could be due to 'age, illness, a troubled mind, or too much grog'. Grog could probably be eliminated because Guy had never drunk much, apart from those exuberant martinis of Manhattan days, but to judge by the splatter of capitals and exclamation marks the other possibilities seem likely, together with failing eyesight: he turned eighty that year. But the main message comes across clearly. Guy was asking for an acknowledgement from Wiseman that the dinner table incident Viereck described had never taken place: '...the story about you and I dining at a house where you smiled while I squirmed...you know nothing of the sort ever happened'.

Guy recalled the arrival of the two gumshoes in New York and how they had found no one ready to take an interest in them. He described the bizarre scene of Wiseman sobbing in the Biltmore. Apart from such entertaining reminiscence, the letters put Wiseman on notice that Guy had not only received approaches from 'the three big Universities' in the United States but the *Saturday Evening Post* was offering to publish his original documents. He did not mention that there were no documents.

Troy was inclined to think the letters were a kind of blackmail attempt and in one of them Guy does mention the word. 'I am no blackmailer but these people have come to me ... I personally don't want to publish....'. All he wants, he repeats, is for Wiseman to disavow the Viereck story: 'just a wire Yes or NO'.

The letters make the troubled mind a near certainty, Not the version so glibly put about by the Foreign Office but a temporary failure of equilibrium caused by the shattering loss and humiliation for which the bureaucrats themselves were responsible. And a horrifying tragedy.

In the early part of 1949, the year which was to end with him firing off those erratic letters to Wiseman, Guy had been seared by a backblast from the past. The first Lady Gaunt burned to death in her bed. Margaret had never really given up Gaunts Wood. The divorce left her maimed in spirit and she became a genteel recluse. During the war the house had been taken over as a convalescent centre. She stayed on in the wing her father added that had a fine view of the valley. In 1945 her brother persuaded her to let the place be sold and go to live with him in Bath, where he was Town Clerk. Three years later she saw that the property, renovated and re-landscaped, had become the Manifold Valley Hotel and moved back into her old room, as a permanent guest. On the cold winter's night of February 8 she seems to have followed her usual practice of pulling her divan bed up to within a foot or two of the fireplace. She would sprinkle paraffin on the coals and bank them up, hoping the fire would last the night. The owner of the hotel, Joseph Blackhurst, was on his way back from the village when he saw the flames and called the fire brigade. The main part of the building was saved but not the extension. Accidental death, said the coroner. She was seventy-nine.

Defamation

If all of that had not been enough to jar Guy off balance, a letter was mistakenly delivered to him addressed to Commander Lancelot Gaunt. His explosive reaction blew both brothers right into the High Court.

Guy, his sensitivity about standing and station rubbed raw by events, took the letter to mean that Lance was trying to pass himself off as having been a commander rather than the rank of lieutenant RNR to which he had reverted after his brief American posting. And a commander RN at that, since only permanent service officers—like himself—were entitled to use their rank in retirement. The two had not spoken for years and even now Guy did not attack Lance directly but wrote to Violet, asking with leaden sarcasm,

Has your husband promoted himself to captain RN on the retired list? Why doesn't he go the whole hog and call himself 'Admiral'?

Somewhere in the unedifying barrage that descended on poor Violet there may be a clue to the brothers' estrangement. 'You can tell your husband,' Guy ranted, 'that I have left orders for all his debts to me to be cancelled on my death.' Debts? Lance had been wealthy before his attempts to get into Parliament almost beggared him and was still far better off than Guy. Did the indebtedness go back to their time together in the United States? Even earlier—to Samoa? The wardroom mess bills Guy paid for him in old *Porpoise*? Whether or not anything had been stirred in the depths of Guy's troubled mind, Lance did what lawyers do best. He sued.

The *Gaunt* v. *Gaunt* libel action was heard in January 1951. The King's Counsel acting for Lance, Mr C P Harvey, told Mr Justice Cassels the two brothers had fallen out over a personal matter some years earlier and 'by mutual agreement' saw no more of each other. Admiral Gaunt had clearly suggested that Mr Gaunt attempted to 'masquerade' as something he was not and that he was unwilling to pay a debt he owed. Both these assertions were gravely injurious to Mr Gaunt's reputation and he therefore asked for damages.

Lance took the witness stand, an impressively correct figure with an early-model hearing aid suspended around his neck. His deafness was now severe although he had been an air raid warden during the recent hostilities, patrolling the streets of Kensington, where he now lived in an impressive block of flats that still stands on the north side of the High Street. Led by Harvey KC, he said that the letter addressed to him as 'Commander' had been entirely inadvertent. He had never described himself in that way, although he was aware that others had. Nor, Lance insisted, had he ever owed his brother money. Guy's threat to mention the matter in his will had been one of his main reasons for bringing the action. As *The Times* explained

The Gaunt family being a distinguished one, with an honourable naval and military record, the matter would, on Admiral Gaunt's death, probably receive publicity and it would be published abroad that he (Mr Gaunt) owed his brother money, whereas he did not owe, and never had owed, him anything.

Uncharacteristically, Guy chose not to show up in court. No defence was offered beyond the contention by his barrister, Roger Winn, that the words complained of were not defamatory. Mr Winn conducted a cautious cross-examination. He avoided referring to other instances in which Lance had been described or addressed as 'Commander' and not, apparently, objected.

Judge Cassels did not see *Gaunt* v. *Gaunt* making judicial history. He conceded that Lance had a case even though the libel had been published only to Mrs Gaunt. Guy was ordered to pay an unimpressive £200 damages and 'being a man of honour, would restrain himself from further expressing to others, on paper, his views, whatever they might be, of his brother'.

These two, the last of their extraordinary generation since Clive died in 1942, never met again. Violet died soon afterwards and Lance moved to a retirement home in Braintree, Essex, where Yvonne Gaunt remembered him, insulated in his deafness, pottering about feeding pheasants in the hope of keeping them away from a nearby shoot. Despite those vicarious proclivities he was, by all accounts other than Guy's, a charming and agreeable man; probably just the youngest of the pack trying to keep up with the high-powered rest.

Days after being ordered to pay for his provocation Guy left for Australia on a passenger carrying freighter, SS *Zealandic*. He did his usual breezy stand-ups in Melbourne and Sydney. The only hint of eccentricity was a photograph in the Sydney *Daily Telegraph* of him dressed in a kind of half-length fur coat even though it was summer, a pair of binoculars hung around his neck. Pictures at the David Jones lunch, however, show him in a respectable three-piece suit, stern and seamanlike. No visible oddness except eyeglasses moored to his breast pocket with a gaudy ribbon.

Wily Willy

Wiseman never said anything publicly about the Viereck account; had probably long since forgotten about it. He had spent part of World War Two in the United States but missed out on the part he wanted to play. In the early days, with America on the sidelines once again, her intentions unclear, he told the director general of the SIS, Stewart Menzies, that 'or £100,000 he could set up 'the best possible intelligence service in the United States' that Britain could have. Menzies reported that 'both his predecessors had had very strong views about Sir William Wiseman and had recommended that he should on no account be employed by His Majesty's government'.

He retired from Koen, Loeb and at the time he heard from Guy he was getting the second part of his archive ready for Yale, documents that mainly dealt with the war years. In London he lived at the Ritz Hotel. With his customary deftness at inserting himself into positions of leverage he had already provided advice to the historian Charles Seymour, who took on the task of editing Colonel House's diaries into a coherent narrative. That became the main source, outside his own papers, about the part he played in those great events, whether it was as star or understudy. He was still in touch with friends and admirers from The Cause. When Guy began to stir up the past he wrote to Willert: 'We should be prepared with a suitable answer when he publishes something crazy.'

Wiseman also wrote to Arthur Murray, now Lord Elibank, having succeeded to a modest Scottish viscountcy, who made some favourable references to him in a 1946 memoir, *At Close Quarters*. The book consists largely of correspondence between Arthur and 'Willie' long after both had left government service. They are good letters on both sides, well written and soundly reasoned accounts of the people each of them had seen or listened to. High class gossip but gossip nevertheless. These old comrades had not been decision makers or takers. They were political courtiers who flattered their superiors by endorsing their opinions, passing along snippets that were often just hearsay or rumour, trading off hints and information with interested parties on all sides.

The precautionary tale that Wiseman encouraged Willert to go to work on came out in 1952, a year after Guy's return from Australia. A shameless testimonial to Wiseman entitled *The Road to Safety: A Study in Anglo-American Relations*, it was produced by a small firm run by a former diplomat and MI6 agent, Derek Verschoyer, that specialised in spook memoirs and sex. Andre Deutsch, a proper publisher who took the business over, wondered where the money to set it up could have come from. His associate Diane Athill remembered Verschoyer as 'a raffish figure, vaguely well-connected ... lolling with his feet up on his desk, used to take pot shots at the local cats out of his window with a .22 which he kept on the desk'.

Willert's transformation from journalist to diplomat had been seamless; there was little difference between what he wrote for *The Times* or for the government. After his stint with Northcliffe's mission he had been picked up by the newly created Ministry of Information and went on to become Head of News at the Foreign Office. In retirement, he was kept on the payroll for public lectures and other PR work.

For all that he might have wanted to portray Wiseman as the saviour of the Western world, Willert found the going hard. There were, of course, the House diaries with their effusive references but little to go on beyond that except for Wiseman's own papers. By page seventeen he was already lamenting that

> Wiseman's name appears in most of the British books by or about those with whom he worked, but with one exception only incidentally. The second Lord Reading, in his life of his father, alluded to him as 'an Intelligence officer of great talent attached to the Embassy', but does not bring out the extent to which his father relied on him.

It was the same on the American side 'with the difference that some of the allusions to Wiseman are mischievous and misleading'. In Willert's approach, even omissions could be converted into plugs. Lloyd George had spoken of Wiseman as 'a young officer ... attached to our Embassy in Washington where he developed remarkable ability as a diplomatist'

> but omits to relate how much he relied upon him for American guidance; how, for instance, he had him to dinner on the eve of the Paris Peace Conference and, armed with a pencil and a writing pad, and fortified by champagne, catechised him for two hours about

Woodrow Wilson, his ambitions, ways of thought, family and friends, and how he was best handled.

In a deft exercise of fact-stretching, Willert managed to associate Wiseman with all the significant episodes of 1915 and early 1916: the Archibald documents, the Albert briefcase, the mad Canada invasion scheme, the expulsion of Papen and the other German envoys, the exposure of the Hindu conspiracies, and plenty more.

Wiseman's duties included counter-espionage, the prevention of sabotage of supplies in factories, on the docks, in ships by incendiary bombs, of the poisoning of mules and horses. Of the placing of shavings of steel in bales of hay to tear the guts of animals to pieces, of the placing of little fish-hooks in cans of food to do the same to humans, of the smuggling of messages by agents in and out of the country, and so on and so on. In those cases most of it was pioneer work.

Indeed it was pioneer work but most of it had been done long before Wiseman got started. All the instances Willert cited were joint triumphs of Guy and Voska. Voska himself had no doubt about who his British connection had been. His 1941 biography detailed 'the set-up with which we carried on until February 1917. It was a triangle—Gaunt at one corner, I at another, and John R. Rathom at the third'.

Neither did Guy's action-man partner Thwaites have any doubt about who had been running the show when he joined it. As Willert told it, Thwaites took his orders from Wiseman—who had indeed recruited him— and merely 'passed as working for Gaunt'. Thwaites did not remember it that way. In his own story, *Velvet and Vinegar*, published in 1932, he wrote of Guy as his 'boss' and described his misgivings when he was told that would no longer be the case. Recalling his summons to London in late 1917, after Wiseman had gone over before him, he wrote

> The section for which I had been working ever since 1916 was under the Admiralty. We had built up an organisation of which we were proud but the proposal had been made that henceforth we should be under the direction of the War Office.

Under the SIS, actually, although Thwaites was still an army officer and 'War Office' might be taken to mean any of those interlaced alphanumerics.

Until I had received instructions in writing from my superiors I could not act in the matter. My obduracy annoyed certain officers, and I was summoned to the War Office to give an account of myself. In other words, I was 'on the mat'.

Which had been promptly whipped from under him when he was sent back to New York with the distinctly lightweight task of making sure that British servicemen visiting the United States behaved themselves. By that time Wiseman was preoccupied with his House connection but still determined to keep Kell's MI5 from muscling in on the intelligence operation, as he showed by his plan to keep The Cause afloat with a secret secret service.

Nor was there much in the way of official gratitude for Willy. Lloyd George laughed off the idea that he might be made ambassador to the United States and also declined to recommend him for a Privy Council place. He was appointed a Companion of the Order of St Michael and St George, the lowest ranking in that standard Foreign Office decoration, and a Companion—together with Guy—in that brim-full Bath.

Even if he did not always get his due from those who were supposed to have benefited from his advice and intervention, there is no doubt that Wiseman was an effective force in British-American relations—*after* the time that it was clear to all concerned that the United States would, sooner or later, join the war on the Allied side. That had been settled as a result of British propaganda, espionage and counter-espionage which had either achieved its objectives, or clearly marked them out well before Wiseman was installed in New York in 1916. Beyond any question it had been accomplished by Guy Gaunt and the other two points of the triangle, Victor Voska and John Rathom, with an indulgent nod to Gilbert Parker's letter-writing campaign. All were now dead—Voska in 1960 after the ghastly irony of having been imprisoned for 10 years by the communist regime that took over the Czechoslovakia he had done so much to create—and the Foreign Office old boys were determined that their man should get the credit. One who should have known better, Bruce Lockhart, who had been a bold diplomat-spy in Russia during the dangerous revolutionary years, was at it as late as 1989. In an article for the *Royal United Services Institute Journal* he wrote

Wiseman's 'Directive' from Cumming—if indeed there was one—is not available, but from what is known of his activities, it was probably along the following lines:

'If indeed there was one....'.

Even more fancifully, Lockhart went on to list what he thought the lines 'probably' were:

He was not to spy on the Americans.

He was to find out as much as possible about the activities of the Central Powers in the US and in particular about their clandestine activities.

He was to prevent sabotage in the docks and the factories of goods going to Britain.

He was to penetrate the Irish and Indian sedition groups.

He was to counter the massive propaganda effort run by the German Ambassador, von Bernsdorff, but not initiate propaganda on his own.

He was to get on the friendliest terms with the US Intelligence, Security and Police Authorities.

Could Lockhart really have had no idea of what Guy and his accomplices had been doing long before Wiseman arrived on the scene? At least they would have learnt how to spell von Bernstorff. Nevertheless, this was the line adopted by the Foreign Office and its old spooks brigade, with Guy's operation never referred to. The American popular historian Richard Spence followed it without much question in a 2004 article for the journal *Intelligence and National Security* that tried to unscramble the rival claims. His account is also shot through with qualifications and assumptions: might, may have been, perhaps, possibly, probably, could have. Nevertheless he concluded—with unscholarly relish—that the 'raffish' Gaunt was pushed aside by C's man, Wiseman. Of course he was. But Wiseman moved no mountains, changed no great ship's course. He was an advisor, not a player.

1953. The difference in age between Guy and Sybil had become marked. He was eighty-four, she only fifty-six. Their address, Bridle Gates, Hogshill Lane, Cobham, Surrey, sounded smug and semi-rustic but it was a shabby cottage barely worth ordering addressed stationery for, although such aids to appearance were as indispensable as school fees for Penelope and Shirley, fifteen and thirteen respectively, and Guy's subscription to the Senior. Out there, Guy might be just another old warrior marching around in the muddy lanes but in Town, inside the magnificent clubhouse, other men of rank knew who he was and what he had been. He went there as often as he could afford to. Sybil was glad to get him out of the house. Whatever his state of mind earlier, Guy was now entering his dotage, or so it must have seemed when he allowed himself to be elected president of the Cobham Pigeon Racing Club.

The Gaunts could afford a Ford Prefect which Sybil drove, a reminder every time she took it out of her circular journey from bank manager's daughter to chauffeured memsahib to titled lady then back to the sort of life she had avoided by marrying a man with thirty-five years on her rather than a mere twenty-eight. Whatever she might have missed out on as Mrs Jordan of Cairo there had been leisure and luxury, idyllic climate, soft-footed, white-robed servants. Most of the Tangier years had also been good. Those bare-back rides she bragged of may have been a fantasy but in the walled-off wonderland of the Zone a European woman had been able to live life much as she pleased. It did not please her to be dragged away to the dreary wartime landscape of little England to live on whale meat and spend all her clothes ration coupons on clunky underwear.

They made friends in the counties. Violet Tremlett was a divorcée, close to Sybil in age but rather more tolerant than she had become by then of Guy's eccentricities and chatter. Stories that had become tiresome background noise to the family amused Violet. He would sometimes pay her a visit alone, politely dropping a line to say when to expect him. A small collection of letters in the Maritime Museum at Greenwich suggests an affectionate and easy-going understanding between the three. In one note Guy tells 'Vi' he is coming over to show her a treasure, the gold cigarette case engraved 'Guant' that had been kept in his London bank with the knightly regalia and his dress sword. Because, typically, the letter is undated it is not clear if that was the fatal visit. But on 18 May Guy collapsed in Vi's house. An ambulance took him to hospital in Woking where he died of 'cerebral thrombosis and generalised arterio-sclerosis': massive stroke and hardening of the arteries, a classical old-age death eight days short of his 84th birthday.

The Admiralty sent Captain James Parrington Gornall to represent it at the post-cremation service. He had recently retired but he came up from Hampshire in full funeral rig—dress uniform, no sword—and, Guy might not have been pleased to see, a DSO glinting on his chest. Also among the mourners was Mr Lance Gaunt.

Within days, Sybil wrote to Vi saying she would telephone soon but

It is easier to write things that are close to one's heart than to say them.

I feel I cannot ever thank you for all you have done for us—not only recently, but, for a long time. Your kindness to Guy—I think some of his happiest times during the last year or two have been spent with you and your understanding and patience with him far surpassed mine.

I am sorry for your sake that his final illness happened in your house but I am so thankful that it <u>was</u> with you it happened & not in the street or Club as it easily might have been. Your help and kindness during the past 10 days has made all the difference to that rather wearing experience.

I am lucky in my friends. With love from us all.

The women went on exchanging visits and letters; warm, civil letters in firm middle-class handwriting, always with an affectionate sign-off. By the end of 1955 Sybil was drifting into genteel poverty. Guy's estate amounted to £822 which she had to split with his solicitor. Her share barely covered their bills. His pension had been £2,190 a year; she received a third of that. She and the girls moved to Oxshott, now an expensive notch in the stockbroker belt, then best known for some smoky brickworks. The cottage they rented was due to be demolished within months and she was looking around yet again for a place they could afford. And for anything she could sell. Vi offered to do what Sybil would not, take the Guant cigarette case to be valued. The Army and Navy store confirmed that it was 14-carat gold—a common American rating, about 60 per cent—but under some arcane trade regulation of the time second-hand items of that standard could not be put up for sale, only smelted. The offer was £22. 'This seems to me to be a great pity,' Vi wrote

so I am going to make you a proposition and beg you not to be offended. Will you accept the enclosed cheque [for £22] and allow me to keep the case on the understanding that you can have it back whenever you want it. This could be of use to you at the moment and the case would still be retrievable should circumstances arise that make you regret having parted with it. Alternatively, it would be available if you heard of anyone who might give you more for its interest above its intrinsic value.

Sybil was briskly grateful.

Guy always imagined his possessions were worth more than they were from other people's point of view .... I do appreciate your suggestion but I would feel I was 'borrowing' the money and that would worry me.

She was happy to accept the cheque; it was nearly equal to two weeks' pension.

Perhaps because Captain Gornall turned in a sympathetic report and someone at the Admiralty thought amends were due, Sybil was invited to apply for a Grace and Favour apartment, a privilege reserved for those who had rendered conspicuous service to the Crown and were now impoverished, or their posthumous dependents. These virtually rent-free residences were scattered around various royal domains and after a lengthy ordeal of affidavits and interrogations by underlings of the Royal Chamberlain, Sybil was put on the waiting list for a 'warrant', in the euphemistic vocabulary employed, to be given one of the fifty-three suites at Hampton Court Palace. The wait for someone to 'resign' and leave a vacancy was longer than usual and it was June 1965 before she and the girls were able to move into the vast Tudor citadel by the Thames. Theirs was Apartment 32A, seven huge and gloomy rooms on two floors overlooking the Clock Court. They had nowhere near enough furniture and the place was impossible to heat but it made for a powerful letterhead. The other residents, except for a couple of old courtiers, were the widows of captains and colonels, generals and royal gofers. A place in the hierarchy depended on the rank of the late husband and a knighted admiral was well up there.

There was plenty of room for both daughters; most of their friends as well, come to that, but Penelope was often away. In the Swinging Sixties she found herself a swinging job, one in the family tradition: she went to sea. The P&O line had only to hear the name to take her on as a Junior

Assistant Purser. She spent two years in the SS *Oronsay* on the Australia run then in 1962 was assigned to the more glamorous *Canberra* for her maiden voyage in 1962. A shapely slab of gleaming white with a pair of jaunty little yellow funnels like twin tail fins, the *Canberra* was the pride of the post-war passenger fleet. She took Penny around the world in her father's wake: over to New York, through the Panama Canal, around the Pacific. Pursers, hotel staff, ran the passengers rather than the ship: the women wore white uniform by day, blue and white cap, skirt just above knee. In the evenings they played hostess in deck-length navy blue.

In the middle of 1966 the *Canberra* was going nowhere. She docked in Southampton in May after a long cruise around the Americas and the deck crew walked off. The seamen's union had called a national strike and every ship in a British port was stuck where it lay. As voyage after voyage was cancelled pursers were sent on leave and Penny could enjoy the grace and favour of Hampton Court. Tourists were seen off the premises at six o'clock and for the rest of the long summer evenings the residents had the greensward and redbrick wonders on their historic doorstep to themselves: the gardens, the Maze, the Chapel Royal. Soon though she missed her shipmates. Sybil no longer had a car but she rented a Mini-Minor, the four-wheeled icon of the time, so they could go visiting while they were all at home. On the morning of 3 June, Penny drove down to the *Canberra*. She wanted to pick up some clothes and catch up with gossip. The little green car bowled along the wharf where the ship was berthed, swung in to park near the foot of the gangway and shot straight over the edge of the pier into the harbour.

Charles Robbins, a fifty-one-year-old taxi driver waiting for his fare to come down, jumped into the water beside the floating Mini. So did Fred Jerram, a Seamen's Union organiser who had been supervising pickets. At eighteen stone he made almost as big a splash as the car. The men tried to pull the passenger side door open but it seemed to be locked. Mr Robbins gestured to Penny to wind down her window but, he later told the coroner, she seemed frozen. Lines were thrown down but the car was sinking too fast for the men to tie them on. In Apartment 32A, where Sybil was wondering why it was taking Penny so long to get to get back, the new brown-and-beige telephone, incongruous in the vaulted salon, began its shrill portent. At the inquest Robbins said it seemed to him that Penny's foot must have slipped off the brake pedal. Death by misadventure.

Old William's family tree had been hacked back almost to the trunk. The astonishing generation he and Elizabeth bred came to an end when Lance fed his pheasants for the last time in 1959. There were fresh tendrils. Shirley married and had children. Clive's son David won the Military Cross with the Australian 7th Division in the Middle East. Ellinor became chief archivist at the Commonwealth Scientific and Industrial Research Organisation in Melbourne and lived until 1979. Some inherited the taste for exotic parts: Ernest's daughter Yvonne, whose memories of them remained laser sharp into her nineties, married one of the last colonial administrators and lived in several of the African territories until World War Two was well under way. After the war her brother John went out to Rhodesia and became chief censor of the rebel regime of white colonists that took the country over, banning *Playboy* for fear it might corrupt the natives. But the World had changed. That British World—Anglo World—of roads to unknown parts, stairways to glory and slippery slides to nowhere was reshaped by the upheavals of the two world wars and their aftermath. Courage became formalised, low cunning commercialised, travel commonplace: distant horizons no longer beyond reach. There was no place for that galloping generation of Gaunts, impatient to get where few had gone before, of gold dust and gunpowder, high seas and low company, reckless opportunism and exhilarating folly. A pity that for most of them, especially Guy and Minnie, it had been better to travel than to arrive at the journey's end.

Background

Apart from the various Gaunts' own accounts of their lives—Minnie's being the most numerous, Guy's the least reliable—their activities have been tracked by interviewing descendants and sifting archives. Only a few irretrievably loose ends have been spliced together by logical inference. I am especially indebted for their recollections to Yvonne Patricia Gaunt, Admiral Ernest's daughter, and James Read, Guy Gaunt's son-in-law. The main records consulted were in the files of the Admiralty, War Office and Foreign Office in the National Archives at Kew; at Churchill College, Cambridge; the National Maritime Museum, Greenwich; the National Archives of Australia, Canberra; the Historical Society of Victoria, the Museum of Chinese Australian History, the Australian Manuscripts Collection at the State Library of Victoria, the William Wiseman Papers at Yale University's Sterling Library; *The Times Digital Archive* via the British Library. Ian McLaren produced an annotated bibliography of Mary Gaunt's work that is a paragon of scholarly devotion. Margaret Bradstock wrote an exemplary entry for Minnie in the *ADNB*, Bronwen Hickman a sparkling MA thesis that led to wider publication. Beyond those I read or consulted

Allen K. *Lusitania Controversy* http://www.gwpda.org; Bellech, J. *Replenishing the Earth: The Settler Revolution and the Rise of the Angloworld*; Bennett, Gill. *Churchill's Man of Mystery*; Birkett, D. *Spinsters Abroad: Victorian Lady Explorers*; Blainey, G. *The Rush That Never Ended: A History of Australian Mining*; Blee, J. *Eureka: The Story of Australia's Most Famous Rebellion*; Bradstock, M. 'Mary Gaunt in China', *Southerly*, vol.53, No.3; Bragadin, M-A. *The Italian Navy in WWII*; Broome, R. *Victorians arriving*; Davison, G. A. *The Rise and Fall of Marvellous Melbourne*; Epstein J. A. *German and English Propaganda in World War I*; Fowler W. B. *British-American Relations, 1917–18: The Role of Sir William Wiseman*; Grigg, J. *Lloyd George, War Leader*; Harvey, J. T. *Eureka Rediscovered: In search of the site of the historic stockade*; HMSO *Official history of the operations in Somaliland, 1901-04*; Jones, J. *The German Secret Service in America*; Judd, A. *The Quest for C*; Lansing R. *Memoirs*; Landau, H. *The*

Enemy Within; Markus, A. *'Chinese immigration under the White Australia policy',* in Paul Macgregor (ed.), *Histories of the Chinese in Australasia and the South Pacific;* Markus, A. *Fear and Hatred: Purifying Australia and California 1850-1901;* McAdoo, W. *The Crowded Years;* Morison, E. *Admiral Sims and the Modern American Navy;* Mullins, R. E. *Sharpening the Trident: The Decisions of 1889 and the Creation of Modern Seapower (PhD diss);* Naftali, T. *Men of Secrets;* Nickles, D.P. *Under the wire: how the telegraph changed diplomacy;* Peterson, H.C. *Propaganda for War;* Ramsay, D. *Blinker Hall, Spymaster;* Rintelen, Franz von. *The Dark Invader;* Serle, G. *Another golden age: a history of the colony of Victoria, 1851-1861;* Shore F. J. *Notes on Indian Affairs;* Simpson, C. *The Lusitania;* Smith, N. C. *The Redcoats at the Eureka Stockade 1854;* Spence, R. *Englishmen in New York: The SSB American Station 1915-21;* Thwaites, N. *Velvet and Vinegar;* Tuchman, B. *The Zimmerman Telegram;* United States National Intelligence Centre *website;* United Nations Organisation. *Mixed Claims Commission (United States v Germany);*Voska, E .V. *Spy and Counter-spy;* Walsh, P.K. & J. W. Hooton. *Australian Autobiographical Narratives 1850-1900.*

As ever, any errors and opinions in this story are due to me and me alone, but I must record my lasting gratitude to Simon Blundell, the masterful librarian of the Reform Club, and to William Ham Bevan and Revel Barker for their peerless editorial eye.

Images

Guy Gaunt. Ernest Brooks, The National Library of Scotland

Tulia the Samoan Girl. Charles Kelly, The Powerhouse Museum Sydney

Lady Cruise—Margery. Bassano, National Portrait Gallery, London

Index